Varieties of Southern Religious History

Varieties of
Southern Religious History

Essays in Honor of Donald G. Mathews

EDITED BY

Regina D. Sullivan *and* Monte Harrell Hampton

The University of South Carolina Press

Published by the University of South Carolina Press
Columbia, South Carolina 29208

www.sc.edu/uscpress

Manufactured in the United States of America

24 23 22 21 20 19 18 17 16 15
10 9 8 7 6 5 4 3 2 1

Library of Congress Cataloging-in-Publication Data
can be found at http://catalog.loc.gov/.

ISBN 978-1-61117-488-5 (cloth)
ISBN 978-1-61117-489-2 (ebook)

For Elizabeth Farrior Buford

Contents

Acknowledgments

We would like to thank the contributors for their eager participation, hard work, and patience with what has been a lengthy process. We are also indebted to those who made the publication of this festschrift possible. David Moltke-Hansen, Alex Moore, and Linda Fogle of the University of South Carolina Press gave this project a home. We would like to acknowledge the particular support and kindness of Alex Moore throughout the publication process. We also thank the anonymous readers for their critiques, which made this volume stronger. Elizabeth Farrior Buford and the Department of History at the University of North Carolina at Chapel Hill provided essential administrative help, and we thank them sincerely. Finally we would like to recognize our families, without whose support this project would have been impossible

This book is dedicated to Elizabeth Farrior Buford, not only for her assistance with this volume, but also for her enduring generosity. She graciously and unselfishly shared her husband with us, and all of Mathews's students, during his years at the University of North Carolina at Chapel Hill, and we remain deeply grateful.

Introduction

A Historian of "Humble Access"

When the editors shared with their mentor the news that their proposed festschrift had been approved for publication, Donald G. Mathews responded with characteristic humility. After expressing his gratitude, his reply turned quickly to his own sense of deficiency. "I have not always been as good a mentor or advisor . . . as I should have been," he lamented. Many times, he disclosed, "I have mumbled the words of the confession ('and there is no health in us') and the prayer of humble access." This was not the only occasion upon which Mathews expressed himself in words taken from the Episcopal Book of Common Prayer: "We have left undone those things which we ought to have done; And we have done those things which we ought not to have done; And there is no health in us."[1] As Mathews is a former Methodist minister who converted to Episcopalianism, the basic sentiments conveyed in these hoary liturgical phrases have informed much of his engagement with his academic worlds, whether the world of his historical subjects, which he entered through the craft of interpretive scholarship, or the world of present relationships, which developed through countless hours of advising his students over the years. These sentiments of human inadequacy have manifested themselves in a deep-seated skepticism toward historical claims of human righteousness and beneficence (especially by those "on top"), and this has served his scholarship well, enhancing his historical vision with lenses of incisive scrutiny and uncommon sensitivity. When it comes to his contribution as a mentor, however, this sensibility has most certainly distorted his vision.

This wide-ranging collection of essays, all of which were contributed by his former students, should correct this distortion.[2] Examples of his flexibility and consistency as an adviser also abound in the list of dissertations overseen by Mathews, which is included in the appendix of this book. The sheer range, topical as well as temporal, covered by this body of scholarship belies his feelings of inadequacy; clearly, there was not *too* much that was "left undone." And his influence transcends the indelible imprint left upon his own students, extending to countless others who have quietly drawn inspiration from his work. Mathews, it should be mentioned, proved a natural interdisciplinary scholar. Interested in both religion and history, he earned a B.D. from Yale Divinity School before taking a Ph.D. in history from Duke University, where he studied with both the historian of the South Robert Woody and the scholar of religion H. Shelton Smith. Numerous scholars of these and related fields, though not having benefited from Mathews's direct mentorship, have nonetheless expressed admiration for his vast sway over the fields of their own scholarship. It was, for example, an admiring colleague rather than a former student, who, upon the occasion of his retirement, honored him with a paper reflecting on the lasting influence of his *Religion in the Old South*. No doubt countless others would have lined up for the opportunity to applaud him by acknowledging the impact of his work upon their own.[3] When it comes to assessing the contribution of Mathews as a guide and inspiration to historians, then, it must be observed that a great gulf stretches between the deep appreciation of the many protégés whom he has directly or indirectly influenced, on the one hand, and his own assessment of inadequacy, on the other.

This same alertness to human inadequacy, this appreciation of the dearth of human sufficiency, has suffused his scholarship, and here its effects have been much more salutary. This awareness has lent to his historical studies a compelling but rare combination of sensitivity and skepticism. The former can be seen in his taking seriously the widely varying forms of human religiosity with which the student of the past must come to terms. That the religion of bygone southerners, for instance, may have lacked resonance with the personal beliefs and priorities of the historians who proposed to study them did not, in Mathews's view, excuse scholarly inattentiveness. In a 1998 essay on the past and future of southern religious history, he noted that synthetic histories of the South, with few exceptions, had given surprisingly scant attention to religion. Admonishing his colleagues, he counseled contrition for this historiographic negligence. Invoking words of Episcopal liturgy, he wrote, "Perhaps historians should have knelt at the altar of Clio to confess with the old prayer book, 'we have left undone those things which we ought to have done.'"[4] Repeating this counsel three years later, Mathews wrote, "Religious life is the portal to an imagined sacred and moral reality that historians distort if they nurture an aloof and naïve incredulity when approaching it." Instead he advocated for "openness to the moral dimensions" of past lives, which he characterized as "an approach to our subjects through the 'prayer of humble access.'"[5] This deep awareness of human finitude and fallibility, of his own finitude and fallibility, helped foster in Mathews a refusal to dismiss those dimensions of the past that do not yield readily to the expectations and mental framework of present academic discourse; yet his approach of "humble access" has ironically multiplied knowledge by bringing into the light countless remote dimensions of the past.

If, fifteen years later, his refrain of insufficient scholarly attention being paid to southern religious history now sounds passé, then this welcome change has resulted in large part from his own prodigious contributions. His pathbreaking and still crucial *Religion in the Old South*, for example, exhibited this humble openness in its approach to the evangelical faith of both blacks and whites in the antebellum South. Mathews looked beyond the formal thought systems and moral record of the region's white theologians and preachers in order to take seriously the religious experience of African American evangelicals, whose voices the custodians of the peculiar institution (and many of the historians who had studied them) so often squelched. He did so, however, without succumbing to the temptation to judge the evangelical faith of slaveholders by the alien standards of late twentieth century liberal historians. Instead the book, characteristic of Mathews's work on religious history, held all of his subjects to the moral standards they themselves had created; he took their moral universe on its own terms. He did not assess them by the standard of an abstract "Christianity," since the multiple potentialities of this faith were patently evident in the diverse ways slaves, slaveholders, and non-slaveholding whites appropriated and altered the evangelicalism that they all held in common. Rather he measured southern religionists by the logic of their own evangelical discourse, the expectations of their own moral vision. If across the span of the antebellum era numbers of white southern evangelicals had migrated from the margins of the southern polity to the hegemonic, slaveholding center, and if later evangelicals came to defend the very worldly order their fathers' evangelical faith had emboldened them to reject, then this newer slaveholding "Christianity" must still be held to the standard that white evangelicals had earlier established in the South. But the standard-bearers for that kind of evangelicalism, he showed, were now the slaves. As the status and incidence of slaveholding increased among white evangelicals, they forgot the question with which they had once wrestled—whether the profound sense of liberty they had found in the crucified yet victorious Christ might extend to their enslaved brothers and sisters. Increasingly Christian responsibility to slaves meant seeking only to convert them; it no longer involved questioning the institution that kept them in bonds. White evangelicalism had changed: self-righteousness replaced self-examination; lust for Christian order eclipsed liberty in Christ. "By the secession crisis," Mathews noted, "white Evangelical leaders had cast their whole history and destiny into the world which their grandfathers had fled."[6] But their slaves now lived in that world, the original evangelical cosmos. While white evangelicals may have redefined evangelicalism in ways that restricted liberty and affirmed the authority of the slaveholding status quo, their black brothers and sisters extended the logic of the original evangelical ambience, which renounced the seemingly immutable values of the present social order, trusted biblical promises of a coming divine inversion of that order, and found sustenance in a liberty won through the suffering and victory of the cross of Christ. In Mathews's words, "The religious-social continuum of black Christianity created a mode of survival and sense of victory that was much closer to the original message of Evangelicalism than the mood and institution of whites."[7] Indeed, he asserts, "The full model of southern Evangelicalism was the creation of the blacks themselves; it was they who made southern religion different." African American evangelicals held more truly to the essential spirit of the evangelical impulse, an impulse that spoke especially to the marginalized rather than the mainstream, the downtrodden rather than the dominant.[8]

But why privilege *this* version of evangelicalism? After all Mathews himself has noted the slippery, ever-changing nature of evangelicalism in American history and has confessed the "sin," which he believes he committed in his earlier days, of treating evangelicalism as a monolithic "abstraction."[9] So how have the experiences of those on the bottom, those at society's margins—rather than those in power—come to command such a right to define, to function normatively, in his historical interpretation? To pose this question is to ponder one of the most elemental impulses that has vitalized and shaped Mathews's scholarship, namely, his conviction that all moral claims "must be understood before the Cross—that is, in such suffering as that of the God of victims." The cross symbolized both the suffering that victims endured and also the possibility of transformative victory through suffering. As God both bore and transformed the worst suffering of human existence, so by focusing on the crucified God the believer (and the religious historian) became aware of both the victims of suffering and also victory over suffering. The quotation above comes from the revealing, and courageous, autobiographical essay published in 2001, in which Mathews explained how such reference to suffering, sacrifice, and the God of victims came to frame his study of religion. Perhaps his appreciation of the capacious human proclivity for inflicting suffering (and for spinning the stories that rationalize such oppression) was here again intertwined with the theological conviction that "there is no health in us." If, as he admitted, "doing history" was in some ways "doing religion," it was because he perceived an "inversion of value and the valuable that lay within both history and religion." Exploring the dimensions of this inversion was the unrelenting burden of much of his work. "If the crucified sensibility attempts to evaluate institutions and relationships from the standpoints of those least benefitted by them and is therefore a continuing moral commitment," he declared, "it spares no one—including the self and nothing." As his curriculum vitae makes plain, much of Mathews's work has reinverted "value and the valuable" by foregrounding those who challenged, or were victimized, by the majority, the status quo, the powerful—whether slaves, white evangelicals who preached to slaves, abolitionists, or women. Indeed Mathews's pioneering analysis of gender and religion in his early work led to the award-winning study of the Equal Rights Amendment, *Sex, Gender, and the Politics of ERA: A State and the Nation.*[10] Here he not only offered a new understanding of religion and a fresh approach to historical interpretation; he also contributed to the development of a new and powerful category of analysis, gender.[11]

How this "crucified sensibility" came to constitute the theological and moral logic underlying his approach to the religious and social experience of southerners occupies several pages of his autobiographical essay. The factors involved in its formation include an upbringing overshadowed by the multigenerational effects of his paternal grandfather having been lynched in early twentieth-century Oklahoma. None of this needs recapitulating here. One reads of it only with great difficulty; one cannot imagine having experienced its effects. Nevertheless he has identified this horrific event as the ultimate reason he came to study religion in the South. Though its effects were many, it generated a family culture that found knee-jerk hatred and violence repellent and was constitutionally suspicious of stereotype, scapegoating, and the supposedly sacrosanct morality of the majority.[12] During his high school years, Mathews often heard his Methodist minister, Dallas McNeil, quote from Howard Thurman's proto–civil rights classic, *Jesus and the Disinherited* (1949). Further delving into the book while an undergraduate at the College of Idaho, he encountered a reading of the Gospel that took for granted that mainstream religion—whether the ancient religious authorities who had executed Jesus or the modern Christianity that had left African Americans "with their backs against the wall"—might be the oppressor and saw coming to the cross of Christ as a means by which society's "disinherited" might find inner, transformative deliverance from the clutches of hatred, fear, and violence. Others influenced the development of Mathews's sensitivity to victims.[13] To identify some of those who have contributed to his penchant for providing a megaphone to the marginalized is not to imply a greater unity among those influences than was actually there, and it hardly suggests that he subscribed to their every theological or interpretive position. Yet he saw in these and other influences something that his family's story had already taught him—that the meaning of religion and morality could not be grasped without the perspective and experience of society's victims.

To speak of victims, however, is to speak of victimizers. The "crucified sensibility," of course, evokes most elementally the Crucifixion, an act of horrible violence perpetrated in the name of religion by people confident of their own righteousness. That in its wake societies have produced so many victims, and that they have so often justified their victimization of others by appeal to religion, resonates with the prayer of confession to which Mathews has so often referred: "we have done . . . we have left undone . . . there is no health in us." In addition to fostering sensitivity toward the silenced and subjugated, then, this "crucified sensibility" has also conferred upon his work a concomitant skepticism toward the moral claims of those in power, of the majority. In this regard Mathews has acknowledged the early influence of H. Richard Niebuhr on his study of religious history, particularly neo-orthodoxy's suspicion of the human tendency to cloak self-interest and narcissism in the robes of religion. Concerning this influence, he wrote, "A neo-orthodox understanding that Christianity is one of many religions under suspicion of idolatry before judgment of the Cross made all historical judgments as relative as a postmodern mystic could wish and revealed most pretense to purity as delusional." To argue whether some practices were "Christian," he contended, was to miss the point. Christians, like all human beings, lived lives embedded in the socioeconomic, cultural, and intellectual matrix of a particular place and time. Hence Christians have considered all sorts of activities—from slaveholding and slave trading to crusades and genocidal slaughter—to be the will of God. "All moral judgments in history are so relative to position and knowledge," Mathews averred, "that they must be understood before the Cross . . . the standard of judgment is not 'Christianity,' but the Cross."[14] Many late nineteenth- and early twentieth-century southerners understood the practice of lynching to be somehow connected to religion, as well, and much of Mathews's latest scholarship has taken up the task of showing how even this horrific phenomenon did not take place in spite of religion but because of it. He has noted that Lillian Smith, author of the 1949 novel *Killers of the Dream*, saw the white supremacy and segregation surrounding her as connected to southern whites' notions of holiness. If her southern white contemporaries were scandalized by so explicit an identification and regarded her criticism as a heresy against the assumptions of southern orthodoxy, Mathews has developed this insight into a wide-ranging argument: That, in the practice of lynching, southern whites were (somewhat unwittingly) atoning for the "impurity" of blackness that had violated the margins of their sacred order, epitomized in their minds by whiteness. This perceived intrusion usually took the form of supposed sexual impropriety, which whites alleged black men to have committed against white women. Evidence was not always necessary. In a world where whites had long marginalized blacks as the impure "other," the slightest suspicion sufficed, because southern whites had already freighted white women with the burden of symbolizing the innocence and holiness of the South. While the scholarly community eagerly awaits the complete version of this thesis in Mathews's forthcoming book, it may be noted here that, for him, even lynching comes within the analytical purview of the cross. Indeed he argues that southern white notions of atonement, articulated by figures such as Robert L. Dabney and deriving ultimately from Anselm's medieval theology, lie at the bottom of the explanation of lynching. Just as their own individual sins could be atoned for only by Christ's sacrificial death, which bore the punishment deserved by sinners, so the purity and salvation of the southern polity could be maintained only through similar punitive means. Though the perpetrators and supporters of southern lynching may not have realized it, in essence they were projecting upon the single victim, whose tree of torture suspended him between heaven and earth, all of the impurity that whites believed the African American population embodied.[15]

On the ground, as practiced and conceptualized in time and space, morality and religion have meant many things and have taken many different forms. The impressive body of work that Mathews has gifted to those scholars who study these and related fields of history has amply demonstrated this. He has brought his "crucified sensibility" to bear on the dominant and the disinherited, the victims and the victimizers. With a sensitivity and skepticism borne of the conviction that "there is no health in us," he has modeled a historiography of "humble access."

NOTES

1. Book of Common Prayer (1928). These words come from the "Daily Morning Prayer" section and are part of the "General Confession." See http://justus.anglican.org/resources/bcp/1928/MP.htm, accessed July 19, 2013. The prayer of humble access, written by Thomas Cranmer in the sixteenth century and included in some later versions of the Book of Common Prayer, originally expressed the humility and unworthiness of those receiving the Eucharist.

2. The present list of contributors to this volume began with an inquiry by the editors to the Department of History at the University of North Carolina at Chapel Hill asking for a list of Donald Mathews's former advisees. Constraints of time and previous commitments prevented some contacted students from joining the ranks of those participating in the project. Still other former students, who for whatever reason were not included on the list and therefore were not immediately available to the editors, doubtless could have further augmented the volume in terms of their appreciation of their mentor and also by the quality of their work.

3. The speaker at Mathews's retirement celebration was Kurt O. Berends of the University of Notre Dame, and his tribute was titled "*Religion in the Old South*: A Twenty-Five-Year Retrospect."

4. Donald G. Mathews, "'We Have Left Undone Those Things Which We Ought to Have Done': Southern Religious History in Retrospect and Prospect," *Church History* 67, no. 2 (1998): 307.

5. Donald G. Mathews, "Crucifixion-Faith in the Christian South," in *Autobiographical Reflections on Southern Religious History*, ed. John B. Bowles (Athens: University of Georgia Press, 2001), 22.

6. Donald G. Mathews, *Religion in the Old South* (Chicago: University of Chicago Press, 1977), 184.

7. Ibid., xviii.

8. Ibid., 250.

9. Mathews, "Crucifixion-Faith," 25, 26.

10. Donald G. Mathews and Jane Sherron De Hart, *Sex, Gender, and the Politics of ERA: A State and the Nation* (New York: Oxford University Press, 1990). The book was cowinner of the American Political Science Association's 1990 Victoria Schuck Award, which honors the best book on women and politics.

11. Ibid., 22–25.

12. Ibid., 17–21.

13. Howard Thurman, *Jesus and the Disinherited* (1949; Boston: Beacon, 1996), xix–xx, 17–19, 23, 36–47. The others include G. Bromley Oxden, a Methodist minister and Social Gospel proponent. Mathews informed the editors of the influence of Thurman and Oxden in private conversation.

14. Mathews, "Crucifixion-Faith," 22, 24.

15. Mathews has posited this interpretation of lynching, in varying portions and aspects, on several occasions. See "The Southern Rite of Human Sacrifice: Lynching in the American South," *Journal of Southern Religion* 3 (2000), http://jsr.fsu.edu/mathews .htm; "Crucifixion-Faith"; "Lynching Is Part of the Religion of Our People," in *Religion in the American South: Protestants and Others in History and Culture*, ed. Beth Barton Schweiger and Donald G. Mathews (Chapel Hill: University of North Carolina Press, 2004), 153–94; "Lynching Religion: Why the Old Man Shouted 'Glory,'" in *Southern Crossroads: Perspectives on Religion and Culture*, ed. Walter Conser Jr. and Robert M. Payne (Lexington: University Press of Kentucky, 2008), 318–53; and "The Southern Rite of Human Sacrifice: Lynching in the American South," *Mississippi Quarterly* 61 (2008), a 2009 rewrite of the *Journal of Southern Religion* article.

MONTE HARRELL HAMPTON

"The Greatest Curiosity"

Race, Religion, and Politics in Henry Evans's Methodist Church, 1785–1858

Few would guess that the Evans Metropolitan AME Zion Church in Fayette-ville, North Carolina, a church that today proudly claims to be the "third oldest African Methodist Episcopal Zion Church in the world" and the second oldest such church in the South,[1] was once renowned for its racial integration. But in its formative years during the late eighteenth and early nineteenth centuries, whites and blacks together crowded into the modest frame chapel to hear the exhortations of Henry Evans, the free African American shoemaker-preacher who founded it. William Capers, the prominent Methodist bishop whose preaching circuit brought him to Evans's church in 1810 shortly before Evans's death, called the African American preacher "the father of the Methodist Church, white and black, in Fayetteville" and "the best preacher of his time in that quarter." Indeed, Capers noted, "distinguished visitors hardly felt that they might pass a Sunday in Fayetteville without hearing him preach." He was the city's "greatest curiosity."[2]

Evans was indeed a "curiosity," especially considering the historical context in which this black preacher carved out his biracial church. Fayetteville, like most of the South, found itself strained by racial tension in the late eighteenth century. Both the republican ideology that sparked the Revolution and the social disorder that was left when the smoke cleared set off a wave of insurrectionary activity among North Carolina slaves. Natural rights philosophy had so pervaded the populace that a Granville County slave named Quillo had planned in 1794 to have a slave "election," after which he would lead slave troops from his own county as well as nearby Person County in a quest for "equal justice." They would be prepared if necessary to "clear . . . out" any whites who stood in their way.[3] To their great consternation, whites discovered that they were not the only ones in whom the spirit of '76 had inspired libertarian dreams. The "contagion of liberty" had infected blacks as well as whites. In Chowan County in 1783, in New Bern in 1792, and in Wilmington in 1795, black revolutionaries roused fellow slaves to take violent action against their white oppressors.[4]

Though these outbreaks had little lasting military effect, they had tremendous psychological effect on whites. Moreover precisely when whites were beginning to imagine the terrifying ways in which this ideology of freedom might assume a more tangible expression, the successful revolution of Haitian slaves and the concomitant demise of thousands of white slaveholders confirmed their worst fears. The news of their West Indian brothers was not lost on slaves throughout the American South; word of the slaves' victory and of the arrival of thousands of fleeing ex-slaveholders in American ports traveled quickly.[5]

Regarding the prospect of proselytizing whites, Henry Evans came to town with two distinct disadvantages. First, he was a free black man. If merely being black would not have sufficiently vitiated his efforts among Fayetteville's whites in this period of intense racial suspicion, the preacher's "free" status would have. The social disorder wrought by war with England had opened niches of economic opportunity that enterprising African Americans began to fill. According to Sylvia Frey, a new economic aggressiveness characterized both free blacks and slaves who hired themselves out in local labor markets. This postrevolutionary assertiveness manifested itself most clearly in the South's urban areas.[6] Whites in these locales responded with legislation curtailing—and in some cases prohibiting—such public activities of blacks, both slave and free. In 1785 the North Carolina General Assembly decreed that "it shall not be lawful for any slave in the towns of Wilmington, Washington, Edenton, or Fayetteville, to hire her or himself out, without first producing a permission in writing . . . and the commissioners shall cause a . . . badge to be affixed to some conspicuous part of the outer garment of such a slave."[7]

Second, Henry Evans was not just a free black preacher; he was a free black preacher who happened to be *Methodist*. Since the First Great Awakening in the early to mid-eighteenth century, Methodists—arguably more than any other religious movement except the Quakers—had questioned the morality of slavery. Early on blacks had found in Methodists' message a millenarian hope of deliverance from bondage. Even some planters, emboldened by evangelical zeal to follow the egalitarian implications of their theology, did not shrink from denouncing the very slaveholding culture that had enriched their estates and elevated their status.[8] Hugh Bryan of South Carolina, for instance, preached "the destruction of Charles Town and Deliverance of the negroes from their Servitude" and (though he recanted) was punished by the state assembly for his actions.[9] Indeed the Methodists in 1784 went so far as to pass a "slave rule" forbidding church members, upon penalty of expulsion, from holding slaves. Though the measure did not receive solid support and was summarily rescinded, the antislavery cloak fit a sufficient number of Methodists to warrant, in the minds of many whites, extreme vigilance. It was into a Fayetteville characterized by this ostensibly inhospitable climate that Evans arrived late in the eighteenth century, and it was in this seemingly infertile soil that he planted Methodism.

Little is known of Henry Evans's background. According to both Bishop Capers and John H. Pearce, a parishioner who later became a preacher in Evans's church, he was born in Charles City County, Virginia.[10] En route to Charleston, he arrived in Fayetteville sometime prior to 1789.[11] Capers wrote that Evans chose to stay in Fayetteville because his "spirit was stirred at perceiving that the people of his race in that town were wholly given to profanity and lewdness, never hearing preaching of any denomination, and living emphatically without hope and without God in the world."[12]

Early on Evans's efforts to instruct the chattels of Fayetteville whites met with the stout resistance that might be expected given the anxiety over racial order that was prevalent at the time. When he began his evangelistic efforts, Evans was promptly jailed. Pearce later remembered that white authorities had arrested Evans as a "mover of sedition and insurrection among the slaves."[13] Capers recalled that "the town council interfered, and nothing in his power could prevail with them to permit him to preach."[14] Yet Evans was eventually released and proceeded to preach at clandestine meetings outside of town in the "sand-hills . . . changing his appointments from place to place."[15] If little record of Evans's background is extant, even fewer of his own words survive. Among these few words, however, is a kind of final message to the black members of his congregation, delivered in the last days of his life, in which he recalled that during his earliest days in Fayetteville he had endured the hostility of relentless mobs who hounded him from warren to warren. Encouraging his charges to emulate his trust in Christ, he reminded them, "Three times I have had my life in jeopardy for preaching the gospel to you."[16]

Despite the hazards inherent in preaching to slaves against their masters' wishes, however, Evans persisted, and by 1802 he had effected what Capers reported as a noticeable "change in the current of public opinion." Capers attributed this to a perceived improvement in the "public morals of the negroes."[17] Whatever its cause, such a shift had indeed occurred, and it was reflected in new municipal legislation passed in 1802 that allowed for limited amounts of assembling for religious purposes by area African Americans. To be sure the magnitude of this change should not be overstated, for this new Fayetteville ordinance still "strictly prohibited . . . nightly meetings of negroes, under the pretense of religious worship." Concerned whites in positions of power maintained their interdiction of blacks secretly gathering to absorb the homilies of a free black man in settings beyond the control of the master class. Yet the same ordinance proceeded to make provision for black preachers to preach to blacks "on every Sunday only, between the rising and setting of the sun," so long as the preacher obtained a "license" from the magistrate.[18] Whereas white authorities had initially forbidden Evans to preach to black audiences, they now extended him a modicum of clerical latitude, even if it was highly regulated. Granted his license, Evans continued in earnest to convert fellow African Americans.[19] When itinerant Methodist evangelist

James Jenkins visited Fayetteville in 1802, he found "no white [Methodist] society there," but he did report a "small society of colored people, under the care of a colored man by the name of Evans."[20] In all probability some from the area's considerable free black population participated in this society along with slaves.[21]

Remarkably between 1803 and 1810 this church—founded and led by a black preacher and composed of black congregants—actually made inroads into the white community. A certain "Mrs. Maulsby" was the first white person to cast her lot with Evans. She left the predominantly white Presbyterian church, which was meeting in the State House, and joined Evans's black Methodist church.[22] Over the next three or four years, the church continued to grow, gradually adding white converts to its numbers. Significantly Francis Asbury, who preached at the church in 1805 and 1806, described these white converts as "people of low estate."[23]

The real breakthrough for the addition of white members came in 1807. Pearce later noted that success among whites was relatively slow until, in that year, "a mortal sickness raged among the people," at which point "multitudes flocked to hear the Word delivered by the unlettered man of colour."[24] Though the nature of this "mortal sickness" is unknown, it is certain that between 1807 and 1810 the trickle of whites swelled into a torrent. Pearce recalled that "twenty came forward at one time and gave him their hands," and the white membership increased to "over one hundred souls."[25] In 1808 Asbury welcomed Evans's congregation into the Methodist Episcopal Church, and the church's "General Minutes for 1810" tallied "110 whites" and "87 colored members."[26] Bishop Capers also noted the extraordinary attraction that Evans's preaching held for white religionists, whose growing presence at his services between 1807 and 1809 had begun to crowd out the original black members. "The negroes seemed likely to lose their preacher, negro though he was," Capers wrote, since "now there was no longer room for the negroes in the house when Evans preached." To accommodate both races in the modest structure, "weatherboards were knocked off and sheds were added to the house on either side, the whites occupying the whole of the original building, and the negroes those sheds as part of the same house." Any suspicions that whites' attraction to this church was somehow in spite of, rather than because of, Evans's presence there are dispelled by the location of his domicile, which in this same construction project was built on to the pulpit end of the church. Evans not only preached at this biracial church; he lived there.[27]

Due to failing health, however, Evans gave up his pulpit in 1809. When he died in 1810, "his funeral," Capers noted, "was attended by a greater concourse of persons than had been seen on any funeral occasion before."[28] Moreover by 1814 the church Evans founded had grown sufficiently prominent to warrant its hosting of the 1814 meeting of the South Carolina Conference of the Methodist Episcopal Church.[29]

How can the enigmatic success of Evans's Methodist church be explained? What interpretation can make sense of a situation so mercurial that in the space of ten to fifteen years the response of Fayetteville's whites to his religious activity could shift from adamant proscription to ambivalent permission to ardent participation? One clue lies in Caper's description of how the church handled its burgeoning white membership. White parishioners willingly endured tight crowds and, no doubt, the opprobrium of many fellow whites as they gathered in what was called "the African Meeting House" to be exhorted by a black evangelical, whose ecclesial success had come only by flaunting the interdictions of white authority. Yet the same newly arrived whites accepted the relegation of their black brothers and sisters to segregated seating, apparently free of misgivings about disparaging those Christians who had striven valiantly to build the fledgling congregation in the face of white opposition. The manner in which this newly biracial church handled its biracial complexion suggests a religious community—at least a white religious community—with its mind not quite made up about the complex racial implications of evangelical religion, republican political thought, and the economic imperatives of slavery. The community was being pulled in opposite directions by two contrary impulses; it was living and worshipping at the cusp of two worlds—the waning world of an early evangelicalism that could take antislavery and libertarian ideology quite seriously and the waxing world of a newer evangelicalism that would less equivocally accommodate, even legitimize the culture of mastery and the calculus of slavery while relegating the unwieldy question of its morality to the realm of individual conscience. If the former opened windows of possibility for racial brotherhood and occasionally even hinted at African American equality, the latter began to close them, gradually affirming the control of white over black.[30]

Another part of the answer may lie in the *kinds* of whites who were being attracted to Evans's church. As John Boles has noted, southern evangelical churches comprising mainly lower-class whites among whom the incidence of slaveholding was relatively low—such as "the early Baptist and Methodist churches"—had more readily viewed black Christians as their true brothers and sisters than had more elite southern Christians.[31] But what was the social composition of the white portion of Evans's church? Though little direct contemporary testimony regarding this church survives, a useful (if incomplete) reconstruction of its white constituency emerges from tracking the income and status trajectories of the individuals who attended meetings of the Fayetteville Methodist Church, the earliest records of which date from 1808. By indicating the number of slaves owned, U.S. Census returns provide clues as to the wealth and racial views of Fayetteville's white Methodists, thereby providing at least a shadowy portrait of the white membership in Evans's church. Examining the incidence of slaveholding among white members of the church for two specific times—1810, around the death of Evans, the last black preacher in this biracial church, and 1820—reveals a distinct trend from lesser to greater wealth and social prominence among white church members as the nineteenth century unfolded.

The names of twelve white parishioners who participated in meetings of the Fayetteville Methodist church between 1808 and 1810 appear in the 1810 Census, and the average number of slaves held by each was .75. In 1820 thirteen white attendees of Methodist meetings appear on the Census. Ten more years into the nineteenth century (and some fifteen years after the time when Asbury could characterize the white Methodists in Fayetteville as "men of low estate"), white members held an average of 3.4 slaves each. To be sure, achieving anything like a scientific sample is difficult given the paucity of names known to be members of Evans's church. This difficulty notwithstanding, a fourfold increase in parishioners' slaveholding, at the very least, strongly suggests that the status of white members was rising while their racial views were hardening.[32]

There are other indicators of this trend as well. While the church owed its origin, its growth, and its incursion into the white community to the magnetism and unflagging persistence of a black preacher, beginning in 1808 a number of white pastors begin to show up in church records. While this development may reflect simply the constraints of clerical resources in the context of Methodist polity, it may also suggest that whites were liberating themselves from the evangelical compulsion to consider the egalitarian implications of their Christianity. Certainly the leadership of white ministers would inflict fewer pangs of conscience than the ambiguous spectacle of a black preacher exhorting white slaveholders from the pages of a book abounding with potentially leveling language— promises to bring "liberty to the captives" and assurances that "the last shall be first." But the increasing presence of *slaveholding* ministers would even more vigorously decide any ambiguity in favor of white dominion. When ill health forced Henry Evans to step down in 1809, he handed over his pulpit to Thomas Mason, a white minister who owned no slaves as of the 1810 Census. By 1820, however, Mason had acquired two slaves. Moreover two other ministers in the church—Jonathan Jackson and John H. Pearce—also had become slaveholders by 1820. The white ministers of a biracial church that only recently had exhibited a racial consciousness sufficiently flexible and munificent to sit at the feet of a black preacher now held in bondage their black brothers and sisters in Christ. The growing prevalence of slaveholding among Fayetteville Methodist ministers reflected the trend in nineteenth-century Southern Methodism—and southern Christianity—generally. Person County slave James Curry (born in 1817) grew up around a different strain of Methodism than slaves two generations before were likely to have experienced. Curry's furtive reading of scripture convinced him that "slavery was contrary to the revealed will of God," though he had seen "a [white] member of the Methodist church" violate the sanctity of slave marriage with apparent impunity. A Virginia slave named Madison Jefferson was convinced that "all the Methodists, even the preachers, are slaveholders, and think no harm of it." And Aaron Robinson, a Georgia slave born in 1829, observed that it was "frequently the case" that Methodist preachers held slaves.[33] Though exceptions could certainly be found, Southern Methodism tended toward acceptance of slavery as the nineteenth century progressed. Fayetteville Methodism reflected this tendency.

In the 1850s, as William Capers prepared his memoirs, his recollection of the white families who had composed the Methodist Church in Fayetteville in its early days actually focused on their considerable economic means. With prominent families such as the "Blakes, Coburns, Lumsden, Saltonstall, McDonald, Thomas, Eccles, Price, and others" in the church's midst, Capers postulated wistfully that, but for unfavorable denominational policy and fiscal disorganization, Fayetteville Methodists could have succeeded in building a parsonage. "With such names as I have mentioned," he wrote, "it should seem that there must have been abundant means" to build an "ample accommodation for the preachers."[34] Indeed George Eccles, of the "Eccles" family referred to by Capers, increased the number of slaves he owned from three in 1810 to five in 1820. Thomas J. Robeson, a member mentioned in church records, augmented his slaveholding from three to seven over the same period and by 1815 had purchased advertising space in the *American,* announcing that he had "recently opened his store in Fayetteville, on the south side of Hay Street."[35] Clearly the congregation that Asbury characterized as "people of low estate" had become a church of considerable means in relatively short order.

Though a dearth of evidence renders conclusions about the nature of worship and religious experience at Evans's church—and how it may have evolved over time—less than certain, extant testimony does suggest a similarly rapid shift from the more demonstrative religious expression associated with early evangelicalism (and with its rekindling during the Great Revival) toward the more staid, socially acceptable expression befitting southern white notions of honor and gentility. Of course ecstatic "trances," "shouts," and rapturous conversion experiences characterized Great Revival Methodism.[36] Indeed the initial white convert to Evans's church, "Mrs. Maulsby," who "had been led out of the public [Presbyterian] congregation for shouting," asked Rev. James Jenkins "if she might come in among the negroes" who were worshipping with Evans, presumably because her "shouting" would not be out of place there.[37] And Capers's description of the local reputation of John H. Pearce—a former deist whose embrace of Christianity had led him to Evans's church—further suggests the kind of overtly emotional religiosity for which the Methodists had become known. Capers reported that many Fayetteville whites considered Pearce "eccentric and enthusiastic." Capers was undoubtedly accustomed to such dismissive characterizations of Methodists. He believed, however, that such open, vulnerable, demonstrative religiosity—discouraged in the Presbyterian church that Mrs. Maulsby left but no doubt encouraged by the expressive preaching style of Henry Evans—was evidence of the authenticity of Pearce's Christianity. Pearce "was enthusiastic, as a matter of course," Capers bristled, "for he loved the Lord his God with all his heart . . . which the world and half-fashioned Christians have ever held to be the height of enthusiasm."[38] Capers's association of emotional expressiveness with authenticity is significant, for this very culture of expressiveness may have encouraged a sense of radical transformation in a way that silent religious observance or the cognition of didactic homilies could not. However "eccentric" to outsiders, the "enthusiasm" and "shouting" in Henry Evans's church may have catalyzed a self-authenticating sense of the reformulation of the self, a sense of being lost and then found.

Moreover if whites found this openly expressive religious experience internally authenticating, they may also have found authentication for this kind of Christianity in its apparent ability to bridge the gaping, seemingly immutable racial divide so endemic to their world. Could white and black be so different after all, when the religious experience of a Maulsby and a Pearce ostensibly appeared to differ little from that of the black members of Evans's church? To be sure, it would be too much to say that the racial chasm so ubiquitous in the South disappeared completely inside the church's walls. As has been noted, racially segregated seating, with whites occupying the preferred seats, had characterized the worship assemblies from the advent of white participation. Moreover Capers noted Evans's "humble and deferential deportment toward the whites," manifested in his acceptance of whites' expectations regarding his manners, dress, and social bearing.[39] While Capers himself interpreted Evans's deference more as a calculated move to maximize opportunities to preach the Gospel in a white-controlled world than an indication of an obsequious disposition, such a demeanor might still serve to undergird assumptions of white supremacy, thereby calming white anxieties concerning any radical implications of Evans's preaching.[40] Nevertheless whites were sitting at the feet of a black man, a black man who had not too long ago effectively defied white prohibitions of his religious activities. Now they eagerly gathered to hear their racial "other" speak to concerns embedded deep within their breasts, far below surfaces of white skin and black skin. Indeed this obstinate sense of racial otherness functioned all the more to backlight the strange, otherworldly sameness that was evident as blacks and whites experienced their faith. What was shared between these two otherwise diverse races seemed to confirm its authenticity. While they did not surrender their racism, they willingly allowed the spiritual feelings brought forth by African American preaching to trump their racism during those moments of preaching.

John Pearce's conversion and association with Evans's evangelicals had carried little weight with his brother, Oliver Pearce, whose refusal to convert to

Christianity may have stemmed from a sense that his brother's new tack did not square with the decorum, orderliness, and self-mastery worthy of a gentleman. After all Oliver had much to lose. Capers observed that he enjoyed "first place in the community as to wealth and worldly respect."[41] Apparently the movement toward "first place" in the southern sociocultural cosmos weakened the impulse to reexamine one's place in the spiritual cosmos. Accordingly the "eccentricity," "enthusiasm," and "shouting" associated with Evans's Methodist church did not appeal to the wealthy, respectable Oliver Pearce. It is interesting to note, however, that by 1812, when some of the church's members had begun moving toward social respectability, Oliver's name at last began to show up in the church meeting minutes.[42]

The course taken by Evans's Methodist church into the antebellum decades followed a path that diverged even further from its origins in an earlier evangelicalism when the tension between white mastery, on the one hand, and Christian brotherhood and a republican ethos, on the other—had been real and palpable. The events of the last three decades before the Civil War resolved this tension in favor of the former. As a strident antislavery message thundered out of New England in the 1830s, defensive white southerners redoubled their effort to protect and vindicate their way of life. In 1835, the same year that the new North Carolina constitution revoked black suffrage, the members of Evans's church left the original meeting site for a "large and handsome new building" at a prominent location on Hay Street. Whatever the reasons for this move, one wonders whether it symbolized, for many white members at least, a psychological departure from the legacy of Henry Evans. The old meeting place, after all, had been inaugurated by this free African American. He had personally built its first church building, known locally as the "African Meeting House." He had lived on its premises and now lay in repose under its chancel. In 1845 the new Hay Street Methodist Church took what could only have been regarded by its black members as another step away from Evans's legacy by joining the schismatic Methodist Episcopal Church, South—a new society summoned from its spiritual siblings by the shibboleth of slaveholding. Shortly after this, most of the black members left and returned to the site of the Evans Meeting House. The records of the Hay Street Methodist Church hardly highlight this momentous event, but an effort to tally the church's numerical accomplishments on the fiftieth anniversary of its 1808 admission into the Methodist Episcopal Church led the record keeper to confess it. Whether with a tone of tragedy or triumph or simple indifference—it is difficult to tell—the entry simply states, "At the close of the first fifty years there were 219 members," all of whom were "white, as most of the colored members preferred worshiping at Evans' Chapel."[43]

Whatever the inflection behind these words, they solidified the final divorce of two races that had once stood together, linking arms before a preacher whose ability, message, and historical moment had brought about a remarkable religious marriage. In his final address to the African American members of his church in 1810, Evans had said, "I have come to say my last word to you. It is this: None but Christ." He reminded them that from the early days of intense opposition, even mortal danger, he had trusted only Christ. "And now, if in my last hour I could trust to . . . anything else but Christ crucified," he concluded, "all should be lost, and my soul perish forever." Whatever the extent to which blacks adhered to this "word" from Evans, it is clear that many whites would soon place the bulk of their trust in something considerably more earthly. They would increasingly tune their ear to the message of wealth, status, order, and mastery. They would forget an earlier way of being evangelical when—to use one historian's apt description of late eighteenth-century evangelical egalitarianism—"for one valiant moment blacks and a few whites appear to have seen and heard the same thing."[44]

NOTES

1. See the church's website: http://www.nvo.com/evansmetropolit, accessed June 28, 2013.

2. William Capers, "Autobiography," in *Life of William Capers, D.D., One of the Bishops of the Methodist Episcopal Church, South; Including an Autobiography*, by William M. Wightman (Nashville: Southern Methodist Publishing House, 1858), 124.

3. Trial of Quillo, April 1794, Granville County Papers, North Carolina Division of Archives and History, Raleigh. Qtd. in Jeffrey J. Crow, "Slave Rebelliousness and Social Conflict in North Carolina, 1775 to 1802," *William and Mary Quarterly* 30 (1980): 79.

4. Crow, "Slave Rebelliousness," 93, 94; Sterling Stuckey, *Slave Culture, Nationalist Theory, and the Foundations of Black America* (New York: Oxford University Press, 1987), 99, 100.

5. Sylvia R. Frey, *Water from the Rock: Black Resistance in a Revolutionary Age* (Princeton, N.J.: Princeton University Press, 1992), 228, 229.

6. Ibid., 223–25.

7. Colin McIver, ed., *Laws of the Town of Fayetteville: Consisting of All the Acts, and Parts of Acts, Now in Force, Passed in Relation to Said Town, by the General Assembly of North Carolina, from A.D. 1762 to A.D. 1827, Inclusive; and All the Ordinances, and Other Proceedings, Now in Force, Passed by the Board of Commissioners of the Said Town, from A.D. 1785 to A.D. 1828, Inclusive* (Fayetteville, N.C.: Evangelical Printing Office, 1828).

8. Donald G. Mathews, *Religion in the Old South* (Chicago: University of Chicago Press, 1977), 66.

9. Qtd. in Sylvia R. Frey, "The Dialectic of Conversion: Shaking the Dry Bones," in *Black and White Cultural Interaction in the Antebellum South*, ed. Ted Ownby (Jackson: University Press of Mississippi, 1993), 26. This paragraph draws heavily on pages 25–27.

10. John H. Pearce, "Negro Preacher of Great Power," *Christian Advocate and Journal of New York* (n.d.); rpt., *North Carolina Review*, December 4, 1910, 10; Capers, "Autobiography," 124.

11. Though Pearce ("Negro Preacher," 10) dates Evans's arrival at 1795, William Blount, who, during the 1789 North Carolina Ratification Convention in Fayetteville, was unexpectedly called upon to oversee the funeral arrangements for Governor Caswell, noted that the funeral processed from "the Church"; Blount Papers, qtd. in John C. Cavanaugh, *Decision at Fayetteville, the North Carolina Ratification Convention and Assembly of 1789* (Raleigh: Division of Archives and History, North Carolina Department of Cultural Resources, 1989), 22, 39n. Since there were no other church buildings in Fayetteville at this time, this church was almost surely Evans's church. This conclusion was suggested by Roy Parker. C. Franklin Grill dates Evans's arrival "soon after" 1784; Grill, *Methodism in the Upper Cape Fear Valley* (Nashville: Parthenon, 1966), 14. Annette Billie without explanation dates his arrival in 1780; Annette Billie, *The History of Evans Metropolitan African Methodist Episcopal Zion Church: A Chronicle of Events* (Fayetteville, N.C.: A.B.C., 2006), 5.

12. Capers, "Autobiography," 125.

13. Pearce, "Negro Preacher," 10.

14. Capers, "Autobiography," 125.

15. Ibid.

16. Ibid., 129.

17. Ibid., 126.

18. "An Ordinance to Restrain the Irregularity of Negroes, When Assembling Nightly, for Religious Worship," in McIver, *Laws of the Town of Fayetteville*, 63.

19. Pearce, "Negro Preacher," 10.

20. James Jenkins, *Experience, Labours, and Sufferings of Reverend James Jenkins of the South Carolina Conference* (N.p., n.d.), North Carolina Collection, Wilson Library, University of North Carolina at Chapel Hill, 120.

21. According to the U.S. Census, Fayetteville and the surrounding countryside of Cumberland County had 122 free black heads of household and 1,723 slaves in 1800; cited in Roy Parker Jr., *Cumberland County: A Brief History* (Raleigh: Division of Archives and History, North Carolina Department of Cultural Resources, 1990), 43. While statements by Pearce and Capers indicate that Evans worked among slaves, Evans's status as a free African American strongly suggests the possibility that other free blacks in the area participated in his religious exercises.

22. Jenkins mentions her as the first convert (Jenkins, *Experience*, 136); Capers includes her among "the [white] first fruits" (Capers, "Autobiography," 126).

23. Qtd. in Grady L. E. Carroll, ed., *Francis Asbury in North Carolina: The North Carolina Portions of the Journal of Francis Asbury* (Nashville: Parthenon, 1964), 219, 220, 226. Asbury recorded in his journal, "I was invited to preach in the State house [the current Presbyterian meeting place], but it did not suit my mind at all; the object of our visit was a Methodist congregation and society. Home is home: ours is plain, to be sure; but it is our duty to condescend to men of low estate; and therefore I felt justified in declining the polite invitation" (220).

24. Pearce, "Negro Preacher," 10.

25. Ibid.

26. Excerpt from church records, in Elizabeth Lamb, ed., *Historical Sketch of Hay Street Methodist Episcopal Church, South* (Fayetteville, 1934), 12. "Hay Street Methodist Church" was the name given to the church Evans founded when it moved to a new location in the 1830s.

27. Capers, "Autobiography," 125. Evans may have even owned the real estate and building used by his church. In his will—the only other communication from him that I know to be extant—he bequeaths the property on "Cool Spring Street" to the church. Since the church building was on Cool Spring Street, it is difficult to determine whether he is willing to the church the property it was then using or another parcel adjacent to the church building. Evans's will is reproduced in Lamb, *Historical Sketch*, 25.

28. Capers, "Autobiography," 125.

29. Stephen B. Weeks, "Henry Evans and Negro Methodism," *Southern Workman*, December 1914, 91, North Carolina Collection, University of North Carolina at Chapel Hill.

30. Aspects of this tension are treated in Christine Leigh Heyrman, *Southern Cross: The Beginnings of the Bible Belt* (New York: Knopf, 1997), 206–25, and Mathews, *Religion in the Old South*, 74–77, 82, 83.

31. John B. Boles, "Introduction," in *Masters and Slaves in the House of the Lord: Race and Religion in the American South, 1740–1870*, ed. John B. Boles (Lexington: University Press of Kentucky, 1988), 9.

32. This analysis is based upon the U.S. Censuses of 1810 and 1820, as well as church records compiled in Lamb, *Historical Sketch*. The first official record of the Fayetteville Methodist church dated from 1808 (*Historical Sketch*, 8).

33. John B. Blasingame, ed., *Slave Testimony: Two Centuries of Letters, Speeches, Interviews, and Autobiographies* (Baton Rouge: Louisiana State University Press, 1977), 131, 129, 218, 498. As Donald Mathews has noted, such evangelical sanction of slavery had paralleled evangelical misgivings about slavery all along; *Religion in the Old South*, 74, 75. As the revolutionary age gave way to the early national and antebellum period, however, the former increased at the expense of the latter.

34. Capers, "Autobiography," 121, 122.

35. U.S. Census Returns for 1810 and 1820; *American*, November 10, 1815.

36. Frey, "Dialectic of Conversion," 35–37; Frey, *Water from the Rock*, 299, 304.

37. Jenkins, *Experiences*, 136.

38. Capers, "Autobiography," 121–22.

39. Ibid., 127, 128.

40. Capers seems to have understood Evans's respectful tack among whites as a kind of diplomatic strategy designed to secure a greater hearing for his evangelism. Recounting Evans's early violations of laws proscribing his public preaching, Capers reported that he "avowed the purity of his intentions" and "even begged to be subjected to the scrutiny of any surveillance . . . anything, that he might be but allowed preach" (Capers,

"Autobiography," 127, 128). Moreover Capers qualified his observation regarding Evans's deferential bearing with the disclaimer: "Henry Evans was a Boargenes; and in his duty feared not the face of man" (128).

41. Ibid., 121, 122.
42. Lamb, *Historical Sketch*, 13.
43. Ibid., 45.
44. Billie, *History of Evans*, 8; Mathews, *Religion in the Old South*, 71.

Philip N. Mulder

Strangers in a Wilderness

Lorenzo Dow and John Taylor on the Religious Frontiers of the Early American Republic

Longing to escape stifling restrictions on his movements, Lorenzo Dow determined "to go farther into the country," away from the Methodist districting and supervisors that would otherwise direct him. It was his chosen solution for the moment in 1796 when he was a restless new itinerant preacher, but one he repeated continuously throughout his career. Departure was his resolution during a lifetime of ministry, and the one that became his identity: he labeled himself the "cosmopolite" and called his published journals "The Life, Experience and *Travels* of Lorenzo Dow" [emphasis added], and he titled multiple essays "Cries from the Wilderness"—his repeated critiques of the many problems that prompted his movements. Ultimately he identified with no place. He was at home only as he moved. He detached himself from many of his contemporaries, including other Methodists and rival Baptists. Dow's mission was to be an alien in any country he delved. He isolated himself from everyone, including his own wife, Peggy, who remained alienated from Lorenzo's virtual home. He frequently left her behind when he traveled, but even when she accompanied him, they were in different mental and religious landscapes.[1]

Dow never met John Taylor, a Baptist preacher whose own restless discontent prompted his departure from Virginia into the western territories.[2] Taylor served a series of Baptist congregations as he drifted away from the coast. He seemed to follow Dow's path, at least metaphorically: he had escaped westward and used the distant perspective to critique the corruptions he intended to leave behind, and he was as distant from his peers, including his own wife, as Dow had been. Taylor ranged from Virginia to Kentucky, temporarily tending several churches—ten in all—until disputes drove him from one to the next. Like Dow, Taylor acted out of dissatisfaction and marched away into America's geographic expansiveness. Both Taylor and Dow went further into the country attempting to escape their kindred.

They ranged through many of the same states and territories—the two were combing common ground for converts—but several things separated them from each other. They happened not to cross paths, but had they met, the encounter would have sparked a debate. Dow spoke contemptuously of Calvinism's determinism and taunted Baptists on the issue. Taylor was equally quick to confront doctrinal differences. Both were disputatious with people of all religious persuasions, including members of their own churches. Even if they recognized their shared discontent and wanderlust in the wilderness, they would have reverted to their differences and perpetuated their singularity. It was the same impulse that drove them into the wilderness.

The preachers represented two compulsions shaping religion in the early West and the developing United States. Taylor and Dow believed they served larger causes, missions that spread their versions of Christianity in unfamiliar lands and set corrective examples for the mistakes they left behind. But their particular causes splintered their relationships in the very locations where they hoped to foster fellowship. They populated places with people like themselves, whose sole possession of the truth fragmented the wilderness. They fantasized about reconciliation and an ecumenical ideal, a movement from corruption toward improvement, from sin toward salvation, from divisiveness toward unity and truth. Dow claimed to be John Bunyan–like in his travels, a pilgrim who progressed toward his redemptive goal. But his burden clung to him, and this, not his destination, mattered most. The concerns, arguments, and resentments propelled the preachers but then did not disperse when they did.

Dow's and Taylor's intentions were inverted. The two wanted to highlight the destructive consequences of the populated places and the beneficial influences of the alternative. Although their efforts actually extended the disruptiveness, the notion of constructive wilderness has lingered. Their dreams have persisted in one form or another, resurrected to shape memories of the spread of Christianity in the early West. Dow, Taylor, and their contemporaries published their own journals and histories to advocate their individual causes, shaping subsequent perspectives with their self-serving claims that their travels were productive. Nineteenth- and early twentieth-century historians echoed the claims, celebrating the effects of Christianity in blunting the crudeness—the sinfulness—of settlers who were strangers to moral and religious influence and checking the "savagery" of Indians whose presence implied unbelief and violence. Twentieth-century historians modified these points to place the preachers onto a "frontier." In this formulation the crude and degenerative experiences were simply the rough edges masking a more significant, beneficial change. In the West, at the margins, a new civilization grew from the creativity of settlers toiling under the demands of the wilderness. They were assertive and independent, and they applied their energies in the short run to the building of self-governing settlements and in the long run to the growth of a distinctive ideology and culture. Theirs was a new working American democracy that would replace traditional pomp and deference, accomplishing the transformation almost imperceptibly as actions outpaced awareness of the changes.

Democratization permeated and transformed Christianity in America, according to Nathan O. Hatch in his study of the early Republic, and preachers such as Dow and Taylor were consciously and intentionally leveling, pacing the transformations. Revolution and expansion combined to create an atmosphere of independent thinking, religious choice, and assertive and defiant personal opinions. Dow and Taylor rode directly into the battles raging over religious authority in the early Republic. Participants in the Second Great Awakening, the religious excitement the two helped ignite, were very deliberately creating a democratic religious culture. They were fully aware of their revolution and its revolutionary influences, and they rejected and attacked the foundations of previous religious structures. Calvinism, education, and presumed authority were the antitheses of democracy and were to be discarded and replaced in the new individualistic culture.[3]

The process was reconstructive, too, an idea Donald G. Mathews captured when describing the Second Great Awakening as an "organizing process." Dow, Taylor and their peers were steadily structuring societies in the early West by organizing churches and voluntary groups. Their work was practical, and their goals required more action than reaction. Rebuilding defined the Second Great Awakening, for the First Great Awakening of the eighteenth century had already introduced the practice of challenging and tearing down traditional religious authority. The crucial characteristic of the Second Great Awakening in the early Republic, according to Mathews, was the *extension* of church life carried out by proselytizing Baptists and Methodists. They spearheaded a movement that, in the aftermath of revolutionary disruption and dislocation, sought to rebuild and reunify the organizations they so craved and prized.[4]

Dow and Taylor did happen to rebuild churches and societies and extend existing organizations into the West. But these were partly unintended results, for they had favored building over rebuilding, tearing down the existing structures and starting anew, with a different foundation, elsewhere. But their removals accidentally became extensions, and as the ministers recognized their continuing burden, they tried to detach themselves evermore and sank further into the loneliness that was their constant companion on the pilgrimage.

Lorenzo Dow was a restless Methodist. From his first religious impulses, during his conversion, and throughout his preaching career, he wandered, generally edging toward the margins. As a child he obsessed over illness and mortality. And then death closed in on him: livestock and close acquaintances died, and he had his own severe bout of sickness, deepening his sense of physical and spiritual peril. He became more intense, serious, and regularly gloomy. He questioned his fate, both the timing and prospects of his death, and the thoughts filled his every conscious and unconscious moment. In one dream the prophet Nathan predicted Dow's death at age twenty-two. More dreams and daydreamed thoughts added to the urgency: he might tumble off a chair and fall into hell. He hung from a thread, and in one moment he despaired that nature itself wished he were dead. Dow did not fall off the face of the earth, but he could not linger while death loomed. Dreams, reflections, and speculation removed him from the comfort of a cohort. He could not wait for those who did not share his compulsion: he did not play with other children because they were frivolous and reeked of the wickedness that might ensnare Dow. Adults were equally problematic when they were consistently unable to answer his urgent questions. Occasionally a bit of reading or conversation would inspire ecstatic relief, for even the hint of resolution offered release from the bonds that dragged him from his world. In such instances he rebounded entirely, temporarily swinging from despair to delight. Yet even there he remained removed, for he was transported to another realm: new dreams put him in the Garden of Eden. And when merciful forgiveness quelled his misery, suddenly everything appeared so good, so lightened, that his feet hardly touched the earth as he walked. He was transported nearly to heaven, again detached from those who could not comprehend either low or high. He swung like a pendulum from idea to idea as he contemplated only himself.[5]

A host of preachers and others were readily available to offer ideas. Dow took from them their ideas and weighed the messages and messengers critically and detachedly. He questioned whether one minister actually worked for God, and he regularly lampooned the teachings of Calvinists, whose determinism he disliked from first encounter. The Methodists, whom Dow soon embraced, were initially quite troublesome to him. He found their message novel and at odds with other more prevalent teachings. He wondered if Methodists spread a "divisive spirit" with their distinctiveness.

Their singularity attracted Dow, whose own dreams had set him apart. He visited and heard various preachers, but he returned again and again to the Methodists, drawn and repulsed repeatedly as he struggled with his attachments. Methodism held Dow's impulses. Like Dow Methodism's founders, John Wesley and his cohort of students at Oxford, had glared judgmentally at their sinful selves and momentarily despaired of their place in any moral universe. Then they swung toward resolution, determined to distinguish themselves with their intense devotions and obsessive behavior. Here were the outcasts Dow could join. Their peers had applied the label "Methodist" to mock the habits of the students who arose early and studied and prayed systematically. As they rebounded from their despair, their feet climbed to heights matching Dow's own leaps—Methodists would reach heavenly perfection, Wesley taught in his doctrine of sanctification.

Dow began his journey as a Methodist by jumping to the front of the pack. He started sharing his own experiences in religious meetings, exhorted others to try the faith, and steadily increased his public speaking. Dow was becoming a Methodist preacher, and despite some initial nervousness, the role pleased him entirely.

It satisfied his impulse to accomplish his moving mission, for he envisioned seekers everywhere in "fields without end." Methodists promoted traveling preachers who rode circuits, preaching from place to place without locating anywhere. They further scorned local attachments by rotating itinerants to new circuits every six or twelve months. Potentially one man could find himself in one year ranging around North Carolina and Virginia and, in the next, central Pennsylvania, New England, or Canada. In practice Bishop Francis Asbury tended to keep preachers in a region, but even with that concession, a person such as Louther Taylor was obligated to roam western North Carolina, Tennessee, Kentucky, and much of Ohio in the course of four years. Senior preachers worked to make sure that prospective travelers were prepared for the rigors of itinerant life, and acting as conference supervisors, they required of initiates months on trial before sending them to circuits on their own. But Dow dashed off immediately through Connecticut, Rhode Island, Vermont, and Massachusetts. His superiors had not confirmed his readiness to represent Methodism so far afield; they urged a more lengthy trial period during which Dow would preach within their earshot. Dow shrugged off the oversight and bolted from place to place, complaining that Satan, among others, was pursuing him. He schemed to blunt his critics, "to set out for some distant part of America, out of sight and hearing of the Methodists" until he could return after a year with proof of his success.[6]

Dow created another crisis as he approached the cusp of approval from the Methodist leadership. Claiming exhaustion from his race away from his critics, he felt his health failing. Dreaming again that he was dying, Dow made another, more extreme escape. He sailed to Europe, hoping that a visit to Ireland might resolve his several problems. He recognized the irony of a risky, strength-sapping voyage in his state. But it was not simply his physical health that concerned him. He remained trapped where he was, and only another departure could ease his burden. "To tarry is death; to go, I do but die," he wrote as he contemplated the trap that allowed him neither comfort nor prospects. He echoed the conundrum in a phrase that belied his attitude toward movement and solitude: "I am now going to a strange land, to be a stranger among strangers." Once again he anticipated visiting "a strange country, without friends." He kept departing "to go farther into the country." His words mixed bravado with sighs. The "wilderness," wherever he might pursue it, both exiled and elevated him. There he could be alone, like John the Baptist, one step removed from Jesus, who himself was a stranger in this world.[7]

When in company, Dow strove to set himself apart by cultivating a reputation as "crazy." He dramatized his preaching with sudden appearances, dramatic gestures, and humorous shocking anecdotes that confronted and mocked his hearers. Early in his preaching career, he began publishing his journals, a practice that he continued through hosts of separate pamphlets, newspaper accounts, and numerous editions of his collected experiences and works. Initially he used these to expand his reputation and help build anticipation of his visits; the publications became a way of creating a persona that transcended personal experience. Dow was quite convinced that remote readers wished to track his special experiences and that sharing would be "for the benefit of mankind." The extreme efforts garnered larger audiences and heightened his singular reputation. He became even more distinctive, such that people could not identify him with any group. Rumors in one area tagged him "Quakerized, others said I was too much of a *Methodist*," and still others concluded he was a "*mystic.*" Dow might be a guiding star for his earthly followers.[8]

Dow blazed in a different universe than most, including his wife, Peggy. He left her for weeks at a time while he rode his circuits. She regularly stayed with relatives or friends when he made his forays, but the separations left her anxious and depressed. If she were to be with him at all, she was obligated to travel. And on occasion she tried to move into his world. What Dow relished, however, Peggy dreaded. He embraced the forays into the wilderness, reveling in the adventure of roaming and preaching and embracing the nickname "Crazy" with his expressive presentations, frank conversation, and distinctive appearance. He wore his hair long, parted down the middle in an androgynous style. He was deliberately unkempt, avoiding combs and wearing the same plain suit until it literally wore through, prompting his followers to donate new clothes—not for appearance but for the simple function of covering and protecting him. He stopped short of wearing animal skins, perhaps only because that might associate him with the Indians his audiences despised. Dow loved adventure, and he cultivated an unmistakable image that removed him from any association with company. Peggy differed. She presented herself in plain but tidy dresses and bonnet. She was utterly unenthusiastic about Dow's favored places. Camping with him inspired mostly fright as her mind wandered through dreadful dreams of "wild beasts and savages." She resigned herself that Dow's pursuits would become her burden. So with reluctance, Peggy became experienced in Dow's West, such that she became with her husband an icon of adventuresome spirituality. As she edged closer, he maintained space between them, overly sensitive to criticism that he began to take rest days and had "grown lazy" and that marriage had slowed and diverted him from his mission. Peggy preceded Dow in death by fourteen years, releasing some of the tension that lingered in their partnership. Dow worked to reconcile their lives and visions after her death, mostly by publishing the journals she began to keep in imitation of his self-promotion. Still when Dow published her writings—either by themselves or in combination with his own collected works—he gave a nod to their differing forms of edification: his portion went by *The Dealings of God, Man, and the Devil;*

as Exemplified in the Life Experience, and Travels of Lorenzo Dow, a title that exuded adventure; Peggy's, by contrast, was titled *Vicissitudes of Life*, a sign of her lingering distance from Dow's physical and spiritual world.[9]

Dow continued to defy the oversight of the conference, reveling in the reputation of a maverick. Like most other itinerants, he bragged about the extremes of his travels. All struggled through miles of travel through all weather extremes to reach hapless souls in distant settlements. Preachers embraced the reputation of faithful sufferers for a higher cause. But Dow offered himself as the traveler who went farther than all the others. When he was supposed to be a local initiate, for example, he broke away from the restraints and flung himself into the itinerant's life, riding out to the hinterlands of Vermont. His initial escape from oversight he presented as the most earnest quest to pursue far-flung souls. He would continue the pattern throughout his career, hustling himself away while publicizing his distant exploits so that everyone knew the hardest-working preacher who operated on the margins of health and sanity.

Inspired by John Wesley's original vision, Methodists built a movement of itinerants who transcended locality. Wesley himself, having been refused access to many parish churches, stepped out of the Church of England's system of local clergy and became a wandering visitor, calling no place—but every soul—his own. Methodism had always employed local class leaders and exhorters to facilitate discussion and worship while the circuit riders were elsewhere on their rounds, and Methodists used local groups to foster intensely personal conversations about spirituality and behavior. Wesley's own religious transformation had begun with a small cohort at Oxford. The impulse to share, however, added the layer of travelers, and these itinerants gained mythic status. Methodism became a system of strangers supervising class groups, a delicate balance of distance and intimacy. Steadily Methodists incorporated local affiliations into their circuit structures, adding district and conference designations to supersede their close association of place designated by circuit labels. In these new forms, state, city, and other geographical designations competed with the Methodists' own ideal sense of space. Wesley sent teams of preachers to the American colonies to chase after people roving through the vast lands. Itinerants kept pace with the migrants and converted thousands, organized them into fellowships, and even constructed church buildings in more populous places such as Philadelphia and New York. Preachers began concentrating their efforts on the growing numbers of Methodists clustered together in more compact settlements. Some former itinerants became unconvinced they had to forsake home, marriage, and land ownership to serve. Others naturally slowed or settled, too tired to travel. But no matter, they thought, there were proximate congregations to be served, and no one minded a convenient ministry. Methodist leaders celebrated as they tallied their growth.[10]

Some Methodists did, in fact, take issue with convenience. Dow, who defined his own success according to hardships, shared no interest in readily clustered congregants. He had been critical of those who did not keep pace with his excessive travels. He implied that lack of traveling made itinerants effete, unworthy of the standards he set. In his counting there were far more lost souls to be found, and they were far-flung, drifting beyond the reach of Methodism. Dow added his singular voice to a small chorus of other itinerants. Together they published screeds critical of the taming impulses in Methodism and the preachers who drifted toward towns, cities, gathered congregations, established meeting times, comfortable homes, and regular rest. The only numbers that mattered to him were the ears that had *not* heard Methodist preaching and, more important, the number of miles he must travel so he could be heard. Dow and his audiences—the lonely and the isolated—were the ones who truly counted. His sacred obligation impelled him to pursue the souls of settlers scattering across North America and not to conform to the sedentary style of settled ministers from Methodism or any religion. Expansive circuits invigorated dedicated itinerants and were the sacred spaces of Methodism for Dow. Debates continued among Methodists about fellowship and place, a constant set of negotiations that grew within a larger context of Methodists' competition and arguments with Baptists over religious relationships.[11]

"All looked gloomy to me," lamented Baptist preacher John Taylor as he surveyed the Ohio River Valley, his new home. He found the place bereft of towns, people, and churches—quite unlike the Virginia he had left behind in 1795. Worse, filling the voids were people whose efforts were counterproductive. This "wilderness," complained Taylor, was being filled with a "savage rage."[12] Unlike Dow, Taylor associated wilderness more with problem than solution. He identified several sources of the crudeness and sinfulness: scattered settlers who struggled daily for subsistence, entirely indifferent to culture and morality, and Indians, whom the settlers associated implicitly with threat and violence, oblivious to their own continuing encroachments and offensive presence. "Not one family [was] free from Indian danger."[13]

Taylor was daunted but did not despair. Rather than be paralyzed by the challenges, he confronted them, working to nurture the infant congregations and build communities, resolutions that contrasted with Dow's. Starting from thirteen members in one Ohio church, Taylor happily reported that his settlement grew to sixty, including "many of the good-old, peaceable disciplinarians" who brought respectability as well as population density to the place. He repeated the process many times, ultimately recounting in his memoir ten churches he had helped, beginning in Virginia, continuing in Ohio, and extending to Kentucky. Yet Taylor, like Dow, claimed the greatest obstacle—the greatest source of "savage rage"—was not sinners and Indians but rather the religious themselves.[14]

Taylor shared with Dow a basic discontentedness, one that diverted him from his fantasy of a steady religious course. His participation in multiple churches belied a spiritual wanderlust that matched Dow's physical travels. Taylor roamed from church to church, driven along by the churchgoers who disappointed him at every stop. *They* were the ultimate source of the "savage rage," exceeding Indians or the social disruptions of revolution and relocation. The religious themselves spread their conflicts into the West, perpetuating patterns established in eastern churches. Taylor meandered through replicas of the religious landscapes he had departed, searching for happiness in loving fellowship but instead finding loneliness and gloom in a "wilderness" of conflicts.[15]

Expanse had been Dow's salvation, but it was Taylor's demon. He struggled with his surroundings like an adversary and tried desperately to outnumber his foes with allies, local groups and relationships that would fill the spiritual void he felt in vast spaces. The "country," in which Dow found automatic relief, was to Taylor a foreboding place. Dow envisioned perfection in the universal transcending all boundaries. Methodists erased political and ecclesiastical boundaries with their own vocabulary of the movement and mission circuit riders; they spoke of country, continent, and land. But Taylor talked of congregation, church, and community. He found comfort in local spaces, sharing the perspective of many Americans in the early Republic whose minds and allegiance bound them to localities and states more than nation or continent. Taylor was a Virginian, and from his vantage point, Ohio and Kentucky were foreign places. They were another landscape, a different affiliation, and a separate people. Taylor could speak for many contemporaries who shared his detachment from their new western homes.

Taylor built with his Baptist faith a series of walls that further isolated him. The first layer was simple: Baptists distinguished themselves from non-Baptists. They should live apart, their churches and congregations removing participants from the wider world. Taylor was dismayed with members of one Virginia Baptist church who failed to live any differently from their neighbors. Taylor knew several beliefs and practices that easily distinguished Baptists from others. Moral character and behavior should obviously separate them from the irreligious, something Baptists tracked with regular meetings, investigations, transgressions, and discipline. They could inquire, admonish, and remove from fellowship those who were impure.[16]

Baptists set another perimeter designed to wall out other Christians. Distinctive to them were practices such as adult immersion, a form of the ritual of baptism in which people who were of an age to make their own determinations chose to affiliate with a Baptist church and symbolically died to their old lives and prepared themselves for a new one by cleansing themselves entirely. Baptists also valued determinedly their local churches, fellowships formed from the mutual commitments and agreements of the participants who bonded together according to common beliefs and practices. In a vigorous nod to the legacies of the Reformation, Baptists claimed that local churches helped stave off established churches or any form of imposition on conscience. Baptists held these and other treasured ways deliberately to set themselves apart from other Christians, most of whom allowed for baptism by sprinkling water and subordinated or affiliated churches through some more centralized authority.[17]

Distinctive Baptist beliefs separated Baptists from non-Baptists, but they just as effectively alienated Baptists from other Baptists. Internal debate among the multitude of independent churches ultimately created as much disunity as unity. Intensely committed to locality, Baptists insisted that their churches grow out of the mutual commitments of members whose common beliefs and assent created and sustained their fellowship. Ideally an integrative force, Baptist localism was intended to support community, but it could also disrupt fellowship. Taylor, like others, treasured the opportunity to seek out people with whom he agreed, and he resisted efforts to force conformity among local churches. The opportunity— really the requirement—to debate and form fellowships according to particular choices inspired intensive discussions and obsession with distinctions. Taylor moved from congregation to congregation hoping desperately for a comfortable fit, but satisfactory fellowship eluded him. By his claim it was the fault of those around him who fell into theological disputes. He grew dismayed by the patterns of argumentativeness and would leave in search of a better situation. Removing west to Ohio and Kentucky extended Taylor's pattern of roaming widely after his ideal locale. Alienated by spats in Virginia, Taylor the estranged went off to embrace strangers. New communities, forming territories and states, and established settlements gave Baptists such as Taylor abundant options to seek better alternatives. Some purer place must be in the next territory, but Taylor became lonelier every time he moved and did not find community.[18]

Arguments engulfed the congregations. Baptist churches chose their preachers by the selection and vote of the congregants. When multiple candidates presented themselves, or when a newcomer offered greater potential than the incumbent, churches split. Numerical growth could create its own problems. One of Taylor's churches was flourishing and was considering fostering a branch fellowship. But the minister tried to block the plan, and the group fell into "devastation," Taylor lamented.[19] Members of another congregation guarded their growth carefully by arguing vehemently over the evidence applicants offered for membership. One faction in the Clear Creek Church in Kentucky was put off by the confident and energetic confession given by George Dale and was inclined to reject him because he was overly confident of his salvation. In another situation uncertainty caused the problem: factions quarreled over "doubtful" accusations in a discipline case. The stakes heightened because some congregants were overly eager to excommunicate, Taylor judged. So he began to distance himself from people who called themselves "Christian" because they were perpetually embroiled in disputes. "I had once thought [that] if all the people on the earth could be Christians we should have a paradise here," but the converted themselves dispelled that dream. The endearing term "brother" became an "epithet" to Taylor, who was losing faith in fellowship. "Two men can scarcely quarrel but others will take sides somewhere. This produces faction and much destroys the peace of the church of Christ. These things not only made their appearance but sprang from the church at Clear Creek. Accusation in the church became very common and [were made] for very trivial things. . . . Human nature is of that base quality that it will not bear to huddle much of it together."[20]

Efforts to mediate and negotiate among factions intensified the fighting. In attempts to temper the arguments and pursue consensus, Baptist churches occasionally—but often reluctantly—attached themselves to more expansive organizations that shared and recommended resolutions to local crises and queries. Churches voluntarily formed associations on a regional basis, expanding Baptist boundaries fitfully in the early Republic. They had to overcome objections from other independent-minded congregations and from rival associations holding divergent beliefs. Clustering of churches around favorite collections of doctrines such as the Philadelphia Confession and later statewide conventions added another strand to the web of Baptist relationships in the eighteenth and nineteenth centuries. Everywhere Taylor traveled, he encountered the divisions between Regular, General, Separate, and Particular Baptists, the largest factions of associated Baptists. Throughout the twenty years Taylor had contact with the churches in the Elkhorn Association, members there fought over their affiliation and title, with the South Elkhorn group splitting into two distinct churches over the issue. Taylor himself repeatedly wished for unity, but he remained deliberately affiliated with the Separates, even reminding his Regular Baptist peers in one community that he was a Separate Baptist when they seemed to be overlooking the distinction.[21]

Taylor created a default when all the other options for fellowship crumbled. He decided to marry. Unlike Lorenzo Dow, who imbibed the Methodist misogyny that viewed women as tempting impediments to their holy absences, Baptist ministers such as Taylor found parallels between personal domestic life and the local fellowship they so desired. As his fantasy of a churchly paradise evaporated, Taylor turned to a more consolidated substitute. He did warn his bride that she would face especial difficulties because of his chosen profession of preacher who traveled frequently. Yet he returned to the benefits he would gain: he "concluded" that "changing my station to a married life" might make him "more happy in this wilderness of sorrow." Giving credit to divine will, he made a "conjugal contract" with Elizabeth Kavanaugh—a "girl" with an appropriate Baptist background— that endured nearly forty years. With that survey of their life together, he hardly mentioned her again, except to note her difficult delivery of their son, Ben, soon after they had struggled from Virginia to Kentucky. Elizabeth and Ben did merit mention as attendees in one of the new churches Taylor constituted; the Taylor "family" had swollen after Taylor inherited seven enslaved people from an uncle. Strength of numbers bolstered his role in congregational votes. Taylor claimed to have consulted his family when he made crucial decisions, but as the free male head, he remained the sole representative of the group, alone in charge of the family. One of his churches once responded to a query whether a woman of ability should be invited to pray or prophecy in church that it would be foolish to "lose any gift that is among them merely because it is found in a female." The inclusive sentiment was lost, however, in a wilderness of arguments that choked out resolution.[22]

Taylor and Dow did not experience the renewals they expected in the wilderness, but their denominations did. Taylor went from congregation to congregation seeking quiet and cooperative fellowship. But he despaired as arguments filled each of his new churches, extending the very debates that had prompted his departures. Dow ran from restrictions so he could release his singular talents and let people experience the amazing stranger they had met in print and rumor. He wanted to shock his audiences and exceed their expectations for this crazy preacher. His confrontational impulses restrained him, however, and he chafed at the successes of his own church and the Methodist structures that grew around the thousands of converts. Denominations were renewing themselves in the wilderness, re-creating what had driven Dow and Taylor to depart. The wilderness they sought shrank and shifted from physical to mental as the men struggled again to isolate themselves from impurities. They felt more and more alone as their churches enveloped them.

NOTES

1. Lorenzo Dow and Peggy Dow, *The Dealings of God, Man, and the Devil; as Exemplified in the Life Experience, and Travels of Lorenzo Dow, in a Period of over Half a Century: Together with His Polemic and Miscellaneous Writings, Complete. To Which Is Added the Vicissitudes of Life, by Peggy Dow*, 2 vols. in 1 (New York: Nafis & Cornish, 1849), 1:20. The theme of Dow's singularity and isolation is one that Charles Sellers introduced in *Lorenzo Dow: The Bearer of the Word* (New York: Minton, Balch, 1928).

2. Although he did meet another John Taylor in New England.

3. Nathan O. Hatch, *The Democratization of American Christianity* (New Haven: Yale University Press, 1989). Many other critiques of the frontier thesis develop the active role of Native Americans and their perspectives in the centuries of encounters.

4. Donald G. Mathews, "The Second Great Awakening as an Organizing Process, 1780–1830: An Hypothesis," *American Quarterly* 21 (1969): 23–43. As with my previous effort to explore further the notion of "evangelical," this article might serve as a footnote to Mathews's insights into religious expansion in the early West.

5. Dow and Dow, *Dealings with God*, iii, and 9–14.

6. Ibid., 13–25. *Minutes of the Methodist Conferences, Annually Held in America; From 1773 to 1813, Inclusive*, vol. 1 (New York: Daniel Hitt & Thomas Ware for the Methodist Connexion in the United States, 1813).

7. Dow and Dow, *Dealings with God*, 34–56; quotations from 35–37.

8. Ibid., 46, 50, 56; Hatch, *Democratization*, esp. 36–40.

9. Dow and Dow, *Dealings with God*, quotations from 104 and 220–21.

10. *Minutes of the Methodist Conferences, Annually Held in America; Jesse Lee, A Short History of the Methodists, in the United States of America* (Baltimore: Magill & Clime, 1810; rpt., Rutland, Ver.: Academy Books, 1974).

11. See, for another example, Peter Cartwright, *The Autobiography of Peter Cartwright*, ed. Charles L. Wallis (New York: Abingdon, 1956).

12. Chester Raymond Young, ed., *Baptists on the American Frontier: A History of Ten Baptists Churches of Which the Author Has Been Alternately a Member*, annotated 3rd ed. (Macon, Ga.: Mercer University Press, 1995), 111.

13. Ibid., 261.

14. Ibid., 263–64.

15. Ibid., 261; D. W. Meinig, *The Shaping of America*, vol. 1, *Atlantic America*, and vol. 2, *Continental America* (New Haven: Yale University Press, 1986, 1993).

16. Young, ed., *Baptists on the American Frontier*, 121.

17. Ibid., 192.

18. Ibid., 172–79, 205–6.

19. Ibid., 172.

20. Ibid., 172, 183, 189, 193, 205.

21. Ibid., 91–95, 129, 175. Young, editor of Taylor's account, suggests that within the Elkhorn Association an argument festered over a disputed exchange of two enslaved people.

22. Ibid., 155–57, 159, 207, 279, 346, 356.

Larry E. Tise

"Taking Up" Quaker Slaves

The Origins of America's Slavery Imperative

One of the most persistent questions for historians of the American past is a truly bedeviling concern: How could Americans have practiced slaveholding and also actively blunted the efforts of those who came to oppose owning slaves from freeing their own? Take, for example, the Quakers. Valiant Friends, from the beginning of their brand of Christianity in the late seventeenth century, decided that the owning of slaves by Quakers was a practice to be avoided. By the end of the eighteenth century, the Society of Friends in Pennsylvania, North Carolina, and elsewhere determined that any Friends who persisted in this sin should be severed from the Society. But when these Quakers began to emancipate their slaves, they ran into problems. Although there have been many forays into the topic of Quakers and slavery by historians of religion and by others looking for the origins of antislavery thought, little attention has been given to the subterfuges devised by slaveholders to undermine and even annul Quaker emancipations.[1]

Among the most surprising and demoralizing efforts to halt Quaker manumissions occurred in the colony and state of North Carolina under an unlikely legal rubric called "Negroes taken up." One of the most revealing sets of such records appears among the legal papers on free people of color and Indians from Perquimans County—one of North Carolina's oldest. An entire collection of jumbled records between 1777 and 1803 documents the legal actions taken by county officials to re-enslave dozens of freed Quaker slaves. Since North Carolina was home to America's second largest community of Quakers (the largest being in Pennsylvania), records provide a rich mine of documentation that sheds new light on the long and often tortured history of Quakers and their slaves.

But even more fundamentally, these records open a new window for understanding the complex and frequently surprising twists and turns of America's travail with slavery. Free people of color were a complicating factor in a developing slave society.[2] Thus elected officials in North Carolina moved decisively to "take up" or to eliminate those freed persons that resulted from Quaker actions of benevolence. Slavery in America, in addition to being a system for providing labor, was also a mechanism for managing what was perceived as an alien population. Here is that harsh story again in one of its starkest forms.

Among the hodgepodge of records for Perquimans County were a great variety of legal actions relating to free people of color. There were receipts from the county sheriff, Richard Skinner, who took a wide medley of persons in hand in 1788. On September 9 he issued a receipt to Thomas Creecy and William Arrington Jr. for "Three Negroes One by the Name of Primos formerly the Property of Caleb Winslow & Reuben Wilson, Teney formerly the Property of William Townsend Deceased." On October 4 he gave another receipt to the same two individuals "for a Negroe Man Named Mingo formerly the Property of John Haskett Supposed to be Set free by the Sd. Haskett." On the same day, he gave yet another receipt to these two busy men for "two Negroe Women Fanny & Hagar formerly the property of William Robinson."[3]

In the same body of papers were a variety of legal notices sent by Sheriff Skinner to particular residents of Perquimans County indicating that their former slaves were presently residing in the county jail. One was addressed to a Mr. Robert Newby under the date of July 8, 1788, as follows: "Sir, I hereby Give You Notice that there is a Negro Man Named Dave, in Hertford Gaol, Said to have been Your Former Property That will be Sold Sum Time of July Court at Heartford, If You have a Claim to him You will Make it known the first Day of Court."[4]

When these cases went to court, and the persons thus notified by Sheriff Skinner did not show up to make a claim, the county court gave a new directive to the sheriff. He was to issue a summons to the presumed former owner of these slaves to appear before the court: "You are hereby commanded to Summon Thos. Newby Senr., Josiah White & Exum Newby, personally to be and appear before the justices of the County Court of Pleas and Quarter Sessions to be held for the County of Perquimans at the Court House in Hertford n the 15th & 16th Days of July then and there to testify . . . in a certain matter of controversy in the said Court . . . between Thomas Creecy, Wm. Arrinton Senr. Plaintiffs, and Certain Free Negroes are Defendants."[5]

No penalty was provided in the summons for failure to appear. However, all parties knew what the consequences would be. When the persons thus summoned did not appear, the court authorized Sheriff Skinner to sell the sequestered former slaves immediately. There were thirteen such persons offered for sale to the highest bidders on October 17, 1788. When Sheriff Skinner completed his accounting for the business transacted that day, the results were revealing. The expenses involved in "taking up" these freed slaves and selling them on October 17 were as follows:

To Noticing the former Owners	1.14.8
To Summoning 21 Witnesses	2.16.0
To Paid for feeding [prisoners] to Chas Moore Esqr	19.7.6
Paid the States Atto[rney] his fee for Sale of 12	24.0.0
Paid for Guarding the Gaol	7.4.0

Comm[ission] for selling £763.14 @ 2/&Ct	19.10.0
Paid Free holders for apprehending Negros	137.2.6
Due to Public Balance this account which is in Bonds, the Sale being on Credit	<u>£548.10.0</u>
By Amount of Sales of Negros Sold by order of Court of this date	£763.14.0[6]

When looking at the expenses of this business transaction, it appears many profited. The subcontractors got paid for jailing and feeding the thirteen detainees. The state attorney got his cut. The sheriff got a 2.5 percent commission on the entire transaction. But even more notably, the citizens who took up the suspects got paid 25 percent of the sales price for apprehending them. The citizens who did the taking up were sheriff's deputies—whose relatives in most cases ended up buying the individuals for bottom price at the public auction. To add insult to injury, the sales—all of which were final—were done on credit with no indication of terms of credit or periods in which the bonds were to be repaid. If all of this looks a little suspicious, one must remember that this was the normal way for business to be handled in most local governments. The business of "taking up" slaves without masters was a good one.

Some of the individuals summoned to appear at court were told that the sheriff was detaining a person who had been manumitted or freed illegally. For example Samuel Moore was informed on May 4, 1791, that "a Certin Negrow Woman Named Nanny and Child was taken up and Delivered to Me as one set free by you Contrary to Law and is now confined in the Gaol of this County." Some of the receipts reveal a similar legal infraction: one of October 4, 1788, for "two Negroe Women Fanny & Hagar formerly the property of William Robinson Supposed to be Manumitted or set free By the said Robinson"; and another of July 8, 1789, for "Two Negroe Women by the Name of Sarah & Nanny and Children which were taken up . . . as set free and are said to be set free by Jacob Winslow Contrary to Law."[7]

The documents also revealed who was committing these crimes. One of the notices, to Robert Newby of July 8, 1788, was given the generic title "The Quakers Notice," and its language was then repeated in the other notices of that year. A public notice of July 14, 1789, was more graphic: "The Sheriff having made Return of Sundry Negroes Taken up and Deliv'd him, as Manumitted by the (People Called Quakers) in express [violation] of the Law . . . in Compliance with the Law it is ordered that the Sheriff on Friday the 14th Instant at the Court House Door in Hertford Between the Hours of one and 4 oClock in the afternoon, expose to Sale to the Highest Bidder the said Negroes."[8]

While most of the documents did not reveal that all of this taking-up activity was directed against one group of believers, there were enough snippets and patterns to prove that the process of taking up former slaves was to deal with a perceived problem caused by Quakers. One of the receipts written by Sheriff Skinner contains a notable tagline: "Received September 23rd 1788 of Richard Woodard and Miles Elliott Two Negroes, one Named Dick said to be Manumitted by John Smith, The other a Negroe Woman Named Hagar said to be Manumitted by Joshua White which Negroes were Taken up by the said Richard Woodard and Miles Elliott agreeable to the Act of Assembly—to Prevent Domestic Insurrections." And the public notice of July 14, 1789, for auctioning taken-up folk contended that the "People Called Quakers" had manumitted their slaves "with an intention to Disturb the Peace of the State."[9]

The idea that the manumission of slaves by Quakers could be perceived as something quite different from a philanthropic act was made crisply clear in a separate set of records maintained in adjacent Pasquotank County. Indeed in the summer and fall of 1793, when a reign of terror was reaching its peak in revolutionary France and when Haitians were flooding into the ports of the United States from the bloodiest slave revolt in history, a grand jury was called in Pasquotank to deal with the crisis of further Quaker manumissions. In the presentment to guide its deliberations, the grand jury described in the starkest terms the crisis that beset the slaveholders of northeastern North Carolina: "The Jurors . . . do present, that the County of Pasquotank, is reduced to a Situation, of great perrel and danger, in consequence of the proceedings, of the Society of people, called Quakers."[10]

The problem was that the Quakers talked so much about emancipation among their own slaves that they and their slaves were infecting the minds of enslaved people throughout the slaveholding regions of North Carolina. In fact, "The Grand Jury, are so perfectly Sensible, the infatuate enthusiasm of the Quakers as to partial & general emancipation, that they see a present alarm amongst the minds of the people, and for [the] prospect of imminent to impend, by the influence and designing attempts of the Quakers to this purpose, which unless prevented must burst with destruction, around the Citizens of the State." The grand jury minced no words as to why the threat was so great at that particular moment in time. Its members were fully cognizant of "the Miserable havock and massacres which have lately taken place in the West Indies [i.e., Saint-Domingue or Haiti], in consequence of emancipation." They also believed that some of the Quakers who lived among them were filled with "the infatuated enthusiasm of Men Calling themselves religious" and "conceive it a duty they owe to themselves . . . to present the people called Quakers and their abettors as the Authors of the Common Mischief in this Quarter of the World."[11]

After the grand jury conducted its due deliberations, it came to the conclusion that "the Destressing Inconvenience the good people of the district lay under [was] from the Inefficiency of the Laws intended to restrict the Emancipation of Slaves." It also concluded that "the people called Quakers in other respect good

Citizens, have by their Conduct, made that Species of property [slaves] not only of small Value, but have Rendered it dangerous to the person at Safety of the proprietors of Negroes and those who live in the Vicinity of them."

Immediate action was necessary, they thought. Their solution was characteristically American: "They . . . require their representative in the next general Assembly, to lay this their presentment before the Legislature . . . trusting that Measures will be taken so to modify the religious Enthusiasm which pervades their Quaker Neighbours."[12]

These folks meant business. They were scared to death that the distemper exhibited by the National Assembly in France had emerged among local Quakers. The National Assembly had just extended liberty, freedom, and equality to every citizen of France and had also declared that even those slaves who had been killing their masters in Haiti had rights equal to every other citizen. Local Quakers, it seemed, were trying to do the same thing for their slaves. Not only were they emancipating them through manumission and thus releasing them into a slave society; they simply would not stop talking about the need for all citizens to unburden themselves from the curse of slavery. They preached this passion among themselves, among their neighbors, to their slaves, and via their slaves to other slaves. And when they set one of these slaves free, they were, in essence, setting loose a potential insurrectionist.

When the North Carolina General Assembly next met, the delegates from Pasquotank and Perquimans Counties—who thought they were surrounded by Quaker antislavery enthusiasts—found others from the slaveholding regions of the state who shared their fears. In fact over the next year, they led a movement in the general assembly to rectify North Carolina's laws on the manumission of slaves and to provide a new legal framework for the activities of any free people of color living in the state or thinking about coming into the state. In the 1795 session of the general assembly, they were able to address both the problems of refugees from Haiti and other Atlantic islands and of free people of color who might somehow appear in North Carolina. Titled "An act to prevent any person who may emigrate from any of the West India or Bahama islands, or the French, Dutch, or Spanish settlements on the southern coast of America, from bringing slaves into this state," the general assembly wanted to close off any possibilities that slaves or emancipated slaves could be dumped in the state.

In true legislative political style, the assembly tacked onto this easy-to-pass law a further act "for imposing certain restrictions on free persons of colour who may hereafter come into this state." No one from any of the prohibited territories could "land any negro or negroes, or people of colour, over the age of fifteen years" under severe penalties for disobeying the law. Those who reported the arrival of any such persons were to share one-fifth of monies recovered from any prosecutions. A process was established for free people of color to arrive as refugees, but each such person had to have a sponsor who would post a bond. But the law also stipulated that whenever "any number of negroes or other slaves, or free people of colour, shall collect together in arms, and to be going about the country, committing thefts, and alarming the inhabitants of any county," a local militia was to be called out "to suppress such depredations or insurrections . . . under the same rules and regulations as in cases of invasion and Insurrection."[13]

As soon as the threat of foreign invasion by hordes of Haitians had been addressed, the general assembly next addressed the domestic problem of Quaker manumissions. Since Friends were emancipating slaves due to matters of conscience, the state legislature reemphasized and slightly modified the grounds for manumission: "No slave shall be set free in any case, or under any pretense whatever, except for meritorious service to [be] adjudged of and allowed by the county court, and license first had and obtained therefor." This strategy sounded fair and logical—except for the fact that strict Friends would not go to the county court to take out a license and would not take the oaths and other strictures necessary to demonstrate that a particular manumission was for meritorious service and not for mere matters of conviction. The law also granted persons "as aforesaid liberated [shall have] all the rights and privilege of a free born negro." But manumitees did not become citizens. They merely became freed slaves and had to live under the strictures that applied to that class of persons.[14]

Several strands of concern thus converged in 1793. The revolutions going on simultaneously in France and its colonial island Saint-Domingue proved that the world was a very dangerous place. White refugees from Saint-Domingue were pouring into North American ports with their slaves. Emissaries of revolution from both France and Haiti were abroad in the land preaching subversion. Dangerous ideas were being brought into America from these places that were sure to cause unrest and insurrection among the enslaved. And on top of all of this, those oddball Quakers had decided at this very moment to flood northeastern North Carolina with a band of freed slaves imbued with dangerous ideas implanted in them by their masters. The Quaker emancipators had to be stopped, thought their fellow slaveholders, whatever the cost. And if they persisted in giving up their slaves, then it was incumbent upon the state of North Carolina to "take up" those who no longer had masters. These freed people must be kept under the control of slavery. And further, means needed to be found to control those free people of color who were already spread across the land. From the point of view of a slave society, the Quakers could not have picked a worse time to attempt to unburden themselves of slaves.

The idea of "taking up" slaves without masters was not new in 1780s North Carolina. Nor was using this strategy to undermine and annul Quaker manumissions. Taking up those freed was a legal process created by slave societies to deal with runaway slaves, with fugitive slaves from other states, or with suspicious characters plying illegal arts. But the fundamental purposes for "taking up" free people of color, and the manners in which they were taken up, may have been unique in North Carolina. As laws and methodologies for seizing free persons of color advanced in North Carolina, this legal mechanism was used to achieve objectives that would never be obvious from a mere reading of the law.

The first law authorizing the taking up of freed slaves appeared in North Carolina in 1723, perhaps borrowed from similar laws adopted at that same time in Virginia. At that time the Lords Proprietors of Carolina approved an act requiring that "Inhabitants" who chose to free one or more of their slaves must also make sure that these freed persons left the colony within six months after their emancipation. But then:

> If any Slave or Slaves being so freed and set at Liberty . . . shall presume to return back into this Province, it shall and may be lawful for any Person or Persons whatsoever to apprehend and *take up* such Slave or Slaves so offending, and carry him or them before some Magistrate . . . [and] shall then sell him or them for Seven Years, at Public Vendue, to the highest Bidder; and the Money arising by the said Sale, after Charges paid, shall be applied, the one Half to the Apprehender, and the other Half towards defraying the contingent charges of the Government.[15]

And thus were set forth the concept and basic principles relating to the taking up of former slaves that would remain the essential ingredients of the process in North Carolina until slavery was abolished in the midst of the American Civil War.

By 1741 North Carolina had moved from being a mere appendage held in thrall between Virginia and South Carolina to being rife with land speculation, from Governor Gabriel Johnston down to virtually every county commissioner. In order to provide an apparatus for taking massive amounts of land from Indians and bringing in hordes of immigrants, there needed to be a clear legal structure concerning indentured servants and slaves and, of course, free people of color. Governor Johnston and the general assembly adopted such a law and spelled out in minute detail the whole process of taking up former slaves without masters. The 1741 law titled "An Act Concerning Servants and Slaves" expanded the description of "taking up" former slaves to portray the special role of the "Taker up" (supplanting the term *Apprehender* from the 1723 law).

The focus of this law was on runaway slaves and not on those who might be manumitted and sent forth into society. Indeed the section introducing the subject of taking up was entitled "For the Encouragement of all Persons to take up Runaways." The further the runaway slave was from his or her master's home, the larger the "Reward to the Taker-up." If the runaway slave resisted the "taker up" or showed "obstinacy" or refused to give the name of his or her owner when delivered by the "taker up" to a constable, an elaborate procedure was outlined for making sure that this person, runaway or not, would not be able to go free and to make sure that everyone got paid for all the efforts—including, of course, the "taker up." All of this was to be handled at the local level, according to the proclivities and practices of the local court.[16]

All of this had to do with runaway slaves. Another section of the 1741 law dealt with manumissions. According to this provision, "No Negro or Mulatto Slaves shall be set free, upon any pretence whatsoever, except for meritorious Services, to be adjudged and allowed of by the County Court, and Licence thereupon first had and obtained." The only legal manumissions were thus those obtained in this manner. If they were done in any other manner, authority was given to the "Church Wardens of the Parish wherein such Negro, Mulatto or Indian shall be found, at the Expiration of Six Months, next after his or her being set free, and they are hereby authorized and required, to *take up* and sell the said Negro, Mulatto or Indian as a Slave, at the next Court to be held for the said County at Public Vendue" (emphasis added).

The monies coming from such sales were to be "applied to the Use of the Parish, by the Vestry thereof." In a sense one philanthropy (manumission) was to be converted into another (support of the church parish), in the case of illegal manumissions. But no "taker up" was to profit from such action. And the sole authority for taking up and carrying out the action was the church wardens.[17] This addition to the 1741 North Carolina law, in actuality, replicated the law that had been in existence in Virginia since 1723.[18]

It is quite unlikely that this 1741 revision of North Carolina's laws relating to taking up former slaves had anything to do with the activities or testimonies of local Quakers.[19] The law prescribed for the first time a procedure to be used in the case of manumissions. "Negro or Mulatto Slaves" could be set free for no reasons other than "for meritorious Services, to be adjudged and allowed of by the County Court." All decisions on merit were to be determined at the local level, including those circumstances in which it could be determined whether a "Negro, Mulatto or Indian Slave" had been freed improperly. In addition to keeping the decision making at the local level, the 1741 law for the first time brought former Indian slaves into the same legal situation as slaves of African descent.[20]

Quakers were strongly present in North Carolina throughout its colonial era. Despite the fact that they maintained a strong role in the governance of the colony, laws regarding the treatment of servants, slaves, and free people of color seem not to have been affected by their presence until the period of the American Revolution. While Quakers were having an intramural debate on the propriety of slaveholding by Friends (and whether to dispose of their slaves if their inner voice were offended), this fitfulness of conscience did not spill over into the public arena. Antislavery Friends visited North Carolina regularly and urged caution and reformation among their brethren. George Fox had gone there in 1672 just after the first Quakers arrived at what they saw as a safe haven where they could practice their religion. John Woolman went there in 1759 after he had seen the light on the subject of slavery. Other Quaker antislavery voices—Benjamin Ferris and John Griffith—went in 1765. All of these urged North Carolina's Quakers to abandon their involvement in slave trading and slaveholding.[21]

And they got a response. In 1768 the North Carolina Yearly Meeting concluded that "the having of Negroes is become a Burthen to such as are in Possession of them" and condemned the participation of any Friend in slave trading for a profit. Between this year and 1775, attitudes among North Carolina Quakers regarding slave trading and slaveholding underwent a dramatic change. Each year brought new pronouncements on the evils of Quaker involvement in slavery.

In 1772 the North Carolina Yearly Meeting even appealed to their associates in London for advice on the subject and got a response that their devotion to God would eventually bring them a resolution. In 1775 the yearly meeting gave as "their advice and Judgement, that all friends that find themselves under a Burden and uneasiness on account of keeping them in Slavery may Set them at Liberty." The yearly meeting assigned to local monthly meetings the responsibility of appointing "proper persons to assist such friends in drawing Instruments of writing for that Purpose." Opinions on slavery among North Carolina Quakers advanced so rapidly that by 1776, and the onset of the American Revolution, the positions of Pennsylvania and North Carolina Friends were virtually identical.[22]

Over this same period of years—when Americans were determining whether or not they wished to continue being a part of the British Empire—some of North Carolina's most prominent Quaker slaveholders decided that they could no longer countenance the owning of slaves. It was perhaps not merely that they underwent a change of mind and heart; it was rather that, in some cases, these Friends went almost overnight from trading in slaves and using slaves like everyone else—to get rich—to a public and overt stance against slaveholding. Thomas Nicholson, a large slaveholder in Perquimans County, wrote an open letter in 1767 to North Carolina Friends urging them to consider the gradual emancipation of their slaves. He had gotten eighteen or twenty slaves himself by inheritance and came to the conclusion that slaves were a "Snare" to those who inherit them and that owning them only provoked "pride, Idleness and a Lording Spirit over our Fellow Creatures." Although the laws of manumission in North Carolina were difficult, he thought he could free his slaves gradually and pay the costs of doing so.[23]

Eight years later in 1775, however, Nicholson had come to the conclusion that, "having been deeply distressed in my mind for several months Principally on account of the unjustifiableness of the Practice of keeping Negroes in Bondage, and Slavery," he could keep his slaves no longer. He wrote another open letter to North Carolina Friends titled "Considerations on Slavery." In this new treatise he announced that, despite North Carolina's antimanumission law, for Quakers to continue to keep slaves "would lay us under the Guilt of obeying Men more than God." In his mind if his freed slaves should be taken up under North Carolina law, the sin of holding men and women in bondage would be transferred to the takers up, the court officials who sold them, and the new owners who would then hold them as slaves.[24]

Meanwhile another landowner in Perquimans County, George Walton, converted to Quakerism in 1772 after a dream. By 1774 he was attempting to persuade other Quakers in the area that they must free their slaves. In a letter to one of the most prominent Friends and slaveholders in the area, Thomas Newby, Walton urged him to free his slaves—even if it was necessary for him to break North Carolina's complicated manumission law. Newby, who owned fourteen slaves in 1775 and was the largest slaveholder in the county, took the matter seriously. He applied, as the yearly meeting had directed, to his monthly meeting in Perquimans for guidance. A committee was appointed to assist him. It reviewed his reasons for freeing his slaves, determined if his slaves would be able to support themselves, and helped him draft a manumission document.[25]

Between the time Newby asked the Perquimans Monthly Meeting for guidance and the time they rendered their full advice at the end of 1775, the world in which these Quakers were seeking to salve their consciences changed completely. Shots were fired at Lexington and Concord in April 1775. North Carolina's last royal governor fled to a royal navy vessel anchored in the Cape Fear River for protection. A revolutionary provisional government was formed in North Carolina. The Continental Congress meeting in Philadelphia established a Continental Army under the command of George Washington. As tempers frayed throughout the American colonies—some leaning in the direction of American independence and others toward loyalty to Great Britain—everyone worried about what side the thousands of slaves would take if the colonies should declare their independence.

When Gen. George Washington—one of Virginia's great slaveholders—refused to reenlist black soldiers, including those patriots who had fought at Lexington and Concord, a wedge was opened in the campaign for slave loyalty. Governor Martin, from his ship in the Cape Fear River, hinted that Britain might use slaves to beat back patriot traitors. In November 1775 Virginia's royal governor, Lord Dunmore, promised freedom to any slaves who escaped from their rebel masters and joined the British Army. Lord Dunmore's hastily assembled army—consisting of white loyalists and of escaped slaves from both Virginia and North Carolina—marched on the port of Norfolk on January 1, 1776, where they were met by patriot troops also from both Virginia and North Carolina. While the Continental Congress had not yet declared independence, a civil war between patriots and loyalists, whites and blacks, slaves and escaped slaves had already begun.

It was in the midst of this bedlam that Newby, with the advice and counsel of his Quaker associates, decided to manumit ten of his fourteen slaves—six men and four women. Under the date of March 3, 1776, he signed and sealed "of my own free will and out of a tender Scruple of Consience" in the presence of two witnesses, a "manumission or Instrument of Writing" in which he "most freely Set at Liberty Six Negro men on their paying me or my heirs the Sum of twenty Shillings a year." They were manumitted totally but also conditionally on the payment of the annual fee and on demonstrating persistent good behavior. If they should fail in either respect, they would revert to Newby or his heirs and could then be sold as slaves.[26] In addition to the slaves freed by Newby at this time, Thomas Nicholson manumitted five of his slaves, Mark Newby emancipated four, Benjamin White another four, and more by others for at least thirty-one slaves in Perquimans County alone.[27]

The Quakers of northeastern North Carolina could not have picked a less propitious or more dangerous time to free their slaves. The barely united colonies were launching into a very risky war for independence. Already hundreds, and perhaps thousands, of slaves had escaped their masters to join the British enemy. And now the Quakers—known pacifists who would not take up arms to support any side—were releasing slaves who would remain in the community. These newly freed people could easily become free agents to spread disaffection among slaves and also serve as the fomenters of slave insurrection against all white masters.

The newly formed revolutionary provincial assembly for North Carolina wasted little time in countering the Quaker threat. The assembly reinvented its 1741 law, designed to deal specifically with runaway slaves, and added a new statute to deal specifically with the sudden spate of extralegal Quaker manumissions. Noting that there was an armed revolution going on across the land at that very moment, the assembly titled the new law "An Act to prevent domestic Insurrections, and for other Purposes." It also opened the revision with a telling preface: "Whereas the evil and pernicious Practice of freeing Slaves in this State, ought at this alarming and critical Time to be guarded against by every friend and Wellwisher to his Country." Something, of course, had to be done about the unleashing of potential traitors and insurrectionists. The 1741 law put the handling and prosecution of nonlegal manumissions in the hands of "Church Wardens" for the parish in which the illegal procedure had occurred. But not this new enactment.

The 1777 law was punitive. It adapted the procedure for dealing with runaway slaves to that of nonconforming manumissions. It made it "lawful for any Free holder in this State, to apprehend and *take up* such Slave [the manumitted person], and deliver him or her to the Sheriff of the County" (emphasis added). As in the 1741 law, the manumitee was to be held in "Gaol of the County" for sale at the next court date. In the interim period, however, the sheriff was required to "give Notice in Writing to the last Owner or Owners, or the reputed Owner or Owners" of the apprehension and pending sale. If the owner did not appear to claim his or her property, the sale was to proceed. In a major variation from the 1741 law, "the net Proceeds of the Money arising by such Sale" would not go to the church parish. One-fifth "thereof shall be paid to the Takers up of such Negroes or Mulattoes," and the residue went into the public coffers. Whereas the 1741 law converted one attempted charity into another, the 1777 law introduced a predatory incentive—rewarding takers up.[28]

North Carolina Quakers reaped the whirlwind in 1777. Pursuant to the new law, the thirty-one slaves manumitted illegally by Quaker owners in Perquimans County were "taken up" in the spring of 1777. The "takers up" got receipts from Sheriff Skinner so that they could receive their just rewards. Sheriff Skinner duly notified the former Quaker owners that their former slaves would be sold if they were not claimed. The former owners, believing that they were just in their motives and also technically correct that their 1776 manumissions predated the 1777 law, went to court with the fledgling state of North Carolina. They hired three of the finest jurists produced by North Carolina to defend their actions. Two of them, in fact, helped to give shape to the new American nation. Samuel Johnston of Edenton had been a member of the Continental Congress and had, in fact, been chosen as the first president of the United States in Congress under the Articles of Confederation. James Iredell, also of Edenton, eventually became one of the earliest justices of the U.S. Supreme Court.

Johnston, Iredell, and the third attorney, Jasper Charlton, represented the thirty-one manumitted slaves at the county court in Hertford, on July 22, 1777. Although the three attorneys made elegant arguments that their Quaker masters had freed these slaves prior to the enactment of the new law and that under North Carolina's Bill of Rights persons could not be made subject ex post facto to a new law, they failed to persuade more than two of the five sitting judges. The court held that the slaves should be immediately sold. On the next day, July 23, 1777, all thirty-one of the manumitted slaves were sold at auction for a total of £3,797.5 or for an average of £122.5 per person. Of the total amount of the sale, a handsome sum of £759.5 was paid to the takers up.[29]

For all of their continued efforts to manumit their slaves outside the procedures of North Carolina law between 1776 and the era of the French and Haitian revolutions in the 1790s, a total of at least 134 manumitted slaves were taken up, the takers up paid, and the slaves resold in the three principal Quaker counties of eastern North Carolina—remonstrances, court appeals, public pronouncements, and creative legal maneuvers by the area's Quakers notwithstanding.[30] The process by which the concept and practice of taking up manumitted slaves got into North Carolina procedures and practices was rather straightforward. Pursuant to a 1723 Virginia law, which was almost surely copied into North Carolina, church wardens were given the authority to take up improperly manumitted slaves. But it was evidently only in North Carolina, where Quakers were flagrantly avoiding the state's legal process for manumitting slaves, that the punitive and predatory process used for apprehending runaway slaves got folded into the settlement of manumission cases. It seems clear that when North Carolina Quakers sought to bypass North Carolina's manumission law (at the height of revolutionary anxiety) that the punitive taking-up procedures came to be applied in perhaps their sharpest form.

Once the process of taking up free people of color became entrenched in the North Carolina legal system, it appears that it became possible to use the same concept and procedure to address many different situations relating to free people of color during the first half century of North Carolina's statehood. Between 1778 and 1835 laws were enacted to

Permit sheriffs to search for "lurking" slaves who had been illegally manumitted.

Restore slaves illegally manumitted by Quaker Mark Newby during his lifetime to his heirs in perpetuity.

Limit the rights of manumitted persons to the severely limited "rights and privileges of a free born negro."

Provide special rewards for taking up runaway slaves living in North Carolina's Great Dismal Swamp.

Provide rewards for taking up free people of color who migrated into North Carolina.

Provide slave patrols with authority to identify persons who should be taken up when patrolling the homes of slaves and free people of color.

Provide laws for taking up persons of color who arrived on ships harboring in North Carolina ports.

Enact laws for taking up free people of color unable to pay fines levied against them.

Implement laws for regulating the lives of all free persons of color and for taking up any who did not strictly adhere to these laws.

In short the "taking-up" system unleashed in North Carolina led to the creation of a web of laws and practices that were designed to trip up free persons of color and to place them in danger of being re-enslaved.

It also seems clear that North Carolina's Quakers picked the wrong moment to begin manumitting their slaves. Perhaps in a slave society there would, by definition, be no good moment to manumit numbers of slaves. But certainly the revolutionary moment with its intense insecurity and social and military upheaval was the worst possible time. Why did North Carolina Quakers make this choice? Given the ancient struggles between North Carolina Friends and the established

Anglican Church for the control of North Carolina, perhaps the Quaker defiance against state law was a historic inheritance. There had been plenty of rivalries and even bloody wars over control of the colony from 1680 up through the 1720s. Also North Carolina's Friends not only adhered to a theology radically different from that of their established adversaries, they also remained in constant contact with Quaker communities in Philadelphia and London. Listening closely to what other Friends were thinking and doing hundreds and thousands of miles away meant that they often remained aloof from the social and political conditions in the places where they lived. Challenged by Friends living in other places and social settings, North Carolina Quakers faced potentially explosive problems when they began tampering with the fabric of an emerging slaveholding culture.

In the last quarter of the eighteenth century, these Quakers chose an inopportune historical moment to free their slaves. And because they refused either to acknowledge or to follow a legally defined process for manumitting their slaves, it is likely that they ended up doing more to entrench slavery in North Carolina than to advance awareness among North Carolinians of the inherent evils of slavery. Further they placed those slaves they tried to manumit in North Carolina in an ambiguous and untenable legal limbo. One could easily conclude that the principal goals of North Carolina's Quakers during the American Revolution, and soon thereafter, were neither to free society of slavery nor to establish freed slaves as citizens in American society. Their main goal was cleansing themselves of the sin of slaveholding immediately. Quakers did much, and would do more, for both the antislavery and abolitionist movements. But at this time—at least in North Carolina—their efforts to free themselves of the sin of slavery did not result in the liberty of those who had been held captive. Instead their actions helped to provide the impetus to establish laws that put all people of African ancestry—those born free and those recently manumitted—at legal risk for re-enslavement.

NOTES

1. Among the studies of Quakers and their problem with slavery are several classics: Stephen B. Weeks, *Southern Quakers and Slavery: A Study in Institutional History* (Baltimore: Johns Hopkins Press, 1896); Thomas E. Drake, *Quakers and Slavery in America* (New Haven: Yale University Press, 1950); Jean R. Soderlund, *Quakers and Slavery: A Divided Spirit* (Princeton, N.J.: Princeton University Press, 1985); and Hiram H. Hilty, *By Land and by Sea: Quakers Confront Slavery and Its Aftermath in North Carolina* (Greensboro: North Carolina Friends Historical Society, 1993). The classic studies of Quakers and slavery in the broader context of the rise of antislavery and abolitionism in Europe and America are David Brion Davis, *The Problem of Slavery in Western Culture* (Ithaca: Cornell University Press, 1966) and *The Problem of Slavery in the Age of Revolution, 1770–1823* (Ithaca: Cornell University Press, 1975). The dilemmas of Quaker interactions with other forces in seeking to abolish slavery in Pennsylvania and North Carolina are outlined in Gary Nash, *Forging Freedom: The Formation of Philadelphia's Black Community,*

1720–1840 (Cambridge, Mass.: Harvard University Press, 1988); Noeleen McIlvenna, *A Very Mutinous People: The Struggle for North Carolina, 1660–1713* (Chapel Hill: University of North Carolina Press, 2009); and Beverly C. Tomek, *Colonization and Its Discontents: Emancipation, Emigration, and Antislavery in Antebellum Pennsylvania* (New York: New York University Press, 2011).

2. On the development of a slave society in the Chesapeake region and the Carolinas, see Ira Berlin, *Generations of Captivity: A History of African American Slaves* (Cambridge, Mass.: Harvard University Press, 2003), 55–81.

3. Rd. Skinner's Receipt for Free Negroes to Creecy & [?] 2 Negroes, September 9, 1788; William L. Byrd III, *North Carolina Slaves and Free Persons of Color—Perquimans County* (Westminster, Md.: Heritage Books, 2005), 168–69.

4. Ibid., 167, with similar notices, 165–67.

5. Ibid., 172, with similar summons, 172–75.

6. Ibid., 183–84.

7. Ibid., 168–69.

8. Ibid., 165–66.

9. Ibid., 165, 168.

10. Presentment, Grand Jury of Pasquotank County, Henry Lankester, Foreman [October 1793], in ibid., 390–91.

11. Ibid.

12. Ibid., 391–92. An interesting additional note at the end of this presentment was a statement that the North Carolina General Assembly needed to act with all due haste so that "the Citizens of this District may Enjoy a full participation of a Constitution which they have assisted to raise Vizt. A protection of their Personal Liberties and Properties." This was undoubtedly a reference to the recent battles to ratify the U.S. Constitution in North Carolina. North Carolina had refused to ratify the Constitution until a Bill of Rights had been added to it that would protect those "Personal Liberties and Properties" referenced in the presentment. One of the movers and shakers in the ratification movement in North Carolina was the veteran member of the Continental Congress and governor of North Carolina Samuel Johnston, who may have been the member of this grand jury meeting in Edenton listed as "Saml. W. Johnston" in the Byrd transcription.

13. William L. Byrd III, *Against the Peace and Dignity of the State: North Carolina Laws Regarding Slaves, Free Persons of Color, and Indians* (Westminster, Md.: Heritage Books, 2007), 130–32.

14. Ibid., 132–33.

15. Ibid., 10–11 (emphasis added). There is no evidence that this 1723 enactment was in response to any actions or proposed actions on the part of Quakers in North Carolina. However, it should perhaps be noted that it was in 1722 that the first reference to slaveholding was documented at a southern yearly meeting. The 1722 Virginia Yearly Meeting added a query to its deliberations asking: "Are all Friends clear of being concerned in the importation of slaves or purchasing them for sale, do they use those well they are possessed of, and do they endeavor to restrain from Vice, and to instruct them in the principles of the christian religion?" See Weeks, *Southern Quakers and Slavery*, 201. The North Carolina law may also have been in response to the enactment of a 1723

manumission law in Virginia, which does not appear to have been replicated in North Carolina at the time.

16. Byrd, *Against the Peace*, 25–27.

17. Ibid., 34. One of the interesting sidelights on this law was that it addressed other issues of "taking up" persons for sale into slavery. The law, in fact, specified that no "Turk or Moor" who had previously been free in a Christian country could be taken up and sold and that children of free parents could not be taken to other counties to be sold. See pp. 23, 34.

18. Thomas D. Morris, *Southern Slavery and the Law, 1619–1860* (Chapel Hill: University of North Carolina Press, 1996), 392–93.

19. Weeks, *Southern Quakers and Slavery*, 201, does mention correspondence between the Virginia and North Carolina Yearly Meetings in 1739 and 1740 concerning the use of their slaves and making sure "to use them as fellow creatures" and to make sure that Friends did not participate in slave patrols. But these seem to have been private matters without public aspects.

20. Byrd, *Against the Peace*, 23, 34.

21. Weeks, *Southern Quakers and Slavery*, 198–204.

22. The evolution of antislavery views and practices among North Carolina Quakers is outlined in Weeks, *Southern Quakers and Slavery*, 206–8. For greater detail see Michael J. Crawford, *The Having of Negroes Is Become a Burden: The Quaker Struggle to Free Slaves in Revolutionary North Carolina* (Gainesville: University Press of Florida, 2010), 76–81. It is Crawford's judgment that the positions of the North Carolina and Pennsylvania Yearly Meetings were identical by 1776; see p. 9.

23. Crawford, *Having Negroes*, 73–75.

24. Ibid., 84–86.

25. Ibid., 37–48, 82–83.

26. Ibid., 87–88.

27. Ibid., 118, contains a partial list of those who were manumitted by Quakers at this time in Perquimans County.

28. Byrd, *Against the Peace*, 67–68.

29. The names, the documents, the names of the slaves, the purchasers, and the amounts paid are found in Crawford, *Having Negroes*, 113–19.

30. Ibid., 100–105, 120–21.

DAVID J. VOELKER

Presbyterian Orthodoxy and the Dilemma of Pluralism

The Battle over Kentucky's Transylvania University, 1800–1830

The story of the remarkable rise and fall of Transylvania University under the leadership of Horace Holley has frequently led historians to bemoan the negative influence of Presbyterians on higher education in the South during the early national period. Holley's tenure as president, from 1818 to 1827, has been called "Transylvania's Golden Era" by one historian. During this period the school gained recognition as the preeminent institution of higher education west of the Appalachian Mountains, with student enrollments that rivaled eastern universities.[1] Holley rapidly transformed an anemic college into an important regional university, with a law school and a thriving medical school, and he helped to quadruple student enrollment.[2] During Holley's presidency Lexington remained the intellectual and cultural center of the trans-Appalachian West, even as it lost its former economic prominence to river towns such as Louisville and Cincinnati. Despite his many triumphs, Holley faced persistent enemies. Lexington Presbyterians had opposed his election as president. Over the years they launched a succession of attacks on him until at last they found an effective strategy: they supplemented their longstanding argument that Holley, a Unitarian, was an infidel —"a Socinian of the worst order," to quote one Presbyterian minister—with accusations that he was also a dissipated elitist and that Transylvania University had become an aristocratic institution. Once this polemic gained traction and was appropriated by the governor, the state legislature was all too eager to defund the university in favor of devoting state monies to turnpikes.[3]

Historians have drawn a moral from this story that echoes Holley's own sentiments, which he expressed in his final report to the university's board of trustees in 1827. He explained his departure by noting that "our personal and local jealousies, our political contentions and sectarian divisions, have thus far prevented a result which all enlightened men must acknowledge to be eminently desirable," namely, the proper funding of the university.[4] Historians have agreed that Holley and his university became the victims of both religious and political factionalism. Niels Henry Sonne, in his classic 1939 study of this controversy, concluded that Holley's defeat meant that "the idea of a great central state university, open to all religious denominations, and conducted on liberal principles, had been effectively quashed."[5] Following in Sonne's footsteps, Richard Hofstadter and Walter Metzger recognized the Holley conflict as "the classic case in which the denominational spirit and popular leveling combined to destroy the work of a liberal educator." John D. Wright, a historian of Transylvania University, likewise concluded: "The failure of Holley to establish at Transylvania a liberal state university was really the failure of Kentuckians and their state legislature to overcome the divisive forces of [religious] sectarianism, class jealousies, and political rivalries."[6] As these comments suggest, historians have focused their attention on the tragedy of Holley's demise, emphasizing the unfortunate impact of "bigoted attacks," to use the words of Kentucky historian Thomas D. Clark, on the development of higher education in the West.[7]

While there are good reasons to lament the demise of the Holley administration, this incident raises other issues central to early U.S. religious history. Why, in the words of Hofstadter and Metzger, would Presbyterians have "nourished education with one hand while throttling it with the other"?[8] Answering this question requires understanding the battle over Transylvania University as part of a lengthy struggle by Presbyterians to come to terms with the growing religious diversity that frustrated their ambition to play a preeminent role in public life. In the religious tumult of the early American Republic, Presbyterians found it necessary to sacrifice both numerical growth and public influence in order to maintain doctrinal purity. The demands of rigorous orthodoxy undermined Presbyterian attempts to extend their prominence in the young state of Kentucky. Their attack on Transylvania University under Holley neither restored the institution to their control nor advanced the interests of higher education. It would be a mistake, then, to interpret Holley's downfall as a clear victory for Kentucky Presbyterians over and against the more enlightened thinking of Holley and his supporters.[9] Rather the Presbyterians were in the midst of learning a difficult lesson: their attempt to dominate public higher education and their larger project of arbitrating religious and moral life in Kentucky was doomed to failure. To be sure the Presbyterian churches in Lexington and elsewhere remained important religious and social institutions, but Presbyterian standards of orthodoxy held little sway in a western state where Methodists and Baptists increasingly dominated the religious scene and in a nation where no single denomination could expect to gain exclusive privileges or majority standing.[10]

American Presbyterians had accepted the principle of religious liberty and the constitutional prohibition of a national religious establishment, but they clung to the idea that they could influence the larger public.[11] In the 1780s the national

Presbyterian General Assembly had been quick to adapt to the emerging religious order of the new nation, in which churches operated without government support and membership was strictly voluntary. Nevertheless the orthodox mindset of Presbyterians made it difficult for them to see themselves as merely one denomination among many. Because of their strict Calvinist standards, Presbyterians tended to think of themselves as the rightful stewards of Christian truth.[12] Furthermore, believing that moral virtue flowed from piety, which in turn depended on correct belief, they took it for granted that anyone who denied orthodox Christian principles lacked regenerating grace and remained in a state of original corruption. The orthodox thus chafed against pluralism—the willing acceptance of diversity that was rapidly reshaping the religious ethos of the early United States. The Presbyterian campaign against Horace Holley, understood within the larger context of their struggle to come to terms with diversity and the denominational system, suggests the nearly insurmountable difficulty of reconciling orthodox principles with religious pluralism.[13]

Presbyterians played a prominent role in the founding of Transylvania University, which began its life as a modest grammar school chartered by the Virginia legislature (before Kentucky statehood) in the early 1780s and funded through land grants. Originally located in Danville, Kentucky, Transylvania Seminary, as the school was initially named, moved to the more promising site of Lexington in 1788. Presbyterian advocates of education both initiated the legislation to found the school and also served as its first trustees and teachers, but the original charter defined the institution as a "public school" and required no religious tests of its teachers and students.[14] When Kentucky became a state in 1792, its bill of rights specified: "no preference shall ever be given by law to any religious societies or modes of worship."[15] For any denomination to control the university for sectarian purposes would have violated both public sentiment and the state constitution.

Nevertheless Presbyterians, with the most highly educated clergy in the state, attempted to exert as much influence over the institution as possible. Although Presbyterians could not use the public school to train ministers, they did use it to provide a formal education for future clergy—a requirement that they insisted on maintaining despite the frontier conditions. Presbyterian supporters of the school became understandably discontent in 1794 when they failed to prevent the election as president of Harry Toulmin, an English Unitarian who was an associate of both Joseph Priestley (a prominent English Unitarian who had also moved to the United States in 1794) and Thomas Jefferson—two men routinely attacked as infidels by orthodox Christians. Believing Toulmin to be an infidel (because of his Unitarian belief in the mere humanity of Jesus) and a political radical (because of his association with the democratic and pro-French republicanism of Priestley and Jefferson), the Presbyterian board members bolted and founded a competing Presbyterian academy. Frustrated both by Presbyterian opposition and by his low salary, Toulmin resigned in 1796. Two years later Presbyterians successfully merged their own academy and its substantial assets with the public institution to create Transylvania University.[16] This merger bolstered the Presbyterian sense of stewardship over the university, which nonetheless remained a public rather than a sectarian institution.

Over the next two decades, Presbyterians continued to be dominant on the university's board of trustees, and Presbyterian minister James Blythe served as acting president from 1804 to 1816. In 1805 the Presbyterian-controlled board announced that the university would "guard against the baneful influence of skeptical principles" and that "the great leading doctrines of Christianity would be warmly inculcated," albeit without any sectarian emphasis.[17] The following year the university adopted a new seal and motto that declared *Pietate et Doctrina tuta Libertatus*—"Piety and Doctrine Guard Liberty."[18] This motto reflected the Presbyterian assumption that Christianity, rigorously defined, played an important civic role. No doubt the Presbyterian trustees and president believed that it served the public interest to have orthodox Christians at the helm; but the fact was that Blythe was an unpopular president who never secured enough support from the board to gain a permanent appointment, and the university failed to thrive under his leadership.

Part of the problem was that Blythe's views of the proper relationship between religion and politics deeply offended many Lexingtonians, especially Republicans who sympathized with Jefferson's idea that a "wall of separation" should be maintained between church and state. Blythe articulated a common Presbyterian critique of this separationist position in an 1815 sermon, "Our Sins Acknowledged," which he delivered on the national day of prayer and fasting declared near the end of the War of 1812. He expressed dismay that the Kentucky legislature met "without once acknowledging God in all their ways, that he might direct their steps." He decried the notion "that it matters not whether the man who is to legislate for us be an atheist, a deist, a spendthrift, a debauchee, or a christian"—an ideology that became known as political atheism. To the contrary Blythe argued that governments "must soon crumble to dust, or grow up into tyranny, unless consolidated by religion, unless administered by men whose hearts have felt the benevolence of the gospel."[19] This position that truly virtuous politics could not be separated from heartfelt Christian belief and piety continued to be compelling to orthodox Protestant Americans for many years.[20] Although Blythe and other orthodox Protestants denied that their standards were sectarian in nature, they in fact understood Christianity rather narrowly, explicitly denying Christian status to Unitarians and Universalists and often implicitly excluding Arminians and other "heretics" from the fellowship of Christianity.[21]

Blythe's sermon reflected the fact that Presbyterian ministers defined their church and established their authority through their support of orthodox doctrine, to which they attributed an important public function. They preached and published sermons saturated with the fine points of orthodoxy, they schooled children in and examined prospective members on the tenets of the Westminster Confession of Faith, and they regularly published periodical literature in which they exposed heresies.[22] Their insistence upon orthodoxy, however, did little to augment the membership lists of Kentucky's Presbyterian churches. Presbyterians hoped to recruit new members in the rapidly growing settlements of the West, including Kentucky, but they soon recognized that joining in the revivals would mean throwing orthodox doctrine to the wind. In fact within several years of the famous 1801 Cane Ridge revival, which had begun under Presbyterian sponsorship, the Synod of Kentucky found it necessary to shear off hundreds of members who no longer adhered to orthodox standards.[23] Despite their inability to compete with the growing ranks of Baptists, Methodists, and "New Light" revivalists, Presbyterian leaders continued to insist that their clergy and laity subscribe to the Calvinistic tenets of the Westminster Confession.

Presbyterians believed that sound doctrine—a correct understanding of God's plan—was tightly interwoven both with God's gift of saving grace and with moral behavior. Right belief thus lay at the heart of their conception of a Christian society.[24] The main requirement of Presbyterian orthodoxy was to accept the spiritual and moral truths revealed by the Bible without judging them using human reason or human standards. From the orthodox point of view, unaided human reason was incapable of gaining the spiritual knowledge that humanity needed for salvation. To be sure it was necessary to use reason to comprehend divine revelation, but Presbyterians denied that Christians could pick and choose from the doctrines and principles that they found in the Bible, as Unitarians and other advocates of "higher" biblical criticism were beginning to do.[25]

While biblical revelation was the ultimate source of spiritual truth, learned Reformed Protestants had distilled the core tenets taught by scripture into the Westminster Confession. According to the Westminster Confession, all human beings were morally depraved because of original sin and therefore all justly deserved damnation. God, in his mercy, however, had arbitrarily predestined some souls for salvation and others for damnation. The sacrificial death of Jesus Christ atoned for the sins of the "elect," those destined to be saved. In other words sinful human beings were utterly unable to earn salvation, but a merciful God had sacrificed his son (who, according to the doctrine of the Trinity, was a part of the Godhead) in order to rescue the elect.[26] The confession that so clearly articulated these doctrines held a status second only to the scriptures. In 1812, when Archibald Alexander gave his inaugural address as Princeton's first professor of theology, he noted: "Our own salvation is involved in the right knowledge of [the Bible]." The entire point of the Confession was "right knowledge" of the Bible, thus the Confession itself functioned as an instrument of salvation.[27]

The Presbyterian doctrine that correct belief was a central component of being a Christian, paired with the assumption that only recipients of God's saving grace could consistently maintain virtue, meant that they resisted disentangling religion and politics or, for that matter, religion and education. By Presbyterian lights both individual salvation and a virtuous polity depended on the truths of Christianity. This position generated substantial opposition in Lexington once Blythe had stated it so clearly.

Despite Blythe's denial that Presbyterians were calling for an establishment of religion, his sermon evoked fierce criticisms. In May 1815, several months after Blythe gave his sermon, "A Native Kentuckean" issued a critique in the *Lexington Reporter*. The author argued that something needed to be done about the "declension of the University," which he claimed had once rivaled the great schools of the East. The Kentuckian criticized Blythe for his sectarianism, to which he attributed the school's problems: "The parents of the western states are not yet quite ready to pay the earnings of their labor in exchange for principles, such as are zealously inculcated by the reverend gentleman [Blythe] who has for fifteen years had the superintendance of this school." Blythe's sermon revealed nothing less than "a cringing subserviency to sect and party," which the citizens of Kentucky would not accept.[28] The pseudonymous author exaggerated the glory of the university prior to Blythe's presidency, but he was surely correct that most Kentuckians opposed Presbyterian efforts to insinuate their religion into public education.

Within a year and a half after Blythe's sermon, the Presbyterians were the target of another accusation that they were attempting to dominate the public university in order to inculcate their own particular tenets, with their goal being the gradual union of church and state. A reader writing to the *Reporter* in July 1816 warned that the attempt of some parties to join church and state was not confined to New England, but that groups with similar goals "have not been less systematic and determined" in Kentucky. "One of those means," claimed the critic, was "to get into the possession and under the control of the clergy of a particular sect the public Seminaries of learning," particularly of Transylvania University. The critic gave evidence of the Presbyterian effort to control the school: "In the Transylvania University no professor, in any of the important branches, can be admitted who is not of the favored sect, nor any president appointed who is [not] a clergyman of that sect." To make the matter even more serious, the university, according to the critic, saw a "rapid and alarming decay, under their [the Presbyterians'] government."[29]

The backlash against Blythe's sermon precipitated a concerted Republican effort to deprive the Presbyterians of control over Kentucky's public university.[30] The Presbyterian-dominated board of trustees foundered between 1815 and 1817 as it attempted to remain in control of the institution while also locating an alternative president to Blythe, who eventually resigned amid the tumult in March

1816.[31] During this period the board elected a Presbyterian and a Baptist minister president, but both declined the position. Opponents of sectarian education in Lexington and the legislature, however, had other plans. Ninety-three citizens of Lexington signed a petition recommending the election of Thomas Cooper as president. Cooper, an English-born Unitarian and friend of Joseph Priestley, was as distinguished for his work as a chemist as for his democratic and anticlerical views. He had shown open hostility toward the "aggressive Presbyterians" who wanted to control education. (He had also been imprisoned under the Sedition Act in 1789 for his criticism of Federalist president John Adams, and he was a vocal supporter of Jefferson, who was also a known enemy of Presbyterian sectarianism.) Although Cooper was not elected, the support for him indicated that the non-Presbyterian advocates of the university were mobilizing to push the institution in a new direction.[32]

In 1817, after failing to agree on Cooper, the trustees elected as president Horace Holley, minister of the prestigious Hollis Street Church in Boston.[33] The Presbyterians on the board initially supported Holley because of their mistaken belief that he was an orthodox divine. Holley's Yale degree was an excellent orthodox credential, but the fact was that he and his congregation were "liberal," which is to say that they were moving in the direction of Unitarianism. Upon realizing their error about Holley, the Presbyterian trustees made the strategic mistake of rescinding his election.[34] This obviously sectarian action drew increased attention from the state legislature, which had been investigating the university since 1815. A legislative committee deemed it unacceptable that the trustees had rejected Holley not because he was unqualified but because, as the investigators stated it, he "did not exactly quadrate with Calvinistic orthodoxy."[35] The committee condemned the board's "decision in favor of sectarian tenets" and described this sectarianism as "an ulcer, cancerous in its nature, which if not thoroughly . . . healed, will not only vitiate, but totally consume this system."[36] Although the trustees reelected Holley as president in a last-ditch effort at appeasement, the legislature voted overwhelmingly in late 1817 to reorganize the board of trustees and remove the Presbyterian members.[37] Thus began the long Presbyterian struggle against Holley.

Despite his Yale degree, president-elect Holley had abandoned his orthodox roots. After his graduation from Yale, he had studied theology under Timothy Dwight, a well-known orthodox Calvinist divine.[38] At first true to his orthodox training, Holley in 1805 took the pulpit of the Congregational Church of Greenfield Hill, in Fairfield, Connecticut, where Dwight himself had once been minister. Soon after Holley's arrival, the congregation adopted a new, Calvinistic confession of faith, which Holley likely drafted. Eventually, however, Holley looked to Boston in search of a more lucrative pulpit that would allow him to support his family comfortably.[39] He was installed as the minister of the Hollis Street

Church in 1809. His move to Boston hinted that his sympathies were migrating toward Unitarianism, a shift also indicated by the fact that he served as a member of Harvard University's board of overseers during his time in Boston.[40] In 1812 Holley gave a discourse on the death of the Reverend Joseph Stevens Buckminster, the founder of higher biblical criticism in the United States. Holley's praise for a man who sought to apply historical and textual analysis to the scriptures, in part to undermine Calvinism, revealed that he had foregone orthodoxy.[41]

Holley's support of freedom of inquiry for university students further signaled his rejection of orthodox principles and revealed his hostility toward Presbyterian sectarianism. In an 1813 article published anonymously in the *General Repository and Review*, he criticized American colleges and universities that favored particular sects in their instruction of religion. Quoting a rule from Princeton, a Presbyterian institution, he argued that the school infringed upon a student's freedom of thought: "'The faculty shall be empowered *to dismiss* from the seminary any student who shall prove *unsound in his religious sentiments.*' What an effect must this have upon a student's inquiries after truth?" After criticizing several other institutions, Holley praised Harvard, a Unitarian institution, "as the great defender of the true Protestant cause, as the source of rational, catholic, and evangelical Christianity, and as the glory of your age, and the hope of posterity." Central to Holley's religious identity was the distinction that he made between "catholic" and "sectarian." Holley used the word *catholic* to describe schools that "adopt the Bible as the rule of faith without any supplement, and whose system of instruction favors rational and simple Christianity." In contrast, he argued, "Any man is a sectarian, whether Papist or Protestant, who insists upon others subscribing [to] a creed, or standard, of his own or his party, beside the Bible." Holley thus criticized Christians who created creeds, judged the beliefs of others using those creeds, and insisted that others agree with their creeds. His major targets in this article were the Presbyterian and Congregational universities, which he described as particularly intolerant. These schools, he argued, needed to "come back from Calvin to Christ."[42]

The sermons that Holley preached to the students of Transylvania University likewise suggest his departure from the orthodox Calvinist theology of predestination and atonement. He clearly believed that human beings played a role in effecting their own salvation. In a sermon that he preached on July 4, 1819, titled "What Must We Do to Be Saved?," he noted that "a state of salvation [is not] an arbitrary condition, without any reference to character & conduct—this is not believed by any class of enlightened christians."[43] In a later sermon, he reiterated that natural religion teaches "that we shall be happy or miserable [in the future life] according to our character."[44] In yet another sermon, Holley went so far as to make morality the central element in his definition of religion, saying that "religion is a moral obligation."[45]

Holley's views reflected the Unitarian Christianity that was taking shape in the Boston area at this time. Unitarianism was emerging out of New England congregationalism, with Rev. William Ellery Channing leading the way in the attempt of New England liberals to distinguish themselves from English Unitarians (including Priestley and his various followers). While English Unitarians asserted the pure humanity of Jesus, a view known as Socinianism, Boston Unitarians tended to see Jesus as having an intermediate status between humanity and God, a view known as Arianism.[46] Furthermore, as Channing noted in his seminal 1819 sermon "Unitarian Christianity," Unitarians also openly rejected the Calvinist doctrine of the atonement—the belief that "Christ's death has an influence in making God . . . merciful"—because Unitarians thought that such a notion cast a shadow over God's "pure goodness."[47] While rejecting the atonement, Unitarians nevertheless believed that Jesus's miracles, as recorded in the New Testament, validated the divine status of his moral teachings, which could inform and inspire individuals so that they might cultivate Christian virtue through their own free will.[48] For his part Holley avoided taking a firm stand on the nature of Jesus. One sermon outline declared, "reject Arianism and Socinianism," but this mandate probably derived more from Holley's distaste for extrascriptural authority than from his opinion about Jesus.[49] Holley certainly dismissed the idea that God and Jesus were equivalent, but Transylvania's senior class, defending him in 1823, asserted that he always "mentioned the name of our Saviour with the utmost reverence."[50] For Unitarians such as Holley, Jesus's teachings made him "the Christ"—the savior—albeit through the mechanism of moral influence rather than through atonement.

Be that as it may, Unitarian positions on Christ, human nature, and salvation galled Presbyterians and other orthodox, whether in New England or in Kentucky. If orthodox Calvinists neglected to acknowledge the distinction between Arianism and Socinianism, it was because they correctly saw that the Unitarian denial of Christ's atonement for the sins of humanity shifted the agency of salvation from God to humans. In short the orthodox believed that Unitarians deprecated divine sovereignty and overestimated human virtue, with the result of replacing piety with an ineffectual moralism—in the sense that historian Joseph Haroutunian used the term in his classic work, *Piety versus Moralism*. The Presbyterian leadership in Kentucky tried to stem this tide of moralism that they believed was washing over the nation, sweeping up not only Unitarian rationalists but also many evangelical Christians. They insisted that God's grace, warranted by Christ's sacrifice, was the only sure foundation for an upright Christian life. In rationalism—whether it had religious trappings or not—they discerned both spiritual and moral danger.[51] From the Presbyterian perspective, Unitarians discarded Christianity's distinctive doctrines, including Christ's divinity and his blood atonement for human sin. Even if Holley was not technically a Socinian, he did sever the connection between Christ's death and the salvation of humankind. Furthermore he talked much more about the human capacity for moral behavior than about the necessity of special grace. From the Presbyterian perspective, his advocating of a facile, natural morality made him every bit as dangerous as Thomas Paine, with whom they explicitly compared him.[52]

Kentucky Presbyterians—who had opposed Harry Toulmin in the 1790s, had resisted the doctrinal slippage inherent in revivalism, and had long strived to defend Calvinist orthodoxy—envisioned their battle against Horace Holley as "but part of the great contest, which has been carried on, time immemorial, between the God of Israel and Belial; between Christ and Antichrist," to use the words of one of Holley's critics.[53] As president Holley exercised significant intellectual, religious, and social influence in Lexington. An important teacher at the university, he had responsibility for the senior class and taught mental and moral philosophy, a capstone course that included both moral philosophy and natural theology.[54] In 1824 a hostile pamphleteer reminded Holley of his importance: "As I heard you say at a commencement, you are to be diffused through [the students], and they are to diffuse you wherever they go."[55] Precisely because of his influential position, Holley for many years stood as the primary target of a Presbyterian campaign against infidelity. His enemies believed that he abused his position of authority by inculcating "principles upon his students . . . which were . . . considered by all denominations except his own, hostile to the christianity of the Bible."[56] Presbyterians believed that Holley's lax theology, which they saw as only nominally Christian, inevitably led to immorality. Holley, therefore, was purportedly unfit to hold a position that gave him influence over the minds and morals of young men. His principles and his personality were spiritually and morally dangerous.

Without exception the leaders of the anti-Holley movement were Presbyterians. John McFarland, a Presbyterian minister in Paris, a town in Lexington's orbit, published a series of pamphlets titled *The Literary Pamphleteer* between December 1823 and March 1824.[57] McFarland's printer in Paris was Joel Reid Lyle, a Presbyterian elder and brother of Rev. John Lyle. Robert Stuart, who under the pseudonym "Citizen" made a major contribution to McFarland's pamphlets, was the Presbyterian minister at Walnut Hill, six miles east of Lexington. Nathan Hall and John Breckinridge Jr., who refused to cooperate with Holley's plan for religious instruction for the university and also made contributions to McFarland's pamphlet series, were the Presbyterian ministers of Lexington. Of the five Presbyterian graduates of Transylvania University who testified that Holley inculcated his unorthodox opinions, three of them later became Presbyterian ministers.[58] McFarland's pamphlets and those from a few others made such an extensive attack on Holley that one Lexington inhabitant referred to the "presbyterian war against the administration of the University."[59]

Presbyterians treated their assault on Unitarianism—which they insisted upon identifying as the heresy of Socinianism—much as they had their earlier campaign against the deism of Paine. In 1808 Archibald Alexander alerted the ministers and elders of the general assembly to the changing nature of the infidel danger. As the orthodox often did, he incorrectly equated Unitarianism with Socinianism, the total rejection of Christ's divinity: "Most of those speculative men, who were lately inclined to deism, will now fill the ranks of Socinianism, or Unitarianism, as they chose to denominate their religion." Alexander noted that while Paine had spoken crudely and seductively to the popular ear, the Socinians posed more danger, "because they [had] for their abettors the learned and powerful of this world."[60] The new enemy, it might be said, had graduated from Harvard and was using guile to win adherents.

While the deists had promoted their ideas in public through open denunciations of Christianity, Unitarians, it was believed, gained adherents more stealthily. Orthodox sentinel Jedidiah Morse, in an 1815 review of Thomas Belsham's *American Unitarianism*, raised the alarm over the Unitarian "defection from those doctrines of the Bible, which have usually been denominated orthodox," and accused Unitarians of working "for most part in secret," using "artifice" to promote "apostasy from Christianity." Morse declared that Unitarians were "unbeliever[s]" who would be condemned to hell because their "denial of the divinity and atonement of the Savior" amounted to a denial of God.[61]

Although Kentucky was a long way from Boston, its Presbyterian ministers believed that the "gangrene of Socinus" plagued their own state.[62] Blythe, writing as editor of the Lexington-based *Christian Register*, identified Kentucky as a center of infidelity, paralleling it with Boston, the home of Unitarianism: "It is well known, that in no part of America, except in the neighbourhood of Boston, are the soul-destroying errors of Socinus, and Arius, so industriously circulated as in Kentucky, and the adjacent states."[63] In 1823 the *Christian Register* published a five-article series attacking the heresy of Unitarianism.[64] Blythe and his colleagues identified Socinianism as a serious threat because they saw it as a "general system of unbelief," perhaps more insidious than deism but every bit as pernicious in its effects. McFarland, writing in the anti-Holley *Literary Pamphleteer* in 1823, spelled out the Socinians' theological offenses: "They do *not* believe that Jesus is truly Divine; that he existed before he was born of the Virgin Mary—that he made an atonement for sin. They do *not* believe in the personality of the Holy Spirit—in the necessity of his renovating operations, and in the doctrine of the fall and depravity of our nature."[65] Having rejected so many articles of faith, including the belief that Christ was the savior, Unitarians were not, in Presbyterian eyes, Christians. Writing in 1805, David Rice had warned Kentuckians that Socinianism was particularly dangerous because it makes "God so merciful, and the way to heaven so easy, that in time it naturally lulls the mind to sleep, and makes it indifferent about all religion."[66] Unitarianism, then, like deism, rejected the necessity of Christ's saving grace. Unitarian theology jettisoned both fear of and dependence upon God, breeding a spiritual complacence that could only lead to immorality.[67]

Presbyterian critics assaulted Holley as an infidel who wore only a thin Christian disguise. One pamphlet writer, "Omega," compared him to Paine: "Like Thomas Paine, one of your first attacks commenced with extolling the book of Nature." But in Omega's eyes, the "book of Nature" failed to reveal most of the central elements of the Bible, as it did not "give a hint of the beginning, nor the end of the world[;] the fall of man, nor his recovery by the Son of God; the resurrection of the body; the last judgment, nor the final state of the righteous and the wicked." Holley emphasized natural religion, Omega argued, precisely so that he could "set aside the need of a Saviour, his divinity & atonement" in favor of Unitarian heresy. Holley's treatment of Jesus particularly disgusted Omega: "Does he not degrade the Saviour of the World to the level of a Socrates, a Plato, and a Zoroaster?" Holley could not deny these crucial Christian doctrines, Omega continued, and still pretend to honor the Bible, which, "as revelation from God, . . . must stand or fall as a whole."[68] Holley, then, was a deist in disguise. His enemies thus pleaded with the public: "Will you pay the President of a University to laugh and brow beat your sons out of the little religion which they may possess?"[69] Further evidence of Holley's plot to indoctrinate students in his infidel beliefs was raised by "Citizen" (Robert Stuart), who decried the "Socinian pamphlets" that Holley had given to the university library. (The university library did in fact obtain the sermons of Unitarian luminary William Ellery Channing in 1824.)[70]

Presbyterians opposed Holley's presidency from the moment that they discovered his Unitarian sympathies, but it was his 1823 eulogy sermon for an important benefactor of the university that incited their full-scale campaign against him. In his *Discourse Occasioned by the Death of Col. James Morrison*, Holley revealed, through his praise of Morrison, the religious qualities that he most admired. He lauded Morrison for his simple, undogmatic, and tolerant religion: "He cared little for works of mere criticism, for technical defenses of principles or dogmas, for authorities collected and arranged to support unnatural, uncomfortable, and injurious systems of belief, and for narrow and exclusive purposes." Holley also admired Morrison for his interest in morality over doctrine: "Colonel Morrison was a christian in his sentiments and practice, but did not consider the peculiarities of any of the sectarian creeds in religion . . . as ornamental to his character. With him, a life of virtue was the most acceptable homage to the Deity."[71] In part because Morrison had been affiliated with a Presbyterian church, the *Literary Pamphleteer* found the eulogy to be an assault on them and on Christian faith. Holley allegedly put words into Morrison's mouth when he praised the colonel for his tolerant, "catholic" religion: "To all that he has said respecting the deceased, as a man, a soldier, a citizen, and a benefactor of his country we offer no dissent; but when he brings him forward as a christian, and makes him shoot off, whatever he himself wishes, from the magazine of infidelity and Socinianism, we consider him at once grossly injuring the dead, and insulting the living."[72] Holley, according to this accusation, lied about Morrison in order to spread his own religious heresies.

Presbyterians argued that Holley's spreading of dangerous errors in the guise of a eulogy revealed him to be a contemptible unbeliever and a skilled practitioner of deceit. Just as he misrepresented Morrison, he had pretended to be something he was not. His enemies repeatedly accused him of misrepresenting himself from the beginning in order to fulfill his ambitions. Omega explained that Holley "took some pains to convince" the university trustees that he was "an orthodox divine." Such deceit and disguise, important tools of Satan himself, were employed by infidels of all ages, wrote Omega. Being well acquainted with this tendency of infidelity, Presbyterians, unlike the other Christians in Lexington, had not been fooled. Quoting the archinfidel Voltaire, Omega described Holley's strategy as akin to that of other infidels: "Strike, but hide the hand."[73]

Holley's alleged deceit was only the first of many supposed moral flaws. Omega argued that the university paid him an excessive salary, which he squandered to keep himself "shining in silk." Thus, through his example, Holley ruined his students, who would naturally find their teacher's ways "irresistible."[74] Five Presbyterian graduates of the university purported to expose his "loose and dangerous" morality in word as well as deed. They claimed that Holley, when speaking in class one day about the passions, had said: "Young gentlemen, whatever you find within you, cherish it, for it is part of your nature—restrain it not."[75] It is impossible to know exactly what Holley said or how he might have contextualized or qualified such a comment, but it is likely that he meant much the same thing as Channing meant when he spoke of the human "likeness to God," by which he meant the "divine principle" in the soul.[76] To Calvinist ears such words encouraged moral license by suggesting that students should give free rein to their most corrupt passions and desires. This immoral counsel followed directly from Holley's theology and moral philosophy. He had been "frequently heard extolling the rectitude of human nature" and was "disposed to laugh" at the idea of Satan. Holley feigned support of Christian ethics but, as Omega contended, "this is the usual cant of deists; they will praise [the Bible's] ethics, but not practise them." They could not do so because they failed to take evil seriously. It was no wonder that Holley's life, as Omega put it, confirmed the orthodox rule "that all have sinned."[77]

The arguments against Holley's appropriateness as a moral role model for students focused on his alleged idle and extravagant habits. According to Citizen, he frequented "all those places to which the vain and dissipated resort," including "the Theatre, the Ball room, [and] the Card table." "Thus by both precept and example," Citizen opined, Holley was "well qualified to lead youth in the way of the destroyer."[78] Consistent with the Presbyterian understanding of morality, Citizen thus united Holley's flawed beliefs, his "precept," with his immoral behavior, or his "example." Holley's alleged moral violations were banal or nonexistent in the eyes of many Lexingtonians, but Presbyterian polemicists took his urbane sensibility and his "catholic" or undogmatic approach to theology as evidence of his moral corruption and deception.

The Presbyterians thus asserted that what people believed about religion and morality crucially shaped how they lived. The renowned orthodox minister Timothy Dwight, Holley's former teacher, articulated this understanding of moral philosophy when he explained why one's moral opinions mattered: "All volitions of the mind are of course accordant with the prevailing dictates of the understanding; and all the actions of men spring from their volitions. Such, then, as is the moral nature of the opinions of a man, will be the nature of his moral conduct." He concluded: "Obedience to error is vice; obedience to truth is virtue."[79] According to this theory of moral philosophy, a direct relationship existed between one's moral opinions and one's moral conduct, and Holley's views did not bode well. In 1825 the *Western Luminary* printed a generally positive letter about Holley, but in their own commentary the editors used the letter to denounce his spiritual state. The author of the letter, who had heard Holley "deliver a course of Lectures on morals and manners," did not doubt that he was a Christian. The author also believed that he served the university well. Although he saw no danger in it, the author did doubt one thing, that Holley "was acquainted with *vital Religion.*" By this phrase he meant "a Supernatural communication from God." Agreeing with this point, the editors turned it against Holley's moral character: "The *morals of a gentleman* [Holley] *may possess,*—while yet of *Christian* morals—or, of morals founded on *vital religion*—he may be entirely destitute."[80] A superficial morality might satisfy the unperceptive, but Holley's Presbyterian critics demanded more from a public figure.

The Presbyterians began their campaign against Holley by criticizing his religion and character, but they did not achieve success until they attracted the attention of Kentucky's governor, Joseph Desha, with political criticism. When Governor Desha turned against the university in 1825, he made three major allegations that derived directly from the polemics of the *Literary Pamphleteer.* Rather than emphasizing Presbyterian religious concerns, however, Desha echoed the largely insincere, populist rhetoric supplied by the *Pamphleteer.* First, he alleged (unfairly) that the school had drawn too liberally "from the funds of the people." Second, Desha objected to the fact that the university paid its president a salary twice that received by the highest state officer, namely the governor himself. And third, because of its "extravagant" spending, particularly on its professors' salaries, the university had raised its tuition, so that only a small portion of the "young men of Kentucky" could afford to attend. In short the university had become an aristocratic institution that lined the pockets of its president and professors and worked for the "benefit of the rich, to the exclusion of the poor; and . . . the only result is to add to the aristocracy of wealth, the advantage of superior knowledge." Rather than continuing to waste money on "the sons of the wealthy," Desha argued, the state should "put into operation a system of Common schools."[81] To achieve this end, he proposed that the legislature divert the state's educational funds to pay for new turnpikes. The tolls from these roads, he promised, would then "be for ever sacredly devoted to the interests of education." This rhetoric, however, proved empty: the plan was designed not to fund education but to build roads, and it ultimately only delayed the creation of a common school system.[82]

Unfortunately for Holley, he and the university were unwittingly embroiled in a larger political controversy over banking policy in Kentucky. Holley opposed the debtor "relief" position of Desha, in no small part because relief policies had eliminated the important income that the university received from stock in the Bank of Kentucky, which it had been granted by the legislature. Ironically, then, the trustees had been forced to raise tuition in part because of the banking policies of Desha's faction of the Republican Party.[83] Upon hearing Desha's first hostile address, Holley realized that the legislature would no longer provide adequate support for the university. Having lost faith in Kentucky's dedication to higher education, he left the presidency in 1827.[84] He had endured years of criticism for his religious beliefs, but it was the hostility and apathy of the governor and legislature toward the university that convinced him of the futility of his labors. He had no time, however, to make a new future for himself: shortly after leaving Kentucky, Holley died of yellow fever, while sailing from New Orleans to New York City.[85]

At last Kentucky Presbyterian leaders had succeeded in their campaign to rid Transylvania University of President Holley. As a result of their efforts, both the prestige and the enrollment of the university plunged. Over the next dozen years, three ministers—a Baptist and two Episcopalians—served as president, but they were unable to reverse the losses incurred by Holley's departure and the simultaneous reduction of state funding.[86] The governing class of Kentucky had turned its back on public higher education, and Presbyterians had been instrumental in leading them to do so. Irony thus marred the victory over Holley: the cause of higher education, which Presbyterians valued so greatly, was set back in Kentucky by decades.

Holley's Presbyterian opponents, it should be noted, had not defeated him with their religious and moral arguments. While their understanding of Holley as an "infidel" motivated their assault, it was their faux populist accusations of elitism that enabled the governor and legislature to launch a well-calculated political attack on the university. Historian Niels Sonne thus erred in concluding that the Presbyterian victory over Holley meant that Kentucky was "becoming an increasingly orthodox Christian state."[87] Rather Governor Desha had appropriated Presbyterian arguments for his own political purposes: shifting funding from higher education to internal improvements while eliminating an opponent of his policies.[88]

Presbyterian power was waning rather than waxing. Kentucky Presbyterians had begun to realize that they had to make a choice between preserving doctrinal purity and establishing public dominance; after years of pursuing both goals, they finally chose the former. Writing in the 1840s, Presbyterian minister and historian Robert Davidson noted that after Holley's departure, "the fortunes of Transylvania . . . languished for a series of years." Because the trustees failed to elect "a President in whom the religious community could confide," he continued, "every leading sect in the State was driven to establish a college of its own." The result impeded the cause of Christian education: "instead of a single towering, complete, well-manned and crowded University, deserving of the name, the strength and resources of the country were frittered into fractions." Briefly, from 1840 to 1842, Davidson himself served as president, but by then Presbyterians were too fully committed to their own Centre College to support Transylvania. Davidson expressed no regret at this lack of Presbyterian support, because he believed that Centre had done great service to "the cause of education and the Gospel ministry in the State of Kentucky."[89] Be that as it may, Centre produced only a handful of graduates each year during the 1820s, and as late as 1839 it boasted only a dozen graduates.[90] Its impact paled in comparison to that of Transylvania, which granted well over six hundred degrees during Holley's tenure.[91]

Nevertheless as Davidson surveyed the history of his denomination, he confidently reaffirmed Presbyterian sectarianism. He regretted that Kentuckians had been unable to create a "towering" public university—led by Presbyterians—that was true to Christian values. In light of this failure, he believed that Presbyterians had made a mistake in trying to cooperate with others. Davidson expressed bitterness toward both the state and other denominations and encouraged the Presbyterians to commit themselves fully to their own institutions: "Let [the Presbyterians] at last take warning from the crippled condition of various State institutions, and from the fate of Transylvania and Dickinson, originally founded by the Presbyterians, and now fallen into the hands of the Methodists. Let [Presbyterians] establish Denominational Schools . . . and provide instruction of a superior and commanding character, and they will not despair of support."[92] Going forward, Presbyterians (and other churches) would indeed support denominational schools as training grounds for future ministers and lay leaders alike. Interdenominational cooperation, it seemed, did not work very well when the participants disagreed so vehemently over fundamental beliefs and priorities.

Not surprisingly Kentucky Presbyterians sided with the "Old School" in the schism that wracked the national general assembly in 1837–38, a decade after the Holley controversy. As Davidson put it, Kentucky Presbyterians joined with "the friends of orthodoxy and sound Presbyterianism."[93] In practice this meant that Kentucky Presbyterians continued to insist on the rigorous Calvinism of the Westminster Confession, and they opted out of the interdenominational organizations that were attempting to promote a Christianized—but not strictly orthodox—American society. While the New School Presbyterians outside of Kentucky came to terms with denominationalism by embracing ecumenical missionary and reform work, the Old Schoolers accepted denominationalism only by default, by relinquishing their ambition to public leadership in favor of the narrower project of preserving orthodoxy.[94]

During Kentucky's early decades, Presbyterians had been "first among equals" in the project of establishing educational institutions, and this status clearly emboldened their ambitions for public influence. Their commitment to orthodoxy went hand-in-hand with a dedication to education. They thus achieved initial prominence by helping found Transylvania University and other western schools. After the War of 1812, however, several political and religious developments reduced Presbyterians to mere "equals" on a pluralistic field of competition, alongside other growing denominations that began to develop institutions and promote education as well.[95] Despite having helped oust Holley, Presbyterians had lost their hold over public education in Kentucky, and as a result they retrenched. Many decades would pass, and an entirely new intellectual context would arise—modern, Darwinian science—before orthodox Christians, dubbed fundamentalists, would reemerge as a political force to be reckoned with.

NOTES

The archival research for this essay began many years ago with support from a National Endowment for the Humanities Younger Scholars Fellowship. At the time I was an undergraduate at Hanover College, where I thrived under the guidance of Marsha S. Dutton, the late Frank S. Luttmer, Philip L. Barlow, and George M. Curtis, who advised my senior thesis on the Holley controversy. I also became indebted at that time to B. J. Gooch, the special collections librarian at Transylvania University, and to my friends Tammy Graham and Suzanne Lamb, who provided tremendous support for my work during those years. I continued to explore the history of religious controversy in early Lexington through my M.A. thesis at the University of North Carolina at Chapel Hill, where Donald G. Mathews served as my adviser. He was uniformly rigorous and provocative in his comments to me and was always steady and kind in his support. I am thus grateful to have the opportunity to take part in this collection of essays in his honor. Charles Capper and John K. Nelson also served on my thesis committee and provided excellent suggestions. More recently, as I reframed and refined the argument of this essay, my spouse, Ruth Homrighaus, and my son, James Cormac Voelker, helped me see things through. Regina Sullivan and Monte Hampton have my gratitude for initiating this project and pursuing it with tremendous persistence.

For a more detailed study of Lexington Presbyterians and the Holley incident, see David J. Voelker, "Frontier Infidelity? Antisectarianism at Transylvania University in Kentucky, 1796–1827," Hanover College Independent Study, 1996, Agnes Brown

Duggan Library, Hanover, Indiana; and David J. Graham-Voelker, "Preserving Orthodoxy in the Early Republic: The Failure of Presbyterian Ambitions in Lexington, Kentucky, 1800–1830," M.A. thesis, University of North Carolina at Chapel Hill, 1998, North Carolina Collection, Wilson Library, Chapel Hill, North Carolina.

1. Walter W. Jennings, *Transylvania: Pioneer University of the West* (New York: Pageant, 1955), 99.

2. During the War of 1812, the enrollment had hovered below fifty students. The enrollment, including preparatory and undergraduates, was just over one hundred when Holley arrived in Lexington. Within a few years, the total number of enrolled students exceeded four hundred, with nearly half of the students coming from outside of Kentucky, almost exclusively from southern states. For enrollment data see Jennings, *Transylvania*, 107, and Niels Henry Sonne, *Liberal Kentucky, 1780–1828* (1939; Lexington: University of Kentucky Press, 1958), 146, 174.

3. James McChord, letter to Samuel Corothers, Lexington, Kentucky, February 20, 1816, qtd. in Sonne, *Liberal Kentucky*, 152.

4. John Bradford reprinted Holley's March 24, 1827, report in his "Notes on Kentucky," in the *Kentucky Gazette*. See *The Voice of the Frontier: John Bradford's Notes on Kentucky*, ed. Thomas D. Clark (Lexington: University Press of Kentucky, 1993), 260.

5. Sonne, *Liberal Kentucky*, 260. Sonne's work, particularly his bibliography, proved invaluable to my research.

6. Richard Hofstadter and Walter P. Metzger, *The Development of Academic Freedom in the United States* (New York: Columbia University Press, 1955), 247–48; John D. Wright Jr., "Libertarianism's Loss: The Case of Horace Holley and Transylvania University," in *Freedom and Reform: Essays in Honor of Henry Steele Commager*, ed. Harold M. Hyman and Leonard W. Levy (New York: Harper & Row, 1967), 101–26, esp. 126. More recently Craig Friend has invoked Holley's presidency as a sign that the middle class in Lexington had seized cultural leadership away from more conservative elements—in this case the Calvinistic Presbyterians—under whom the university threatened to languish. Friend does not, however, follow the history of the university through Holley's resignation, which indicates a setback to the cultural prominence of the city's middle class. Craig Thompson Friend, *Along the Maysville Road: The Early American Republic in the Trans-Appalachian West* (Knoxville: University of Tennessee Press, 2005), 176–77, 212–13.

7. Clark, *Voice of the Frontier*, ix. Merle Borrowman goes even further: "By 1825 an agrarian sense of economic exploitation was in league with the forces of religious fundamentalism and frontier anti-intellectualism against Lexington and Holley. With the Jacksonian Democrats and the religious fundamentalists in firm control of the state government, the future of Transylvania was bleak." Borrowman, "The False Dawn of the State University," *History of Education Quarterly* 1 (1961): 18.

8. Hofstadter and Metzger, *Development of Academic Freedom*, 244.

9. Sonne, and to some extent Wright, characterized Holley's resignation as a victory for Presbyterians. See Sonne, *Liberal Kentucky*, 260–61, and Wright, "Libertarianism's Loss," 108.

10. On the social influence of Presbyterians in the Bluegrass region through 1830, see David J. Voelker, "Church Building and Social Class on the Urban Frontier: The

Refinement of Lexington, 1784–1830," *Register of the Kentucky Historical Society* 106 (2008): 191–229.

11. On the revision of the Westminster Confession to make it consistent with the separation of church and state, see D. G. Hart, "American Presbyterianism: Exceptionalism," *Journal of Presbyterian History* 84 (2006): 12–16.

12. For an incisive analysis of the Presbyterian identity, see Mark A. Noll, "What Has Been Distinctly American about American Presbyterians?" *Journal of Presbyterian History* 84 (2006): 6–11. Noll notes the dual importance of the Bible and the Westminster Confession, as well as the Presbyterian ability to engage in ecumenical projects (such as the missionary and reform societies of the early nineteenth century) while also behaving "as if Presbyterian beliefs and practices constituted the only possible stance for faithful Christian commitment" (6). Perry Miller has also argued that although the Presbyterians altered the Westminster Confession in 1789, making it consistent with a separation of church and state, they still opposed the denominationalist idea: "Presbyterianism was so rooted in the theology of the Reformation that it could not easily give up . . . its inherited ideal of THE Church." Perry Miller, *The Life of the Mind in America, from the Revolution to the Civil War* (San Diego: Harcourt Brace Jovanovich, 1965), 43–44.

13. On the postrevolutionary challenges faced by Presbyterians (and other Calvinists), see Mark A. Noll, *America's God: From Jonathan Edwards to Abraham Lincoln* (New York: Oxford University Press, 2002), 256–59. Samuel C. Pearson, "From Church to Denomination: American Congregationalism in the Nineteenth Century," *Church History* 38 (1969): 67–87, explores how New England Congregationalists only very gradually adjusted their identity to come to terms with American pluralism. He noted: "By the early part of the nineteenth century it was apparent that these national churches forged in the midst of a pluralistic society were denominations, i.e., they were voluntary associations of like-minded individuals united to accomplish certain defined objectives" (67). On the churches' uncertainty about their proper function within the new context, see Ralph E. Morrow, "The Great Revival, the West, and the Crisis of the Church," in *The Frontier Re-examined*, ed. John Francis McDermott (Urbana: University. of Illinois Press, 1967), 65–78. For an influential interpretation of the rise of denominationalism, see Sidney E. Mead, "From Coercion to Persuasion: Another Look at the Rise of Religious Liberty and the Emergence of Denominationalism," *Church History* 25 (1956): 317–37.

14. Rev. John Todd, his nephew Col. John Todd, and Caleb Wallace—all Presbyterians—initiated the early legislation in the Virginia legislature establishing Transylvania Seminary (a name that lacked religious connotation at the time). Rev. David Rice, the first Presbyterian minister to establish a church in Kentucky, served as the first chair of the institution's board of trustees. The first teacher, James Mitchell, was a Presbyterian minister. Ernest Trice Thompson, *Presbyterians in the South*, vol. 1 (Richmond, Va.: John Knox, 1963), 264–65; Wright, *Transylvania*, 5–8.

15. Kentucky Constitution of 1792, Article XII, Section 3.

16. Toulmin had strong Republican credentials—recommendations from Jefferson and James Madison—and had support in Lexington from the likes of John Bradford, staunch Democratic-Republican and editor of the *Kentucky Gazette*, Lexington's earliest newspaper. In his *Thoughts on Emigration*, Toulmin revealed why he had immigrated to

America in 1793: "In America you are at liberty to maintain any religion, as God and your conscience dictate. Hence rankling jealousies, furious anathemas, [and] unchristian struggles for ascendency [*sic*], are unknown." Toulmin's experiences proved his hopes wrong. Sonne, *Liberal Kentucky*, 37; Wright, *Transylvania*, 30–32.

17. *Kentucky Gazette*, October 10, 1805, qtd. in Sonne, *Liberal Kentucky*, 76.

18. Friend, *Maysville Road*, 176–77; Wright, *Transylvania*, 50–53.

19. James Blythe, *Our Sins Acknowledged. Being a Sermon, Preached in Lexington, Jan. 12, 1815. The Day of the National Fast* (Lexington: Skillman, 1815), 4–6, 8, 9. "Political atheism" is the notion that citizens (and government officials) should put aside their religious beliefs upon entering the political sphere. The phrase came into common usage—primarily as a term of opprobrium—in the 1830s and 1840s. See, for example, Lyman Beecher's book *Lectures on Political Atheism and Kindred Subjects* (Boston: Jewett, 1852). For a scholarly discussion of this concept, see Patrick W. Carey, "Political Atheism: *Dred Scott*, Roger Brooke Taney, and Orestes A. Brownson," *Catholic Historical Review* 88 (2002): 207–29.

20. Witness Ezra Stiles Ely's call, in 1827, for a "Christian party in politics." See Ely, "The Duty of Christian Freemen to Elect Christian Rulers," in *American Philosophical Addresses, 1700–1900*, ed. Joseph L. Blau (New York: Columbia University Press, 1946), 548–62; Joseph L. Blau, "The Christian Party in Politics," *Review of Religion* 11 (1946): 18–35; and Arthur M. Schlesinger Jr., *The Age of Jackson* (Boston: Little, Brown, 1945), 132–45.

21. For an influential Presbyterian statement on the boundaries of Christianity, see Robert Baird, *Religion in America* (New York: Harper, 1844). Baird starkly divided America's churches between the "evangelical denominations" and the "unevangelical sects." While the former were united in "recognising Christ as their common Head," the latter "either renounce, or fail faithfully to exhibit the fundamental and saving truths of the gospel." Baird freely denounced Unitarians as full of "error." See 219–20, 269, 272–80.

22. Lexington Presbyterians actively advocated for their orthodox positions. Between 1809 and 1829, Presbyterians published four religious journals in Lexington, each of which lasted about a year. They also operated a weekly religious paper, the *Western Luminary*, from 1824 to 1835. Additionally they founded the Lexington Bible Society in 1809.

23. For a brief analysis of the significance of the Cane Ridge revival for Kentucky Presbyterians, see Voelker, "Church Building," 201–6. For a broader analysis of the revival and its impact, see Paul K. Conkin, *Cane Ridge: America's Pentecost* (Madison: University of Wisconsin Press, 1990).

24. During the post-Revolutionary period, Presbyterians influenced more by John Witherspoon than Jonathan Edwards developed increased confidence in the natural ability of human beings; by the turn of the century, however, having faced a number of crises (the Illuminati, Thomas Jefferson, Jacobinism, deism, etc.), "Presbyterians began to inch back toward the belief that something supernatural was required to ground social well-being." This indeed was the case in Kentucky, which became a bastion of Old School Presbyterianism. See Mark A. Noll, "The Irony of the Enlightenment for Presbyterians in the Early Republic," *Journal of the Early Republic* 5 (1985): 167.

25. For an example of the Presbyterian ambivalence toward reason, see Archibald Alexander, "General Assembly Sermon" (1808), in *The Princeton Theology, 1812–1921: Scripture, Science, Theological Method from Archibald Alexander to Benjamin Breckinridge Warfield*, ed. Mark A. Noll (Grand Rapids, Mich.: Baker Book House, 1983), 53. For a more general discussion of the orthodox mind-set of this period, see Joseph Haroutunian, *Piety versus Moralism: The Passing of the New England Theology* (1932; New York: Harper & Row, 1970), 186–87; and Philip F. Gura, *American Transcendentalism: A History* (New York: Hill & Wang, 2007), 35–36.

26. "The Westminster Confession," in *Creeds of the Churches*, ed. John H. Leith, 3rd ed. (Atlanta: John Knox, 1982), 192–229. On the importance of the Westminster Confession of Faith to antebellum Presbyterianism, see Donald S. Fortson III, "New School Calvinism and the Presbyterian Creed," *Journal of Presbyterian History* 82 (2004): 221–43.

27. Archibald Alexander, "Inaugural Address" (1812), in Noll, *Princeton Theology*, 89.

28. "A Native Kentuckean," *Lexington Reporter*, May 31, 1815.

29. "Church and State," *Reporter*, July 31, 1816. This was the same paper as the *Lexington Reporter*, with the name changed.

30. Sonne, *Liberal Kentucky*, 128–34.

31. Presbyterian trustees downplayed their own prominence on the board by noting that some of the "Presbyterian" trustees and faculty members were "associate reformed" rather than regular Presbyterians. See Sonne, *Liberal Kentucky*, 148.

32. Cooper's supporters included Henry Clay and Lewis Sanders, a wealthy trustee. The Presbyterian trustees elected him to be a chemistry professor at a low salary, knowing that he would decline, which he did. See "[A Petition] To the Trustees of Transylvania University," March 1816, Transylvania University Special Collections, Lexington, Kentucky; and Sonne, *Liberal Kentucky*, 143–44. On Cooper's hostility toward Presbyterians, see Elizabeth Flower and Murray G. Murphey, *A History of Philosophy in America*, vol. 1 (New York: Capricorn, 1977), 292.

33. *Journal of the House of Representatives of the Commonwealth of Kentucky* (Frankfort), 1815–16, 201–2. See also Wright, *Transylvania*, 56–60.

34. *Board of Trustees Minutes*, vol. 2, 209–10, Transylvania University Special Collections. On November 15, 1815, the trustees ordered the appropriate committee not to inform Holley that he had been elected president, and they also asked that "each member of this board be requested to obtain information as to the character and standing of Said Doct. Horace Holley and report accordingly at a meeting to be hereafter convened for that purpose."

35. On December 11, 1815, Francis Johnson moved that the legislature establish a committee to investigate the affairs of the university. *Journal of the House*, 1815–16, 35. The report of this committee and the response of the university trustees appear in the *Journal* on January 26, 1816, 201–2.

36. *Journal of the House*, 1815–16, 201–2.

37. *Board of Trustees Minutes*, vol. 2, 310. On October 25, 1817, Holley received six votes for the presidency, but this was not a legal majority, so there was no election. On November 15, 1817, however, the board unanimously elected Holley as president. See

also John Pope, William T. Barry, John G. Breckinridge, and James Prentiss to Horace Holley, Lexington, November 18, 1817, in which the trustees informed Holley of his election. Transylvania University Special Collections. The Senate passed the "Bill to lessen the number and alter the mode of electing the trustees of the Transylvania University" on December 15, 1817. *Journal of the Senate of the Commonwealth of Kentucky* (Frankfort), 36, 51. See also Sonne, *Liberal Kentucky*, 153–58.

38. Roland L. Bainton, *Yale and the Ministry* (San Francisco: Harper & Row, 1985), 73–78.

39. Edward Everett, "[Review of] *A Discourse of the Genius and Character of the Rev. Horace Holley*," *North American Review* 27 (1828): 409–10.

40. Kathi Trask, "Horace and Mary Austin Holley," *Dictionary of Unitarian and Universalist Biography*, accessed June 24, 2014, http://uudb.org/articles/maryaustinholley.html.

41. Charles Caldwell, *A Discourse on the Genius and Character of the Rev. Horace Holley* (Boston: Hilliard, Gray, Little & Wilkins, 1828), 187–89. Caldwell reprinted a selection of Holley's eulogy for J. S. Buckminster. On Buckminster see Jerry Wayne Brown, *The Rise of Biblical Criticism in America* (Middletown, Conn.: Wesleyan University Press, 1969), 19–26. See also E. Brooks Holifield, *Theology in America: Christian Thought from the Age of the Puritans to the Civil War* (New Haven: Yale University Press, 2003), 191.

42. Holley used the phrase "evangelical Christianity" to refer to a Christian faith firmly rooted in the Bible rather than dependent on authorities such as John Calvin. [Horace Holley], "[Review of] *A Contrast between Calvinism and Hopkinsianism*," in *American Higher Education: A Documentary History*, Vol. 1, ed. Richard Hofstadter and Wilson Smith (Chicago: University of Chicago Press, 1961), 182, 187, 188. See John Pierpont, *A Discourse Delivered in Hollis Street Church, Boston, September 2, 1827: Occasioned by the Death of Horace Holley* (Boston: Press of Christian Examiner, 1827), 26, regarding Holley's authorship of this article.

43. Horace Holley, "Sermon 5" (June 27, 1819), in *Sermon Outlines*, 47. Transylvania University Special Collections.

44. Holley, "Natural Religion, 2" (n.d.), in *Sermon Outlines*, 76.

45. Holley, "Natural Religion, 4" (June 2, 1820), in *Sermon Outlines*, 91.

46. On the attempt of Channing and New England Unitarians to distinguish themselves from Priestley and other English Unitarians, see J. D. Bowers, *Joseph Priestley and English Unitarianism in America* (University Park: Pennsylvania State University Press, 2007), 152–59.

47. William Ellery Channing, "Unitarian Christianity," in *Three Prophets of Religious Liberalism*, ed. Conrad Wright (Boston: Beacon, 1961), 76.

48. Holifield, *Theology in America*, 197–217.

49. Holley, "The nature and objects of religion explained" (June 6, 1819), in *Sermon Outlines*, 11.

50. The senior class letter, signed by a committee of five seniors, was published in a Lexington newspaper in 1823 and is in Mary Holley's scrapbook, Transylvania University Special Collections.

51. Admittedly *moralism* is an ambiguous term. Presbyterians themselves were guilty of a certain kind of moralism: witness their criticism of Holley for attending the theater. Presbyterians, however, rejected the type of moralism that put faith in human ability— independent of the divine gift of special grace—to pursue and achieve moral virtue. On the trajectory toward this kind of moralism, see Haroutunian, *Piety versus Moralism*, and James Turner, *Without God, without Creed: The Origins of Unbelief in America* (Baltimore: Johns Hopkins University Press, 1985), 69–72, 82–95. Turner argues persuasively that "moralism crushed Calvinism" (92). He has also shaped my understanding of how the Presbyterians resisted the temptation to sacrifice doctrine to moralism, as many American Christians eventually did in their quest to reinforce Christianity's relevance. See esp. 64–65, 82–84.

52. Omega, *Two Letters Addressed to Horace Holley, L.L.D. President of Transylvania University* (Lexington, 1824), 6. Paine was a favorite bogey of Kentucky Presbyterians. In an 1814 sermon, Blythe had referred to him as "the very dregs of human depravity." See James Blythe, *A Portrait of the Times* (Lexington, Ky.: Skillman, 1814), 18. Two years earlier a Presbyterian magazine had printed a lengthy diatribe against Paine. Salvian, "Some Inquiries Concerning the Writings, Character and Death of the Late Mr. Thomas Paine," *Evangelical Record, and Western Review* (1812): 325, 358, 364.

53. Omega, *Two Letters*, 8.

54. Sonne, *Liberal Kentucky*, 172.

55. Omega, *Two Letters*, 3.

56. *The Literary Pamphleteer: Some Observations on the Best Mode of Promoting the Cause of Literature in the State of Kentucky; and a Review of the Late Administration of Transylvania University. . . . to the Citizens and Legislature of Kentucky*, ed. John McFarland (Paris, Ky., 1823–24), no. 2, 6. The series included six undated issues published between December 1823 and March 1824.

57. *Literary Pamphleteer*, no. 1, 3.

58. On these Presbyterian leaders and their contributions to the attack on Holley, see Lewis Collins and Richard H. Collins, *History of Kentucky*, 2 vols. (Covington, Ky.: Collins, 1878), 1:474, 2:18; and Sonne, *Liberal Kentucky*, 196, 221.

59. Bradford, *Voice of the Frontier*, 245. Bradford quoted from an April 3, 1824, article in the *Lexington Public Advertiser*.

60. Archibald Alexander, "General Assembly Sermon, 1808," in Noll, *Princeton Theology*, 53–54.

61. Jedidiah Morse, *Review of American Unitarianism* (Boston: Samuel T. Armstrong, 1815), 1–2, 15. On Morse's response to Belsham, see Haroutunian, *Piety versus Moralism*, 181–88, and Bowers, *Joseph Priestly*, 167–70. For additional examples of the anti-Socinian tradition in the United States, see Bowers, *Joseph Priestley*, 62–65, 88–89.

62. John McFarland, *The Signs of the Times* (Paris, Ky., 1821), 17.

63. [James Blythe,] "Introductory Remarks," *Christian Register*, June 1822, 5. Although no actual Unitarian congregations formed in Kentucky until the 1830s, Presbyterian leaders nonetheless feared their influence. Blythe was thinking not only of Holley but perhaps also of Barton Stone, an apostate Presbyterian himself, who promulgated a

form of the heresy in an unusual New Light–rationalist mix. On Stone's quasi-Unitarianism (or Socinianism), see Conkin, *Cane Ridge*, 132–34.

64. "Extract from Dr. Miller's Letters on Unitarianism," *Christian Register*, January–May 1823.

65. *Literary Pamphleteer*, no. 3, 7. David Rice had made this point almost two decades before McFarland wrote. In his 1805 *Epistle to the Citizens of Kentucky, Professing Christianity*, which was reprinted in 1824, Rice argued that people who had accepted Arianism (the belief that Jesus was more than human but not divine) had "freed themselves from all the distinguishing features of the Christian religion, and . . . become Deists." See David Rice, *Epistle to the Citizens of Kentucky, Professing Christianity*, rpt. in Robert Bishop, *An Outline of the History of the Church in the State of Kentucky, . . . Containing the Memoirs of Rev. David Rice* (Lexington, Ky., 1824), 331.

66. Rice, *Epistle*, 333.

67. Such moral condemnations of Unitarianism were cliché in New England as well. Elizur Wright Jr., a Yale graduate and teacher at Massachusetts's Groton Academy, characterized Unitarians in a mode that was repeated at about the same time in Lexington. Writing to his parents in 1826, Wright noted: "[The Unitarians] would no doubt be pleased if I would attend balls and parties instead of religious meetings, if I would quote the North American review instead of the Bible, if I would talk about liberality and candour and good feeling, instead of the necessity of being born again, if I would not pray in my school, or at least, say nothing about sin in my prayers." In a letter the next year, Wright pointed to the theological errors behind Unitarian dissipation, asserting that they "hoot out of the world the idea of the regeneration of the world by the Holy Spirit." See "The Trinitarian Indictment of Unitarianism: The Letters of Elizur Wright, Jr., 1826–1827," ed. Lawrence B. Goodheart and Richard O. Curry, *Journal of the Early Republic* 3 (1983): 289, 292. See also "Which Society Shall You Join, the Liberal or the Orthodox?" *Spirit of the Pilgrims* 1 (1828): 245–46.

68. Omega, *Two Letters*, 6–7.

69. *Literary Pamphleteer*, no. 1, 15.

70. Ibid., no. 1, 13. On the acquisition of Channing's sermons, see manuscript 1819-U-158, Transylvania University Special Collections. (The date of the manuscript number is misleading; this bill from Wells and Lilly booksellers is dated December 24, 1824.)

71. Horace Holley, *Discourse Occasioned by the Death of Col. James Morrison* (Lexington, Ky.: John Bradford, 1823), 17, 19–20.

72. *Literary Pamphleteer*, no. 5, 8–9.

73. Omega, *Two Letters*, 4–5.

74. Ibid., 22.

75. *Literary Pamphleteer*, no. 4, 5.

76. William Ellery Channing, "Likeness to God," in *Works of William E. Channing* (Boston: American Unitarian Association, 1886), 291–302.

77. Omega, *Two Letters*, 6–7.

78. *Literary Pamphleteer*, no. 1, 13–15.

79. Timothy Dwight, *The Nature and Danger of Infidel Philosophy* (New Haven, Conn.: Bunce, 1798), 44. These views were widespread. See, for example, Blythe, *Our Sins*

Acknowledged, 9. Likewise in a fast-day sermon preached upon the opening of the War of 1812, Jedidiah Morse had asked his audience: "How can an infidel, who fears not God, nor believes his word, nor regards his law, be a minister of God for good?" Jedidiah Morse, *A Sermon, Delivered at Charlestown, July 23, 1812* (Charlestown, Mass.: Samuel Etheridge, Jr., 1812), 31. On the theological challenges associated with maintaining consistent Calvinist beliefs along these lines, see Conkin, *Cane Ridge*, 134–43.

80. Letter by Robert B. Semple Jr. (and accompanying editorial comments), *Western Luminary*, May 25, 1825, 734–35.

81. Joseph Desha, Message to the Legislature, December 7, 1825, in *Journal of the House*, 1825, 16–17.

82. Joseph Desha, Message to the Legislature, December 4, 1826, in *Journal of the House*, 1826–27, 17. See also Thomas D. Clark, *A History of Kentucky*, 6th ed. (Ashland, Ky.: Jesse Stuart Foundation, 1988), 222–23. On the failure of Kentucky to support a common school system, and on Desha's diversion of education funding to internal improvements, see Frank F. Mathias, "Kentucky's Struggle for Common Schools, 1820–1850," *Register of the Kentucky Historical Society* 82, no. 3 (1984): 214–34, esp. 218–19.

83. On the bank policy controversy in Kentucky and its impact on university finances, see Sonne, *Liberal Kentucky*, 242–54; Wright, *Transylvania*, 109–10; and Wright, "Libertarianism's Loss," 112, 121–23.

84. Holley first resigned on December 23, 1825, two weeks after Desha's initial hostile comments about the university, but the trustees convinced him to stay until the spring of 1827.

85. Holley died at sea on July 31, 1827. Wright, *Transylvania*, 116.

86. On the declining enrollments, see Sonne, *Liberal Kentucky*, 255, and Wright, *Transylvania*, 123, 147. Wright noted that enrollment did improve somewhat in the late 1820s, but the effect was short-lived. By the time that Robert Davidson was president, the academic department had only twenty-eight students, a figure comparable to the enrollment nadir that accompanied Holley's departure.

87. Sonne, *Liberal Kentucky*, 261. Sonne was likely misled into this conclusion by two factors. First, on the national level, American Protestants were in the process during the 1820s–40s of consolidating what William Hutchison has called the "informal establishment of the Protestant religion." The Old School Presbyterians of Kentucky effectively opted out of this "benevolent empire" rather than make the theological and ecclesiastical compromises entailed by interdenominational cooperation. See Hutchison, *Religious Pluralism*, 82. Second, Sonne was perhaps misled by the religious politics of his own time. The rise of a politically engaged "fundamentalist" Christianity in the early twentieth century perhaps distorted his understanding of early nineteenth-century Presbyterians. As George M. Marsden has noted: "Historians during the early twentieth century, in the midst of their own emancipation from Protestant intellectual and moral dogmatism, emphasized the tolerant and the progressive in America's national tradition. Evangelicalism, which in the opening decades of this [the twentieth] century was usually masked in the robes of militant fundamentalism, appeared retrograde and obscurantist." See George M. Marsden, *The Evangelical Mind and the New School Presbyterian Experience: A Case Study of*

Thought and Theology in Nineteenth-Century America (New Haven, Conn.: Yale University Press, 1970), ix.

88. On Holley's opposition to Desha's relief and "New Court" policies, see Sonne, *Liberal Kentucky*, 244–59.

89. Robert Davidson, *History of the Presbyterian Church in the State of Kentucky* (New York: Carter, 1847), 318–21.

90. Hardin Craig, *Centre College of Kentucky* (Louisville: Gateway, 1967), 11–13.

91. Sonne, *Liberal Kentucky*, 256.

92. Davidson, *History of the Presbyterian Church*, 322–23.

93. Ibid., 350.

94. For an analysis of the Old School–New School schism, see Marsden, *Evangelical Mind*, 59–87; James H. Moorhead, "The 'Restless Spirit of Radicalism': Old School Fears and the Schism of 1837," *Journal of Presbyterian History* 78 (2000): 19–33; and Lefferts A. Loetscher, *A Brief History of the Presbyterians* (Philadelphia: Westminster, 1983), 73–100. Bradley J. Longfield put the disagreement between the Old School and New School thus: "While the Old School was convinced that false doctrine produced the greatest possible threat to a lost world, New School clergy, insistent on the priority of evangelism over strict confessionalism, had no difficulty with doctrinal innovations that increased the revivalistic harvest." Longfield, *The Presbyterian Controversy: Fundamentalists, Modernists, and Moderates* (New York: Oxford University Press, 1991), 133. Mark Noll notes that the core of the Old School tendency was "a full and frank promotion of historic Calvinist confessionalism" and suggests that the Old Schoolers had adjusted poorly to the realities of the American situation, including the "separation of church and state." See Noll, *America's God*, 124–30, 308–11. The issue of slavery, of course, loomed in the background, but it was not until 1861, as the Civil War began, that the Presbyterian Old School divided into northern and southern parts. On the slavery debate within the Presbyterian Church in Kentucky, see Andrew Lee Feight, "James Blythe and the Slavery Controversy in the Presbyterian Churches of Kentucky, 1791–1802," *Register of the Kentucky Historical Society* 102 (2004): 13–38; and Walter B. Posey, "The Slavery Question in the Presbyterian Church in the Old Southwest," *Journal of Southern History* 15 (1949): 311–24.

95. On the "allure of respectability" that motivated other evangelical denominations to support higher education, see Nathan Hatch, *The Democratization of American Christianity* (New Haven, Conn.: Yale University Press, 1989), 201–6.

Wayne K. Durrill

Nat Turner and Signs of the Apocalypse

Between 1827 and 1831, Nat Turner, the man who led the largest slave revolt in American history, saw numerous signs pointing to the end times, when slaves might expect to be released from their bondage. Specifically he saw white and black spirits dancing on the horizon in an east to west line; a darkened sun; a loud rumbling that he described as thunder; blood flowing in local streams; a second round of spirits dancing on the horizon that he described as men in "different attitudes"; drops of blood found on corn plants; and leaves with hieroglyphic characters written in blood. When Turner told a local poor white man named Etheldred Brantley about all this, Brantley himself broke out in apocalyptic signs. He promptly developed sores all over his body and began to sweat blood as Jesus did on the cross. Shortly thereafter, in May 1828, Turner heard a "loud noise" in the heavens that the Holy Spirit told the slave came from an immense serpent, the sign of the devil himself now come as the Antichrist to begin the time of tribulations. Finally, on February 12, 1831, a sign appeared that led Turner to begin planning his own end times for Southampton County, Virginia. On that day he saw in the sky a sun that turned almost completely black about 10:30 in the morning, changing day into night and summer into winter as the temperature fell rapidly. As Turner pointed out in his *Confessions*, he never had any thought of raising a slave insurrection until that moment, but afterward he devoted himself to no other pursuit.[1]

White southerners writing during the Southampton Insurrection considered Nat Turner to be a misguided religious lunatic and cited his account of the signs he had seen as proof of his lunacy. According to one Southampton resident, "Our insurrection, [whether] general or not, was the work of fanaticism—General Nat was no preacher, but in his immediate neighborhood, he had acquired the character of a prophet."[2] They argued that he was, in fact, a conjurer or trickster, a religious charlatan who used simple tricks to fool the gullible. One white man from Southampton County, for example, accused Turner of faking the power to spit blood on demand in order to prove his powers as a prophet of the Christian god.[3] The man claimed that Turner, in fact, had put in his mouth a piece of dye root, used to dye cloth the color red, and after chewing on it spit out a red liquid. Southern whites writing after the insurrection, however, never challenged

Turner's claims to having seen some strange things. After all the eclipse of February 1831 could not be denied. Therefore southern whites argued that Turner was not necessarily delusional but rather misguided, allowing his prophetic pretensions to overwhelm his common sense. His lunacy lay not in what he saw but in how he interpreted what he had seen.

Historians have simply ignored Turner's visions, choosing to recount them as part of the story of his upbringing and progress toward rebellion but making little effort to assess their credibility or significance.[4] A major exception to this rule is Donald G. Mathews's *Religion in the Old South*. In a pioneering chapter that deals with the religious experiences of slaves in the antebellum South, Mathews argues that slaves "of necessity became premillennial quietists," patiently but anxiously waiting for the end times that would spell the destruction of slavery. He further argues that religion among evangelical blacks focused more on the hereafter than on the present and provides evidence in abundance from prayers and spirituals to that effect. A focus on the future, moreover, led black Methodists and Baptists to center much of their religious life on the coming apocalypse, an aspect of black religion that Mathews argues has been woefully neglected by scholars. Sad to say more than thirty years later, this is still the case. Most scholars writing on Nat Turner and his rebellion simply recite without comment Turner's visions as they appeared in the *Confessions*. Even those who more recently have taken his role as a prophet seriously tend to focus on his theology rather than the means by which Turner acquired his premillennial ideas and later propagated them. As Mathews noted in *Religion in the Old South*, "It is the Apocalypse that is missing from most evaluations of black religion."[5]

About 1825, according to Turner's own account, he suddenly became religiously active for the first time in three years when he had a vision that conflated several natural phenomena that actually occurred in 1827 and 1828, combining them into one prophesy in which he "saw white spirits and black spirits engaged in battle, and the sun was darkened, the thunder rolled in the heavens, and blood flowed in streams."[6] The strange sights that Turner reported, in fact, began in September 1827 when the Aurora Borealis could be seen on the Atlantic coast for the first time in decades as far south as Charleston.[7] In Norfolk on Tuesday, September 25, 1827, between about eight and ten o'clock in the evening, the celestial display "illuminated the northern sky, for about 30 degrees above the horizon, so brilliantly as to produce an effect similar to that of the moon when the canopy is slightly overcast with light flitting clouds." The lights had a "translucent appearance," and during the aurora's greatest brightness, "the stars in that quarter of the heavens," meaning to the northwest, "were scarcely visible to the naked eye." By about ten o'clock that evening, the celestial display "became less and less brilliant, shedding a faint crepuscular light on objects beneath, much resembling the first rays of the morning."[8] On that same night, residents in Petersburg witnessed "a full display of that wonderful phenomenon, the Aurora Borealis, or the northern lights." "Such was its brilliancy, that the moon gave only a faint light altho' she was unobscured by any intervening cloud."[9] These displays in the sky continued through at least the end of October 1827. The lights were no doubt the "white and black spirits engaged in battle" on the northern horizon that Turner reported seeing in his 1825 vision.[10]

About the same time, the immense storms on the sun that had produced a view of the Aurora Borealis in Virginia also became visible as huge black spots on the sun. Beginning in August 1824, astronomers noticed a black spot "on the disc of the sun, about half-way between the sun's centre and its southeast limb." By July of the next year, ordinary individuals as well could discern dark patches on the sun. According to a correspondent writing to a Boston newspaper, "For more than a year spots on the sun have been very frequent, but we have rarely seen one of the magnitude of that now visible on the disc of that luminary; indeed such is its size, that it is easily discovered by the eye, protected by a dark glass, without the assistance of a telescope."[11] In 1827, however, the number of spots multiplied until they appeared sometimes to cover most of the sun. By April an "Astronomical Correspondent" writing to the *Charleston Courier* reported, "There is now visible near the centre of the Sun's disk, twenty six spots, which may be distinctly counted with the aid of a telescope." Viewers with a telescope of lesser power, as well as persons looking at the sun with the naked eye, saw what "might be mistaken for three large spots."[12] It was most likely these three large spots to which Turner referred when he spoke in his *Confessions* of a darkened sun.

The third sign in Turner's 1825 vision, thunder that "rolled in the heavens," probably refers to the earthquake felt in Virginia on the evening of March 9, 1828. A newspaper in Richmond reported, "On Sunday night, about 11 o'clock, we had a distinct shock of an Earthquake in this city. Many citizens were roused from their slumbers," and "those who were awake at the time, describe it as continuing for four or five seconds, shaking window-shutters and window frames, bed-steads and other moveable articles of furniture, in a very perceptible manner." In Fredericksburg the earthquake "consisted of two distinct shocks, occupying something less than half a minute; the first much more severe than the second." Houses in the town "rocked so violently that persons who had retired for the night, and were asleep, sprang terrified from their beds, and were with difficulty persuaded to return to them." In Brunswick County just west of Southampton, the earthquake created "in some places . . . no inconsiderable chasms made in the earth." The earthquake caused no major damage, but it produced what Turner described as thunder that "rolled in the heavens." In Fredericksburg the shocks were "accompanied by a loud rumbling noise, not unlike that produced by the rapid passage of many carriages over a pavement." In Richmond "the vibration seemed to be from North to South" and also produced "a rumbling noise."[13]

The final portion of Turner's 1825 vision, blood he reported that "flowed in streams," also must have had a factual basis in nature, but direct evidence of such a phenomenon occurring in Virginia has not turned up except in the *Confessions*. It is reasonable to conjecture, however, that the red liquid Turner saw in his vision may have been a rare phenomenon called blood rain that had resulted from a severe drought in Virginia in 1826. During a blood rain, red drops of water fall from the sky, the drops having been created by dust storms that sometimes gather up into the atmosphere dirt from plowed fields of desiccated red clay. In 1826 and 1827, there were many such fields in the piedmont counties to the west of Southampton County that, following the prevailing summer winds that blew southwest to northwest, may have caused blood rain to fall in eastern Virginia.[14]

Whether Turner actually saw all these natural events in a vision two or three years before they occurred, of course, remains open to question. When he dictated his *Confessions* in 1831, he may simply have attached memories of natural events in 1827 and 1828 to a spiritual crisis he had endured in 1825 so as to explain to himself how all this began. Whatever the case, it is certain that something in 1825 set Turner on the road to becoming a prophet, not just a preacher. For the moment, however, he found his religious experiences more puzzling than enlightening, and therefore secluded himself in what amounted to a religious retreat, determined to understand the meaning of his vision with the help of the Holy Spirit. As Turner said in his *Confessions*, "I now withdrew myself as much as my situation would permit, from the intercourse of my fellow servants, for the avowed purpose of serving the Spirit more fully."[15]

A couple of years later, the Holy Spirit appeared to Turner again and reminded him "of the things already shown" to him, presumably in the 1825 prophecy. The Holy Spirit then promised to reveal to Turner "knowledge of the elements, the revolution of the planets, the operation of the tides, and changes of the season." These subjects constituted roughly the contents of any natural history textbook then in use at the College of William and Mary or the University of Virginia, and Turner's story suggests that he may have had access to such books. When local notables in Southampton County examined him after the insurrection, they found that he "had much knowledge of these subjects and was well acquainted with the movements of the planets, etc."[16] In short Turner believed that the Holy Spirit had returned to give him the intellectual means with which to accomplish things for his people that would improve their lives in the here and now, not in some heavenly future. Perhaps then Turner's vision of the end of the world did not end in judgment and retribution but rather signaled the beginning of a new era in which the existing world would be made anew.[17] Only after Turner had mastered the specialized knowledge of the natural world did the Holy Spirit return to give him his final training in religion. As Turner put it in his *Confessions*, "After this revelation in 1825, and the knowledge of the elements being made known to me,

I sought more than ever to obtain true holiness before the great day of judgment should appear, and then I began to receive the true knowledge of faith."[18]

Having seen many wonders in the sky in 1827 and 1828, Turner now puzzled over the meaning of such strange events. "I wondered greatly at these miracles, and prayed to be informed of a certainty of the meaning thereof." He did not immediately get his wish but instead was confronted with additional wondrous signs. "Shortly afterwards, while laboring in the field," Turner later recalled, "I discovered drops of blood on the corn as though it were dew from heaven." Then he "found on the leaves in the woods hieroglyphic characters and numbers, with the forms of men in different attitudes, portrayed in blood, and representing the figures I had seen before in the heavens."[19]

What Turner interpreted as drops of blood on the corn probably resulted from blood rain, and the men in different attitudes were, as he explained in his *Confessions*, simply another manifestation of the figures he had seen in the Northern Lights. But why did Turner see hieroglyphic characters and numbers? Most likely this passage in the *Confessions* marks the period in which he began communicating in coded language with others at some distance, perhaps abolitionists. And in fact there is considerable evidence to suggest that Turner used coded writing. For example when after his revolt some white men in Southampton County seized his personal papers from his wife, they found what they themselves described as hieroglyphic writings and symbols on a number of the papers. In addition when a black leader in New York wrote a letter to Turner in late August 1831, the author included several obscure symbols at the bottom of the letter, presumably to authenticate the document.[20] In short Turner's mention in the *Confessions* of seeing figures and numbers in blood on leaves in the woods may simply be a metaphor for his introduction to the practice of sending and receiving coded messages.

Why did Turner so willingly see signs from God pointing to the end times? Such expectations, in fact, had been stoked among both blacks and whites by a mountain of books and pamphlets predicting the end of the world and soon, many of which had been excerpted in American newspapers during the 1820s. Some of these apocalyptic works argued that most of the predictions in the Gospel of St. John had been fulfilled in the time of the Roman Empire, and therefore God now had exhausted those revelations and there was little more to be done except to end the world immediately. Others saw what they believed to be the growing power of the papacy as a signal that the end times had come, identifying the Pope himself as the predicted Antichrist who would reign over the coming thousand years of chaos and evil. Still other writers pointed to the return of Jews to Palestine. In the late 1820s, after the Ottoman Empire had lost its grip on that area and before Egypt took control, thousands of Jews from all around the Mediterranean Sea and southwestern Russia flocked to Constantinople and from there to the Holy Land, seeking to settle and make a home for themselves. Many Christians in Europe and America saw in this development a sure sign that the last and most important portent of the end times had been revealed. Finally many religious writers pointed to recent political events, especially the rise of Napoleon and the recent decline of Ottoman power in Egypt and Palestine, as the fulfillment of the final prophesies. In short there existed an extensive and respectable literature produced in America and Europe on the apocalypse lending credence to even the most extreme predictions of the imminent demise of the world.[21]

Sometime in 1828 Turner saw yet another sign confirming his view that the end times were about to begin. "I heard a loud noise in the heavens, and the Spirit instantly appeared to me and said the Serpent was loosened, and Christ had laid down the yoke he had borne for the sins of men." In the book of Revelation, Satan takes the form of a serpent or dragon, and his appearance signals the beginning of war in heaven after the opening of the seventh seal, the last act before the apocalypse is to commence. The Holy Spirit also told Turner that he "should take it on and fight against the Serpent, for the time was fast approaching when the first should be last and the last should be first." In doing so the Holy Spirit cast Turner in the role of Michael, the archangel who "led his angels fighting against the dragon" in Heaven. This was not a pleasant prospect, of course, because both Satan and Michael lose their place in Heaven and fall to earth where the battle continues and the serpent makes war "on those who keep the commandments of God and bear testimony to Jesus."[22]

The loud noise in the heavens that Turner claimed to have heard, in fact, probably resulted from one of several large meteors that plunged to earth in the American South from July through October 1828, some of which created the appearance of a serpent in the sky. For example at 10:15 on the evening of August 31, 1828, in Huntsville, Alabama, "a number of citizens, while seated before their doors, on the east side of the public square, were thrown into a stupor of astonishment on finding all the objects around them, streets and houses, suddenly illuminated with the dazzling effluence of noon-day." Looking about for the cause, the Huntsville residents instantly concentrated their gaze on "what appeared to the naked eye a blazing serpent, of about twenty feet in extent and three in breadth, gliding through the air from east to south, its first appearance at an elevation of nearly fifty degrees." The editor of the local newspaper identified the unusual phenomenon as a meteor, but for some persons their "amazement at the scene enforced the belief of its being a real serpent."[23] The most likely candidate in Turner's case was a meteor that fell in eastern Virginia, a part of which landed in Chesterfield County twenty miles or so west of Richmond and fifty miles northwest of Southampton County.[24]

After hearing the noise of a serpent in the sky, according to Turner's account, the Holy Spirit told him that "by signs in the heavens . . . it would be made known to me when I should commence the great work." In the meantime he was enjoined to "conceal it from the knowledge of men" and wait patiently "until the first sign appeared," the words *first sign* implying that there would be more signs to come before the "great work" could begin. Finally, upon the appearance of the first sign, according to Turner, "I should arise and prepare myself and slay my enemies with their own weapons."[25] In fact Turner did nothing from 1828 to 1831, telling no one of his mission, while he waited patiently for the first sign to appear.

On February 12, 1831, beginning about 10:30 in the morning, the first sign of the end times appeared, at least in Turner's view, an annular eclipse of the sun that became visible in Southampton County for about forty-five minutes. The eclipse had begun in northern Mexico and then passed over southwestern Louisiana, the black belt of Alabama, piedmont Georgia, South Carolina, North Carolina, and eastern Virginia before moving out to sea along the southern Delaware shore. The center of the line of this eclipse passed directly overhead in Petersburg, meaning that residents of Southampton County saw a nearly total eclipse. Beginning about 10:45 in the morning, Turner therefore must have viewed a solar disk that appeared almost entirely black except for a sliver of sunlight in the form of a crescent on one side of the solar disk equaling about one forty-eighth the sun's total width.[26]

Why did Turner take this particular celestial event as a sign from God? After all the eclipse came as no surprise to anyone in 1831. Beginning in mid-1830 newspapers in Virginia and elsewhere had repeatedly printed articles that detailed the exact date on which the sun would be blotted out, and even printed illustrations of what the eclipsed sun would look like. But as one northern newspaper put it disapprovingly, "On such occasions, people now-a-days . . . look for portentous signs, for ghastly gleamings of fiery comets, the rushing up, with dire intimations, of the 'northern lights,' and expect to perceive 'Clouds of dark blood to blot the sun's broad light, And angry meteors shroud the world in night."[27] It would be surprising then if Turner had not connected the eclipse with earlier signs pointed out to him by the Holy Ghost.

Turner, however, also may have had specifically religious reasons for seeing the 1831 eclipse as a sign from Heaven urging him to raise a revolt against slaveholders in the South. Five references to a darkening sun occur in the Old Testament, and in all but one, the Book of Joel, a dark sun specifically signals God's displeasure with wicked rulers and other powerful men. In Amos 8, for example, God vows to destroy Israel because its rich men have abused the poor, and, he says, the sign of his displeasure would be a darkening of the sun. "And it shall come to pass in that day, saith the Lord GOD, that I will cause the sun to go down at noon, and I will darken the earth in the clear day."[28] Similarly, found in Micah 3, God promises to punish the leaders of Israel for their abuses of ordinary people, those leaders "who also eat the flesh of my people, and flay their skin from off them; and they break their bones, and chop them in pieces. . . . Therefore night shall be unto you, that ye shall not have a vision; and it shall be dark unto you, that ye shall not divine; and the sun shall go down over the prophets, and the day shall be dark over them."[29]

Moreover two books in the Old Testament connect a darkening sun specifically with God's fearsome response to the evildoing of slaveholders. In chapter 13 of the book of Isaiah, for example, the prophet foretells the downfall of the Babylonian leaders who held Jews in captivity, God's vengeance to be signaled by a darkened sun: "Behold, the day of the LORD cometh, cruel both with wrath and fierce anger, to lay the land desolate: and he shall destroy the sinners thereof out of it. For the stars of heaven and the constellations thereof shall not give their light: the sun shall be darkened in his going forth."[30] Similarly in Ezekiel 32 the prophet tells of a time when God will unleash all manner of calamities upon the Pharaoh of Egypt for holding his people, the Jews, in slavery. The sign of God's hand in this work was to be a darkening of the sun. "And when I shall put thee out, I will cover the heaven, and make the stars thereof dark; I will cover the sun with a cloud."[31]

Turner may also have had in mind millennial references in the New Testament to a darkened sun. In Mathew 24, for example, Jesus's disciples, after they had left the Temple and gathered on the Mount of Olives, asked him bluntly, "What shall be the sign of thy coming, and of the end of the world?" In a lengthy answer, Jesus warns of a period of desperate difficulties for both the wicked and the pure of heart, after which he will return to earth, the sign of his coming to be a dark sun. "Immediately after the tribulation of those days shall the sun be darkened," and when this sign appears, his return will follow shortly and all earthly existence will end. "When ye shall see all these things, know that it is near, even at the doors."[32]

Finally the book of Revelation associates a darkening sun, not specifically with the second coming of Jesus but with the larger apocalypse that will follow his return to earth. In chapter 6 "the Lamb," presumably the Lamb of God, meaning Jesus, opens seven sealed documents containing the secret will of God. Each opening then unleashes a new devastation upon the people of the earth to avenge the wrongs done to previous generations now in Heaven. The next to last of these sealed documents was said to reveal the "wrath of the Lamb." This would be God's final judgment on all the peoples of the earth, and it would be signaled by multiple cataclysms, including a darkened sun. "And I beheld when he had opened the sixth seal, and, lo, there was a great earthquake; and the sun became black as sackcloth of hair."[33]

After the 1831 eclipse, Turner told four fellow slaves, as he later recalled, "in whom I had the greatest confidence" of "the great work laid out for me to do." Shortly thereafter Turner, Henry, Hark, Nelson, and Sam began organizing a local insurrection. As Turner said in the *Confessions*, "Many were the plans formed and rejected by us."[34] But why would Henry, Hark, Nelson, and Sam sign on to participate in an action that was both illegal and highly dangerous, and why now? Perhaps because Turner's visions about the end of the world as slaves knew it had become plausible as a result of recent events. As the economic depression of the 1820s continued into its twelfth year, hundreds of thousands of Virginians—those who had fared worst, especially blacks, women, and poor whites—flocked to camp meetings and then to church revivals when they, like Turner and his four followers, turned their attention to the coming millennium.[35]

Beginning in December 1830, the purpose of these revivals changed as the religious exercises increased in size and intensity. What had begun as an effort to organize a new missionary Baptist church in Virginia and North Carolina (as opposed to strict Calvinism of the Kehukee Association) suddenly became a mass millennial movement. At a four-day meeting in Buckingham County west of Richmond, for example, the Reverend James Fife from Goochland County who had been among the earliest organizers of the 1831 revival suddenly shifted the focus of his sermons away from the advantages of conversion to the punishment that awaited those who failed to heed his words. In the words of one eyewitness, Fife "called upon the people, now that God was compassionately drawing so nigh, no longer to neglect the mercies, and thereby provoke the wrath of him, whose hatred is worse than death." Another minister at the same meeting made the point more explicitly by using as the text for his sermon Revelation 6:17: "For the great day of wrath has come, and who can stand before it?" The passage refers to the consequences to follow after the Lamb of God, or Jesus, opens the sixth seal of the scrolls revealing the will of God now that the Apocalypse drew near. In short by early August 1831, Baptist ministers in Virginia urged sinners to avail themselves of their last opportunity to save their souls before the end of the world came.[36]

With the millennium fast approaching, Turner began to plan how he and other slaves in the neighborhood could help it along. By late June he and his fellow conspirators had settled upon July 4, 1831, as an appropriate date to begin, probably for two reasons. First, there was the immense symbolic value. That day, of course, marked the anniversary of the promulgation of the Declaration of Independence in 1776 and was generally considered the date on which the new nation had been born. To begin a revolt on that day would signal the end of the old nation-state and the beginning of a new nation, at least for slaves. Then there was the practical advantage. On the fourth of July, local notables ordinarily gathered in Jerusalem for a dinner with many toasts, and therefore the attack on plantations could proceed without any white leaders nearby to defend their homes and families. The only disadvantage in attacking on July 4 lay in the fact that the local militia also often mustered and paraded in the county seat on that day. That would place them near a large cache of muskets and ammunition stored in the courthouse that had been dispatched to the county in January 1831 by the governor of Virginia in anticipation of a slave revolt that did not materialize. It was perhaps such difficulties that led the five to procrastinate and caused Turner himself to become so ill that he called off the plan. As Turner later recalled, all this planning "affected my mind to such a degree that I fell sick, and the time passed without our coming to any determination how to commence.[37]

Turner, however, could delay for only so long. In the summer of 1831, signs in the sky that could be read in religious terms came fast and furious. The first sign came in the form of rain. From early June to early July, it rained the biblical forty days and forty nights in eastern Virginia and North Carolina. According to one observer writing in July, "During the late spell of unpleasant weather in which out of about forty days . . . there was not one without shower." In addition some of the showers were quite violent. According to the *Richmond Compiler*, "Different parts of the state have been visited by heavy showers of rain, and copious discharges of electricity," so much so that the spring wheat harvest had been brought to a standstill. About July 1 counties around Southampton experienced a particularly "severe storm of thunder, lightning and rain." This unusual monsoon in turn raised a considerable debate over its origins and meaning. Many thought that the heavy rains should be considered a manifestation of God's will, a product of "the directing agency of Him who sendeth the rain in its season."[38] It was only a short step from seeing the unusual rains of 1831 as a manifestation of God's will to seeing them as a sign from God urging his people to prepare for the destruction of the world.

After skies cleared in the first week of August, a second series of unusual sights could be seen in the heavens between August 4 through 12. During that time nine conjunctions or oppositions of the planets, moon, and sun occurred, a phenomenon that even astronomers at the time considered "an uncommon coincidence." On August 4 Venus and the sun could be seen in opposition, and the next day Mercury and Mars appeared in conjunction along with the sun and Uranus. On August 7 Mercury and Saturn could be seen in conjunction, followed the next day by the moon and Mars, and the day after that the moon and Saturn. On August 10 the sun and Jupiter appeared in opposition, and the next day the moon and Venus appeared in conjunction, followed on the day after by Mars and Saturn in conjunction. As a North Carolina newspaper writer noted, "such occurrences as these" often persuaded some people to predict "great troubles in the political states of empires, kingdoms, &c as also good or bad fortunes to individuals." When Turner saw these unusual sights in the sky, it is likely he interpreted them as the very signs from God for which the Holy Spirit had told him to look after the eclipse of February 1831.[39]

On Saturday, August 13, 1831, Turner saw the final sign in sky for which he had been waiting. According to the *Confessions*, while he and his small band were "still forming new schemes and rejecting them," suddenly "the sign appeared again," a darkened sun that could be seen in the skies over Virginia just as it had been in February. What Turner saw, however, proved not to be an eclipse but a far rarer celestial phenomenon—a blue sun. As one Norfolk newspaper reported, at dawn the sun appeared "a light and lively green and as it was ascended above the horizon, changed first to cerulean, then to silver white, and finally to pale yellow, when its beams no longer permitted the intrusive gaze of the multitude." At sunset the process reversed. "About five o'clock in the afternoon it appeared like a globe of silver through the thick haze which overspread the heavens, shorn of its beams—and gradually assumed the cerulean tint, from which it passed to light green."[40] Americans as far north as Maine and as far south as Georgia also saw a blue sun.[41]

The cause of the blue sun lay in an eruption of several volcanoes around the world in late June, July, and early August. The extraordinary sequence of events began in the West Indies, where, from late June through early August, several volcanoes erupted, including one on Guadeloupe, another on the island of Saint Vincent in Barbados, and a third somewhere in the Lesser Antilles near Barbados.[42] In Europe at least two volcanoes erupted as well in the summer of 1831. On July 10 an entirely new volcano rose from the depths of the Mediterranean off the coast of Sicily. Although at first merely "a mass of boiling water that rose sixty feet above the surrounding surface of the sea," by July 18 the volcano had surfaced and, according to an eyewitness, "was in a constant state of activity, and appeared to be discharging dust and stones, with vast volumes of steam."[43] Further north, on July 23, a small crater inside the ancient caldera of Mount Vesuvius in southern Italy suddenly exploded, and for the next six days "the mountain continued to throw up, at intervals, flames and stones."[44] Finally, during the first two weeks of August 1831, Mount Saint Helens in southern Washington state erupted. According to a Methodist preacher named Samuel Parker who happened to be on the scene, it became quite dark during the eruption "with the exception of a slight red, lurid appearance" in the sky. "So completely was the light of the sun shut out by the smoke and falling ashes, that candles were necessary."[45]

These several volcanoes injected tons of ash into the Arctic jet stream, which carried it to the entire East Coast of the United States, including much of the South. Ordinarily in midsummer the jet stream moves west to east across North America starting in Washington state, swinging north into Canada and dipping back down into the United States around the Great Lakes, and then turning northeastward to exit the continent around Newfoundland. This route usually leaves most of the Midwest, Northeast, and South sweltering in heat and humidity during July and August. In the summer of 1831, however, the jet stream moved hundreds of miles to the south, producing cold, rainy weather along much of the Atlantic Coast.[46] A newspaper editor in the village of Washington, North Carolina, located on the coastal plain, reported in mid-July that "for the last forty-seven days we have had nothing but rain, rain, rain! The weather has been so disagreeable that winter habiliments have been resumed; and on Sunday last we found the fire-side very desirable." The same jet stream also funneled volcanic dust directly from Mount Saint Helens and other volcanoes around the world to all the states on the Atlantic Coast from South Carolina to Maine, thereby producing the blue sun that Turner interpreted as a sign from God.[47]

Turner was not the only person along the Atlantic Seaboard to see the blue sun as a sign of things to come. At Fredericksburg, Virginia, for example, according to a local observer, "some of the good folks" there were "considerably alarmed at the phenomenon," and many "took it for granted that war is at hand." Others saw the blue sun as a commentary on the low state of political discourse in the country, specifically "the disgraceful circumstances recently developed at Washington" resulting from Andrew Jackson's dismissal of most of his cabinet members.[48] In Macon, Georgia, some local residents believed that the blue sun portended yet more rain, while others thought it meant a "sickly" season must be on the way.[49] For blacks in southeastern Virginia, however, the dark sun meant that the time had come for revolt aimed at ending slavery in America. At an immense camp meeting held at Cooke's Mill in Sussex County just north of Southampton on Sunday, August 14, a crowd of three thousand blacks were told to prepare to revolt on Monday, August 29, when a "black sun was to rise in the east," and afterward there would be "oceans of bloodshed &c.," according to one informant writing from Petersburg after the insurrection.[50] In the end no dark sun appeared on Monday, August 29, as predicted, but by that time it did not matter. Nat Turner had begun his revolt a week earlier, it had failed, and bloody chaos had ensued from Delaware to Louisiana.

Between 1827 and 1831, Turner saw and heard a series of unusual natural phenomena—an eclipse, sunspots, the Aurora Borealis, the rumbling of an earthquake, blood rain, a meteor, and finally the rarest of all celestial events—a blue moon. And from these signs, he deduced that the end times were about to begin and that he should lead the way. Was this an unreasonable conclusion to draw in eastern Virginia during the late 1820s? Certainly the local notables in Southampton County and other officials and writers thought so. For every sign that Turner read as a signal from the Holy Ghost, they could point to a scientific explanation or, in the case of the blue sun, a pseudoscientific (and dead wrong) explanation. But in fact those white gentlemen who wrote accounts of the Southampton Insurrection did not represent the views of many people in the state or the nation. Virginians in particular, during the later 1820s, saw the same signs that Turner did and drew much the same conclusion—the Apocalypse was near and almost palpable. Baptists and Methodists who attended camp meetings and revivals in those years fervently believed that the world was about to end, and they confirmed that fact with near hysterical worship. Moreover there existed a large printed literature often written by very respectable clergymen and other professionals supporting the idea that signs of the end times had already occurred or were now occurring. Beginning in 1827 these signs became part of widespread premillennial discourse at camp meetings and revivals throughout Virginia and eastern North Carolina.

It should not be surprising then that Turner and many other blacks in Virginia saw the unusual natural events of the late 1820s and early 1830s as signs from God indicating that the world as they knew it was about to end. In fact, of course, they were right. The slavery into which they had been born did end, not in 1831 as Turner and many others had hoped, but thirty years later at nearby Fortress Monroe, where a Massachusetts politician and militia general named Benjamin Butler defined slaves as contraband of war, thus paving the way to free every slave who passed through Union lines. For slaves in America, the Civil War was their Apocalypse. It brought the destruction of a system of oppression for which they had prayed for generations and reconstituted them as new men and women, redeemed collectively and individually just as Turner had hoped, and just as the signs of a coming Apocalypse had predicted to him.

NOTES

1. Thomas R. Gray, ed., *The Confessions of Nat Turner* (Baltimore: Gray, 1831), hereafter cited as *Confessions*. Anthony Santoro makes a compelling case for Nat Turner as a prophet working within a prophetic tradition in Virginia in "The Prophet in His Own Words: Nat Turner's Biblical Construction," *Virginia Magazine of History and Biography* 116 (2008): 114–49. On blacks and the Baptist Church in southeastern Virginia from the Revolution to Nat Turner's revolt, see Randolph Ferguson Scully, *Religion and the Making of Nat Turner's Virginia: Baptist Community and Conflict, 1740–1840* (Charlottesville: University of Virginia Press, 2008), especially chap. 4. See also Sylvia Frey and Betty Wood, *Come Shouting to Zion: African American Protestantism in the American South and British Caribbean to 1830* (Chapel Hill: University of North Carolina Press, 1998). On black religion and resistance, see Albert J. Raboteau, *Slave Religion: The "Invisible Institution" in the Antebellum South* (New York: Oxford University Press, 1978), chap. 6.

2. *Richmond Constitutional Whig*, September 26, 1831, rpt. in Henry Irving Tragle, ed., *The Southampton Slave Revolt of 1831: A Compilation of Source Material* (Amherst: University of Massachusetts Press, 1971), 92.

3. Stephen B. Oates, *The Fires of Jubilee: Nat Turner's Fierce Rebellion* (New York: Harper & Row, 1975), 38.

4. Ibid., 35–41; Scully, *Religion and the Making of Nat Turner's Virginia*, 35–41.

5. Donald G. Mathews, *Religion in the Old South* (Chicago: University of Chicago Press, 1977), 223, 231. On Nat Turner and prophesy, see also James Nathaniel Mitchell, "Nat Turner: Slave, Preacher, Prophet, and Messiah, 1800–1831: A Study of the Call of a Black Slave to Prophethood and to the Messiahship of the Second Coming of Christ," D.Min. diss., Vanderbilt University, 1975. On thinking about the Second Great

Awakening in broad terms, see Nathan O. Hatch, "The Second Great Awakening and the Market Revolution," in *Devising Liberty: Preserving and Creating Freedom in the New American Republic*, ed. David Konig (Stanford: Stanford University Press, 1995), 244–64.

6. *Confessions*, 10. On Turner and his apocalyptic ideas, see also Mathews, *Religion in the Old South*, 231–36.

7. *Monitor*, June 1, 1823, 205.

8. *Norfolk (Va.) American Beacon*, November 27, 1827.

9. *Raleigh (N.C.) Register*, October 2, 1827, reprinting an article from the "Petersburg Rep."

10. *Washington (D.C.) Daily National Journal*, October 24, 1827, reprinting an article from the *Charleston (S.C.) Courier* dated October 15.

11. *Portsmouth (N.H.) Journal of Literature and Politics*, August 6, 1825, quoting a letter to the *Baltimore Gazette*, July 27, 1825; *Essex (Mass.) Register*, August 1, 1825. This was the first sighting of sunspots in Virginia since 1816. See the *New York Spectator*, June 10, 1828.

12. *Middlesex (Conn.) Gazette*, April 18, 1827, quoting the *Charleston Courier*. The number of spots declined in 1828 to about eleven and then evidently disappeared the next year. See the *New York Spectator*, June 10, 1828. The last report of sunspots I have been able to find for the 1820s occurred in February 1829. See *Providence (R.I.) Patriot*, February 14, 1829, quoting the *Baltimore Chronicle*.

13. *Macon (Ga.) Telegraph*, March 24, 1828, reprinting an article from the *Richmond Compiler*; *Delaware Patriot and American Watchman* (Wilmington, Del.), March 18, 1828, reprinting an article from the *Fredericksburg (Va.) Arena*. For the geographical scope of the earthquake on Lower Canada, see the *Baltimore Patriot*, March 14, 1828; on Washington, D.C., see the *Daily National Intelligencer*, March 11, 1828; on eastern Ohio, see the *Chillicothe Scioto (Ohio) Gazette*, March 13, 1828. On the effects of the earthquake in Brunswick County, see John Herbert Claiborne, *Seventy-Five Years in Old Virginia* (New York: Neale, 1904), 17–18.

14. Blood rain, of course, has been reported occasionally since ancient times, and in recent years scientists have confirmed that it results from dust carried up into the atmosphere before a rain storm. For a recent scientific explanation of blood rain, see, for example, Constantino Criado Pedro Dorta, "An Unusual 'Blood Rain' over the Canary Islands (Spain): The Storm of January 1999," *Journal of Arid Environments* 55 (2003): 765–83. For a scientific description of blood rain in the American South during the nineteenth century, see F. P. Venable, "Fall of Blood in Chatham County," *Journal of the Elisha Mitchell Scientific Society* 1 (1884): 38–39.

15. *Confessions*, 10.

16. For an example of such a natural history textbook, see Patrick Kerr Rogers, *An Introduction to the Mathematical Principles of Natural Philosophy: Adapted for the Use of Beginners, and Arranged More Particularly for the Convenience of the Junior Students of William & Mary College* (Richmond, Va.: Shepherd & Pollard, 1822). Rogers taught chemistry and natural philosophy at William and Mary in the 1820s. See the *Daily National Journal*, October 28, 1826, for Turner's knowledge of natural history.

17. William Sidney Drewry, *The Southampton Insurrection* (Washington, D.C.: Neal, 1900), 30n2.

18. *Confessions*, 10.

19. Ibid.

20. *Macon (Ga.) Telegraph*, October 8, 1831, reprinting an article from the *Richmond Compiler*; Hannibal to Mr. Nathaniel Turner, August 25, 1831, Freemont Rider Collection, Manuscript Library, Syracuse University, Syracuse, New York.

21. See, for examples, Georg Croly, *The Apocalypse of St. John, or Prophecy of the Rise, Progress, and Fall of the Church of Rome; the Inquisition; the Revolution of France; the Universal War; and the Final Triumph of Christianity* (Philadelphia: Littel, 1827); Elias Boudinot, *The Second Advent, or Coming of the Messiah in Glory: Shown to Be a Scripture Doctrine, and Taught by Divine Revelation, from the Beginning of the World* (Trenton, N.J.: Fenton & Hutchinson, 1815); the anonymous *A Count and Conjecture or Two on the Number of the Beast* (New York: Mercein, 1819); and William C. Davis, *The Millennium, or, A Short Sketch on the Rise and Fall of Antichrist* (Columbia, S.C.: Davenport, 1813). On the validity of natural signs as a guide to prophecy, see the sermon titled "The Signs of the Times" in Albert Barnes, ed., *Sermons on Important Subjects by the Rev. Samuel Davies*, vol. 3 (New York: Dayton & Saxton, 1842), 100–128. On the eighteenth century origins of this literature in the United States and Britain, see Susan Juster, *Doomsayers: Anglo-American Prophecy in the Age of Revolution* (Philadelphia: University of Pennsylvania Press, 2003). On Jews moving to Palestine in the 1820s and the Christian movement in England to encourage that move, see Sarah Kochav, "The Evangelical Movement in England and the Restoration of the Jews to Eretz, Israel," *Cathedra* 62 (1991): 18–36. On the American Society for the Condition of the Jews, which advocated "the restoration of the Jews" among other things, see *Israel's Advocate*, April 1824, 64. For detailed newspaper reports of Jews moving to Palestine, see the *Fayetteville (N.C.) Carolina Observer*, April 29, 1830; the *Raleigh Star*, April 8, 1830; and the *Connecticut Mirror*, January 16, 1826.

22. *Confessions*, 11. See Revelation 12.

23. *Hillsborough (N.C.) Recorder*, October 8, 1828, reprinting an article from the *Huntsville (Ala.) Southern Advocate*. Many other newspapers printed versions of this story, but the version in the *Hillsborough Recorder* appears to be the most complete available.

24. *Richmond Enquirer*, June 14 and 15, 1828. Turner in the *Confessions* gives May 12, 1828, as the exact date on which he heard the "loud noise in the heavens," but I have been able to find nothing in the newspapers on that date to fit the description. For reports of other meteors falling in the South in 1828, see *Pittsfield (Mass.) Sun*, July 31, 1828, referring to reports in the Charleston, South Carolina, newspapers about a "very brilliant meteor" that passed over the city on July 11; *South-Carolina State Gazette and Columbia Advertiser*, July 19, 1828, reporting a sighting of the July 11 meteor in Georgetown, South Carolina; the *Washington, D.C., National Intelligencer*, September 30, 1828, copying a report from the *Huntsville (Ala.) Advocate*, telling of a "dazzling" meteor that appeared on August 31; and the *Raleigh Register*, November 14, 1828, summarizing an article from the *Nashville Banner* that told of a "shooting star" seen over Nashville on October 29.

25. *Confessions*, 11.

26. *Richmond Enquirer*, February 15, 1831. For other reports of the eclipse in the South, see *Lynchburg Virginian*, February 14, 1831; *Raleigh Star*, February 17, 1831; *Fayetteville Carolina Observer*, March 3, 1831, reprinting an article from the *Western Carolinian*;

Washington, D.C., *Daily National Intelligencer*, February 14, 1831. On the eclipse see also Louis P. Masur, *1831: Year of Eclipse* (New York: Hill & Wang, 2001), chaps. 1–2.

27. *Liberator*, February 26, 1831.

28. Amos 8, esp. verse 9.

29. Micah 3, esp. verses 3 and 6.

30. Isaiah 13, esp. verses 1, 2, and 10.

31. Ezekiel 32, esp. verse 7.

32. Matthew 24, esp. verses 3, 29 and 33. The same story appears almost verbatim in Mark 13, especially verses 4 and 24. The book of Luke also refers to a darkening of the sun in conjunction with the death of Jesus. See Luke 23, especially verses 44 and 45. This story in turn is recalled in the later book of Acts as proof of the divinity of Jesus. See Acts 2, especially verses 16 and 20.

33. Revelation 6, see especially verses 5 and 12. For a contemporary view of the opening of the sixth seal, see the *Fredericksburg Virginia Herald*, October 26, 1831, for a poem by the English poet Thomas Gray titled "Opening of the Sixth Seal," which was reprinted from a popular almanac, the *Token of 1832*. See also *Christian Examiner and General Review* 8, no 2 (1830): 150–52, for an article titled "The Apocalypse of St. John . . ." that reviews four recently published books on the book of Revelation. Pages 150–52 deal specifically with the sixth seal.

34. *Confessions*, 11.

35. On hard times in Virginia during the 1820s, see Thomas J. Wertenbaker, *Norfolk: Historic Southern Port*, 2nd ed. (Durham, N.C.: Duke University Press, 1962), 151; and Tommy L. Bogger, *Free Blacks in Norfolk, Virginia, 1790–1860* (Charlottesville: University Press of Virginia, 1997), chap. 4.

36. *Richmond (Va.) Religious Herald*, July 22, 1831. On the reorganization of evangelical churches in Virginia during the 1820s, see also Charles Frederick Irons, "'The Chief Cornerstone': The Spiritual Foundations of Virginia's Slave Society," Ph.D. diss., University of Virginia, 2003, chap. 3.

37. *Confessions*, 11.

38. *Fayetteville Carolina Observer*, July 27, 1831.

39. *Fayetteville Carolina Observer*, August 17, 1831. In this newspaper report, Uranus was called Herschel, the name used at the time for the planet. Uranus had been discovered in 1781 by the British astronomer Sir William Herschel and was originally named for him.

40. *Norfolk Herald*, August 15, 1831. See also William S. Forrest, *Historical and Descriptive Sketches of Norfolk and Vicinity* (Philadelphia: Lindsay & Blakiston, 1853), 192–93; and *Charlotte Miners' and Farmers' Journal*, August 31, 1831, reprinting an article from the *Richmond Compiler*.

41. On reports of a blue sun seen in Georgia, see *Macon Telegraph*, August 20, 1831.

42. The volcano on Saint Vincent was the Soufriere volcano, which is still active today, and the one in the Lesser Antilles was an unnamed submarine volcano. John Milne, "Seismological Observations and Earth Physics," *Geographical Journal* 21, no. 1 (1903): 13–14. On the eruption on Saint Vincent, see *Proceedings of the Royal Institution of Great Britain* 29 (1936): 621. On the submarine volcano, see Péter Hédervári, *Catalog of Submarine*

Volcanoes and Hydrological Phenomena Associated with Volcanic Events, 1500 B.C. to December 31, 1899 (Boulder, Colo.: World Data Center A for Solid Earth Geophysics [for] U.S. Dept. of Commerce, National Oceanic and Atmospheric Administration, National Geophysical Data Center, 1984). On Soufriere see also G. J. Symons, ed., *The Eruption of Krakatoa* (London: Trübner, 1888), 396.

43. "New Volcanic Island," *Mirror*, October 8, 1831, 241–44. The eyewitness, Cmdr. C. H. Swinburne, master of the sloop *HMS Rapid*, sent a letter dated July 22, 1831, Malta, to Vice Admiral Henry Hotham—reprinted in the *Mirror* article—describing the volcano. By late October the volcano had disappeared into the sea. See also the *American Magazine of Useful and Entertaining Knowledge* 3 (1837): 245.

44. *Rural Economy*, September 1, 1832, 409–10. On the 1831 eruption of Vesuvius, see also, Symons, *Eruption of Krakatoa*, 396.

45. Rev. Samuel Parker, *Journal of an Exploring Tour beyond the Rocky Mountains*, 4th ed. (Ithaca, N.Y.: Andrus, Woodruff & Gauntlett, 1844), 337–38. Parker's report notes that the eruption was confirmed later by a British naturalist named Dr. Gardner who was nearby at the time with a man employed by the Hudson Bay Company. The 1831 eruption of Mount Saint Helens, in fact, began a four-year series of eruptions at that volcano. See Mika Kohno and Yoshiyuki Fugii, "Past 220 Year Bipolar Volcanic Signals: Remarks on Common Features of Their Source Volcanic Eruptions," *Annals of Glaciology* 35, no. 1 (2002): 217–23.

46. Cold, rainy weather was experienced in New Orleans, the black belt of Alabama, northern Georgia, and Charleston in June and early July 1831. Only cities in the far southeast such as Mobile, Tallahassee, and Savannah experienced normal summer weather in 1831. On the southern limit of the rains in the summer of 1831, see *New-York Spectator*, July 26, 1831, quoting an article from the *Savannah Georgian*, July 9, 1831.

47. On the cold and rain in Washington, North Carolina, see *New-York Spectator*, July 29, 1831, reprinting an article dated "Washington (N.C.) July 16."

48. *Lynchburg Virginian*, August 25, 1831, quoting the *Fredericksburg Arena*.

49. *Macon Telegraph*, August 20, 1831.

50. *New-Hampshire Patriot and State Gazette*, September 26, 1831. The article is reprinted from the *New York Enquirer* and is titled "Extract of a letter from a friend, dated Petersburg, Sept. 10, 1831."

RUTH ALDEN DOAN

"Neither Cult nor Charisma"

William Miller and Leadership of New Religious Movements

Joseph Smith dug in the hills of upstate New York and told of golden plates and revelations. Marshall Herff Applewhite had himself castrated and left this world with thirty-eight people in tow. Even William Miller's successor of a sort, Ellen G. White, had explosive religious experiences and heard directives straight from her God. Miller, compared with his fellow leaders of new religious movements, was just plain dull. He grew up in rural New England. His family farmed, and he became a respectable enough citizen to receive appointment as justice of the peace and to join the Masons. Although he stepped out of the mainstream by becoming a deist in his youth, for most of his life he followed the evangelical Christianity of many of his neighbors and relatives. Except of course that his version of evangelical Christianity included his anticipation that he would see Jesus return "about A.D. 1843."[1]

Precisely because he was so un-extraordinary in so many ways, Miller can provide an object lesson to students of new religious movements. Like the popular media, scholars are often tempted to follow the story that offers a bit of what seems bizarre—not to mention the story that includes sex and drugs or at least the high drama of visions.[2] Yet Miller receives acknowledgement as a member of the category of "sect and cult leaders" and leaders of new religious movements.[3] To walk through some of the scholarship of new religious movements with Miller at the center of our story, therefore, allows us to think about generalizations often applied to new religious movements and to broaden our understanding of such work.[4]

MILLER AND MILLERISM

Born February 15, 1782, in Massachusetts, William Miller lived most of his life on the border where Low Hampton, New York, and Poultney, Vermont, almost touched each other. As a boy he lived on a farm where he chopped wood, plowed fields, gathered sap, and slaughtered hogs. He traveled around a limited neighborhood to sell surplus goods or to join in militia training. His education was perhaps more limited than he would have liked, but he took to reading so that he could explore ideas further on his own and with neighbors who would eventually include infamous deists and skeptics. In his youth, however, he was exposed to evangelical Christianity through his grandfather, a Baptist preacher, and through his mother.[5]

In 1803 Miller married Lucy Smith, and their own farm in Poultney—at least at first—differed little from the farm on which he grew up. As Rowe has noted, however, Miller did not aspire to remain an ordinary farmer. He moved his family to the center of Poultney. He joined the Masons. He took an interest in Democratic-Republican politics. He received appointments as constable and sheriff.[6] Miller also embraced deism publicly and reaffirmed his loyalty to the skeptical by making fun of Christians, including his own grandfather.[7] Miller's service in the War of 1812 may have been a turning point in his system of belief. He suffered not only the chaos of battle but also witnessed a series of deaths from typhus of people close to him on the battlefield. When he retired from the military, he returned to Low Hampton, New York, and, as Rowe implies, to identification with his family of origin.[8] In Low Hampton, Miller finally accepted Christianity.

As a Christian, Miller took it as his duty to understand the Bible, and he carried out a two-year study. At the end of that time, Miller concluded, famously and infamously, that Jesus would return, suddenly and personally, about the year 1843. Miller did not immediately go forth to share his new insight, however. He stayed in the same local area, discussed religion with his family and with his minister, and continued to do his work. Not until 1831 did he accept what he understood as a call to carry his message throughout the land. Through the 1830s he traveled largely from small town to small town to teach and to preach.[9] Although invitations arrived steadily, Miller was right to suspect that not all of his hosts believed in his chronology. His reputation for inspiring conversions probably led to most of his opportunities to speak.

The pace of the Millerite movement accelerated at the end of the 1830s. Certainly the closer approach of the date, 1843, brought in more audiences. Equally important, Joshua V. Himes chose to set himself up not only as a believer but also as Miller's lieutenant. Himes became the media genius of the movement, ordering up the Great Tent as an attraction at revival meetings, publishing newspapers, and advertising lectures as he sent Miller to cities as well as towns.[10] As the number of believers in the "soon appearing of Christ" multiplied, and as a network of lecturers spread out to feed the flames of anticipation, the movement spun beyond anyone's control—Miller's or Himes's. Some followers added eccentric ideas and actions to the central notion that Jesus would soon appear: annihilationism, manifestations of the spirit, communalism, and so on. Overworked, turning sixty, and faced with such chaos in his own movement, Miller fell ill and spent much of 1842 and 1843 at home in Low Hampton. Even in retreat he heard the appeals of followers to take stands on issues that agitated the movement. He balked at approving the "come-outer" movement that urged separating believers from existing churches. Miller, however, did speak and write in favor of a more specific date: he argued that the return of Jesus would happen in the Jewish year 1843, which would run from March 1843 until March 1844.

That year, 1844, became the year of disappointment for Miller. When March passed, he issued no new predictions for Christ's return. As he followed his own advice to watch and wait, another Millerite, Samuel S. Snow, developed a new chronology. The day of the return, Snow ultimately argued, would be October 22, 1844. Miller's discomfort with the new date did not stop others from embracing it. The pressure mounted for him to accept the new date, and finally in October he wrote, "I see a glory in the seventh month which I never saw before," and he prepared with his family for the day when he hoped to see the "King of kings." Legend has it that Miller waited on "Miller's rock" for Jesus to break through the clouds.[11]

The chaos in the movement before the predicted dates was matched by the chaos that followed the Great Disappointment. Some left the movement in disgust. Some added new ideas and behaviors. Some recalculated dates. Most wanted Miller to come with them in their own reinventions of Millerism. Miller did flirt briefly with the "shut door" theory—the idea that October 22 had indeed been the date when God had put an end to possible salvation for sinners. For the most part, however, he distanced himself from reinterpreters and continued to say that he anticipated the return of Jesus at any time. He did not found another movement. But he did ultimately follow Himes in rejecting the shut door theory and in bringing together a conference at Albany in the spring of 1845 that was clearly a move in the direction of establishing a separate sect on Millerite grounds. Miller also wrote an *Apology and Defense* through which, according to Rowe, he was "claiming a personal legacy and passing it on to a new generation."[12] Although Miller lectured in 1845, 1846, and 1847, he was a tired old man with increasing health problems. He stayed home in 1848 as those problems multiplied and his eyesight failed. When he died on December 20, 1849, Himes was there to close his eyes.

Growing Up without Psychopathology

In the media, in the popular mind, and among a good number of psychologists, new religious movements grow out of the pathologies of individual leaders. The History Channel named an exploration into new religious movements *Cults: Dangerous Devotion*.[13] Internet sites provide many opportunities to see "cult leaders" as at least deviant and probably insane.[14] YouTube offers a video list of "Most Evil Cult Leaders"—the word *psychopathic* flashes repeatedly across the screen.[15] The tendency is so widespread that David G. Bromley and Anson D. Shupe put perception of leaders of new religious movements in the context of what they call a "subversion mythology" that includes a picture of "arrogant gurus who claimed or were attributed divine stature by followers."[16]

Alexander Deutsch focuses on "the psychotic leader" in his essay "Psychological Perspectives on Cult Leadership" but draws most of his conclusions from a single case study.[17] For the most part, however, psychologists and psychiatrists have paid more attention to followers than to leaders of new religious movements.[18] The Group for the Advancement of Psychiatry, in their report *Leaders and Followers: A Psychiatric Perspective on Religious Cults*, almost sidesteps the issue of leaders. Granting the possibility that leaders of new religious movements might be frauds,[19] this report goes on to outline ideal types of cult leaders: the Hero, the Outsider, the Narcissist, the Charismatic Figure, and the Entrepreneur.[20] Without further exploration this list shows us little about leaders. Similarly, as James R. Lewis has pointed out, the *Diagnostic and Statistical Manual of Mental Disorders* fails for the most part to cite studies of the leadership of new religious movements but nonetheless noted the likelihood that those with "Paranoid Personality Disorder" must be "overrepresented among leaders of mystical or esoteric religions."[21]

Much other work on leaders emphasizes syndromes rather than psychopathologies but focuses on the deviant nonetheless. Anthony Stevens and John Price, in *Prophets, Cults, and Madness*, conclude that leaders of new religious movements exhibit symptoms similar to those of schizophrenics. Stevens and Price refer to what they call the schizotypal leader who, in their interpretation, shares a genetic predisposition to see visions, which then become the basis for a reinterpretation of reality shared by followers.[22] When psychologist Len Oakes surveyed leaders of new religious movements in Australia and New Zealand, he found a pattern of narcissistic personality disorder.[23] Although Oakes asserts that the creation of the new religious movement is a productively adaptive response to narcissistic personality disorder,[24] the disorder is at the forefront of his interpretation.

Many scholars of new religious movements approach the psychopathology explanation with skepticism. Rodney Stark has asserted directly that "there have been precious few examples for which there is any persuasive evidence that the founder of a new religious movement had any symptoms of mental problems."[25] Resisting the tautology that visions or revelations are by definition pathological (and thus that they are evidence of the pathology that has as a primary symptom visions and revelations),[26] such scholars recognize the difficult personal and psychological backgrounds of some leaders without positing that psychopathology is necessary to the emergence of a new religious movement.

On Miller's personal development, family life, and psychological state, we can follow the lead of David Rowe. Rowe does indeed find much in Miller's early life that helps to explain his interpretation, his leadership style, and his successes in building a movement. Two themes that Rowe focuses on are the problem, for Miller, of pleasing his father and of becoming a father himself, and the problem of balancing the two cultures from which his parents emerged—the evangelical Christianity of his mother and his maternal grandfather and the political and skeptical bent of his father's associates. Rowe also recognizes in Miller a tendency toward "melancholy."[27]

According to Rowe, one of Miller's lifelong struggles could be summed up in this way: "How could Miller, having been a disobedient son, hope to be a worthy father"?[28] Because his father died while Miller was in his rebellious, mocking, deistical phase, the son suffered from the lack of any opportunity to make amends. Perhaps it is not surprising, then, if Miller's conversion received its spark from an invitation to read a discourse at the Baptist church on the "importance of parental duties."[29] Miller worked both within his nuclear family and within his extended family and neighborhood to "authenticate his fatherhood."[30] As Millerism spread into a region-wide movement, the movement itself functioned, according to Rowe, as a platform for his wrestling with the roles of good son and good father. A child of God who had become the metaphorical "father . . . of thousands," Miller could play out personal anxieties on a public stage.[31]

If Miller's struggles with fatherhood helped to give form and impetus to his movement, those struggles also intertwined with the problem of reconciling his dual heritages. His maternal grandfather, Elnathan Phelps, was a Baptist pastor in Pittsfield, Massachusetts. Rowe points to Miller's mother as a model of "personal piety" in the family.[32] But through his father, Miller had the opportunity to meet Matthew Lyon, an intellectual, writer, political agitator, editor, and deist. Although he attended church and gave evidence of piety in his youth, Miller avowed himself a deist after he moved to Poultney, Vermont, in the early 1800s.[33] Miller's creative resolution of the two traditions became clear in Millerism: strong biblical literalism meant to Miller both the embrace of Jesus and his miraculous return and also the embrace of "Bible facts" and a logical, empirical approach to anticipating the dramatic, supernatural end.[34]

The one problematic part of Miller's personality is what Rowe characterizes as his "melancholy." Miller himself suspected that his friends found him "hypcondrical" and understood that "he appeared 'moross and ill natured.'"[35] Rowe raises the issue without finding a single interpretation for this melancholy. First he hypothesizes that the melancholy arose out of "guilt over rejecting his parents and their teaching"; later Rowe asserts that "continuing depression was but a signpost of a developing conversion," and yet Miller's melancholy persisted after he came to a resolution of both his parents' religious heritage and his own conversion.[36] Without an examination of whether Miller's testimony actually points to a diagnosis of depression, we are left with an incomplete picture.

What Rowe's characterization points to, ultimately, is a man with some not at all unusual struggles in his path toward adulthood. Resolving tensions between revealed religion and skepticism, between the heritage of his mother's family and of his father's circle, seeking a path to a meaningful role as a father and leader in his community—later in his movement—these were all very real challenges to

Miller, but challenges of the sort that young people face frequently and in the normal course of life. Miller showed no signs of psychopathology, and few possible signs of syndromes that would require psychiatric treatment. Instead he struggled through the difficulties of youth and the quest for a meaningful and stable adult life. Interestingly for students of American religion, his struggles led him to conclude that he needed to warn his neighbors that Jesus Christ would return "about A.D. 1843."

WHERE IS THE CHARISMA?

Once Miller had developed his insight into the Bible and its promises for the future, he set about sharing his message with others. Accounts of his public presence, of his roles as preacher and leader, leave us a mixed picture. Among the characteristics that he displayed, however, charisma could not be counted. The focus of both popular and scholarly views of new religious movements on charismatic leaders returns us to the starting point of this essay: the temptation to focus on the exotic, the dramatic. The question of charisma also hints at the possibility that the bias of scholars as well as that of popular commentators is against seeing new religious movements as viable religious options. Seeking an explanation for why anyone would believe so differently from oneself, an observer might be tempted to conclude that others must have been led astray by Svengali-like figures.

Max Weber proposed "charisma" as one of three types of authority. Weber defines charisma as "a certain quality of an individual personality by virtue of which he is set apart from ordinary men and treated as endowed with supernatural, superhuman, or at least exceptional powers and qualities."[37] Thus for Weber charisma begins within the individual leader—it is a personal characteristic—but charisma also must be validated by followers. Indeed, Weber asserts, "It is the recognition on the part of those subject to authority which is decisive for the validity of charisma."[38] In his study of the Rajneeshee, Charles Lindholm elaborates on Weber's point: "Individuals possessing charisma are portrayed by Weber as above all else passionate and intrinsically compelling . . . to the followers, whatever the charismatic leader says is right not because it makes sense or because it coincides with what has always been done but because *the leader says it*."[39] The followers of Bhagwan Shree Rajneesh "felt they were in a direct, intimate, and passionate relationship with Rajneesh," and thus charisma arose out of the interaction between the individual with an extraordinary "capacity for enchantment" and those who followed him.[40]

William Miller was neither charismatic, in the popular sense, nor meek and mild-mannered. He exemplified, rather, strong but not extraordinary local leadership before his years as a prophet carried him out into a broader world. He received an appointment as sheriff in 1809—such an appointment required the posting of bonds that give testimony to the respect in which neighbors held him.

Miller may have gained personal popularity as well as respect, in part through his habit of mimicking preachers, including his own grandfather Phelps.[41] After his return from the War of 1812, and after his initial conclusion that the personal, premillennial return of Christ was imminent, he lived a respectable life that Sylvester Bliss characterized thus: "He was a good citizen, a kind neighbor, an affectionate husband and parent, and a devoted Christian; good to the poor and benevolent, as objects of charity were presented; in the Sunday-school was teacher and superintendent; in the church he performed important service as a reader and exhorter."[42] Miller remembered that, as he began to tell his neighbors about the "evidence of the nearness of the advent," he was basically ignored.[43] Baptist elder Truman Hendryx, on the other hand, remembered Miller's reputation as someone "hard on ministers who differed with him." Hendryx later excused Miller's harshness by claiming that it only landed upon the heads of those who demonstrated "a spirit of self-importance," but he did not deny the point about Miller's propensity to deal shortly with those that he judged to be out of line.[44]

The public phase of Miller's life opened in 1831. When Miller carried his message of the end soon to come across the northeastern states, his followers found him persuasive but not charismatic. Followers nicknamed him "old father Miller" or "Father Miller," and the nickname summarizes the dominant view of Miller within the movement.[45] He was, indeed, in his fifties by the time he began the itinerant preaching life, and the aches and pains of that tiring existence probably made him seem more the old father than he might otherwise have appeared. Miller himself reinforced the image of the old father, supposedly asking Joshua V. Himes, for example, "What can an old farmer do?"[46] As the years passed, he rounded out but did not go gray.[47] Nonetheless the old farmer image must have intensified when, for example, Miller suffered bouts of illness during the key year 1843. One observer noted even after his recovery that he remained "affable and attentive"; as Arthur Whitefield Spalding later noted, Miller's "kind and fatherly ways" contributed to his image as much as did the simple fact that "he was old."[48] Rowe asserts that illness and retreat only reaffirmed Miller's role as "patriarch" and source of "fatherly wisdom."[49] Old he may have been, but he was nonetheless an effective public speaker. As Rowe summarizes, the shared perception of Miller seems to have been a man who was "lucid, erudite, and effective."[50] Sylvester Bliss quoted a journalist's account that praised Miller as "one of the most interesting lecturers," a man who "labors . . . diligently to inculcate" his doctrine with "candor and fairness."[51] Diligent and interesting hardly adds up to the intense magnetism of the charismatic leader.

More recent scholarship on charisma also leaves Miller on the far side of the divide. One scholar whose work may help to explain his lack of charisma is Philip Smith. In his article "Culture and Charisma: Outline of a Theory," Smith argues that charisma can be understood not in the context of social structures and psychological theories, within which most scholars have explored the concept, but in the context of autonomous culture.[52] For Smith necessary foundations for charismatic authority include "narratives which implot events within a salvation framework"—certainly a foundation that made it possible for Miller to attain charismatic authority. On the other hand, Smith also asserts that "the symbolic logic of charisma hangs upon binary codings" and that "images of 'evil' must be present in the forest of symbols surrounding each charismatic leader."[53] It is oddly difficult to see Miller working within such a binary logic or identifying "evil, negatively charged symbols" around which his followers could build a community.[54] Certainly he believed in a literal devil. Yet for all of his willingness to place the rise and fall of Satan within his chronology of the end, he never identified agents of the devil in his community.

Charismatic leadership is not the only option, of course—it is simply the option most often identified with the emergence of new religious movements. Weber himself saw charisma as one of three sources of authority, an alternative to rational/legal and traditional authority. For Weber traditional authority passed from generation to generation in a process based neither on the qualities of individuals nor in overarching principles. Rational/legal authority, on the other hand, rested on uniform principles rather than on tradition or on the visionary leadership of a compelling individual.[55] Miller derived his authority not from a sense of the god within, not from a sense of his own embodiment of the divine, but rather from a rational, empirical reading of the Bible. He announced that "we have sought to spread the truth, not by fanatical prophecies arising out of our own hearts, but by the light of the scriptures, history, and interpretation."[56] Thus Miller's authority resided outside himself and could be broadly shared—shared with any who opened their eyes to see how to read scripture aright. In fact one of the greatest appeals of Millerism seems to have been the participatory nature of the movement—all could follow biblical numbers, all could do the arithmetic, all could apply their reason to the largest questions and derive the answer to the problem: 1843.[57]

Drawing on Culture and Community

William Miller grew up in an eastern New York and a Vermont that offered a number of social and religious paths to a boy and young man. Vermont in his lifetime saw agriculture both successful and unsuccessful, a "sheep craze," and the emergence of small-scale textile industry.[58] Religious persuasions that offered Miller worldview and community include Congregationalism, Episcopalianism, Methodism, Baptism, and deism.

Historians have paid some attention to the cultural and social contexts of the emergence of new religious movements in the first half of the nineteenth century. Whitney Cross's famous study, *The Burned-Over District*, identified the home ground of such movements as the Mormons and the Oneida Perfectionists not as frontier areas but rather as maturing economies boosted by the completion of the Erie Canal.[59] Gordon Wood focused on Mormons, not Millerites, in an important 1980 essay, but the context to which he pointed could apply to a great extent to Millerites as well: new religious movements drew on the broader evangelical culture and the energies unleashed by the Second Great Awakening.[60] Nathan O. Hatch tied new religious movements and revivalistic Christianity to broader developments in the new nation in *The Democratization of American Christianity*.[61]

Many scholars of new religious movements, on the other hand, have taken a sociological turn and rooted leaders and founders in social groups. As Rodney Stark has asserted in a discussion of recipients of new revelations, "A recipient's ability to convince others is proportionate to the extent to which he or she is a respected member of an intense primary group." He goes on to elaborate that "revelations cannot be sustained and transformed into successful new religions by lonely prophets, but are invariably rooted in preexisting networks having a high level of social solidarity. Indeed, new religious movements based on revelations typically are *family* affairs," or at least affairs based in "a durable, face-to-face, network with very high levels of trust and affection."[62]

Although William Miller did not receive a new revelation, he developed a new interpretation of existing scripture. As with a new revelation, a new interpretation must find a willing audience. Thus it is important to return to his biography, and to note that during the 1820s Miller expanded and reinforced his close, local circles while adhering to but not yet preaching his anticipation of the second coming. Rowe characterizes Miller's home as a "rural community tightly knit by blood, bond, and mutual need."[63] His household and extended family were large. He fathered ten children, eight of whom survived. In the New England tradition, he took others, unrelated by blood, into his household. He lived near his mother, his sister, his brother, and his sister-in-law.[64]

Miller's connections in the church community were rooted in his ancestry and in habits that preceded his conversion. He attended services at the local Baptist church, especially when he was asked to read a sermon or homily himself.[65] After his conversion and his later-famous two-year Bible study, Miller became a major figure in the Hampton Baptist Church, both as a relative of the pastor and in his own right. His church ties expanded the circle of his personal acquaintance as he won election to the newly formed Washington Baptist Association, and Miller reinforced those ties through membership in the missionary society.

In the broader community, Miller attained a measure of respect. As a member of the Masons, he associated with the men who were the primary leaders and decision makers in his community. His ties to the Democratic-Republicans meant he ran in political circles. His appointments as constable and as sheriff both signaled the respect in which he was already held in his community and gave him further opportunities to build his social and political networks.

All of Miller's networks of association—in family, in church, and in public affairs—served him well when, in 1831, he went public with his prediction of the impending end. Unfortunately we do not know who his first converts to the second advent doctrine were. We do know that he wrote to his sister Anna Atwood on the subject. His first invitation to preach took him to Dresden, where his sister Sylvia lived.[66] It is tempting to speculate that Miller's power in his own congregation in Hampton led to the exit of pastor Leman Andrus, who gave no sign of accepting Miller's doctrine, and his replacement by Truman Hendryx, who embraced Miller's views of the end—but the sources offer nothing but speculation on this point.[67]

MILLER AFTER 1843

One factor that promotes the survival of a new religious movement is the establishment of loyalty to the founder and the continuation of that loyalty in some form after the founder's death. All Scientologists—not to mention many non-Scientologists—recognize L. Ron Hubbard as the founding force of the Church of Scientology. Equally important, Hubbard's presence continues today, both in his image in larger-than-life form in Scientology institutions and meetings and in the efforts of the new leader, David Miscavige, to establish his credentials as providing continuity with Hubbard. Similarly the Church of Jesus Christ of Latter-Day Saints (Mormons) has effectively spread a new sacred history among its adherents that places Joseph Smith at the center of the rediscovery of the ancient history of the Americas and the connection of that history with the ongoing promises and demands of the church.

William Miller's place as founder and leader of a new religious movement is somewhat more problematic than those of Hubbard and Smith. Certainly the hope that Jesus Christ might return about the year 1843 became the center of a movement named for Miller. But as the movement spread in the late 1830s and early 1840s, during the period when George Knight perceives the shift from Millerism to Adventism, the place of Miller at the center became tenuous.[68] The energy of spreading Adventism came from Joshua V. Himes, in particular, and no longer from Miller himself. Nonetheless Himes found it necessary to defer to Miller, at least in word if not in deed. He sought the credibility offered by Miller's approval of a variety of measures such as the use of the Great Tent. Himes reminded Miller of the founder's importance: "The whole enterprise demands the influence and help you can give it." If Himes forgot whose movement it was, audiences reminded him; when Himes showed up to preach in Miller's stead on at least one occasion, the people stayed away in droves.[69] And when Himes feared that the movement would shatter in the whirlwind of 1844, he looked to Miller to provide a stable center. "Never," he wrote, "was there a time when we needed you more."[70]

When Miller's time to look for the end had passed after March 1844, those groping toward a new understanding sought Miller's support. His positive assessment (if not complete acceptance) of the so-called seventh-month movement that predicted the return of Christ on October 22, 1844, was essential to the widespread acceptance of the new prediction among his followers.

After Miller died Himes and others still found it necessary to seek the Miller name to lend legitimacy to their interpretations and actions. As George Knight recounts, Joseph Bates met with widow Lucy Miller in 1853. After she "listened attentively," she commented that "she did not know but the [seventh-day] Sabbath" that Bates and others taught "was right."[71] Even such a lukewarm endorsement was eagerly held up by Bates and other Adventists as evidence that their path was the right one. Even more problematic than Miller's role in the spread and survival of Millerism and early Adventism was Miller's role after his death as a symbolic founder of the Seventh-day Adventist Church. First of all Miller's place within Seventh-day Adventism was based on the assumption that Miller was wrong—or at least half wrong. Seventh-day Adventists in the nineteenth century, and thereafter, accepted the interpretation that the date, October 22, 1844, was correct but the event wrong. The Bible did point to the centrality of the date, Adventists argued. None of Miller's arithmetic was in error. On the other hand, Seventh-day Adventists from Hiram Edson on asserted that the date signified not an event on earth but rather an event in the heavens. The event was not the return of Christ to earth but rather the beginning of the "cleansing of the sanctuary."[72]

Miller's place as one of the founders of Adventism is broadly accepted by both believers and scholars. Yet another way to think about Miller's role is to understand it as a construction of his followers. As James White, Hiram Edson, Ellen G. White, and others assembled the cultural pieces that they brought together into Seventh-day Adventism, they drew on a number of sources. It would be possible, for example, to imagine an Adventism that looked back to Seventh-day Baptists for an origin story. Too, White had been a Methodist before she became a follower of Miller. The choice of Miller as the predecessor or founder of Adventism has had significant effects both on understandings of Miller and on understandings of Adventism.

Local Methodists perhaps ensured that White would not look back upon them as her group of origin. White's family had belonged to the Methodist Church of Portland, Maine. It was in the context of the Methodist Church that the Whites first learned of and experienced conversion and Christian community. But when White's father, Robert S. Harmon Sr., accepted the message of the soon appearing of Christ, he suffered disfellowship. Similarly White herself remembered trying to bring the Millerite prophesy into her Methodist church and, most significantly, being rejected because of it.[73] Whether Millerites became "Come-Outers" on principle or whether they were pushed out, their connections to existing denominations were often cut.

White and her fellow Adventists in the early years of the movement did not describe Miller as the embodiment or sole conduit of a special truth or revelation. Instead they emphasized his rationality, his precision and care in reading and interpreting scripture—it was the scriptures themselves that held the revelation available to all. Nonetheless White and other Adventists did emphasize that Miller had a special role. Although he did not embody a new truth, he found a reading of the old truth that was available in a special way to his—and to Ellen White's—generation. Elder James White posited that just as Martin Luther was "the man for his time," so Miller "in the hands of God, was the man for his time."[74] Later Ellen White went further and proposed that "God sent his angel to move upon the heart of a farmer [Miller] who had not believed the Bible, to lead him to search the prophecies." Nor was this a single spiritual push, in White's view. Rather "angels of God repeatedly visited that chosen one, to guide his mind and open to his understanding prophecies which had ever been dark to God's people."[75] Miller himself had never suggested that he was a "chosen one," nor that he was led quite so directly by angels. Contrary to what one might expect of a new religious movement in its longer-term consolidation, instead of a kind of domestication of the original founder, Miller's image grew toward that of divine, or at least angelic, conduit, or chosen embodiment of truth. For later Adventists Miller became the symbol of the opening of a new era, perhaps a new dispensation. God's choice to touch the human community through Miller provided the foundation for God's choice to reopen spiritual gifts, and especially visions, to White.[76]

Adventists' understandings of Miller also underscore the development of the church's understanding of the role of visions and of the place of White as visionary. Early Adventists had no particular need to assert that White's access to visions was unique. In the enthusiasm of what were assumed to be the end times, gifts could be open to all. In the 1840s and 1850s, therefore, Adventists expended little energy on the distinction between White's visions and the spiritual experiences of Miller and others. Later in the century, however, theologians and leaders focused on White's visions as separate and superior. Thus it is no surprise to the historian to find Adventists denying that Brother A. T. Jones heard White announce that "all can have the gift of prophecy." The confusion that might arise if all could claim visions had to be fended off. In the 1890s a number of claims to visions and prophecy arose among Adventists—perhaps in part because of White's own advancing age. White warned, "You cannot be too careful how you talk of the gift of prophesying" since it was dangerous to "encourage men and women and children to imagine that they have special light in revelations from God, when they have not received such light."[77] In the context of this development, it was even more important that Miller's place in foreshadowing but not experiencing revelation be clarified.

One possible lens for understanding White's turning to Miller for legitimacy is the lens of gender. Scholars know that female religious leaders often turn to direct revelation to provide a basis for their authority—or perhaps it is equally fair to say that revelations or visions open the path for female religious leadership.[78] White provides a kind of case study for this interpretation. Yet the validity of a woman's visions draws not only from the visions themselves but from the contexts in which the visions are understood.[79] White's interpretation of Miller as the first recipient of immediate supernatural direction in the new age of spiritual gifts provides the opportunity to see White's own visions as part of a larger history. White gains legitimacy through the fact that a man had received the first inklings of the new truth.[80] On the other hand, White herself also recognized the visions of African American preacher William E. Foy—a recognition that points to White's reconstruction of early Adventism as a vision-drenched time when God actively touched people of varied backgrounds and statuses.[81]

Although Miller may have sought to base his movement on "Bible facts," others looked to miracles in the heavens as signs that might point to the special nature of Miller's age and to the opening truth to which he pointed. Arthur Whitefield Spalding, in an early twentieth-century book directed to children, noted that Miller's birth came "during the American Revolution, about two years after the sun was darkened."[82] Presumably Spalding did not have to come out and say that the darkening of the sun may be taken as a sign from God that dramatic things were afoot in order to have readers understand the implications of the coincidence.[83]

Although not perhaps a miracle, the opportunity opened to Miller to go and teach his interpretation of the imminent advent certainly seemed to be an opportunity opened by God. Miller himself, as well as his followers, White, and White's followers, all understood this part of the story in the same way: the invitation to preach at Dresden was a sign from God that Miller should go forward and tell the world what he had discovered. Not surprisingly White's story included an echo of Miller's. White's sister Mary and brother-in-law Samuel Foss invited her to visit with them in Poland, Maine. White remembered, "I thought this was an opening from the Lord," just as Miller's invitation to preach had been such an opening. White recounted her first vision at an Adventist meeting in a chapel in Poland during her visit, and "the power of the Lord came upon me and on the people."[84] Nor could Miller receive the ultimate blame for his failure to see the Adventist truth of the date and the event. White bemoaned the inability of Miller to accept the "third angel's message"—the truth, as White saw it, that the event of 1844 was a spiritual and not an earthly event. Human influence and not divine, claimed White, led Miller to be distracted from the truth. Even more, Satan lay behind the human forces that drew Miller astray.[85] Thus Miller could be elevated for his insights, forgiven his errors, and left his role at the forefront of Adventism.

William Miller may have been dull relative to his fellows in the pantheon of new religious movement founders, but he offers opportunity for intriguing research and lively debate. If we can get beyond the categories inherited from Ernst Troeltsch,[86] we can see new religious movements as emerging from a range of social contexts, birthed by a range of types of founders. The real history of new religions is not the history presented by YouTube or even by the History Channel, but a history populated by sad and grumpy old men as well as by prophets, visionaries, and maybe a genuine lunatic or two. And in Miller's case, we have the opportunity to look at a classic but little-understood issue in new religions: how do they go forward after the end?

NOTES

1. William Miller, *Apology and Defense* (Boston: Himes, 1842), 11.

2. James T. Richardson mentions the "nuts and sluts" tradition in sociology, which, he noted, "seems to study 'weirdos' partially for the entertainment value of such work." Richardson, "The Psychology of Induction: A Review and an Interpretation," in *Cults and New Religious Movements: A Report of the American Psychiatric Association*, ed. Marc Galanter (Washington, D.C.: American Psychiatric Association, 1989), 227.

3. Eugene V. Gallagher, *The New Religious Movements Experience in America* (Westport, Ct.: Greenwood, 2004), 42–44; Hannah Cho, "Seventh-Day Adventists," New Religious Movements Homepage, March 12, 2002, http://web.archive.org/web/20060830091838/religiousmovements.lib.virginia.edu/nrms/sevn.html. Countercult and anticult writers also count Miller within their subject: see, for example, Anthony A. Hoekema, *The Four Major Cults: Christian Science, Jehovah's Witnesses, Mormons, and Seventh-Day Adventism* (Grand Rapids, Mich.: Eerdmans, 1989), 89–92; Walter Martin, *The Kingdom of the Cults* (Minneapolis: Bethany House, 2003), 538–42; "About the Millerites," Apologetics Index (http://www.apologeticsindex.org/m10.html, accessed May 16, 2014), which makes the interesting claim that Branch Davidians "are basically Millerites"; "Miller, William," Watchman Fellowship (http://www.watchman.org/cat95.htm#M, accessed May 16, 2014).

4. It seems particularly appropriate to be considering Miller in light of other scholarship after the publication of David L. Rowe's biography, *God's Strange Work: William Miller and the End of the World* (Grand Rapids, Mich.: Eerdmans, 2008). The debt that this essay owes to Rowe will be apparent throughout.

5. Biographical material on Miller, in addition to Rowe's work, is available from William Miller, *Apology and Defence* (Boston: Himes, 1845); Sylvester Bliss, *Memoirs of William Miller: Generally Known as a Lecturer on the Prophecies, and the Second Coming of Christ* (Boston: Himes, 1853); James White, *Sketches of the Christian Life and Public Labors of William Miller, Gathered from His Memoir by the Late Sylvester Bliss, and from Other Sources* (Battle Creek, Mich.: Seventh-Day Adventist Publishing, 1875); Francis D. Nichol, *The*

Midnight Cry: A Defense of the Conduct and Character of William Miller and the Millerites (Washington, D.C.: Review and Herald, 1944); Clara Endicott Sears, *Days of Delusion: A Strange Bit of History* (Boston: Houghton Mifflin, 1924); Everett N. Dick, *William Miller and the Advent Crisis, 1831–1844* (Berrien Springs, Mich.: Andrews University Press, 1994); Wayne R. Judd, "William Miller: Disappointed Prophet," in *The Disappointed: Millerism and Millenarianism in the Nineteenth Century*, ed. Ronald L. Numbers and Jonathan M. Butler (Knoxville: University of Tennessee Press, 1993), 17–35; Ruth Alden Doan, "William Miller," in *Encyclopedia of Protestantism*, ed. Hans Hillerbrand (New York: Routledge, 2001); Ruth Alden Doan, "William Miller," in *Blackwell Dictionary of Evangelical Biography* (London: Blackwell, 1994).

6. Rowe, *God's Strange Work*, 26–31.

7. Ibid., 38–42.

8. Ibid., 61.

9. Miller received his license to preach in 1831.

10. On Himes see David T. Arthur, "Joshua V. Himes and the Cause of Adventism," in *The Disappointed: Millerism and Millenarianism in the Nineteenth Century*, ed. Ronald L. Numbers and Jonathan M. Butler (Bloomington: Indiana University Press, 1987), 36–58.

11. Rowe, *God's Strange Work*, 189–91.

12. Ibid., 217.

13. *Cults: Dangerous Devotion* includes the assertion that "like most cult leaders, Warren Jeffs has been using religion to act out his fantasies."

14. For example, "Cult Leaders," Ananda Awareness Network, accessed May 16, 2014, http://www.anandainfo.com/cult_leaders.html; "Profile of Cult Leaders," The Skeptic Tank, accessed May 16, 2014, http://www.skeptictank.org/hs/cprofile.htm.

15. "Most Evil Cult Leaders 1/5," YouTube video, originally aired by the Discovery Channel, posted by "Janis Joplin," December 3, 2008, http://www.youtube.com/watch?v=PLejgoNRpoA.

16. David G. Bromley and Anson D. Shupe, "Public Reaction against New Religious Movements," in *Cults and New Religious Movements*, ed. Marc Galanter (Washington, D.C.: American Psychiatric Association, 1989), 322.

17. Alexander Deutsch, "Psychological Perspectives on Cult Leadership," in Galanter, *Cults and New Religious Movements*, 147–63. Deutsch bases his conclusions on his own study of the Family and the leader of that group.

18. The nineteenth-century habit of attributing insanity to those who followed marginal religious movements is discussed in William Sims Bainbridge, "Religious Insanity in America: The Official Nineteenth-Century Theory," *Sociological Analysis* 45, no. 3 (1984): 223–39; Ronald L. Numbers and Janet S. Numbers studied cases in which Millerites were labeled insane in "Millerism and Madness: A Study of 'Religious Insanity' in Nineteenth-Century America," in Numbers and Butler, *Disappointed*, 92–117. Neither of these studies focuses on leaders. See also Ruth Alden Doan, *The Miller Heresy, Millennialism, and American Culture* (Philadelphia: Temple University Press, 1987), 158–74.

19. Group for the Advancement of Psychiatry, *Leaders and Followers* (Washington, D.C.: American Psychiatric Publishing, 1992), 6.

20. Ibid., 19–20.

21. Qtd. in James R. Lewis, *Legitimating New Religions* (New Brunswick, N.J.: Rutgers University Press, 2003), 185–86.

22. Anthony Stevens and John Price, *Prophets, Cults, and Madness* (London: Duckworth, 2000). Lewis cites this work in *Legitimating New Religions,* 186. See also Charles Lindholm's study of Bhagwan Shree Rajneesh and his followers: "Rajneesh's extraordinary personality reflected exactly the sort of disintegrative psychic crisis that is commonly found in the life histories of shamans as well as contemporary charismatic figures." Lindholm, "Culture, Charisma, and Consciousness: The Case of the Rajneeshee," *Ethos* 30, no. 4 (2002): 370.

23. Len Oakes, *Prophetic Charisma: The Psychology of Revolutionary Religious Personalities* (Syracuse: Syracuse University Press, 1997).

24. Ibid., 165–75, 190–92.

25. Rodney Stark, "A Theory of Revelations," *Journal for the Scientific Study of Religions* 38, no. 2 (1999): 286.

26. See, for example, William Sims Bainbridge and Rodney Stark, "Cult Formation: Three Compatible Models," in *Cults and New Religious Movements: A Reader,* ed. Lorne L. Dawson (Oxford: Blackwell, 2003), 61.

27. Rowe, *God's Strange Work,* 51, 62.

28. Ibid., 61.

29. Bliss, *Memoirs of William Miller,* 66; Rowe, *God's Strange Work,* 67. Miller often read at Baptist services when there was no minister present, more a sign of his social standing than of any religious status.

30. Rowe, *God's Strange Work,* 101.

31. Ibid., 127.

32. Ibid., 5.

33. Ibid., 38–39.

34. George M. Marsden, "Everyone One's Own Interpreter?: The Bible, Science, and Authority in Mid-Nineteenth-Century America," in *The Bible in America: Essays in Cultural History,* ed. Nathan O. Hatch and Mark A. Noll (New York: Oxford, 1982), 79–100; and Doan, *Miller Heresy,* 93–102.

35. Rowe, *God's Strange Work,* 51.

36. Ibid., 62, 66, 140, 222.

37. Max Weber, *The Theory of Social and Economic Organization,* trans. A. M. Henderson and Talcott Parsons, ed. Talcott Parsons (New York: Free Press, 1947), 358.

38. Ibid., 359.

39. Lindholm, "Culture, Charisma, and Consciousness," 358.

40. Ibid., 369. See also Saul V. Levine, "Life in the Cults," in Galanter, *Cults and New Religious Movements,* 98: "There is a single, overall leader, who is usually imbued by the group with superhuman and mystical powers."

41. Bliss, *Memoirs of William Miller,* 22–23, 29.

42. Ibid., 80.

43. Ibid., 83.

44. Ibid., 93–94. When James White described Miller as a "benevolent, affable, and kind spirit" and as a "humble, Christian gentleman," he probably exaggerated. See White, *Life Incidents, in Connection with the Great Advent Movement, as Illustrated by the Three Angels of Revelation XIV* (Battle Creek, Mich.: Steam Press of the Seventh-Day Adventist Publishing Association, 1868), 25.

45. For example Ellen G. White, *Christian Experience and Teachings of Ellen G. White* (Mountain View, Calif.: Pacific, 1922), 23: "He was indeed rightly called 'Father Miller,' for he had a watchful care over those who came under his ministrations, was affectionate in his manner, of a genial disposition and tender heart." Joshua V. Himes also referred to the founder as "Father Miller" (qtd. in Bliss, *Memoirs of William Miller*, 141). Lynn Davidman and Janet Jacobs point out how common it is for followers in new religious movements to refer to their leaders as "father" in "Feminist Perspectives on New Religious Movements," *Religion and the Social Order* 3B (1993): 179.

46. Bliss, *Memoirs of William Miller*, 140.

47. White, *Life Incidents*, 71–72.

48. Bliss, *Memoirs of William Miller*, 249; Arthur Whitefield Spalding, *Pioneer Stories of the Second Advent Message* (Atlanta & Fort Worth: Southern Publishing Association, 1922), 85.

49. Rowe, *God's Strange Work*, 172.

50. Ibid., 173.

51. The *Fountain* quoted in Bliss, *Memoirs of William Miller*, from White, *Life Incidents*, 69.

52. Philip Smith, "Culture and Charisma," *Acta Sociologica* 43, no. 2 (2000): 101–11.

53. Ibid., 103.

54. Ibid., 104.

55. Weber, *Theory of Social and Economic Organization*.

56. Qtd. in Nathan O. Hatch, *The Democratization of American Christianity* (New Haven, Conn.: Yale University Press, 1989), 136.

57. Doan, *Miller Heresy*, 83–118; Jane Marsh Parker, "A Little Millerite," *Century Magazine*, November 1886–April 1887, 315.

58. P. Jeffrey Potash, *Vermont's Burned-Over District: Patterns of Community Development and Religious Activity, 1761–1850* (Brooklyn, N.Y.: Carlson, 1991); Randolph Roth, *The Democratic Dilemma: Religion, Reform, and the Social Order in the Connecticut River Valley of Vermont, 1791–1850* (Cambridge: Cambridge University Press, 1987).

59. Whitney R. Cross, *The Burned-Over District: The Social and Intellectual History of Enthusiastic Religion in Western New York, 1800–1850* (Ithaca, N.Y.: Cornell University Press, 1950).

60. Gordon S. Wood, "Evangelical America and Early Mormonism," *New York History* 61 (1980): 359–86.

61. Hatch, *Democratization*.

62. Stark, "Theory of Revelations," 296–97.

63. Rowe, *God's Strange Work*, 85.

64. Ibid., 84.

65. Ibid., 65.

66. Ibid., 97–100. Most accounts of Miller neglect to note the family connection to Dresden, presumably because such a mundane cause of Miller's first invitation detracts from the notion that he received a miraculous call to preach from God.

67. Ibid., 96–97. James White, later husband of the prophet, explicitly asserted the importance of family ties to acceptance of the second advent doctrine: whereas before he had looked upon Millerism as "fanaticism," when his "mother, in whose judgment and piety I had reason to confide, spoke to me upon the subject in words of earnestness, candor, and solemnity," he "was now disposed to view the subject as worthy of my attention." White, *Life Incidents*, 15–17.

68. George R. Knight, *Millennial Fever and the End of the World* (Boise, Idaho: Pacific Press, 1993).

69. Rowe, *God's Strange Work*, 172.

70. Ibid., 187.

71. Knight, *Millennial Fever*, 312.

72. James Nix, "The Life and Work of Hiram Edson," M.A. thesis, Andrews University, 1971, 18–20; Ellen G. White, *The Great Controversy between Christ and Satan* (Battle Creek, Mich: White, 1858), 432.

73. Ellen G. White, *Life Sketches of Ellen G. White, Being a Narrative of Her Experience to 1881 as Written by Herself; With a Sketch of Her Subsequent Labors and of Her Last Sickness Compiled from Original Sources* (Mountain View, Calif.: Pacific Press, 1915), 50–53.

74. White, *Life Incidents*, 26–27.

75. *Spiritual Gifts: The Great Controversy, Between Christ and His Angels, and Satan and His Angels, Vol. 1* (Battle Creek, Mich.: White, 1858), 229.

76. Acceptance of White as the central authority of the church, and of her visions as a source of understanding second only to the Bible, took several decades. The emergence of White as prophetess is a process not yet well understood by historians. See Herbert E. Douglass, *Messenger of the Lord: The Prophetic Ministry of Ellen G. White* (Nampa, Idaho: Pacific Press, 1998); Rennie Schoepflin, ed., "Scandal or Rite of Passage? Historians on the Dammon Trial," *Spectrum* 17 (1987): 37–50.

77. "Can All Be Prophets? Ellen G. White Statements That Bear on the Question," Ellen G. White Estate, Inc., accessed May 16, 2014, http://www.whiteestate.org/issues/CanAllBeProphets.html. In the twentieth century, the visions of others led to sectarian divisions within Adventism; by then, however, the unique authority of White was widely accepted in the Seventh-day denomination.

78. Ann Taves, *Fits, Trances, and Visions: Experiencing Religion and Explaining Experience from Wesley to James* (Princeton, N.J.: Princeton University Press, 1999), 158–65; Susan Juster, "Demagogues or Mystagogues? Gender and the Language of Prophecy in the Age of Democratic Revolutions," *American Historical Review* 104, no. 5 (1999): 1574–80; Catherine A. Brekus, *Strangers and Pilgrims: Female Preaching in America, 1740–1845* (Chapel Hill: University of North Carolina Press, 1998), esp. 182–86.

79. Rodney Stark discusses the significance of context for the acceptance of revelations as true and valid in "Theory of Revelations," 289–91.

80. See also Davidman and Jacobs, "Feminist Perspectives on New Religious Movements."

81. William E. Foy, *The Christian Experience of William E. Foy Together with the Two Visions He Received in the Months of Jan. and Feb. 1842*, reprinted with an introduction by Delbert W. Baker (Berrien Springs, Mich.: Andrews University Press, 2005); see also Delbert W. Baker, *The Unknown Prophet* (Hagerstown, Md.: Review and Herald, 1987).

82. Spalding, *Pioneer Stories*, 51.

83. See David L. Rowe, "Comets and Eclipses: The Millerites, Nature, and the Apocalypse," *Adventist Heritage* 3, no. 2 (1976): 10–19.

84. Arthur L. White, *Ellen G. White: The Early Years, Vol. 1 1827–1862* (Hagerstown, Md.: Review and Herald, 1985), 65.

85. Ellen G. White, *Spiritual Gifts*, vol. 1, 257–58.

86. Ernst Troeltsch, *The Social Teaching of the Christian Churches*, trans. Olive Wyon (New York: Harper, 1960).

Cheryl F. Junk

"Ladies, Arise!
The World Has Need of You"

The Widow Bumpass's Newspaper War

Nearly unknown in the present, Frances Moore Webb Bumpass (1819–98) was one of the most important churchwomen in the nineteenth-century South.[1] She worked slowly and gradually from within Methodism and Victorian-era social conventions to expand acceptable notions of what churchwomen could and should do to effect a sweeping agenda of social change. Her conscious goal was nothing less than the moral and spiritual transformation of the world, and the religious weekly that she edited from 1851 to 1871, the *Weekly Message*, was its chief vehicle. The sphere of her paper's influence extended west across the trans-Appalachian frontier to the gold fields of California, up the East Coast of the United States, across the Atlantic to England, and across the Pacific to the mission fields of China.

The pivotal moment in her editorship came when she began to urge church-women to speak in public religious services. From December 1853 to March 1854, she had to fight for her editorial credibility in what one reader called the "paper wars" between her publication and the *Richmond Christian Advocate*, edited by a prominent Virginia Methodist clergyman.[2] This article examines that turning point and, in particular, the relationship between Bumpass and the clergymen who defended her editorship. In the process she and her defenders legitimized her editorship and expanded her authority as a public figure of considerable influence in the church. This work also examines how she used her hard-won authority to create a new ideal for women's church work.

By the time she called white southern Methodist women to "arise" in the 1870s, the widow Frances M. Bumpass was a new woman.[3] In the five decades between her marriage to the Reverend Sidney D. Bumpass in 1842, at age twenty-three, and her death in 1898, at age seventy-nine, her religious experiences radically transformed her life.[4] Near the start of her life as a minister's wife, in December 1843, a woman at Edenton Street Methodist Church in Raleigh, North Carolina, had scolded Frances for failing to give her public religious testimony at a ceremony called the love feast.[5] Methodist preachers' wives were expected to set an example for other women with this kind of public speech. By 1887 Bumpass had become a valued speaker and writer on behalf of the Southern Methodist Woman's Missionary Society and the National Woman's Christian Temperance Union. She had been a charter member of the Missionary Society and a founder of the North Carolina chapter of the WCTU.[6]

Between these poles of her identity—timid preacher's wife and vocal temperance/missionary advocate—she passed through a formative stage as editor (she called herself "editress") of the *Weekly Message* of Greensboro, North Carolina.[7] She had inherited the *Message*—North Carolina's first Methodist-affiliated paper—from her husband, Sidney. His untimely death in December 1851 represented both her greatest personal tragedy and her greatest professional opportunity. As editor she was the only known southern woman before 1890 at the helm of a paper with a doctrinal agenda. For the next twenty years, until 1871, she turned the privilege of editing a religious paper—a privilege previously granted only to clergymen—into a woman's right to be heard. Each week, after she became sole editor in 1852, she chose every article, wrote all of the editorials, chose almost all of the ads, and, after 1854, published the paper herself from the second floor of her Greensboro home.[8] Therefore everything in the *Weekly Message* represents her attempt to influence the religious values of her constituency. As a reflection of its editor's views, the paper also chronicles her personal evolution as a "spiritual virtuoso"—someone who craved an unusually intimate and demanding relationship with God.[9]

Over the course of the 1850s, as Bumpass herself evolved, she turned her paper into a southern center to promote northern Methodist evangelist Phoebe Palmer's version of John Wesley's doctrine of "entire sanctification," alternately called "Christian perfection" or "holiness." Palmer's "Altar Principle" prescribed three steps to sanctification: first, entirely consecrating oneself to God—an inward surrender of one's will and life to God's purposes, on the symbolic altar of faith; secondly, believing that God had accepted this offering and had begun to purify the person's heart, even if one did not feel anything special; and finally, proclaiming in public worship that God had sanctified the person, leaving her in a state of "perfect love."[10] In the process of promoting this Methodist doctrine, Bumpass expanded ideas about respectable white women's activities in the church to include most types of public religious speech, including expounding on a biblical text (informal preaching). The Reverend J. M. Fulton of the northern Methodist church in the California gold fields even gave Frances legitimacy as a holiness preacher. He charged her to "go on, dear sister, and preach through your little paper this glorious old Methodist doctrine!"[11] On the other hand, although her paper was meant for men and women alike, it is clear from the contents that she made holiness a woman's issue. This fact did not seem to deter readers of either sex. A de facto congregation of approximately three thousand readers in all American regions and the mission fields of China voted with their dollars to sustain the *Weekly Message* for two decades.

The *Weekly Message* brings into view a dense network of North Carolina clergymen, lawyers, yeomen farmers, and others who cared so much about holiness that they supported a female editor of a theological paper in spite of her sex because she publicized a doctrine they prized.[12] These men legitimized her editorship based upon her competence. But they also supported her because she walked a fine line between tradition and innovation. We do not know how representative these men were, but they certainly complicate recent assertions by scholars of southern men that relations between the sexes in the slave South were "oppositional."[13] Instead the word *collegial* describes Bumpass's relationship with the clergy and laymen in her constituency.

We cannot begin to understand Bumpass's historical contribution without knowing something about the religious idea and experience that drove her—what she called, interchangeably, "Christian perfection," "entire sanctification," "holiness," or "perfect love." John Wesley and his Methodists were unique among the three main Protestant churches (Baptist, Methodist, and Presbyterian) for working out a scriptural rationale for everyone to attain an inward, or higher, state of redemption that went beyond having one's sins forgiven. Sanctification, Wesley believed and taught, was a second, but necessary, work of grace in the heart, after the new birth (also called conversion or regeneration). In that first event, the believer entered into the ranks of the saved, but he or she was still capable of willful acts of sin or disobedience to God's commands. Only the guilt of sin, not the capacity to be sinful, was removed in rebirth or regeneration. Sanctification, however, removed the ability willfully to commit sinful acts or have sinful thoughts. The heart was made pure in sacred love and was henceforth capable of pure love to God and humankind. For Wesley that pure love in the heart must translate into outward service to God and humankind. Without Christian service holiness was useless and inauthentic.[14]

There was, however, a crucial difference between Bumpass's generation of holiness advocates and John Wesley. Wesley had thought that all regenerate souls would experience sanctification at the moment of death so that it would be a universal experience for all Christians. On the other hand, Bumpass and a small but powerful group of Methodist clergy and laity followed the writings of New York lay evangelist Phoebe Palmer's revision of the doctrine. In the 1840s Palmer changed Wesley's doctrine, altering it to fit the increasingly rapid pace of modern life. She insisted that scripture promised instantaneous sanctification; that a long process was not necessary; and that believers could be sanctified in the moment when they surrendered themselves to God. In the 1850s, when Bumpass was preaching Palmer's doctrine in her paper, the theology had evolved to *require* sanctification in this life if the believer wanted to "see God" in the next.

Bumpass was especially qualified to edit a paper devoted to holiness. She was in touch with North Carolina Methodists of all kinds, so she knew what was on their minds. She went to countless religious services of many different types every year. She started women's prayer meetings in Raleigh, in Greensboro, and at Greensboro Female College. These prayer meetings had immense significance to the women who attended them. Here they could practice verbal prayer, encourage one another to speak aloud, and mentor one another. Bumpass's diary records the makings of a spiritual sisterhood in these meetings. By the time she moved to Greensboro, across from Greensboro Female College, she was functioning as a devoted mentor to the college girls.[15] For more than six decades, she talked with people, prayed with them, and listened to them about spiritual matters. As the widow of a presiding elder, she had wide public recognition in the North Carolina Conference and in the circles of southern Methodism. In short she knew what kind of market niche her paper could fill. That niche—information on the subject of sanctification—also matched her own idea of what people *should* be reading. It was a match, she believed, that was literally made in Heaven by God himself. Sanctification, or holiness, had also been among her husband's editorial priorities. But his editorship had understandably been geared more toward the professional interests of clergy. Instead she made the paper's contents more accessible to everyone, including, but not limited to, clergymen. For Bumpass "everyone" included women.

During the first years after Sidney Bumpass's death, the *Weekly Message* functioned partly as a de facto memorial to its fallen editor.[16] Bumpass herself printed the paper's origin story and lengthy tributes to her late husband several times between 1852 and 1855.[17] The heart-rending account of his untimely death and his widow's courage in continuing to publish the paper served two purposes: First, it paid tribute to a beloved clergyman in the North Carolina Conference, helping to reinforce the Methodist sense of belonging to an extended religious family. One of their own had fallen, and his widow was struggling to support their children. Second, it gave her initial credibility as editor. She told readers that editing was something that both her late husband and God wanted her to do. Her husband had bequeathed her the paper and urged her before his death to keep it going if he should die. But God, she believed, had voted in her favor when the conference had refused to buy the paper from her at the end of 1852.[18] By that time she had become the paper's sole editor. In her second editorial, on December 4, 1852, she formally announced that spreading the doctrine of entire sanctification was her top editorial priority. In other words she took the initiative to keep the paper going.[19]

Indicators also seemed to be positive for the *Weekly Message* itself between December 1852 and August 1853. Bumpass had reported to readers on April 22, 1853, that the paper, "our little dove," was enjoying a "favorable reception, as shown by an increase of about a hundred new subscribers per month, which leads us to hope that the expenses of its mission will no longer be burdensome."[20] The upward trend seems to have started when the North Carolina Conference of Methodist clergymen endorsed her paper at their annual conference in late November and early December 1852.[21] All these were signs, she believed, that pointed to the paper's eventual success, once the original start-up debt was paid off. By its second year, the *Weekly Message* had a large, loyal, and growing constituency of women and clergymen to its credit. In October 1853 the Reverend Thomas Barringer, a North Carolina Methodist minister and advocate for Bumpass's editorship, told her that "ladies especially favor" the paper.[22] Clergymen, too, supported it with their own subscriptions and by acting as agents in the field. These women and clergymen helped Bumpass's "Pet Dove" compete successfully with other church papers, all edited by ministers. Chief among these was the *Richmond Christian Advocate*, organ of the Virginia Conference, and the *Christian Advocate* out of Nashville, organ of the Methodist Episcopal Church, South. The increase of subscribers also helped keep her paper afloat in spite of stiff competition from ladies' magazines, topped by *Godey's Lady's Book*.[23]

The survival of Bumpass's paper depended upon the blessing and assistance of the Methodist clergy, especially in the North Carolina Conference. During the four months between December 1853 and March 1854, some of the clergymen she trusted the most launched a vociferous challenge to her editorial credibility and her paper's right to exist. She did not see the challenge coming, but a group of North Carolina clergy supporters rose to her defense. Thanks to her own polemical skills, her standing in the community, and the eloquent defense by her friends in the clergy, she emerged victorious from these "newspaper wars." This victory, in turn, seemed to have solidified readers' belief in her fitness to edit the paper and preach the doctrine of holiness from what many clergymen recognized as a de facto editorial pulpit.

The skeletal story of the "newspaper wars" emerges in approximately twenty articles from six issues of Bumpass's paper and one issue of the *Richmond Christian Advocate*. All of the other articles have been lost. The existing articles refer to twelve main characters, four of whom used pseudonyms. These were almost certainly Methodist clergymen from either Virginia or North Carolina. Bumpass would likely have known the identities of her pseudonymous defenders because she usually refused to publish an article unless the author provided her with his real name and address for later return. The Reverend Leroy Lee (1808–82), editor of the *Richmond Christian Advocate*, would likewise have known his defenders.[24]

During the week between the editorial on December 8, 1853, when she asked readers to pray for her efforts, and the next issue of her paper on December 15, she received a letter from a clergyman calling himself "Old North State." This letter, and her editorial response, was the first salvo in the newspaper wars. "Old North State" became her staunchest supporter. He told her about Lee's speech to the still-assembled conference in Raleigh, deliberately given after she had to go back home. He expressed both indignation at Lee and concern for Bumpass's fiscal affairs. Lee had charged that her paper was "losing money" every day, was hampered by Sidney Bumpass's initial start-up debt, and was taking subscribers away from his venerable *Richmond Christian Advocate*. This latter charge was Lee's most audacious gambit. The conference had just endorsed Bumpass's paper "provided that" it did not take subscribers away from the other church papers. Lee charged that Bumpass's paper was guilty of doing just that. "Old North State" wanted to defend "Sister Bumpass," but first he needed to know the truth. He gently asked her to give readers an account of her financial situation. She did more than that. She published his letter verbatim in the December 15 issue and gave readers the information he had requested. In the process she turned a discussion among clergy at conference into a topic for public debate. Between January and March 1854, both editors allowed their supporters to form opposing camps and fire rhetorical shots into each other's columns.[25] During the ensuing sixty days, each editor's champions steadily raised the rhetorical temperature until, at the peak of the conflict, they were attacking the motives and Christian character of their opponents.

On the surface the conflict seems like a clear case of jealousy and rivalry among ministers, with a female editor caught in the middle. The story line of the newspaper wars was simple. Its cultural meaning was not. It was not just a sibling rivalry between North Carolina and Virginia Methodist clergy. This conflict allows us to observe church men and women in the act of defending existing gendered boundaries and creating new ones.[26] The question they debated was whether or not Frances Bumpass was really a consecrated and worthy editor of a legitimate religious paper or simply a money-grubbing widow posing as a servant of God.

Boundaries of Gender

Bumpass was glad to have other clergymen defend her paper because it bolstered her case immensely. But in reality she was fighting for her religious reputation and for the right of a woman to practice her occupation even though it encroached upon male territory. Her own battle was primarily about religion and gender. When "Old North State" indignantly reported Lee's heinous actions against her at the conference, she could have kept his letter private. Her decision to go public with the controversy was doubtless difficult. But Lee had thrown down the gauntlet, and her belief in her paper's sacred mission demanded that she pick it up.

Leroy Lee knew better than to attack Bumpass's paper simply as a competitor. Its editor, after all, was not another man but a *woman*. Social conventions demanded courtesy and respect for her solely on the basis of her sex but also required the deference due a widow. Bumpass had become something of a southern

Methodist symbol as the widow of "sainted Brother Bumpass." By virtue of being Sidney Bumpass's widow, she enjoyed the sympathy and support of a wide circle of southern Methodists. They were not neutral about her as a woman, a mother, and a widow. Lee knew that. So he couched his attack in gentlemanly terms, saying that his first concern was for the widow and her family. He argued that the paper was having increasing "pecuniary difficulties." Therefore the conference was doing the widow Bumpass no favors, he argued, by encouraging her in an effort that was doomed to fail. Apparently he never said that she should not be doing this work, that only men had done it before her, or that she was overstepping the bounds of womanhood. Although her attackers took direct aim at her religious motives, even charging that her real "message" was "I want the money" from subscribers, none of them ever cast aspersions on her femininity.[27]

This may seem a bit surprising in an era when literary women were constantly under intense public scrutiny for any signs of slippage from the ideal of "true womanhood." Bumpass apparently never gave the would-be critics cause to question her femininity. They knew that she was a devoted mother as well as a Christian woman of business. The evidence from the newspaper wars, however, takes us beyond the usual list of Victorian feminine qualities of piety and domesticity as they applied to Frances Bumpass. The gendered script in the data is about more than Bumpass and the men who challenged her. It is about larger patterns of interaction between church men and women. The newspaper wars exemplify, perhaps in the extreme, the types of negotiations going on all over the United States about women's place in the church. This evidence complements recent studies about how social movements gain momentum. In particular women and other subordinate groups make slow and steady incremental gains by walking the cultural tightrope between tradition and innovation, not just by sudden visible revolutionary acts.[28]

In the articles about Bumpass as a woman, and in her own editorials on the subject, readers could hear the words they needed to hear—that Bumpass was acting like a woman even though she was doing something only men had previously done. Acting like a woman, however, did not preclude her using pointed argument, sarcasm, and shaming tactics to counter Leroy Lee. Her opening editorial defense on December 15, 1853, in the same issue as "Old North State's" exposure of Lee's actions, not only answered readers' concerns about the financial welfare of the paper, but also laid out a lengthy and eloquent argument that showed her as both warrior and peacemaker. Social convention permitted women to use such voices when defending their families or righteous causes. In this case Bumpass was defending her livelihood and her calling by God. She knew in writing this editorial that all eyes were on her, especially the eyes of women. This is probably the most rhetorically complex of all Bumpass's surviving editorials. She moved smoothly through a series of voices—gratitude, righteous sarcasm, and a patronizing apology for Lee's behavior—all calculated to persuade readers that her paper should exist.

She started by making psychological lemonade out of Lee's sour words, with an ironic tone of sincere gratitude. She *thanked* him for opposing the conference's purchase of her paper in 1853. She was glad they had not bought it. If they had she would have "felt a lone one indeed upon the earth without this cherished object for good, of the dearest departed."[29] Here she spoke in the vulnerable emotional language of a grieving widow, something that reminded readers that she was not only an editor but was Sidney Bumpass's rightful editorial heir. By referring to him and to her grief, she was acknowledging a degree of appropriate dependence upon his memory and his bequest. She was not a woman defiantly striking out on her own, something respectable women should not do.

After the ironic gratitude of the opening, she moved into righteous sarcasm about Lee's speech at the conference two weeks previously: "We doubt not that the esteemed Doctor was . . . successful [in stirring up questions about her paper] at the late Conference." Then she told readers in biblical language that Lee's efforts had actually backfired. Instead of prompting the conference to withdraw its endorsement, Lee had "brought down blessings on the persecuted."[30] In her only reference to state pride, she said that Lee's speech had "rallied the sons and daughters of Carolina" who might not otherwise have worked so hard to "promote the . . . eternal peace of all within their much loved state."

Her most striking defense was neither sarcastic nor ironic. Rather she apologized for Lee's actions. The only women who could safely apologize for gentlemen in the Old South were women in their immediate families. Methodists were well-known for binding members into a surrogate family of faith.[31] One sign of this was that they called one another by familial names—brother, sister, mother, uncle. In this context Bumpass referred to herself as Lee's "younger sister" in Christ. She therefore assumed that she was justified in pointing out his mistake in this matter. Her apology was unique among the articles in the newspaper wars, because Bumpass alone exposed Lee's discrimination of her based on sex. None of the men in the newspaper wars mentioned gender-based reasons for Lee's opposition. Bumpass, however, was not surprised that he expected her paper to fail. After all most male-edited papers failed within a short time. How then could a woman succeed?

"We would apologise for our brother's assertion by saying that as he knew so many men failed who undertook to publish newspapers, he did not see any chance for a woman to succeed."[32] Bumpass followed this patronizing apology by explaining the key to her success—reliance upon God for strength and guidance—and referred to herself in the third person. Alone, she said, she was not "sufficient for these things." "We could not succeed of ourself," she affirmed. "But we doubt not that he who holds all hearts in his hands will cause a sufficient increase of patronage to enable us gradually to diminish the debt of a thousand dollars on which we are now paying interest."

Clergy editors of Methodist papers did not talk about being "sufficient" to edit. They did not need to draw attention away from themselves and up to God. By contrast respectable Victorian women could not engage in public activities for the personal satisfaction it gave them. Or rather they did not speak or think about it that way. There had to be a higher motive, a cause to work for, the public or religious good to promote. Middle-class Victorian women, in general, felt genuine fulfillment by working for the good of others. Methodist women, in particular, had been raised on the Wesleyan theological balance between faith and works.[33] They believed that charitable acts of love were the will of God, and that each person, regardless of age or sex, could discern God's particular will for him- or herself. Discernment of God's will was a type of knowledge that entered the human mind by grace from the Holy Spirit. Wesleyan theology predisposed believers to place great stock in knowing God "in the heart." Wesley also accorded each person considerable authority to interpret God's will, based on both scripture and an inward sense. So when a respected Methodist woman said that God wanted her to edit a religious newspaper, when that paper was meeting a genuine public need, and when it was beginning to climb out of debt, people listened and took her public voice seriously.

Her final argument in this initial editorial of the paper wars tried to make peace and smooth things over, something readers would have expected of a woman. Her stance was submissive, conciliatory, deferential, and practical. She deferred to Lee as her "elder brother" in the Methodist family hierarchy and called for cooperation, not competition. "Let the quiet sister peacefully work by the elder brother, and let them both remember that their work is one and unitedly pray for the success of each other's work." She reassured readers that her paper was no threat, that it "was never designed to interfere with the operation of the church." It was designed rather "to aid" by providing a cheap family paper devoted to the doctrine of "entire sanctification," something that the church, "with all her zeal and labor," had not been able to do. She also gave Lee's paper some free publicity: "Let this paper [*Richmond Christian Advocate*] circulate freely in your midst, as there is work for both it and the Message to do. Yea, more than they can do." Her approach was so eminently sensible that one would have expected it to put an end to the conflict. It did not.

As the conflict escalated, Bumpass had to decide whether or not to write more editorials on the subject. She knew that she would be vulnerable to charges of impropriety if she spoke too much on her own behalf. Victorian women were taught to shun the limelight and to downplay the importance of self. Their subordination also depended upon their being nearly invisible in public. However, Bumpass's vocation kept her in the public gaze. Therefore she was in a very delicate position, a dilemma that she and her male defenders understood well. Her clergy friends rose to the occasion with chivalric gestures and the cultural language of southern honor. It is very interesting to read Methodist clergymen's using this masculine language, because they were frequently scorned for being less than masculine.[34] By 1850 clergymen had spent nearly a century condemning long-accepted practices of "southern manhood" such as dueling, drinking, dancing, gambling, and indulging in fine dress. They were, however, products of the culture they criticized. Therefore it is not surprising that they would have rallied to protect Bumpass from public scorn.

Bumpass was the first to recognize that she needed to fade into the background. In January 1854, one month after the conflict began, she put out a call for champions among the clergy: "If those influential ministers of the Conference who have so ably defended the Message find that such *singular accusations* as have been made injure the paper, we are confident that they will again try to set matters aright."[35] Writing under a pseudonym, "Itinerant" was the first to answer her call and affirmed the need for others to speak for her. He argued that Lee's revealing comments about her fiscal situation had compromised "Sister Bumpass's delicate position." "The publication of so much about Self," he wrote, "must impose . . . a severe tax on modesty." Yet he did not want her to stop publishing the paper during the conflict or to keep the conflict out of the paper. "Instead," he told her, "you can properly allow another to speak for you when it would be improper for you to speak for yourself."[36] After her initial attempt to defend herself and offer Lee an olive branch had failed, she could now withdraw from the field of combat and let the clergymen protect her honor. "Old North State" agreed: "Sister Bumpass richly deserves the protection, sympathy, and warm-hearted support of every friend of woman and every friend of Methodism." His remark clearly implied that womanhood and Methodism were fused in this relationship. Befriend one, and you befriend the other. Oppose one, and you oppose the other.

It would have been understandable for her defenders to stop with chivalric protection of her honor. But they did not. Instead they made it clear that they believed in her not only as a woman and the widow of their beloved friend, but also as a competent editor in her own right. These clergymen actually helped to give Bumpass a new identity, with her credibility based upon competence and divine calling, not upon widowhood. Itinerant's account described Bumpass as a woman who had made a remarkable transition from a timid widow in 1851 to a competent editor with what Itinerant called a "well-cultivated mind." In one impassioned paragraph, he succinctly described her accomplishments as a woman, an editor, and a disciple of Christ: "Without compromise of her womanly delicacy; without interfering with the recognized papers of the church; and with admirable tact and increasing ability, she has conducted the paper through its perilous trial year, given it a position of increasing usefulness in the religious public of North Carolina, and so improved its financial condition as to make it pay the expenses of publication and yield a small interest upon its capital . . . toward the support of her family."[37] Itinerant's interpretation implied that she was as good an editor, if not better, than her male counterparts.[38] To Bumpass's defenders her paper's promotion of Wesleyan Perfectionism mattered more than the fact that she was female. Itinerant and Old North State both argued that the *Weekly Message* must continue to exist because it bound readers "by so many chords" into a "sacred community" around the doctrine of Christian perfection. No other southern paper at the time performed such a function.[39]

We do not know exactly what happened to end the conflict. Several articles and editorials in March 1854 seem to have been particularly influential. The first of these was an unexpected gesture of truce from the opposing side. In March 1854 the Reverend L. W. Martin, one of Bumpass's harshest critics in the "paper wars," proposed that one hundred people give ten dollars each to liquidate the debt, and he contributed the first ten dollars toward the project.[40] In that same issue, Bumpass's editorial had a calming tone. She tried to put a light spin on the whole affair. She admitted, perhaps smiling as she wrote, that the conflict had been good for business. It had called attention to both papers and increased their circulation. Again she thanked readers for the many encouraging letters since the beginning of the conflict, and she humbly prayed for her paper to be even more effective in promoting the cause of holiness. Once again she deferred to God as the paper's true editor in chief, reaffirming her humble position as his "feeble instrument."[41] Readers would have understood her implicit message to them: Here is a brave widow, standing up to strong opposition from a clergyman who is needlessly defensive. She is doing this only because God gave the paper to her as a gift from her husband. She is not doing it for fame, glory, or personal gain. You have to support her.

The last official article in the newspaper war was the Reverend N. H. D. Wilson's measured scolding of all parties. He admitted that the conflict had been good for business in the short run, but it was the wrong kind of publicity. The church was being made to look foolish, like a gang of bickering children. This would not draw people into the fold but would push them away. More important, he could not abide the heartless criticism of religious motives. That subject, he said, should be off-limits. He was shocked at such malicious gossip from alleged gentlemen. Bumpass, he said, was a "worthy Christian sister." To write about her as they had clearly revealed that they did not know her. He defied them to spend time with her—which he knew that they would not do—and then repeat their ridiculous charge that all she wanted was to make money. He could not imagine such a thing. To know Bumpass, he said, was to love and respect her. Wilson's argument, the last in the conflict, dismissed the potentially damning character assaults as the product of ignorance. By all appearances his call for a halt to this "shameful episode" was successful.[42]

Lee's first of three editorials in the next issue of the *Richmond Christian Advocate* (March 16, 1854) acknowledged the need for a cease-fire, although he could not resist blaming Bumpass for starting the conflict. In his editorial "The Weekly Message Controversy," Lee acknowledged that "the controversy he [Wilson] so justly deplores is to be regretted on all hands. But neither the fault of its origin, nor of its character, can be properly charged upon us. It was begun in the Message." Later in this editorial, Lee accepted the olive branch Bumpass had offered in her editorial the previous week (March 9, 1854) and reprinted a large part of her editorial. Notably Lee's third editorial in that issue was an argument that only clergy should edit religious papers because of their training in classical languages, their skills at biblical exegesis, and their divine calling to the ministry. His point was to set clergy editors of official papers off from lay editors of other sorts of papers. This editorial was his oblique way of reminding Bumpass that her paper was in no way "official" and that she was still his subordinate in status and gender, a fact that she knew very well.[43]

In summary although Bumpass perceived that the conflict had started mainly because she was a woman trying to succeed in male professional territory, the newspaper wars did not produce much rhetoric explicitly about gender. Yet all of her defenders fused gender and Christianity to assert that her credibility rested on the fact that she was both a true woman and a disciple of Christ. When they had to choose between the two, they chose to defend Bumpass's editorship on religious grounds. Bumpass the disciple, doing the will of God and being useful to the church, was more important to them than Bumpass the woman doing something unconventional. When it came to spreading the doctrine of entire sanctification, her sex became irrelevant to the men who rallied around her.

Thanks to outspoken clergy friends and to her own flawless instincts about how to defend her editorship, Bumpass emerged from the fracas with her credibility not only intact but stronger than ever. She retained the North Carolina Conference's support because her paper met a genuine need of the readership for information on holiness. She also gained support because she stuck to her story in asserting that God wanted her paper to exist and that anyone who doubted that also doubted God himself.

Rather than shaking her faith, the newspaper wars seemed, if anything, to strengthen it in the long run. Her diary reveals her personal reactions to the conflict without ever explicitly describing what was going on in her editorial life. Soon after the conflict began with that first letter from her faithful friend, "Old North State," Bumpass once again claimed in her diary that she "enjoyed" the state of sanctification, "that love which casts out fear."[44] In late January 1854, after Old

North State and Itinerant came forth to defend her, she wrote in her diary that "friends have arisen to vindicate the Message and at the time needed. The Lord is good. . . . O! That his love may continually fill my soul."[45] By March 1854, near what would be the end of the conflict, she was feeling low, but her faith had sustained her throughout that trial. God's strength enabled her "to love those who most oppose my favorite work, the Message." No matter what the trials, she knew that if God was with her, "all shall be well."[46] In March her spirits were flagging after the brutal attacks on her Christian motives in the *Richmond Christian Advocate*. On March 10, just a week before the truce, she was tempted to think that God "would forsake" her because he was "displeased with my course in conducting the paper." Nevertheless she found consolation in the gospel promise to keep in "perfect peace" those "whose minds were staid on Him."[47] Throughout the paper wars, and in spite of some understandable discouragement, her faith never wavered.

Although her diary recorded what was going on in her spiritual life in early 1854, few issues of the *Weekly Message* survive between April and December 1854, and none explained what was happening in the North Carolina Conference after the paper wars. The minutes of the North Carolina Annual Conference fill in the gap. By the time the conference convened in December 1854, a long-standing lawsuit with the northern church over the Methodist Book Concern had been settled in favor of the Methodist Episcopal Church, South.[48] This meant that money was now available to southern Methodist conferences for publishing initiatives. The time was right for the North Carolina Conference to move forward with its plans to have an official paper of its own, edited by a clergyman. Such a paper would accord them legitimacy in the eyes of their peers, especially those in the state across their northern border, Virginia. In late November 1854, the conference in session in Pittsboro, eight months after the paper wars ceased, resolved to form a joint stock company of clergy and laity to amass the capital for a conference paper and to establish a bookstore and publishing business in Raleigh. They further resolved to send a committee of five clergymen to meet with "Mrs. Bumpass" as soon as two thousand dollars of the stock had been subscribed. They were going to see her to "make [a] proposal. . . to purchase *The Weekly Message*." If she refused to sell, the committee was instructed to go ahead and buy the equipment necessary to publish the *North Carolina Christian Advocate*, at a subscription price of two dollars per year. They expected to issue the first number of the paper on January 1, 1856.[49] Now the proverbial shoe was on the other foot. The ministers urged her to sell them the paper they had refused to buy in 1852. This time Bumpass was the one to say no. She believed that God had left the paper in her hands twice—the first time when Sidney died, and the second time when the conference did not buy it from her. After surviving the conflict, she was not going to relinquish her hard-won but now firm editorial hold on her beloved paper, her "Pet Dove."

The newspaper wars episode illustrates all of the major themes in Bumpass's paper and in her future lifework: the importance of the doctrine of holiness; her desire for women to preach it, proclaim it, teach it in public settings, and write about it for publication; her desire for women to stop caring about what people thought of them and start caring about ushering in the millennium; and the permission clergymen gave Bumpass (and by extension all Methodist women) to be public disciples for the cause of holiness. For its promoters the doctrine of holiness transcended gender boundaries. Bumpass emerged victorious from the newspaper wars because her focus on holiness was more important to her readers than the fact of her sex.

Bumpass and her small cohort of women in the nascent holiness movement of the 1850s devoted their talents to preaching a doctrine especially suited to women. All believed that religion begins in the mind. Therefore they wanted women to think of themselves as speakers and doers for Christ. This small but vocal vanguard of women saw itself as the moral physicians to a world on the brink of moral collapse. Holiness, they believed, was nothing short of a cosmic concern. With holy women leading the army of the faithful, they believed that God would hasten the millennium and fulfill his plans for humankind.

Furthermore the newspaper wars illustrate better than anything else in the *Weekly Message* the fact that the paper, and Bumpass's lifework, were reformist in nature. She and her cohort of churchwomen were active reformers, but not on the northern model of organized urban women's associations or radical political agendas. Rather they worked from within the church and southern society to promote their agenda of women's public speech, women's education, temperance, and social reform. As a result she made significant contributions to the long struggle for women's emancipation in the United States.[50]

The mechanism of reform in the *Weekly Message* was the human voice in print—in particular, the female voice of its editor. This was, as Elizabeth Varon has pointed out, "figurative" public space, as opposed to the "literal" public space of the pulpit."[51] If she had been defending herself in front of a congregation, she would have appeared improper. But from her editorial desk, the position of her own creation and vigorously defended, she was where readers thought she belonged. During the "newspaper wars," Bumpass and her clergy brethren spoke with their pens, loudly and clearly, to all readers. They proclaimed that this woman had the God-given authority to do the work she was doing; that she was a de facto preacher shepherding a congregation of readers larger than most physical congregations; and that she was doing her job better than most men could do. She was, they said, doing something that no other church paper in the South was doing: attempting to foster American Methodism's original mission to "spread scriptural holiness over the land."[52] For her part Bumpass's editorial voice in the "newspaper wars" was alternately maternal, rebuking, stoic, resolute, and deferential. She used all of the tones of voice necessary both for "feminine modesty" and to prosecute her case with the skills of a Harvard lawyer. She was also the only writer in the "wars" who explicitly unmasked Leroy Lee's condescending attitude toward her: expecting her to fail because she was a woman.[53]

Her diary (1841–51), editorials in the *Weekly Message* (1852–71), and her articles for the *Woman's Missionary Advocate* (1878–95) constitute an extraordinary corpus in which we can hear one woman speaking to church people, especially women, for more than fifty years.[54] From her editor's chair, Bumpass fostered a dialogue with readers on holiness. In the process she created a community in print where she inspired church women to change the way they thought about themselves.[55] Any woman reading the *Weekly Message* during the "newspaper wars" would have understood that if Bumpass could speak with authority to clergymen and call women to a new model of Christian discipleship, then they could—and should—follow her lead. Bumpass's actions, and those of her readers, demonstrate that once a woman entered the public realm for religious reasons, both she and the church would never be the same.[56]

NOTES

1. This essay is a reworking of chapter 3 of my doctoral dissertation, "Ladies, Arise! The World Has Need of You: Frances Bumpass, Religion, and the Power of the Press, 1851–1860," University of North Carolina at Chapel Hill, 2005.

2. The *Richmond Christian Advocate* was published under that name from 1837 to 1901 and was the official paper of the Virginia Conference of the clergy in the Methodist Episcopal Church, South. The Reverend Leroy Madison Lee (1808–82) edited the paper for more than twenty-five years. See "Papers of the Methodist Episcopal Church, South," in *Encyclopedia of World Methodism*, ed. Nolan B. Harmon, vol. 1 (Nashville: United Methodist Publishing House, 1974), 57.

3. "Ladies, arise! The world has need of you! . . . Too long we have waited in our appointed sphere!" Bumpass is reported to have issued this command during an 1877 speaking tour of southern Methodist churches as she, and a core of prominent Methodist women, tried to persuade rank-and-file Methodists to support an autonomous woman's missionary society. This quotation is from an unpublished manuscript biography of Bumpass by her granddaughter, Ethel Troy. The manuscript is in the possession of the Brock Historical Museum at Greensboro College, Greensboro, North Carolina.

4. Frances Moore was born in Halifax County, Virginia. The family moved over the border to northern Person County, North Carolina, when she was twelve in 1831. After her marriage to Sidney Bumpass in 1842, the couple had four children, three of whom lived to adulthood. In 1847 the family moved to Greensboro, North Carolina, where Frances lived until her death. Her husband and three year-old son died of typhoid fever in December 1851. Frances Bumpass inherited the *Weekly Message* from her husband and ran it from 1851 to 1871. Thereafter she devoted herself to temperance and missionary causes. She died on May 8, 1898. This sketch is compiled from primary sources in the Southern Historical Collection, University of North Carolina at Chapel Hill; the Brock

Historical Museum at Greensboro College; and the Greensboro Historical Museum, Greensboro.

5. Frances M. Bumpass (hereafter, FMB), Diary, December 4, 1843. #1031. Subseries 3.1. Folder 15. Southern Historical Collection (hereafter SHC). Manuscripts Department, Wilson Library, University of North Carolina at Chapel Hill.

6. Bumpass is listed as a charter member of the Woman's Missionary Society of the Methodist Episcopal Church, South in the *Woman's Missionary Advocate*, June 1882, 3. Her name is ubiquitous in the minutes of the North Carolina chapter of the Woman's Christian Temperance Union between 1883 and 1898, the year of her death (North Carolina Collection. Woman's Christian Temperance Union of North Carolina, *Convention, 1883–1970*, North Carolina Collection, University of North Carolina at Chapel Hill).

7. Hereafter the *Weekly Message* will be referred to as TWM. About women in the editorial profession, see Patricia Okker, *Our Sister Editors: Sarah J. Hale and the Tradition of Nineteenth-Century American Women Editors* (Athens: University of Georgia Press, 1986).

8. Letter from Frances's "Cousin Etta" to "Cousin Bettie," January 25, 1854, Webb Family Papers, Southern Historical Collection, Wilson Library, University of North Carolina at Chapel Hill.

9. The term "religious virtuoso" is original to Max Weber. Here I am using Robert Abzug's interpretation from his *Cosmos Crumbling: American Reform and the Religious Imagination* (New York: Oxford University Press, 1994), 4–5.

10. This summary based upon Richard Wheatley, *The Life and Letters of Phoebe Palmer* (New York: Garland, 1984 [orig. New York: Palmer, 1881), esp. chap. 1. Palmer is the acknowledged mother of today's Holiness/Pentecostal family of churches, which split off from Methodism at the end of the nineteenth century. For more on the impact of her theology in American Protestantism, see E. Brooks Holifield, *Theology in America: Christian Thought from the Age of the Puritans to the Civil War* (New Haven: Yale University Press, 2003). For biographical information on Palmer, see "Life Sketch: Who Is Phoebe Palmer?" in Harold E. Raser, *Phoebe Palmer: Her Life and Thought* (Lewiston, N.Y.: Mellen, 1987), 21–74.

11. TWM, December 4, 1856, 2.

12. Bumpass was the only southern woman before 1890 to edit a paper that preached religious doctrine. Sarah Knowles Bolton, editor of the *Congregationalist* (Boston, published from 1816 to 1934) and Phoebe Palmer (*The Guide to Holiness*) were the only northern editors of religious papers before 1890. See the appendix in Okker, *Our Sister Editors*, 176.

13. Craig Thompson Friend and Lorri Glover, *Southern Manhood: Perspectives on Masculinity in the Old South* (Athens: University of Georgia Press, 2004), xiii.

14. On Wesleyan "perfectionism" see E. Brook Holifield's section "Christian Perfection" in his *Theology in America: Christian Thought from the Age of the Puritans to the Civil War* (New Haven: Yale University Press, 2003), 256–72. See also the discussion in Nolan Harmon, ed., *Encyclopedia of World Methodism*, vol. 1 (Nashville: United Methodist Publishing House, 1974), 489–91. See A. Gregory Schneider, *The Way of the Cross Leads*

Home: The Domestication of American Methodism (Bloomington: Indiana University Press, 1993), 52, for a helpful section on sanctification theology.

15. FMB, Diary, May 15, May 26, June 3, July 7, July 14, August 12, September 22, and September 30, 1843. Diary of William Kennedy Blake: #71-Z, 49, 54, 57. Southern Historical Collection, Manuscripts Department, Wilson Library, University of North Carolina at Chapel Hill. The Reverend William Kennedy Blake, a faculty member at Greensboro Female College in the 1850s, credited Bumpass with creating and promoting the high degree of "religious fervor" among the college girls.

16. James Jamieson, "To the Patrons of the Weekly Message," TWM, December 18, 1851, 2.

17. James Jamieson, "Death of the Rev. Sidney D. Bumpass," TWM, December 18, 1851; S. Milton Frost's account of Bumpass's death, untitled, TWM, May 6, 1852; Frances Bumpass, "He Being Dead Yet Speaketh" (editorial), TWM, April 5, 1855, 2–3.

18. FMB, editorial, TWM, November 27, 1852, 2.

19. FMB, editorial, TWM, December 4, 1852, 2.

20. FMB, editorial, TWM, Friday, April 22, 1853, 2. "Dove," "Pet Dove," and "little Dove" were all nicknames Frances gave to her paper, after the engraving of the dove of the Holy Spirit on the paper's masthead.

21. FMB, editorial, TWM. November 27, 1852, 2.

22. TWM, October 20, 1853. Barringer reported from his circuit that there was a growing interest in the *Message*, especially among the ladies. A cursory glance at the subscription lists for the first several years verifies that probably more than half of the subscribers were women or men who subscribed for women.

23. Steven D. Cooley, *Origins of the Southern Middle Class 1800–1861* (Chapel Hill: University of North Carolina Press, 2004), 47, 49, 52, 53, 248n14), 250n34.

24. Leroy Madison Lee was the younger brother of Jesse Lee, founder of Methodism in New England. He was appointed editor of the *Richmond Christian Advocate*, serving from 1836 to 1837 and again from 1839 until the 1850s. See Joseph Mitchell, "The *Richmond Christian Advocate*, 1832–1840," *Methodist History*, October 1963, 46–47.

25. Bumpass printed "Old North State's" letter in full in the editorial column of December 15, 1853, 2.

26. Two cultural anthropologists have provided background for this analysis of social boundaries: Mary Douglas, *Purity and Danger: An Analysis of Concepts of Pollution and Taboo* (New York: Praeger, 1966), and James C. Scott, *Domination and the Arts of Resistance: Hidden Transcripts* (New Haven, Conn.: Yale University Press, 1990).

27. "Old North State," TWM, March 2, 1854, 2, and N. H. D. Wilson, *Richmond Christian Advocate*, March 16, 1854, 1.

28. Several theorists of social movements, including holiness, have been very helpful in this analysis. In addition to cultural anthropologists Mary Douglas and James C. Scott (see note 27), the dissertations of Lucy Ann Lind Hogan, "The Overthrow of the Monopoly of the Pulpit" (Ph.D., Drew University, 1998), and Diane Cunningham Leclerc, "Original Sin and Sexual Difference" (Ph.D., University of Maryland, 1995), focus on Phoebe Palmer's ministry and movement as examples of this pattern. See also Jean Miller

Schmidt, *Grace Sufficient: A History of Women in American Methodism, 1760–1939* (Nashville: Abingdon, 1999).

29. FMB, editorial, TWM, December 15, 1853, 2.

30. Bumpass is paraphrasing Jesus in the Beatitudes, Matthew 5:10 (KJV).

31. Christine Heyrman, *Southern Cross: The Beginnings of the Bible Belt* (New York: Knopf, 1997), 117–60, 161–205.

32. FMB, editorial, TWM, December 15, 1853, 2.

33. FMB, "Would You Be Holy?" (editorial), TWM, September 23, 1857, 2.

34. Holiness theology pulled men and women into gender-neutral territory. It required men to become submissive to God's will, surrendering all of their control over their lives to God. Such values were antithetical to the culture of honor of masters in the antebellum South. Women, likewise, were required to stand and speak in public worship about their sanctification, to teach others on the path, and to write about their experiences. All of these venues were either proscribed or socially risky for women at the time. Edmund Morgan offers a very astute assessment of this tension in holiness theology and how southern clergymen negotiated it in his review of three classic monographs on southern manhood and the code of honor, Bertram Wyatt-Brown's *The Shaping of Southern Culture: Honor, Grace, and War, 1760s-1880s*, Wyatt-Brown's *Southern Honor: Ethics and Behavior in the Old South*, and Kenneth Greenberg's *Honor and Slavery*. See Edmund Morgan, "The Price of Honor," *New York Review of Books*, May 31, 2002, 36–38.

35. FMB, editorial, TWM, January 12, 1854, 2.

36. "Itinerant," TWM, January 19, 1854, 2.

37. Ibid.

38. In terms of James C. Scott's theory of dominant and subordinate social transcripts, Itinerant was doing an extraordinary thing. He was a member of the dominant group. Yet he was giving someone in the subordinate group a place among the dominant ones. In other words he was announcing that a woman could edit a religious paper in place of a clergyman and do a better job. In the process he changed the dominant transcript to implicitly include not only Bumpass but also any future woman in the same situation.

39. "Itinerant," TWM, January 19, 1854, 2, and "Old North State," TWM, February 9, 1854, 2.

40. L.W. Martin, TWM, March 2, 1854, 2. FMB, editorial, March 2, 1854, 2. Direct evidence is lacking to prove that the debt was liquidated, but it is doubtful that she could have kept publishing if it had not been. Instead the paper ran for another seventeen years.

41. FMB, editorial, TWM, March 2, 1854, 2.

42. N. H. D. Wilson, *Richmond Christian Advocate* (RCA), March 16, 1854, 1.

43. Leroy M. Lee, "The Religious Press" (editorial), RCA, March 16, 1854, 2. Bumpass's editorial from March 9, 1854, does not survive. The only source for her words is Lee's reprint of parts of her editorial in his own response to Wilson.

44. The phrase "Love that casts out fear" is a biblical reference to "perfect love" (1 John 4:18, KJV) that became a euphemism for holiness in coded religious language during the 1850s. It is ubiquitous in the writings of holiness advocates in Bumpass's day.

45. Ibid., January 29, 1854. The timing of these diary entries coincident with the paper wars make it logical to assume that the difficulties she was talking about had to do with the conflict.

46. FMB, Diary, December 31, 1853.

47. Ibid., March 10, 1854. According to the *Minutes of the Annual Conferences of the Methodist Episcopal Church, South for the Years 1853–1854*, 460, N. H. D. Wilson was the pastor of Bumpass's church in Greensboro at the time. Whether or not she talked to him about her discouragement, his article a week later restored the peace.

48. Only eighteen issues of TWM survive between February 30 and the end of the year for 1854. For details of the Book Concern settlement, see James Penn Pilkington, *The Methodist Publishing House: A History*. Vol. 1, *Beginnings to 1870* (Nashville: Abingdon, 1968), 321–22.

49. Manuscript minutes, North Carolina Conference of the M.E. Church, South, Pittsboro, North Carolina, Monday, November 13, 1854. Duke University Special Collections Library, Durham, North Carolina, #F2727, 1846–66. The committee appointed to approach Bumpass about buying her paper was made up of some of her closest clergy friends, including N. H. D. Wilson.

50. Gerda Lerner concluded that many single women in the nineteenth century made significant contributions toward women's emancipation even if they did not embrace radical opinions such as woman suffrage. France Bumpass was among these women who moved women toward emancipation. See Lerner, "Single Women in Nineteenth-Century Society: Pioneers or Deviants?" Review of Lee Chambers-Schiller, *Liberty, a Better Husband*; Carroll Smith-Rosenberg, *Disorderly Conduct*; and Martha Vicinus, *Independent Women*, in *Reviews in American History* 15, no. 1 (1987): 95–100.

51. Varon defines "public" as "a set of physical spaces—literally the world outside the home" and also as "a figurative space—the world of letters." Elizabeth R. Varon, *We Mean to Be Counted: White Women and Politics in Antebellum Virginia* (Chapel Hill: University of North Carolina Press, 1998), 2.

52. "Minutes of Several Conversations," Question 3 in *The Works of John Wesley, Volume 8*, Ed. Thomas Jackson (Grand Rapids, Mich.: Baker Book House, 1978), 299.

53. FMB, editorial, December 15, 1853, 2.

54. *Woman's Missionary Advocate* (Nashville: Woman's Missionary Society of the Methodist Episcopal Church, South, 1888–1910). Between 1852 and 1859, Bumpass printed the writings of twenty-seven women.

55. Virginia holiness preacher Martha Hancock Wheat called the *Weekly Message* "that dear little paper." Diary of Martha Wheat, May 23, 1853, Bedford County, Virginia, 49, Ref. #517.58, Southern Historical Collection, Wilson Library, University of North Carolina at Chapel Hill.

56. Kate Flint, *The Woman Reader: 1837–1914* (Oxford: Clarendon, 1993), esp. "Theory and Reading," 17–46, and "Reading Practices," 187–252. Mary Crawford and Roger Chaffin, "The Reader's Construction of Meaning: Cognitive Research on Gender and Comprehension," in *Gender and Reading: Essays on Readers, Texts, and Contexts*, ed. Elizabeth A. Flynn and Patrocinio Schweickart (Baltimore: Johns Hopkins University Press, 1986), 3–30.

Nancy Gray Schoonmaker

Where Do We Go from Here?

Spiritualism and Eternity in 1850s Nashville

Everyone dies. Since the beginning of recorded time, mankind has turned to religion to explain the mysteries of this world, and every successful religion has promised that the soul, the self, would not be extinguished when we die. Protestant evangelicalism held sway in the antebellum South, and Christians were expected to have faith that belief in Christ's atonement for the sins of mankind would ensure them and their loved ones eternity in Heaven. The New Testament promised a glorious afterlife, although the nature of that "world without end" was veiled in impenetrable mystery. However the mechanics of the afterlife were conceived, Christians were supposed to find comfort in its promise; often they did not. Letters and diaries are full of the anguished confessions of southerners whose faith simply did not offer adequate solace as they coped with the death of loved ones and contemplated their own mortality. In religion as it is actually lived, people often pick and choose from what is available to construct a usable personal faith. Even for Christians the world of the dead could intrude on that of the living, as the persistent belief in ghosts and demons suggests. By the 1850s phrenology, animal magnetism, and spiritualism—explorations of the mysteries of the human mind that had potential religious significance—had made their way to the South. While some southern Christians cleaved to evangelical orthodoxy, others embraced the possibilities of these mysteries. Our understanding of evangelical Christianity in the nineteenth-century South has not adequately taken into account these "other Christians," who alone or in small groups reinterpreted the word of God to fit more comfortably with their individual needs and their understanding of the world.[1]

Jesse Babcock Ferguson of Nashville was one of these "other Christians." His story illustrates what was possible when a sincere Christian, empowered by the spiritual legacy of the Enlightenment—what historian Nathan Hatch called "the democratization of American Christianity"—embraced the right and duty to interpret the Bible as his own inner light revealed its true meaning, as the literal word of God (or not). Conversion and rebirth in the spirit launched young

Ferguson on a career as an itinerant evangelist. His inner light impelled a continuing reconfiguration of personal faith that moved beyond traditional evangelical interpretations of the Bible's teachings about salvation, Heaven, and apostolic gifts. His extraordinary success as a preacher eventually gave him the confidence and opportunity to make public his beliefs, which by 1854 included universal salvation and communication with the spirits of the dead. The support and resistance these beliefs met when he shared them in the pulpit and the pages of the *Christian Magazine* left a paper trail that gives us a window into the beliefs of one community of southern Christians. Some of them feared deviating from the faith of their fathers, but "others" explored new possibilities and reshaped their beliefs while continuing to consider themselves good Christians.

Jesse Babcock Ferguson was the charismatic and influential preacher of the Nashville Church of Christ from 1846 to 1856. His sermons drew such large crowds every Sunday that by 1849 his wealthy congregation built a larger and more elegantly appointed new church for him to accommodate comfortably up to 1,200 souls. Despite the fact that the marriage of slavery and evangelicalism created southern exceptionalism, the story of Jesse Ferguson demonstrates that educated southerners, urban southerners, and their northern counterparts were all very much part of the same community of ideas. The print and transportation revolutions made it so. It was an age of progress, scientific advances—and theological innovation—that excited the interest of an increasingly literate public through evermore available and affordable books, magazines, newspapers, and pamphlets. Ferguson's engagement with this world of ideas, despite the fact that some were also known to be embraced by northern abolitionists, was not as unusual for southerners as older historians had suggested.[2] An early example of Ferguson's interest in progressive if controversial inquiries into the working of the human mind is his experimentation with animal magnetism, or mesmerism.

The idea that an invisible force or fluid moving between the mind of the mesmerizer and his subject had the potential to unlock heretofore unimagined powers in the subject's mind—and that anyone might try to effect this movement—seemed to democratize scientific investigation and sold books and periodicals. In 1842, six years after a Frenchman brought mesmerism to America, Ferguson and his family were conducting their own experiments in animal magnetism on a plantation in Todd County, Kentucky.

Within his trusted family circle, Ferguson's experiments led him to two conclusions about what he called the "laws of mind." The first, simply put, was clairvoyance: one person's mind could perceive the thoughts and sensations in the mind of another person. Ferguson claimed all who participated had observed evidence "of a nature and amount that did not admit of a question." He and his wife, Lucinda, were alone in accepting a second and more startling conclusion. They believed that Lucinda, while in a trance state, had demonstrated that the human mind, "acting apart from its own and all external senses," could hold communion with *disembodied* minds.[3] Lucinda had received communications from the dead.

As a minister of the Gospel, Ferguson should have been satisfied by the New Testament's assurance of eternal life, but he saw in mesmerism—and later in spiritualism—a way to move beyond faith and hope to empirical verification of the afterlife. Ferguson and his family regarded the results of their mesmeric investigations as "promises of future unfoldings, such as we could not definitely describe."[4] Unsure of what to make of it all, and probably of how people would react, Ferguson shared these experiments and his more unorthodox private musings only with family and friends. Publicly he was eloquent, devout, an engaging and inspiring speaker.

Ferguson's considerable talents as a religious orator attracted attention. The same year he began to experiment with mesmerism, the Nashville Church of Christ, which had no full-time minister, invited him to be a guest speaker for two weeks. He so impressed the congregation that they repeatedly entreated him to become their settled preacher. In early 1846 he finally accepted, and soon he also became editor of the Churches of Christ's Nashville-based *Christian Review*, which he renamed the *Christian Magazine, Devoted to Primitive Christianity and Religious Intelligence.*

Primitive Christianity was a term that resonated for the many nineteenth-century American Protestants who were certain that Christian denominations, especially Catholicism, had lost the simplicity and purity of the church begun by Jesus and his disciples. Again and again new faith movements sought to reclaim— to restore—this closer connection to God, uncluttered by creeds and dogmas and rituals. The most effective of these restorationist movements was the Disciples of Christ, or Churches of Christ, who called themselves "the Christians." They followed Alexander Campbell out of Presbyterian and Baptist churches during the great revivals in Tennessee and Kentucky, intending to live by the Bible as the revealed word of God, especially as filtered through the New Testament. Visits from Campbell in 1827 encouraged a breakaway group of Nashville Baptists "fully [to] reorganize in harmony with the ancient Scriptural pattern" and become a Church of Christ. Campbell visited the Nashville church every five years or so and remained an important influence on the congregation. A nineteenth-century writer observed that Disciples of Christ editors wielded power like that of bishops in other denominations. As editor of the *Christian Baptist* and later the *Millennial Harbinger,* Campbell shaped the beliefs of the growing flock of "Christians" in the South and West. His motto was "Where the Bible speaks; we speak; where the Bible is silent, we are silent."[5] The Bible did not mention animal magnetism, and Jesse Ferguson did not mention it in public.

The Nashville Church of Christ prospered under Ferguson. Its congregation included many of Nashville's leading men and their families. Ferguson's sermons were inspirational and uplifting, if occasionally deviating from the interpretations of scripture older members of the congregation (and Campbell) favored. But the church was thriving, and Ferguson always managed to explain away statements that troubled that small minority in a way that reestablished his public posture of "Christian" orthodoxy. Privately he grew evermore heterodox.[6]

The Fergusons' belief that they had communicated with spirits, or disembodied minds, prepared them to accept the tenets of spiritualism. Reflecting in 1844 on their mesmeric experiences, Ferguson had noted in his journal that he foresaw "such a manifestation of the saints, that the veil of flesh will be rent away and the connection will be permanent. . . . The angels of God will ascend and descend as Jacob saw, and as Jesus promised, and the [things] for which Peter asked on the Mount of Glory will be granted to all." In 1849, at about the time the Fox sisters of New York were gaining fame for their communications with the dead, Ferguson published these reflections in the *Christian Magazine*. Privately he and his family realized that if the Fox sisters really had established contact with the spirits, Mrs. Ferguson "is a medium!" That same year someone in a trance state (probably his wife) told him the manifestations were from spirits long dead, "seeking access to the world by the agency of spirits recently departed."[7]

Ferguson considered the implications of these revelations. Campbell and the Disciples adhered to the biblical injunction that anyone who did not accept Jesus Christ during life on earth was doomed to eternity in Hell, and that at the second coming of Christ, "they that are in their graves shall hear his voice, and come forth, and they that have done good, to the resurrection of life, and they that have done evil to the resurrection of damnation."[8] Little by little Ferguson gave hints in his sermons and writings that he was not so sure that was the case. His position was more akin to that of Universalists, who were convinced that a loving God who had created mankind in his own image would not destroy even one of his beloved creatures. "We confess," Ferguson later explained, "that our experiences and observation so deepened and confirmed our faith in the reality and nearness of Spirit presence, that it gave a character to our ministrations that was marked by all, and led, doubtless, to the strange controversy that grew out of the denunciations of heresy and infidelity, that some ephemeral publications and irregular ministers fulminated against us."[9]

In the April 1852 *Christian Magazine*, Ferguson revealed that it was clear in his mind "that Christ by his spiritual nature, or by the Spirit, did preach to the Spirits of the invisible world," assisted by "ministering angels" who brought the gospel to "infants, idiots, pagans, and the countless thousands whose external circumstances remove them far from the light of the blessed gospel" during their lives on earth.

He also averred that he had hesitated for the "past eight years" to express publicly everything he believed, including that he had never "committ[ed] the body of a single human being to the grave, for whom it is not a pleasure for us to know, that his soul has already entered where the knowledge of Christ may be his."[10] Campbell replied in the next issue of his *Millennial Harbinger*, asking Ferguson to clarify whether he did indeed believe the biblical doctrine of future punishment. Implicit in this request was the demand that Ferguson dissociate himself from the taint of Universalism and acknowledge his adherence to Campbell's belief that those unconverted in their lifetimes would in fact be consigned to Hell. This triggered a flurry of articles and pamphlets.

Campbell's July *Millennial Harbinger* featured appropriately disapproving letters from readers reacting to Ferguson's articles. Ferguson's August *Christian Magazine* denied repeatedly that he was a Universalist and devoted a good deal of ink to "the Attack of the Millennial Harbinger upon the Christian Magazine and its Editor," which Campbell then reprinted in the September *Millennial Harbinger*, vowing to "unsheath the sword of our spiritual warfare, and enter into the field." Ferguson accused Campbell of using his position as editor to become a "one-man church court."[11]

Campbell's opposition strengthened Ferguson's resolve to let no man dictate his beliefs. In late 1853 Ferguson and his wife spent six weeks in Ohio, meeting regularly with a circle of spiritualists that included a Methodist minister and other committed Christians. Spiritualist publications at the time claimed everyone was a potential medium. As he had with mesmerism a decade earlier, Ferguson wanted to investigate for himself the phenomena that excited the United States and western Europe. And as he had with mesmerism, he came away convinced that spiritualism offered empirical proof of the afterlife.

Ferguson returned to Nashville and his pulpit. In April 1854 Campbell reprinted a pronouncement by the editor of the Alabama *Universalist Herald* that Brother Ferguson was "a Universalist in the true sense of the term" and predicting that Ferguson would "be known in future ages as a Christian reformer." Everyone who dies, Ferguson believed, goes directly to the spirit world and begins an eternal progression of spiritual growth. "There is a future Spiritual life to all human beings that death cannot destroy," Ferguson averred, and "*that future Spiritual life is progressive to all souls.*"[12]

This idea of spiritual progression in Heaven came from the influential Swedish mystic Emanuel Swedenborg, who groused in 1758 that "today's churchman knows almost nothing about heaven, hell, or his own life after death." Swedenborg wrote at length and in detail of his visits to Heaven and his conversations with angels. Less than a hundred years later, Henry Ward Beecher would claim that no one in America "could consider himself educated who had not read Swedenborg's works." Johnny Appleseed distributed Swedenborgian tracts to the backcountry and frontier. A few Swedenborgian ministers itinerated in the rural South. Swedenborg's tales of Heaven and angels and spirits were told and retold. His description of spiritual progress in a family-centered heaven resonated with many Christians in the nineteenth century, who began to speak of their dead as having gone to the "spirit world."[13] Popular hymns incorporated themes of celestial family reunion and reminded believers that at death they would "fly away." Christians who accepted the burden of original sin and the fear of Hell fretted that their unconverted loved ones would not join them in the hereafter, that their sacred family circles would be sundered for eternity. Swedenborg's eternal progression dovetailed nicely with universal salvation. For Jesse Ferguson it was only reasonable to believe that he never buried a member of his flock who had not already begun to progress to a clearer knowledge of God.

By the summer of 1854, Ferguson had moved beyond universal salvation and publicly proclaimed his belief in the reality of communication with spirits. "I have investigated; and I could neither be an honest man nor a philanthropist, did I not say I know that I have had intelligent and blissful communion with departed spirits." The majority of the Nashville congregation backed Ferguson's right to his religious convictions, making it a strange Church of Christ indeed, but a dissenting minority asked Campbell to come to Nashville to support them. This minority included men who had shared church leadership for several years while the congregation did not have a paid minister. One of these, Tolbert Fanning, had unsuccessfully opposed hiring Jesse Ferguson in 1846. The dissatisfied minority produced a pamphlet exposing Ferguson's many errors.[14]

Fanning and the traditionalists charged that Ferguson had veered dangerously from "the old platform, for which we have been so successfully battling for the last quarter of a century." Ferguson and his supporters thought the minority had, in just a quarter of a century, become hidebound by creed and dogma that blinded them to new spiritual developments and possibilities. "No marvel," sniped the minority authors, "with such ideas of the church of God, that some of Mr. Ferguson's warmest members say there are as [*sic*] good people out of the Church as in it." Interestingly his critics repeatedly accused Ferguson of plagiarism. The men who conspired against him called him "a most servile copyist" of liberal and unorthodox theologians in the North such as Theodore Parker, Henry James, and F. W. Newman, but Fanning and the dissident minority demonstrated that they too knew the work of these writers.[15] They also went to law to regain custody of the church building.

Ferguson, meanwhile, had published a book about his communications with spirits and was sending long reports to the *Spiritual Telegraph*, a spiritualist newspaper based in New York City. Currying national support among spiritualists, he chronicled his persecution and his explorations of spiritualism in Nashville and named many prominent Nashville citizens who joined him in these investigations.

By the 1850s Nashville was a busy port city on the Cumberland River and had become an important center of medicine and publishing. Many of Ferguson's parishioners were nationally recognized businessmen, physicians, jurists, and politicians. That so many of them were willing to investigate publicly spiritualist phenomena tells us that these antebellum southerners were open to new ideas and phenomena that promised to meet their religious needs better than a strict adherence to conventional wisdom.

The majority of Ferguson's congregation still supported him, but the civil courts awarded the church building to the Campbellite minority. In his 1856 farewell sermon, Ferguson claimed he was leaving of his own free will and asked God to "breathe upon our newly awakened faculties thy vision of glory." Shortly thereafter fire consumed the building. Ferguson preached regularly in Nashville venues hired by his supporters, and he traveled and lectured. One of the most knowledgeable historians of the episode claims Ferguson's popularity was "undiminished by controversy." Ferguson was a vocal supporter of the Confederacy and escaped to England when Nashville fell to Union troops. After the war he traveled in Europe with the Davenport Brothers, spiritual mediums who were twice exposed as frauds while he was with them. Ferguson left the tour and returned to America, but his reputation was tarnished. He headed for Washington, bearing spirit messages for President Andrew Johnson from Universalist minister–turned-spiritualist John Murray Spear, and while there he lectured and spoke in support of the president. Returning to Nashville, he found that real estate investments had made him a wealthy man. But Ferguson was not well, and on September 3, 1870, he died.[16]

Christian spiritualism in the South did not die with him. Within a few years, another charismatic minister in another southern city would publicly take up the cause. No one knows how many southerners attempted to lift the veil between this world and the spirit world. Historians have assumed that the South was both too orthodox and too defensive about northern "isms" to let spiritualism take root, but abundant sources reveal evidence linking hundreds of individuals in the South with spirit communication.

Spirit communication could appear to be logical, sensible, and even biblical when bolstered by empirical observation and scripture. *Sola scriptura* did not automatically lead to orthodoxy. Having once turned to biblical proof-texting to counter northern attacks on slavery, Ferguson turned to the Bible for support of his belief that these spiritual gifts were a new dispensation. The Old Testament is rife with visitations from angels, and St. John admonished the faithful to "believe not every spirit, but try the spirits whether they are of God."[17] The Church of Christ that welcomed Ferguson in 1846 had seemed to him to offer fellowship based on shared Christian faith and not "predicated on a vain uniformity of belief." His popularity fed resentment and jealousy, and the eventual schism in the

Nashville church presaged differences that would soon surface throughout the denomination.[18] The Churches of Christ learned that Ferguson was not alone in believing that the meaning of *sola scriptura* could not be dictated by the interpretations of others.

Belying the argument that northern "isms" had little appeal to slaveholders, women's diaries reveal devout southerners who had incorporated phrenology, mesmerism, and spiritualism into their vocabularies. Northern spiritualist newspapers printed letters, stories, and names of subscribers from the South. Southern manuscript collections, the census, city directories, and local and family histories have provided the tools to reconstruct the stories of hundreds of freethinking religious seekers in the nineteenth-century South and to map networks of family, faith, and professional connections through which ideas were shared. Christian spiritualism, whose adherents' private beliefs were uniquely their own and not entirely in accord with either orthodox or evangelical dicta, is best thought of as a religion of families, a religion of intimates. It was only by being so that southern Christians could both preserve Christian fellowship and safely believe what their coreligionists might interpret as dangerous heresy.

NOTES

1. Cedric Mims, *When We Die: The Science, Culture, and Rituals of Death* (New York: St. Martin's, 1998), 342; Catherine L. Albanese, *A Republic of Mind and Spirit: A Cultural History of American Metaphysical Religion* (New Haven, Conn.: Yale University Press, 2007), 9.

2. See, for example, Robert W. Delp, "The Southern Press and the Rise of American Spiritualism, 1847–1860," *Journal of American Culture* 7, no. 3 (1985): 88–95; and Clement Eaton, "The Resistance of the South to Northern Radicalism," *New England Quarterly* 8, no. 2 (1935): 215–31.

3. J. B. Ferguson, *Spiritual Communion: A Record of Communications from the Spirit-Spheres with Incontestible Evidence of Personal Identity, Presented to the Public, with Explanatory Observations* (Nashville: Union and American Steam Press, 1854), 10–11.

4. Ibid., 11.

5. Johnny Tucker, *Like a Meteor across the Horizon: The Jesse B. Ferguson Story* (Fayetteville, Tenn.: Tucker, 1978), 36; Henry E. Webb, "The Power of the Press: The Editor Bishop in a Time of Transition, 1900–1930," in *The Power of the Press: Studies of the "Gospel Advocate," the "Christian Standard," and "The Christian Evangelist,"* by Henry E. Webb, Richard T. Hughes, and Howard E. Short (Nashville: Disciples of Christ Historical Society, 1986), 35; Richard T. Hughes, "The Editor Bishop: David Lipscomb and the *Gospel Advocate*," in Webb, Hughes, and Short, *Power of the Press*, 6; Earl Irvin West, *The Search for the Ancient Order: A History of the Restoration Movement, 1849–1906*, vol. 1, *1849–1865* (Nashville: Gospel Advocate Company, 1974), 46.

6. Ferguson's changing beliefs were heterodox from the perspective of Alexander Campbell. The terms *orthodox* and *heterodox* are contingent on what one believes is

authoritative interpretation of scripture. For the purposes of this project, we presume that each individual might assume his or her beliefs to be orthodoxy and those of anyone who is not of like mind to be heterodoxy.

7. Ferguson, *Spiritual Communion*, 11, 12.

8. Thomas Claiborne, *History and True Position of the Church of Christ in Nashville: With an Examination of the Speculative Theology Recently Introduced from Neologists, Universalists, Etc.* (Nashville: Cannon & Fall, 1854), 13.

9. Ferguson, *Spiritual Communion*, 11.

10. Johnny Tucker noted that "Tolbert Fanning had published a similar article by Ferguson called 'Another State of Probation'" in the October 1845 *Christian Review*, the publication Ferguson renamed the *Christian Magazine* in 1848. It appears the results of Ferguson's experiences with his mesmerized wife and their shared belief that they were in touch with spirits of the deceased had begun leaking into his public utterances by the mid-1840s. Tucker, *Like a Meteor*, 13–14.

11. Ibid., 17; J. B. Ferguson, *Relation of Pastor and People; Statement of Belief on Unitarianism, Universalism and Spiritualism* (Nashville: Union and American Steam Press, 1854), 5.

12. Ibid., 19. The editor was John C. Burruss; Ferguson, *Spiritual Communion*, 12.

13. Colleen McDannell and Bernhard Lang, *Heaven: A History* (New Haven, Conn.: Yale University Press, 1988), 181; Timothy Miller, *America's Alternative Religions* (Albany: State University of New York Press, 1995), 80, 183.

14. Ferguson, *Relation of Pastor and People*, 13; Richard T. Hughes, *Reviving the Ancient Faith: The Story of Churches of Christ in America* (Grand Rapids, Mich.: Eerdmans, 1996), 76; Claiborne, *History and True Position*, 13.

15. Claiborne, *History and True Position*, 27.

16. J. B. Ferguson, *Moral Freedom: The Emblem of God in Divinity and Life; A Discourse, Delivered in Voluntarily Surrendering the House of Worship Built for His Use, to Its Doctrinal Claimants, When Their Claim Could Not Legally Be Sustained, and When Not Authoritatively Demanded* (Nashville: Bang, 1856), 3; John Buescher, "Jesse Babcock Ferguson," *Dictionary of Unitarian and Universalist Biography*, accessed September 2, 2006, http://www.25-temp.uua.org/uuhs/duub/articles/jesseferguson.html.

17. J. B. Ferguson, *Address on the History, Authority and Influence of Slavery* (Nashville: Fall, 1850), supports a predominantly "rational" defense of the enslavement of blacks with some evidence from the Bible; for Ferguson's scriptural defense of spiritualism, see esp. *Relation of Pastor and People*, xxi; 1 John 4, KJV).

18. Ferguson, *Relation of Pastor and People*, 14; Hughes, *Reviving the Ancient Faith*, 70.

Robert F. Martin

Annie Wittenmyer and the
Twilight of Evangelical Reform

The American Civil War was without question the United States' greatest political, economic, and social tragedy. The detrimental consequences of the
bloody cataclysm and its chaotic aftermath haunted the nation for generations. Yet
it was also cathartic and a catalyst for a plethora of changes that were sometimes
stressfully rapid and dramatic and at other times glacially slow and frustrating.
One of the significant, if at first subtle, consequences of the war was its impact
on the place of women in American life. From 1861 into the mid-twentieth century, most scholars and popular writers alike wrote celebratory accounts of the
contributions of women, North and South, to the conflict. During the war years,
recognition of women's roles sometimes helped to foster solidarity for the cause,
while in the postwar era commemoration of their sacrifices played a role in the
romanticizing of the war and sometimes in the reaffirmation of traditional gender
roles. Throughout much of the early twentieth century, scholars continued to
explore the involvement in, and significance of, women's contributions to the war,
but after midcentury the focus of research and interpretation began to shift toward
an exploration of the consequences of the war for the future status of women in
American society.[1]

Among the women who played a significant role in the Union war effort and
for whose postwar life that participation had significant implications was Annie
Turner Wittenmyer. Her work on behalf of the Keokuk Ladies' Soldiers' Aid
Society, the Iowa Army Sanitary Commission, and the United States Christian
Commission earned for her the respect and gratitude of the nation and laid the
foundation for her postbellum activities as writer, editor, and organizer of women's
work for the Methodist Episcopal Church and for her service as the first president
of the Woman's Christian Temperance Union and her contributions as chaplain
and president of the Women's Relief Corps. Although well-known and admired in
late nineteenth-century America, she has been largely forgotten, except by a relative handful of scholars in women's history and Gilded Age American history. In
part, at least, this is due to the fact that, although she stretched the boundaries of

conventionality and the gender norms of her day, her pressure on those norms was more a matter of practical necessity than ideological challenge and her activism was largely a product of her evangelical religious convictions and, in many ways, was more typical of the reform agenda of the nineteenth century than of that of the twentieth. Consequently her story has not always resonated with the ideology and interest of later generations of women. Nevertheless her life and work helped to illuminate women's important roles in the war and the significance of their service for women in the postwar era.

Sarah Ann Turner was born near Sandy Springs, in Adams County, Ohio, on August 26, 1827, to John G. and Elizabeth Smith Turner. Her father's family had been slaveholding planters near Louisville, Kentucky, and her mother believed herself descended from John Smith of Jamestown. Turner's childhood was spent in southern Ohio just across the river from Kentucky. Her family appreciated the benefits of education and was sufficiently affluent to send her to a seminary for young women, where she received an education superior to that of most of her female contemporaries. This early training served her well in her subsequent reform endeavors.[2]

In 1847 Turner married William Wittenmyer, a prosperous merchant of Jacksonville, Ohio, who was considerably older than his bride. Three years later, in 1850, the couple moved to Keokuk, a flourishing town in Lee County, on the Mississippi River, in southeastern Iowa. There they prospered and became an integral part of both the economic and social life of their community. In 1853, with the support of other local women, Annie began a free school for the poor children of Keokuk. Concerned for the religious and moral as well as the secular training of her charges, she soon also organized a Sunday school for their benefit. The school became the nucleus for the emergence of the Chatham Square Methodist Episcopal Church, which served as a notable center for the religious and civic life of the community.[3]

The advent of the Civil War catapulted Keokuk into a city of importance to Iowa's military efforts. Its location on the river meant that it became a major port of embarkation for Iowa troops and supplies bound for the front. It also served as a medical center for the care of sick and wounded Union soldiers and some Confederate ones as well. Given their community's strategic location, it was hardly surprising that the women of Keokuk did what American women had been doing for at least half a century and what their sisters all across the North began to do in the spring of 1861: they organized a voluntary association to meet a critical need.[4] As historian Anne Firor Scott pointed out, "What business and public life were to aspiring nineteenth-century men, the voluntary association was to aspiring women."[5] For several generations prior to the war, women had organized voluntary associations to address the perceived religious, moral, educational, health, and other problems of their society. In doing so they contributed much to early nineteenth-century American life and gained valuable experience unavailable to them through other avenues.

The long apprenticeship in voluntary associations led to the irony that when the guns roared in Charleston Harbor, women were at the outset better equipped for the part they were to play in the great Civil War than men were for their part. In a country that had eschewed a standing army on principle and in which the militia had become principally an outlet for sociability, preparing the male population to fight a modern war was a daunting challenge. Women, by contrast, began at once to use the skills they had been honing for half a century as they undertook to deal with a considerable range of war-related problems that they defined as their responsibility.[6] The women of Keokuk exemplify Scott's point. They served as volunteers in local military hospitals and then in the late spring of 1861 organized the Keokuk Ladies' Soldiers' Aid Society to secure supplies and dispatch them to the front.[7]

While the 1850s was for Wittenmyer a decade of public service, her private life was marred by much sorrow. She gave birth to four children, all but one of whom, her son Charles, died in infancy, and, by the time of the Civil War, she had also lost her husband. Ironically, as a result of her personal misfortune, Wittenmyer was more able than many other women of Keokuk to dedicate her time and energy to the support of the war. Her husband left her a relatively affluent widow, and her parents and a married sister, whose husband was serving in the army, were living in her home in the early 1860s and could therefore provide care for her one surviving child. Given her circumstances and her commitment to community service, it is hardly surprising that Wittenmyer immediately volunteered to help with the care of the sick and wounded. She recalled with compassion and some pride in her 1895 memoir, *Under the Guns*, that she had "closed the eyes of the first Iowa soldier who died in the war." When the women of the town organized the Keokuk Ladies' Soldiers' Aid Society, Wittenmyer played a prominent role, first by helping to coordinate the local acquisition of supplies and then as corresponding secretary by writing to like-minded women in the emerging network of similar aid societies around Iowa in an effort to channel provisions destined for the front through Keokuk. By late summer and early fall 1861, that objective was beginning to be realized, as an increasing volume of goods flowed steadily into the river city and then were shipped down the Mississippi River. Wittenmyer did not see her activities and those of her coworkers as a radical departure from tradition or a challenge to the gender norms of her age. For her work on behalf of the troops in particular and the war effort in general was merely an extension of the Christian benevolence in which she had been involved for a decade. Elizabeth Leonard, in a perceptive essay, has noted that "for Wittenmyer as for countless other middle-class women whose patriotic roots ran deep, responsibility to country merged with responsibility to God." The work Wittenmyer began in the spring eventually took her far from Keokuk and into the heart of battle and provided her with experiences that changed her life.[8]

In August 1861 the Second Iowa Regiment moved south down the Mississippi River, headed for combat. Wittenmyer accompanied the troops in order to better ascertain the soldiers' needs. She then returned to Keokuk and acquired supplies that she accompanied to the front in September. This late-summer trip south was the first of many she made in the following months. Sending a woman on these missions no doubt raised eyebrows in some quarters, since sending a male would have been more consistent with prevailing gender norms. However the women of Keokuk seemed to have had few qualms about Wittenmyer undertaking this task. They had great confidence in the woman who had proven herself a capable and invaluable contributor to their community since her arrival fourteen years earlier. Furthermore in their opinion a woman, by her wide and quick sympathies and by her lifelong experience as nurse in the sickroom, was far better qualified to discover at a glance the wants and necessities of the sick and, with means at her disposal, to supply them with delicate tact and discriminating judgment.[9] In short they believed a woman could do the job better than a man, and Wittenmyer's performance confirmed their confidence in her.

In the fall of 1861, Wittenmyer became the general agent of the Keokuk Ladies' Soldiers' Aid Society. This change in title and responsibility acknowledged the importance and effectiveness of her work and meant that much of her time would now be in the field. She not only coordinated the distribution of relief supplies but also shared news with the folks back home. As she traveled she wrote frequent letters describing the situation at the front and reporting on the condition of Iowa's troops. Her activities and the name recognition generated by her letters, which were widely circulated in the state's newspapers, enhanced her credibility and generated widespread support for the efforts of the women of Keokuk. By the fall of 1861, they had achieved considerable success in coordinating the operations of a network of similar volunteer groups throughout Iowa. Soon, however, they encountered an unanticipated and initially unwelcomed challenge.[10]

The Civil War accelerated the fledgling trend toward organization and bureaucratization already in evidence prior to 1861. This tendency quickly became apparent in civilian efforts to support Union military operations. At about the same time that the women of Keokuk were establishing their own local Ladies' Soldiers' Aid Society, a few hundred miles to the east, in New York City, another group of dedicated civilian supporters of the cause was organizing the United States Sanitary Commission (USSC), the objective of which was to coordinate national relief activities. Despite its well-intentioned and realistic goals, the commission

sometimes ran afoul of the localism and regionalism that traditionally characterized American life. Many mid-nineteenth-century Americans were unaccustomed
to thinking in terms of large-scale national organization, and although the commission got the cooperation of many local groups, others jealously protected their
efforts to support their friends and relatives in combat.[11]

When, in October 1861, Gov. Samuel J. Kirkwood created the Iowa State
Army Sanitary Commission as an auxiliary of the national commission to coordinate relief work in the state, a complicated and confusing struggle ensued. The
problems stemmed in part from the fact that while both the United States Sanitary
Commission and the Keokuk Ladies' Soldiers' Aid Society and similar groups
across the state strove for efficiency in the management of relief efforts, the vision and goals of the former were more bureaucratic and national, while those
of the latter were initially at least more parochial and personal. The situation
was further complicated by what appears to have been the political ineptitude
of Governor Kirkwood, who, when he created the Iowa Army Sanitary Commission, the leadership of which was exclusively male, failed to acknowledge the
work already under way by women not only in Keokuk but across Iowa. Not surprisingly this antagonized many women and resulted in an article in the Keokuk
paper in which local women pointed with pride to the work in which they and
others were already extensively engaged. The article pointed out that their work
predated the creation of the Sanitary Commission and suggested that the new
male-dominated state organization was unnecessary and irrelevant. The author
also suggested a selflessness, purity of motive, and efficiency on the part of the
state's women that might not be characteristic of a male-dominated commission,
which offered opportunities for salaries, plaudits, and a variety of other advantages
aside from simply supporting the troops. The article noted Keokuk women's past
experience as instructive. According to the author, when they tried to provide
educational opportunities for the children of their community's poor, the intrusion of men into this endeavor had led to inefficiency, chaos, and the deterioration
of their educational efforts. Leonard has suggested that the article thus soundly
rejected the constraints of a prewar gender system, which characterized the more
public, administrative aspects of war relief as inappropriate for women and asked
that Iowa's women in general, and the Keokuk Society in particular, be allowed to
continue doing what they had already been doing without interference.[12]

Leonard is correct that these dedicated women were challenging certain constraints of prevailing gender norms, yet their response was perhaps less an overt
challenge to those norms than a sense of indignation that males were intrud-
ing upon an area, that of benevolence, which had been dominated by women
throughout the nineteenth century. The dispute also reflects a persistent belief on
the part of many women in their gender's moral superiority and purity of motive,

characteristics that equipped them to do the job of relief more efficiently and effectively than could men, whose motives were tainted by ambition and a desire for self-aggrandizement.

Governor Kirkwood tried to correct his initial error in judgment and to solicit Wittenmyer's cooperation and that of the Keokuk Ladies' Soldiers' Aid Society through a complimentary letter in which he requested her cooperation with the new Sanitary Commission. However he merely compounded his earlier political mistake by making it clear that he regarded the newly created Iowa State Army Sanitary Commission as Iowa's official relief agency and that the Keokuk and other aid societies should relinquish control of their work to the commission and refocus their efforts toward its support.[13] Wittenmyer and her associates resented Kirkwood's attitude and resisted his call for cooperation.

The existence of two avenues of relief in the state created confusion. Local societies were uncertain as to how best to proceed. Some collaborated with the new state group, while others remained supportive of the Keokuk organization. In early 1862, as part of its effort to establish dominance in the field of relief work, the State Sanitary Commission requested that the financial records of local groups be provided to the commission. The Keokuk Society declined to comply, but the membership worried that this action might negatively affect its credibility. While her Keokuk colleagues had absolute confidence in Wittenmyer's integrity and responsible disposition of supplies and funds, they were becoming aware that accountability of the sort characteristic of the male-dominated business world was becoming the norm in relief work as well. Consequently they asked Wittenmyer to begin to keep more detailed records of the acquisition and distribution of supplies for which she was responsible. Wittenmyer, working tirelessly and at considerable risk among the troops, was apparently at first offended by this request, believing it indicative of a lack of confidence in her honesty and ability. When her associates in Keokuk assured her that the request was a result of the growing bureaucratization and professionalization of relief work and that the society's survival might be linked to compliance with standards characteristic of practices shaped by a male-dominated culture, she somewhat grudgingly provided the information requested and began endeavoring to keep more detailed records, a sometimes problematic task because of the scant information provided by some of the groups that furnished her with supplies.[14]

While the tedium of record keeping may have at times rankled Wittenmyer, she quickly developed a sophisticated understanding of how to operate in a male-dominated world and learned to cope with and adapt to the political, military, and personal challenges of relief work in time of war. She lobbied Governor Kirkwood on behalf of the Keokuk Ladies' Soldiers' Aid Society, pointing out to him the shortcomings of the State Sanitary Commission, which included the accumulation of too few supplies, the failure to distribute those supplies effectively, and the expense of a salaried staff, the results of whose labors were not commensurate with their income. She showed considerable shrewdness and political skill by building and sustaining the support of the military leadership with whom she worked. She arranged with officers that all supplies intended for Iowa troops arriving in St. Louis would be turned over to her or other agents of her group rather than those of the State Sanitary Commission. By the spring of 1862, she had requested and received from the secretary of war, Edwin M. Stanton, a pass signed by Abraham Lincoln authorizing her and her supplies to pass freely along Union lines in the course of her work. She made every effort to see that control of and credit for relief be given to herself and the Keokuk Ladies' Soldiers' Aid Society. In doing so she not only demonstrated a realistic appreciation of the importance of public relations, but also exhibited some of the stereotypical masculine competitiveness and desire for credit for which the ladies of Keokuk had criticized the male-dominated State Sanitary Commission. Within a matter of months, Wittenmyer had become not simply a compassionate ministering angel but also a shrewd and astute agent of an organization whose interests she served, along with those of the thousands of soldiers to whom she ministered.[15]

In 1862, after the failure of his initial efforts to secure the compliance and co-operation of many of the women's volunteer societies, Governor Kirkwood sponsored and secured the passage of a bill to make Wittenmyer co–sanitary agent for the state, along with the Reverend A. J. Kynett of the Sanitary Commission. The legislation provided Wittenmyer with a monthly appropriation of one hundred dollars for salary and expenses. Kirkwood recognized that Wittenmyer's work had widespread support across Iowa, and his appointment of her as a sanitary agent was no doubt an effort to promote collaboration or perhaps eventual union between the commission and private work. If this was his goal, it did not immediately succeed. The continued existence of two groups, and now two authorized relief agents, did not result in cooperation but in continued conflict, controversy, and confusion. Occasionally Wittenmyer found not just her work but herself embroiled in controversy, as in the summer of 1863 when the Reverend Father W. Emonds of Iowa City, an agent of the Sanitary Commission, charged her with selling supplies, including eggs, butter, and sauerkraut, destined for the troops. The allegations may have arisen out of a misunderstanding of an arrangement in which the governor provided funds for Wittenmyer to purchase supplies and resell them at cost to troops in the South. They may have also stemmed in part from Emonds's resentment over Wittenmyer and her associates' refusal to support the commission. Whatever the reason, the charges angered Wittenmyer, who responded in an article in the *Iowa City State Press* in which she noted her many contributions to the war effort and her personal sacrifices on behalf of the cause. She stressed the Christian convictions that underlay her work and reminded readers that she had asked little in return. There was no evidence of any truth in these charges, and Wittenmyer appears to have had the support of the governor throughout the controversy. Nevertheless the incident did put her reputation at some risk and further strained relations between the Sanitary Commission and the independent relief work of the aid societies.[16]

After two years of contentious struggle, a measure of reconciliation and co-operation between private and state-authorized relief efforts was at last achieved when delegates to two "sanitary conventions" in the fall of 1863 organized the Iowa Sanitary Commission. The new body comprised both men and women, but neither Wittenmyer nor Kynett held leadership positions in the new commission. Wittenmyer did, however, continue to serve as an agent of the new organization and, as such, wielded considerable influence, which may explain why she shortly found herself embroiled in another controversy. By early 1864 she commanded widespread respect and support in Iowa and elsewhere, yet she remained controversial in some quarters. Early in the year, critics made an unsuccessful effort to repeal the legislation of 1862 that had authorized her position as a state sanitary agent. Although she no doubt felt vindicated by the support shown her in the legislature, by this time she was already preparing to assume the responsibilities that would make her a nationally known figure. However, before doing so she initiated another project on behalf of the soldiers of Iowa that would survive long after the war.[17]

In the course of her work as sanitary agent, Wittenmyer frequently encountered soldiers who expressed their gratitude for the efforts being made on their behalf by the citizens of Iowa. However those expressions of appreciation were often accompanied by concerns for their families, especially if they, the soldiers, should become disabled or give their lives for the cause. Wittenmyer, herself a widow and a mother, felt keenly the troops' desire that their families be provided for in some fashion and led the effort in 1863 and 1864 to mobilize Iowans in support of the establishment of orphanages for the children of those who died in the war. Thanks in part to her efforts, delegates to a convention, October 7–9, 1863, in Muscatine, agreed to begin raising money and to establish a home for soldiers' orphans as soon as possible. On October 14 an appeal went out to the people of Iowa asking that on the following Thanksgiving Day, November 26, they contribute money and supplies for the establishment and support of the proposed home. Those in attendance at the October convention nominated Wittenmyer as president of the newly created Iowa Soldiers' Orphans' Home Association. The level of political sophistication she had developed during her wartime service is evident from her recognition of the need for state support for the project and her shrewd suggestion that the position, therefore, be offered to newly elected governor William M. Stone. In addition in February 1864 Wittenmyer appeared before the Iowa legislature to speak on behalf of the orphans' asylum. Although she was reportedly received cordially by legislators, her address did not immediately persuade the assembled lawmakers to support the project. Indeed it would be two years before the state assumed full responsibility for its Civil War orphans. Consequently the first facility, established at Farmington in southeastern Iowa in the summer of 1864, was a private venture. The following year Wittenmyer was instrumental in securing for the association the abandoned Camp Kinsman barracks at Davenport, along with a quantity of supplies stored there. Late in 1865 the Farmington facility was closed, and the children were moved to the more commodious lodgings at Davenport. Wittenmyer served briefly first as matron and then as superintendent of the Davenport orphanage until 1867. Meanwhile additional facilities were opened in Cedar Falls in 1865 and Glenwood in 1866, and in the latter year the state assumed responsibility for the homes.[18]

Although Wittenmyer's service among Iowa's soldiers from late 1861 to early 1864 earned for her the respect and appreciation of the men at the front as well as that of many of their families, friends, and supporters back home, it was her work on behalf of the United States Christian Commission (USCC) in 1864 and 1865 that brought her to the attention of the nation. Within a few months of the outbreak of the war, a number of Young Men's Christian Association (YMCA) workers, as well as evangelical clergy and laity, in the Northeast felt a call to provide support to the hundreds of thousands of men who were being mobilized to preserve the Union. They initially perceived the greatest need to be the spiritual nurture of the troops, which the fledgling military chaplaincy lacked the resources to provide. As a result of this growing concern, in November 1861, at a meeting in New York City, representatives of the YMCA and of a number of evangelical groups created the USCC to minister to the spiritual and temporal needs of the soldiers.[19]

The USCC developed a rather elaborate and extensive organizational structure placing several thousand representatives known as "delegates" in the field during the war. These were evangelical Christians, many, though by no means all, of whom were clergy. Those who served undertook a wide range of tasks, some of which were of the most menial sort. Although the emphasis had, at first, been on the provision of Bibles, the Testaments, and other types of religious literature and on assistance to chaplains, whose numbers were insufficient to meet military needs, the commission quickly expanded its role to include such other responsibilities as gathering and distributing supplies, aiding surgeons, working in hospitals, collecting the wounded from battlefields, and burying the dead. Delegates were expected to exemplify the gospel that they espoused and at all times to adhere to the rules and regulations of the military command to which they were assigned. Those who failed to act in accord with commission guidelines were removed from their posts. Relations between the military and the commission were at times strained, but in most instances problems were eventually resolved.[20]

In the winter of 1862, Wittenmyer, in the course of her relief work, discovered her brother in a military hospital in Sedalia, Missouri. He was weak and malnourished because he could not bring himself to eat the unappetizing and often unnourishing food provided the troops in military hospitals. When she saw the piece of bread and slice of bacon swimming in its own grease served to the men for breakfast, she understood her brother's loss of appetite. In time she came to believe that better nutrition could facilitate the recovery of thousands of sick and wounded soldiers. In late 1863 and early 1864, with the approval and cooperation of Iowa relief authorities, she lobbied the United States Christian Commission to underwrite a project to promote dietary reform in military medical facilities and to appoint her as the USCC agent in charge of the project.[21] The leadership of the commission liked the proposal and authorized the system of kitchens envisioned by Wittenmyer. As ultimately implemented the plan was remarkably simple and efficient.

It called for the food for those needing special diets to be prescribed by the ward surgeon. A bill of fare was provided with the patient's name and bed number. These were consolidated by the ward master, and a copy was sent to the superintendent of the diet kitchen. The food was then prepared in the special kitchen, which was a part of the hospital and under the control of the medical authorities.[22]

Since the implementation of this program required both governmental and military cooperation, Wittenmyer sought and received authorization for the work. She recalled, "I laid the matter before Mr. Lincoln, Secretary Stanton, and Surgeon General Barnes. They received the systematic plan of cooperating with medical authorities very cordially, and by special order, official papers and otherwise, afforded every possible facility for carrying out the enterprise."[23]

The first USCC kitchen was established in Nashville in the Department of the Cumberland, followed quickly by scores of others in the departments of the Mississippi and the Potomac. Ultimately Wittenmyer coordinated the work of approximately one hundred diet kitchens and two hundred kitchen supervisors. The women were given very specific guidelines regarding comportment and responsibility. They were to support the surgeons in their efforts to improve the condition of the men, adhere to the rules and regulations of the hospital, and never to distribute food without the surgeon's authorization. They were to "always present an attitude of cheer and Christian sympathy when in the presence of the sick."[24]

The operation was not without problems. Wittenmyer received letters from kitchen managers who complained of officers who wanted no women associated with their hospital kitchens, others who regarded them as "cooks" rather than supervisors, and still others who were corrupt or inept. There were reports of at least a few instances in which army personnel made sexual advances toward kitchen managers and an occasional case of inappropriate behavior or inept work on the part of women workers. Generally, however, once the dietary kitchen program was well established, it had widespread support and proved remarkably successful. The kitchens may have served as many as two million rations during the last year of the war. The nutritious meals delivered by the kitchens are credited with saving the lives of or improving the conditions of thousands of soldiers who might otherwise have perished. Much of this success was a product of Wittenmyer's organizational and political skills and her tireless efforts to establish, supply, staff, and oversee the operations of the kitchens.[25]

Why Wittenmyer took her proposal for dietary kitchens to the USCC rather than to the larger and better-funded U.S. Sanitary Commission is not entirely clear. Perhaps her decision stemmed from her earlier struggles with the Iowa Army Sanitary Commission or from dislike of what she had seen of the U.S. Sanitary Commission's bureaucratic structure and practice as she traveled among the troops in the field. More likely, however, she desired to associate with the USCC because she was comfortable with its essentially religious character. While Wittenmyer's papers contain very few of her own letters from this period, there are many from women affiliated with the hospital work or who wished to become affiliated with it that reflected their perception of the endeavor as fundamentally religious in nature. The work she undertook after the war is definitely indicative of her affinity with evangelical Protestant values and her understanding of the relationship between Christianity and social responsibility.

Immediately after the war, Wittenmyer devoted herself to the Iowa Soldiers' Orphans' Home in Davenport, serving for a time as matron and then as superintendent of the facility. However her war work had established her as a woman of considerable prominence in both religious and benevolent circles. It was not surprising, therefore, that in 1867 Bishop Matthew Simpson of Philadelphia, one of the leading figures in postwar American Methodism, offered her the opportunity once again to serve both church and society at the national level when he invited her to become an organizer of women's work in the Methodist Episcopal Church. Wittenmyer accepted the invitation and sometime in the spring of 1868 left Keokuk for Philadelphia.[26]

Women had played a major role in the benevolence activities of volunteer associations throughout much of the first half of the nineteenth century. The challenges of postbellum recovery and of rapid economic and social change no doubt convinced Wittenmyer that there were even greater opportunities for service in the years to come. She and the women with whom she had worked during the Civil War had taken risks, accepted responsibilities, and exhibited abilities that many of both genders would not have thought proper or possible prior to 1861, and they could surely help the country address the problems that lay ahead.

With the support of Bishop Simpson, in 1868 Wittenmyer began working to establish an organization, soon to be known as the Ladies' and Pastors' Christian Union, that would minister to the physical and spiritual needs of the nation's poor. In these early years, at least, this effort appears to have been more akin to the highly individualistic and personal approach of movements such as the Salvation

Army than to that of the more institutionally oriented emphasis of the Social Gospel later in the century. The union, like the Salvation Army, "attempted to rescue the underprivileged and indifferent outcasts of society." The Ladies' and Pastors' Christian Union was at first an autonomous organization of which Wittenmyer was an influential member of the board of managers. In the early 1870s, the union became an official agency of the Methodist Episcopal General Conference and she became the corresponding secretary.[27]

As early as her years as a seminary student in southern Ohio, Wittenmyer had demonstrated a flair for writing, and this talent proved a valuable asset to her work in the postwar era. To promote women's work within the church, she founded a newspaper known as the *Christian Woman*, which she edited for eleven years, and soon thereafter launched a complementary journal, the *Christian Child*. Meanwhile she became associate editor of *Home and Country*, a magazine published in New York City; wrote a column for the *New York Weekly Tribune;* and contributed articles to the periodical *National Tribune*. In addition to her journalistic endeavors, it was while working in Philadelphia that she began the writing of several books, the first of a body of work that ultimately included *Woman's Work for Jesus, History of the Woman's Temperance Crusade, The Women of the Reformation*, and *Under the Guns*. In all of these writings, she stressed the abilities and responsibilities of women and focused on their contributions to the problems of their age. Meanwhile she broadened the scope of her work to address another of the challenges of her own age, that of intemperance.[28]

Concern over the pervasiveness and abuse of alcohol in American society grew throughout the first two-thirds of the nineteenth century. What at first was often perceived as primarily a problem detrimental to individuals and their families came increasingly to be viewed as a social issue as society became more complex, industrialized, and diverse. It is hardly surprising, therefore, that temperance societies were among the most widespread and active of the voluntary associations that flourished from the 1820s to the 1850s. Women played major, if usually subordinate, roles in these efforts to curb the consumption of alcohol. Because much of the early emphasis in temperance was on alcohol's detrimental consequences for men and their families, and the movement's tactics emphasized moral suasion and the conversion of individuals to temperance or abstinence, there was a logical place for women, usually perceived as more virtuous than men, in the movement. Their role was, however, circumscribed by social convention that routinely precluded their assumption of positions of leadership, limited their ability to speak in public, and excluded them entirely from the political process.

For a time it appeared that the temperance crusade of the second quarter of the century was having the desired salutary effect as consumption of alcoholic beverages declined substantially between 1830 and 1845. However the gains of previous decades seemed to be slipping away by the 1850s as large numbers of Irish and German immigrants, for whom alcohol was an integral part of their culture, flowed into the United States. Americans perceived immigration, the consumption of wine, beer, and distilled spirits, and a rise in urban instability as inextricably linked and inherently threatening. At the same time, the traditional use of moral suasion as the primary weapon in the war against intemperance appeared ineffectual since most immigrants seemed impervious to it. Consequently the 1850s witnessed the first major political crusade against alcohol. A spate of laws was proposed, some of which were passed, but most of which did not withstand judicial scrutiny and were short-lived.

The shift in temperance tactics toward political action posed a significant problem for women since they lacked the ballot and sometimes even the right to speak publically in support of the cause. Consequently they sought greater equality within the movement and an expansion of their role in society. When older temperance organizations were slow to accede to women's demands, they turned to newer, more receptive associations, such as the Independent Order of Good Templars, where they found both a voice and more equitable treatment. Although with the exception of suffrage, by the late 1850s women enjoyed a greater measure of equality with their male counterparts in the temperance crusade. Many were not impressed with a male-dominated political process that had failed to make significant gains in the struggle against the familial and social threats posed by demon rum.[29]

Lacking political power and unimpressed by the success of those who wielded it, some women concluded that there must be a better way to stem the flow of alcohol. Some resorted to a dramatic vigilantism, giving those who dispensed intoxicating beverages the option of abandoning their wicked ways or having their inventory destroyed by ax-wielding respectable women of their community. Such dramatic tactics got public attention and sometimes support but placed the women vigilantes at risk and resulted in questionable long-term benefits. By the late 1850s, other women began to adopt a slightly more genteel approach to the vendors of alcohol, one that lacked the legal and ethical problems inherent in the destruction of property. They, like their more militant counterparts, marched onto the premises of businesses that dispensed alcohol, but their weapons were Bibles and prayers rather than clubs or axes. They marched into saloons, drugstores, and other places that sold alcohol and began to pray with and for the owners and operators of these establishments. This blend of psychological, community, and economic pressure established the pattern that would be followed by the dramatic Woman's Temperance Crusade of 1873 and 1874.[30]

The Civil War diverted energy from the temperance movement, but it also helped to set the stage for postwar activism because of heightened concern over what was perceived as an increase in the excessive consumption of alcohol by soldiers. That perception, coupled with the flow of immigrants into the nation's cities in the decades after the war, stimulated a new and more determined era of temperance activism in the late nineteenth century.

On the evening of December 23, 1873, Dr. Diocletian Lewis, an advocate of a physically active life for women and an apostle of temperance, delivered an address in Hillsboro, Ohio, in which among other things he recounted his mother and her friends' successful use of prayer and persuasion to close a Saratoga, New York, saloon frequented by his father. Lewis had delivered this temperance lecture hundreds of times and had occasionally inspired his audience to action. In Dixon, Illinois, for example, in the late 1850s, bands of local women had gone into the city's saloons, where they asked the proprietors to cease the sale of alcoholic beverages. If their appeals went unheeded, the women remained on the premises engaging in protracted prayer vigils, which were both dramatic and disruptive. Lewis advocated this type of prayerful intervention as a weapon in the arsenal of the postwar temperance crusade. The address galvanized the women of Hillsboro to action, and they quickly began to employ the tactic in their community. Events in Hillsboro served as the catalyst for similar campaigns across Ohio, the Midwest, and the Northeast. This grassroots movement, which became known as the Woman's Temperance Crusade, used a variety of tactics to close hundreds of saloons and stopped the dispensing of liquor at many other commercial establishments. Within a year the success of the crusade led to the founding of one of the most significant women's organizations of the late nineteenth century.[31]

On Wednesday, November 18, 1874, 135 women from sixteen states gathered at the Second Presbyterian Church of Cleveland, Ohio, for the first national meeting of the Woman's Christian Temperance Union (WCTU). Delegates to this organizational meeting committed themselves to the principle of total abstinence, the introduction of temperance education into Sunday and public schools, the continuation of the evangelical methods that had proven effective in the woman's temperance crusade, and the publicizing in every way possible of the cause of temperance. After considerable discussion they adopted several resolutions, including: a refusal to support intemperate men in office; a call for banishing wine and liquor from public banquets and the tables of public officials; a demand for a congressional committee to investigate the liquor traffic; and an admonition to physicians to use care in the prescribing of alcohol as medicine. Some delegates supported a more radical stance, calling for disfranchisement of rum sellers in certain circumstances, censure of the churches for equivocation on temperance, and a suggestion that physicians allow patients to die rather than administer alcohol as medicine. The press sometimes erroneously reported the adoption of the more extreme positions and pointed to them as indicative of the radicalism of the WCTU.[32]

The public perception of the union as radical stemmed largely from the fact that it was an organization comprising and led exclusively by women who were willing to speak out boldly and adopt sometimes unconventional tactics in support of a controversial cause. However, initially at least, many of the women involved regarded themselves as anything but radical, believing that they were acting simply in defense of home and society against corrosive forces related to the manufacture, sale, and distribution of alcohol. That the early WCTU membership was more conservative than many contemporary Americans believed is apparent in the selection of its first president.

Nine names were placed in nomination for the presidency of the new organization, the best known of whom was Wittenmyer. Her Civil War work, service with the Methodist Episcopal Church, and journalistic activities gave her credibility as a potential leader with organizational skills, editorial ability, and commitment to the strategy of "Gospel temperance" in which most of the membership believed. She had followed closely and actively supported the Woman's Temperance Crusade in 1874 and would eventually admiringly chronicle many of its activities in *History of the Woman's Temperance Crusade.* Although not elected on the first ballot and never the unanimous choice of the delegates, she enjoyed the support of a solid majority and presided over the union until 1879. Francis Willard, who succeeded her as president, was elected corresponding secretary and worked closely with Wittenmyer in an increasingly problematic relationship for four of the next five years.[33]

During the first year or so of the WCTU's work, the greatest challenges were organizational and financial. There was no manual to guide those organizing the union at the local level and little money to support the work of the national office or to finance the production of literature. Willard attended to many of the organizational details, corresponding with union workers and interested parties across the nation and preparing the manual. Meanwhile Wittenmyer traveled extensively, sometimes lecturing six days a week and attending all the major WCTU conventions during that first year. The two women initially enjoyed a cordial and productive relationship that facilitated the growth of the WCTU, but there were differences between them that in time became increasingly evident and reflected ideological and tactical divisions within the union.[34]

Although some members would have preferred a more overtly political approach, in its first years the WCTU eschewed politics, supporting neither women's suffrage nor any political party. A majority of the membership, while willing to utilize a variety of tactics sometimes, including legislative action, remained emotionally committed to the efficacy of "gospel temperance." Wittenmyer's own essentially religious understanding of the nature of the campaign against alcohol is nowhere more apparent than in a letter she wrote to Matilda Gilruth Carpenter, an Ohio woman active in the temperance crusade in that state.

My own thought is that God has been preparing the women of this land for work, for a long time. This preparation began in the more liberal education of woman, and was greatly quickened by demands upon them during the late war; and still more intensified by the various home and foreign missionary societies which have been conducted by women in nearly all the Christian denominations in our land. And thus prepared, it pleased the Lord to pour out his Spirit upon his daughters—his handmaidens, (not upon the world), for this special work; and, as on the day of Pentecost, the people were amazed and pricked to the heart.[35]

While she viewed the events of the mid 1870s largely through the prism of her religious convictions, Wittenmyer, like many of her associates in the WCTU, was perceptive and practical in her approach to problems. She was not averse to certain types of legislative action, such as petitioning Congress for an investigation of the liquor industry. In February 1875 she and another representative of the WCTU delivered a petition to Congress, where it was introduced into the Senate and referred to the Finance Committee. After hearing testimony from Wittenmyer and her associate, the committee seemed favorably disposed toward the petition, but the issue of an investigation was not formally docketed prior to the end of the congressional session and thus died. Undaunted, the WCTU president urged the union to continue petitioning Congress until it took steps to investigate the industry.[36]

There were limits to Wittenmyer's pragmatism and to her flexibility with regard to WCTU goals, which in time undermined both her relationship with Willard and her support within the organization. Superficially the differences between the two women seemed tactical, but they in fact differed fundamentally in their vision of women's place in reform, in particular, and society, in general. Willard, a dozen years younger than Wittenmyer, was bright, ambitious, and predisposed by training, travel, and experience as an educator and administrator to see the WCTU's goals and tactics in broader social and political terms than did Wittenmyer.

WCTU historian and Willard biographer Ruth Bordin has suggested that "Willard's primary commitment may not have been to temperance. From the beginning, women's rights probably commanded her deeper loyalty." Temperance may have simply provided her with a means to a larger end, that of expanding women's role in the political process and in addressing the many inequalities inherent in society. While Wittenmyer believed women should play an active role in addressing social issues and had spent years negotiating and stretching the parameters of nineteenth-century gender norms, she was less inclined than her younger associate to challenge openly the ideological foundations on which they rested. For her temperance was also a means to an end, but that end was the preservation of the sanctity of the home, the security of women and children, and the elevation of the moral and religious tenor of the nation.[37]

The differences between Wittenmyer and Willard were indicative of a growing divergence of opinion within the WCTU itself. While officially retaining its commitment to Gospel temperance as fundamental to its work, members of the union had never wholly eschewed legislative efforts, which included striving for local option or state prohibition legislation. The organization had, however, shied away from calls for national prohibition and women's suffrage. In time as WCTU women worked to persuade individuals to pledge themselves to abstinence, they began to understand better the complexities of the social and economic context and consequences of the consumption of alcohol. As a result many became more receptive to the possibility of using other means to achieve their ends.

Willard, who was no longer convinced of the efficacy of Gospel temperance, had for a number of years been convinced of the importance of suffrage to gender equality in particular and constructive social change in general. In 1876 she conceived a creative means of linking the controversial issue of the ballot for women with the noncontroversial one of protecting the home from the corrosive effects of intoxicants. At the convention of the WCTU in Newark, New Jersey, that year, she expressed her personal commitment to what she called the "home protection ballot." Wittenmyer, who shared the platform with Willard, regarded suffrage as itself a potential threat to the home. She, like many in the audience, was surprised by Willard's statement and reportedly muttered, "You might have been a leader but now you'll only be a scout."[38]

Wittenmyer was mistaken. In 1879 Willard defeated her in her bid for reelection as president in part because of the younger woman's charisma and in part because her views resonated with an ever larger proportion of WCTU members. By the late 1870s, increasing awareness of the complexities inherent in the "liquor problem," the sense that Gospel temperance was at best only marginally effective in addressing that problem, and the conviction that women's suffrage would strengthen the temperance crusade and protect the family was becoming more prevalent. In some ways the change in leadership did not represent as dramatic a break with the past as has been assumed. Wittenmyer herself acknowledged that there was a role for government in the temperance crusade and supported national prohibition in her last presidential address in 1879. However, she, like many other more conservative WCTU members, remained emotionally committed to Gospel temperance and opposed to the idea of the ballot for women. She had once told a convention of the WCTU that "this society was born of prayer and must be nurtured and sustained by prayer." Yet for many members politics now seemed a solid rock on which to base the struggle for change. In some parts of the country, the tempo of political action was already accelerating as local and state organizations filed antiliquor petitions, supported prohibition legislation, and advocated women's suffrage. Willard built upon the work of these less conservative and more assertive elements within the WCTU membership to guide the majority toward a broader and more diverse program of political and social action.[39]

After it became clear that the WCTU was moving decisively away from Gospel temperance and toward political activism, Wittenmyer no longer felt comfortable within its ranks and left to concentrate on her church, editorial, and literary endeavors. Soon, however, she found herself involved in the work of yet another national organization to which she was emotionally linked because of her service during the Civil War.

After the war the Grand Army of the Republic (GAR) emerged as an important cohesive force among, and a politically powerful advocate for, Union veterans. In the early 1880s, the Woman's Relief Corps was established as a service auxiliary of the GAR. The relationship between the veterans' organization and its auxiliary exemplified the conventional gender norms of the age. Women were denied membership in the GAR; officers of the corps were generally deferential to their male counterparts; and women understood that their role was to serve. As historian Stuart McConnell has written, "In the static world of the GAR, men marched while women cheered." Yet in fact women's contributions far exceeded those of cheering the past accomplishments of husbands, brothers, and sons. To be sure they cooked and served meals at GAR encampments, but they also raised funds for homes for the destitute and disabled; provided short-term relief to widows, orphans, and veterans; and erected monuments to commemorate the sacrifices of those who had served the nation in its most critical hour.[40]

Wittenmyer was involved in the work of the Relief Corps from its inception. That veterans and their families held her in high esteem is nowhere more apparent than in the corps's selection of her to fill a variety of posts in the national organization between 1883 and 1900. Among the positions she held were those of chaplain, president, national councilor, chairman of the National Relief Corps Home, member of the Andersonville Prison Board, and lifetime member of the National Council of Administration. Her service to the Woman's Relief Corps, for the most part, enabled her to avoid the political complications of her work on behalf of the WCTU, while at the same time it was consistent with her belief that women had the ability and responsibility to make significant contributions to the world in which they lived. One accomplishment that must have been especially gratifying to Wittenmyer was the instrumental role she played in securing the passage in 1892 of legislation that provided pensions for approximately 655 nurses and kitchen supervisors who had served during the Civil War. Many of these individuals, with some of whom Wittenmyer had worked, were aging, and many were impoverished or ill and had heretofore been ineligible for federal assistance. Ironically Wittenmyer herself, now in her mid-sixties and with only modest financial resources at her disposal, was not covered by this or any other pension statute. In

1898, somewhat to her embarrassment, Congress recognized Wittenmyer's service to the nation when it passed special legislation providing her with a federal pension that helped to sustain her until her death on February 2, 1900.[41]

Annie Turner Wittenmyer was born and reared in the second quarter of the nineteenth century in an era when evangelical Protestant values and the social conventions, denominations, and reform associations they nourished were at their zenith in American society. The rural, small-town, evangelical ethos in which she was steeped as a girl indelibly shaped her perspective on the world and her place in it, but a catastrophic war and a host of dramatic cultural, economic, and political changes over the course of her lifetime meant that she repeatedly had to negotiate the shifting landscape between current realities and traditional norms. The Civil War was for her in many ways a transformative experience. She developed skills and assumed responsibilities not dreamed of in her prewar years. In the course of her work on behalf of her community, her state, and the nation, Wittenmyer repeatedly confronted and tested the limits of the cultural and societal constraints imposed upon women of the era. Her activities during the war attest to the fact that she possessed courage, stamina, interpersonal and organizational skills, and political acumen comparable to or superior to that of many men and that she had few qualms about confronting a male-dominated social and political establishment in the interest of the causes she served. However as her postwar work on behalf of the Methodist Episcopal Church, WCTU, and Woman's Relief Corps suggests, her challenge to convention was more practical than ideological. Throughout her life she remained committed to the idea of complementary spheres for men and women, although she attributed to the female sphere a considerably larger and more responsible place in society than had women a generation earlier. In addition even as society began to grow more secular, she saw the hand of God in her own life and in many of the events of the age. A corollary to that conviction was her continued acceptance of the idea that women were generally more religious than, and morally superior to, men and that these characteristics could be marshaled to guard home and society against the deleterious social changes stemming from industrialization and immigration. Wittenmyer recognized that a male-dominated society often failed to appreciate the individual abilities and collective contributions of women and tried to call attention to both in her actions and writings. However because her understanding of society was more organic than individualistic, she thought primarily in terms of women's responsibilities rather than their rights and never seems to have fully grasped the inextricable relationship between the two.

Although by no means wholly forgotten, Annie Wittenmyer's life and work have been eclipsed by those among her contemporaries whose activism is more compatible with the individualistic, secular, and politically oriented values of today. Contemporary advocates of gender equality may admire Wittenmyer's courage, compassion, ability, and selfless dedication to the causes in which she believed, but her opposition to suffrage and Protestant evangelical religiosity and what appears to the modern mind to be her acceptance of a subordinate role for women has meant that she has not, with a few exceptions, captured the imagination of those who have chronicled the gender battles of the last century and a half.

NOTES

1. Drew Gilpin Faust, "Ours as Well as That of the Men," in *Writing the Civil War: The Quest to Understand*, ed. James M. McPherson and William J. Cooper Jr. (Columbia: University of South Carolina Press, 1998), 228–29.

2. Ruth A. Gallaher, "Annie Turner Wittenmyer," *Iowa Journal of History and Politics* 29, no. 4 (1931): 519.

3. Ibid., 519–20.

4. Ibid., 521.

5. Anne Firor Scott, "On Seeing and Not Seeing: A Case of Historical Invisibility," *Journal of American History* 71, no. 1 (1984): 9.

6. Ibid., 12.

7. Gallaher, "Annie Turner Wittenmyer," 521–22.

8. Ibid., 519, 522–24; Annie Wittenmyer, *Under the Guns: A Woman's Reminiscences of the Civil War* (Boston: Stillings, 1895), i–ii; Elizabeth D. Leonard, *Yankee Women: Gender Battles in the Civil War* (New York: Norton, 1994), 53.

9. Leonard, *Yankee Women*, 58; "Report of the Ladies' Soldiers' Aid Society," *Gate City (Keokuk) Newspaper*, April 15, 1862.

10. Tom Sillanpa, *Annie Wittenmyer: God's Angel* (Evanston, Ill.: Signal, 1972), 14–15.

11. Leonard, *Yankee Women*, 57.

12. *Gate City (Keokuk) Newspaper*, October 28, 1861, and November 18, 1861; Leonard, *Yankee Women*, 60–63.

13. Leonard, *Yankee Women*, 64.

14. Ibid., 65–68; Mrs. D. B. Barnes to Wittenmyer, December 17, 1863, Annie Wittenmyer Papers, Iowa State Historical Society, Des Moines.

15. Leonard, *Yankee Women*, 65–69; Sillanpa, *Annie Wittenmyer*, 20.

16. Leonard, *Yankee Women*, 72–78.

17. Gallaher, "Annie Turner Wittenmyer," 532; Leonard, *Yankee Women*, 79–81.

18. Sillanpa, *Annie Wittenmyer*, 27–30; L. O. Cheever, "Annie Wittenmyer," *Palimpsest* 47, no. 6 (1967): 254–55.

19. James O. Henry, "The United States Christian Commission in the Civil War," *Civil War History* 6, no. 4 (1960): 374–75.

20. Ibid., 374–75, 380, 382–84, 387.

21. Wittenmyer, *Under the Guns*, 72–73; Sillanpa, *Annie Wittenmyer*, 24.

22. Henry, "United States Christian Commission," 385–86.

23. Kathleen S. Hanson, ed., *Turn Backward, O Time: The Civil War Diary of Amanda Shelton* (Roseville, Minn.: Edinborough, 2006), 8–11; Wittenmyer to Governor W. M. Stone, January 23, 1864, Wittenmyer Papers; Resolution Order, signed by E. Skinner,

Corresponding Secretary for the Iowa Sanitary Commission, and Approved by Governor William M. Stone, January 23, 1864, Wittenmyer Papers.

24. Wittenmyer, *Under the Guns*, 262; Sillanpa, *Annie Wittenmyer*, 24; Gallaher, "Annie Turner Wittenmyer," 546, 552–54; Henry, "United States Christian Commission," 386.

25. Gallaher, "Annie Turner Wittenmyer," 554–58; Wittenmyer, *Under the Guns*, 264–67; Wittenmyer to Col. R. C. Wood, April 26, 1864, Wittenmyer Papers.

26. Wittenmyer, *Under the Guns*, 251–58; Cheever, "Annie Wittenmyer," 254; Sillanpa, *Annie Wittenmyer*, 31.

27. Sillanpa, *Annie Wittenmyer*, 31.

28. Ibid., 31–32.

29. Jed Dannenbaum, "The Origins of Temperance Activism and Militancy among American Women," *Journal of Social History* 15, no. 2 (1981): 240.

30. Ibid., 246.

31. Ibid., 235; Ruth Bordin, *Woman and Temperance: The Quest for Power and Liberty, 1873–1900* (Philadelphia: Temple University Press, 1981), 15–17.

32. Bordin, *Woman and Temperance*, 36–38.

33. Ibid., 38–39, 47–49.

34. Ruth Bordin, *Frances Willard: A Biography* (Chapel Hill: University of North Carolina Press, 1986), 78–81; Elizabeth Putnam Gordon, *Women Torch-Bearers: The Story of the Woman's Christian Temperance Union* (Evanston, Ill.: National Woman's Christian Temperance Union Publishing House, 1924), 17–18.

35. Letter, December 15, 1874. Qtd. in Jack S. Blocker Jr., "Annie Wittenmyer and the Women's Crusade," *Ohio History* 88, no. 4 (1979): 422.

36. Bordin, *Woman and Temperance*, 55–56.

37. Ibid., 45–46.

38. Bordin, *Frances Willard*, 82, 102–3.

39. Sillanpa, *Annie Wittenmyer*, 34.

40. Ibid., 35; Stuart McConnell, *Glorious Contentment: The Grand Army of the Republic, 1865–1900* (Chapel Hill: University of North Carolina Press, 1992), 218–19.

41. Sillanpa, *Annie Wittenmyer*, 39–41.

Gavin James Campbell

"All Sharers in the Blessed Knowledge"

*Niijima Jō's Transpacific Crusade for a
Christian Japan, 1871–73*

Niijima Jō[1] never questioned his faith, but an Andover Seminary class on Calvinist theology did make him doubt his sanity. He lamented his mind's solid, practical bent and his inability to master Greek and Latin. "It may be the hardest year in the seminary," he groaned, "because it requires so much close attention and thinking."[2] Amid the fog, however, one lesson stood out. "God determined to place us as we are," Prof. Edwards Park told the class, "and then we act."[3] That made living sense. Divine providence and Niijima's own stubbornness seemed the only explanation for his extraordinary path from Japan to the United States. It explained his chance discovery of Genesis, his hurried escape from Japan in 1864, the friendly ship's captain who put him ashore in Boston, and the generous merchant who paid for all that followed: Phillips Academy, Amherst College, and now Andover Seminary. After more than six years in America, he wrote in wonder, "I feel I have been thus far carried by the gentle hand of my Heavenly Father."[4] Now the letter on his desk made it clear that God had placed him at Andover for a reason. Niijima needed to decide if he would act.

The letter confirmed what the Boston newspapers had already told him. The Japanese emperor had ordered a high-ranking diplomatic embassy to go abroad. "At a time when every other country is progressing in all directions," the emperor said, "only our country, being unfamiliar with the situation prevailing in the world, stubbornly maintains old customs and does not seek the fruits of change."[5] The embassy's tour would begin in America, where they planned investigating everything from manufacturing and agriculture to military science and public schools. Niijima knew, however, they had no plans to visit Andover or any other Christian place. Since 1614 every single Japanese ruler had shaken his fist in God's face, banning all Christians foreign or native, and even now as Japan opened to Western influences, Christianity remained illegal. "The Japanese government are desirous that their people be instructed in arts and sciences, in which your country is superior," one official curtly told Western diplomats, "instead of being instructed in religion."[6] To drive the point home, the government defied Western protests and continued persecuting a small band of native Christians. Now Niijima learned high officials from this same government were crossing the Pacific, and the letter invited him to share with them his deep knowledge of American society.

Niijima balked and chafed. On the one hand, he knew "our nation is in trouble because our people have not been introduced to God's teaching." If Japan wanted to modernize, "first we should learn the sacred teaching of Christ to improve ourselves, and teach this to all our people."[7] God had obviously brought the embassy to America so they could understand; Niijima could not remain mute. And yet his courage sometimes evaporated. No one in the embassy knew him personally, so they did not know he had become a Christian. They did not know that if he survived systematic theology, he would soon be an ordained minister. They did not know he planned returning home to unfurl Christ's banner. Quite the contrary, the government had recently begun requiring students heading for Western schools to vow they would never convert. Telling these men Japan needed Bibles more than gunships therefore carried considerable risk. Western powers could defend their missionaries abroad, but Niijima—and his helpless family back home—would stand alone. "I wish you would make [a] special prayer for me, and also for the embassy," he wrote a friend.[8] Then he packed his bags and boarded a train to meet the embassy in Washington, D.C. God, he decided, must have gathered everyone in America for a reason.

Unfortunately historians of nineteenth-century Christian missions have often overlooked native converts such as Niijima or sidelined them as midwives of Western empire. Only recently have we rediscovered their role translating Christianity into new languages and contexts.[9] They often did the heavy lifting, communicating complex ideas and easing major cultural shifts. Overcoming the Japanese embassy's long-held prejudices and crossing barriers of language, culture, and history, for example, required a subtle touch. More skillfully than American Christians, Niijima balanced New England theology with the hard realities of Japanese politics. His trans-Pacific gospel promised steamboats and factories. "Those nations prosper that believe in the one and only God and those nations decline that do not," he said.[10] But he also challenged the embassy to think beyond material goods and national prestige and plan for Japan's moral health. He also challenged himself. Like so many native converts, Niijima stood in between. "My heart is in two places—heaven and Japan," he said once, and "yes, one more place—America."[11] Niijima seized the embassy's visit to claim an equal right to speak for all three.

Old Japan, New Japan

Heading home, the Pacific mail steamer *America* usually carried packages, coolies, and worn-out missionaries. On December 23, 1871, however, it carried Japan's future. Dressed in his official court robes, Iwakura Tomomi led aboard a stately delegation of noblemen, diplomats, researchers, bureaucrats, and five young women for the San Francisco run. "If we would profit by the useful arts and sciences and conditions of society prevailing among more enlightened nations," the emperor had told them, "we must . . . send abroad an expedition of practical observers, to foreign lands, competent to acquire for us those things our people lack."[12] After months of planning, Iwakura and his embassy started a journey that would take more than eighteen months, cover thousands of miles, and begin transforming Japan into a world power.

First, however, they dealt with the low-grade boredom of a Pacific cruise, which set conflicting ideas and personalities boiling. No one could even agree on proper attire and table manners, let alone how Japan might shape its future. Not long after the ship departed, small black buttons began appearing on the restroom floor. Then a yellow pool was discovered near the urinal and a telltale piece of Japanese paper placed over the mess hinted at the culprit. Frustrated by the fumbling necessary to undo their new Western clothes, it seemed some had panicked. Just loosening a sash had been so much easier. Calling a general meeting, a vice-ambassador pleaded with everyone "not to stain the honor of Japan in such a fashion." To prevent further embarrassments, one member with experience abroad wrote a pamphlet about Western table manners. Some thought this was all getting excessive. They snickered about the vice-ambassador's "shitty speech," and one gleefully slurped his soup, bellowed at the waiter, and gnawed on his steak like a caveman. It would be a long journey.[13]

After they reached San Francisco in January, however, Americans kept them too busy to bicker. "We shall inspect with pleasure your manufactures and machinery, your colleges and schools, and your system of justice," they told a crowd of California dignitaries.[14] This news ricocheted to the opposite coast, and Americans across the country got busy showing off. In Saratoga Springs the delegation stayed at a hotel with a thousand rooms and bathed in the famed medicinal waters. In New York City they rambled along Broadway, dumbfounded by the scrum of pedestrians, carriages, and omnibuses that battered their way up and down the street. The noise, one wrote, "rivaled ten thousand thunderclaps, or a gale blowing through a forest of pine trees."[15] Then it was off to Niagara Falls, where the rush of water "scattered like snowflakes and then rose into the air in a huge veil of mist."[16] In Boston they listened to an English chorus ten thousand strong sing "Hail Britannia" while an electrically controlled cannon boomed in time outside the concert hall. In Washington, D.C., they peered into Lincoln's box at Ford's Theater and visited the bone from Gen. Daniel Sickle's amputated leg. In Chicago they watched local firemen set a house ablaze and then come clattering to the rescue in their new Babcock fire extinguisher. Elsewhere they ate watermelon ("it tastes no different from the watermelon in our country"), picked strawberries, and sampled potato chips.[17] They met mayors and businessmen, governors and generals. They toured the White House, Mount Vernon, and Robert E. Lee's old home, chatted with Ralph Waldo Emerson, endured a tributary poem by Oliver Wendell Holmes Sr. ("We welcome you, Lords of the Land of the Sun!"), and spent an afternoon snowed in with Brigham Young. They ascended in a balloon, listened to an opera, watched a surgeon remove a miner's limb, and gawked at a bearded lady and a cow with five legs. They toured countless factories and wondered at machines whirring cotton into shirts, stitching leather into shoes, beating iron into locomotives, and smelting silver into coins. "Nothing is too minute or too dry for their investigation," marveled one journalist.[18] Every member of the embassy agreed that Americans were not an idle people. "We were astounded beyond all expectation," they reported home.[19]

Some things failed to impress them. "Certainly, Westerners have not mastered the technique of shooting fireworks straight up into the sky, or of having one rise upon itself every time it explodes," one noted. "This was a rather disappointing display." While the ingenuity of American factories astonished them, the shoddy results did not. They also lamented how democracy eroded respect for authority. "The lower classes often give expression to their freedom through dissolute behavior, lacking all restraint," one complained, and "because the lowly lack respect for their superiors, their manners are very poor." New York City under gaslight was a nightmare, a "raucous, lewd and licentious place."[20] They were dismayed hearing Americans brag that the embassy admired the United States above all other nations. Our America, a Milwaukee editor bubbled in typical fashion, is "that star of the West that shines refulgent in the eyes of the Orientals, and attracts their attention and admiration."[21] Modesty, the embassy also observed, was not a prevailing American trait.

All the banquets, serenades, speeches, and pamphlets began taking a toll. Few members spoke anything other than Japanese and only a handful had ever left Japan, but every day they would start again trying to catch explanations shouted over screeching machinery and maintain their dignity when gawking strangers hollered through windows, "Show yourselves, you yaller duffers."[22] Sometimes they longed "to enjoy, just once, the simple pleasures of drinking plain water and lying with our heads pillowed on our bent elbows."[23] They needed help.

Initially they relied on Japanese students already enrolled in American schools, but this quickly proved a disaster. Some could still barely understand English, while others saw everything with star-spangled eyes. "I can hardly bear to listen to their light-headed frivolous ideas," one delegate fumed. "Why do these young men adopt everything [American] indiscriminately without regard for whether it is good or bad?"[24] The embassy also tried leaning on the Japanese chargé d'affaires, Mori Arinori. Thoroughly acclimated to American life and boasting top-level contacts throughout the country, at first Mori seemed indispensable. But many in the embassy found him arrogant, hotheaded, and irresponsible. He was no better than the students, one grumbled, scorning "the customs of his own land indiscriminately in the presence of foreigners."[25] Two pictures in Mori's office were especially irritating. One showed the embassy's highest-ranking member, Iwakura Tomomi, in traditional court robes, and Mori had written above it "Old Japan." Another beside it showed Iwakura in Western clothes: "New Japan."[26] When the embassy met President Grant, they all appeared in traditional attire. Mori wore a suit.

The Ramblings of a Lunatic

Mori did at least find Niijima in Andover. Interrupting his seminary studies, Niijima immediately impressed everyone he met. "His kindness and sincerity make him very different from the frivolous and shallow fellows who now advocate civilization at every turn," one wrote. All agreed he was "a man on whom we may depend in the future," and after only a week, the embassy asked him to also join their European tour in the summer.[27] Niijima's future seemed bright.

Suddenly thrust into the center of power, Niijima wondered how to bring up Christianity. "I expect to *stand up for Christ* before the heathen embassy," he had roared in the safety of Andover's bosom, but after a week in Washington he felt more like Peter than Paul.[28] He circled the topic with five young girls the embassy was dropping off for an American education, "teaching them some moral principle in a pleasant way," but he did not mention Christ or recommend the Bible.[29] Around others he said even less. Niijima grumbled that Americans were too scrupulous about Japanese sensibilities and did not say grace before meals, but he did not interject his own. He planned taking one delegate to Sunday school, but a snowstorm intervened, so he canceled and went alone. In contrast another Japanese student studying law in the District of Columbia boldly escorted some embassy members to his Methodist church and explained his new faith and his upcoming baptism.[30] "My active battlefield has come within my sight," Niijima wrote his friends back in Boston; "I am ready to march forward."[31] But in truth God's armor felt rusty.

Niijima had reason for caution. The embassy was sick of Jesus. They had braced themselves for diplomatic pressure to end the centuries-old ban on Christianity but had not anticipated constant appeals from ordinary American believers. They had barely settled themselves on their U.S.-bound ship before a Baptist missionary named Jonathan Goble requested an audience. Flustered, Iwakura Tomomi deputized two young men who sat through Goble's lecture and responded with vague pleasantries but took no notes and filed no report.[32] Goble, in contrast, dashed off a letter saying he had met men "especially charged with the duty of learning all they can of the peculiar doctrines and customs and usages of Christianity." The *Baptist Missionary Magazine* quickly puffed Goble's overblown claim, declaring that their man "was invited to explain the Christian religion" and that Iwakura himself privately assured Goble "his government is well disposed toward Christianity.[33] Iwakura and his embassy had just touched dry ground when

California's governor also rushed in, congratulating them for commencing studies "where the course taught is what we call Christian civilization."[34] Baptist ministers them presented Iwakura with a Bible. On the opposite coast, a Boston paper assured readers the visit "will not fail to advance the interests of the Redeemer's Kingdom."[35] Everywhere they went the embassy heard unsolicited advice about the glories of Christianity and religious tolerance.[36]

The embassy listened politely, but privately they waffled between tearing out their hair and laughing. "When a foreigner comes to their country, they always ask what religion he observes and what god he worships," Kume Kunitake marveled. "Where there is a village, there is a church; where there is a group of people, there is a Bible." As he learned more about the faith, it staggered him that "even rational people well-versed in world affairs" worshipped an executed criminal and believed biblical stories "easily . . . dismissed as the ramblings of a lunatic." Kume thought "it would scarcely take an intelligent scholar to defeat the arguments advanced by the Christians," but he surrendered all hope of rational debate because "even if they lose in argument, their faith is not shaken."[37] The embassy did not want a diplomatic firestorm, so they followed their hosts into churches and Sunday school classrooms. American Christians, however, mistook silence for attention and a captive audience for a captivated one.

For a time Niijima did little but watch and worry. He feared revealing his new faith might make returning home impossible and also cause problems for his family. Thus while American Christians babbled uselessly, Niijima remained silent. And yet with a Calvinist's certainty, he knew God had ordained the embassy's travels. Exposed to Christians and their works the embassy would surely see the same thing he had: "those nations prosper that believe in the one and only God and those nations decline that do not." But overcoming the embassy's long-held prejudices and crossing barriers of language, culture, and history required a subtle touch. Devoted and sincere, American Christians were anything but subtle, and Niijima feared they might unwittingly retard God's advance into Japan. He needed to find some way to make the embassy not simply hear but listen.

To Take Truth Because It Is Truth

In an opportunity he could only attribute to providence, Niijima was assigned to assist the senior deputy education minister, Tanaka Fujimaro. Japan's future, everyone agreed, depended much on Tanaka and modernizing public education. "It will be difficult indeed for us to promote the enlightenment of the common people and to develop their intellects in order to maintain our national sovereignty and prevent any infringement on our independence," an imperial adviser mused, "but nothing has greater urgency for us than schools."[38] Tanaka, however, had never left Japan, spoke no English, and had no expertise in education. Niijima, by contrast, spoke English fluently and after seven years in American schools knew modern education firsthand. Tanaka would lean on Niijima's judgment and experience.

Niijima, Tanaka, and nearly the entire embassy all shared a similar classical education emphasizing etiquette, military training, ancient Chinese and Japanese history, and the Confucian classics. Some like Niijima had also tried cramming engineering, advanced mathematics, physics, navigation, and other "Western" studies when they could, but opportunities were spotty, often at the whim of where they lived and the lord they served. As they began touring American schools together, Niijima advised Tanaka to mothball the old traditional curriculum. Even a short time in America surely showed how badly Japan lagged.

But reform, Niijima insisted, did not mean wholesale destruction. Ethics centered the Confucian curriculum and should anchor its replacement as well. "The strength of a nation is the strength of [the peoples'] virtue and piety," Niijima reminded Tanaka, so Japan's new schools "must provide some means . . . to teach moral principles to the people."[39] Americans provided a new model, using the Bible and daily prayer as the foundation for a powerful nation and harmonious society ironically more Confucian than Japan. "The rich help out the poor, and those with higher status are not arrogant, nor people in lower positions considered unworthy," he pointed out. "People are united to make the nation strong."[40] In contrast though Japanese children memorized all the Confucian precepts, as adults few ever opened an orphanage, insane asylum, penitentiary, hospital, or poorhouse. Though certainly wise, Confucius was just an ordinary mortal, and his teachings therefore lacked "vital power to convert or regenerate the heart of man."[41] Only when students knew their lessons rested on sacred truth would they stake their life and their nation on the consequences. "There is truth in the Christian religion," Niijima said, a power "to make men free, vigorous, and virtuous."[42] Tanaka therefore need not abandon Confucian texts or an education centered on ethics. He need only add the Bible.

After touring American schools, Tanaka confessed that perhaps Japanese schoolchildren should learn the Bible as "virtuous food." He had even begun thinking Christianity might be a better way "to govern a people or elevate a nation." He did not care about what people believed so long as they obeyed the government's orders. Besides, he said, "if there is truth or goodness in one religion more than the others it will prevail after all." As education minister he need only consider pragmatic results, and if the Bible worked better than Confucian classics, he would happily make the trade. He did not care whether students believed one or neither. "I do not know enough to say that we ought to love truth because it is truth, and not use it as a mere instrumentality," he concluded.[43]

Niijima quickly countered. "We ought to take truth *because it is truth*," he responded, "and not as a mere instrumentality."[44] But rather than simply argue the point, Niijima began crafting an itinerary proving American progress rested on

Christian faith. In Pennsylvania he translated the school superintendent's annual report, peppered with details about classroom Bible readings, hymns, and prayers. He and Tanaka visited a Philadelphia penitentiary with buildings designed so that inmates could hear Sunday services without leaving their cells. In New York City they toured a shelter and chapel for indigent newspaper boys, then sat with poor children listening to their daily Gospel message. In Boston they trooped to Sunday school and later called on Niijima's divinity professors at Andover. Niijima also arranged for three days at his alma mater, Amherst College, where the president frankly explained that "the only education which comes to be of any essential value, in promoting the civilization of a people, in the long-run, is that which is founded upon *morality*." A good Confucian, Tanaka knew this already. But the president made it clear that in America "public morality could not be secured without the Christian religion."[45] Niijima's favorite professor, Julius Seelye, joined in: "we pride ourselves upon the triumphs of our industry and our inventions," but "back of these and above them there is a spiritual source from which they come." That wellspring was, of course, "the true religion."[46]

Niijima kept up a tight schedule, and after several weeks Tanaka wondered where his heart stood. Watching Niijima's daily devotionals, surrounded by pious Americans, and seeing the practical effects of Christian education, he felt a little overwhelmed. He started kneeling during Niijima's morning prayers and then asked guidance reading the New Testament. "I [have] become [a] Sunday-school teacher," Niijima reported proudly. Exhausted but exhilarated, he accepted Tanaka's invitation to continue with the embassy in Europe. "I may possibly do some service for promoting Christ's kingdom in his heart, hence to Japan," he told a friend.[47]

Led Away by a False Method of Worship

After a quiet trans-Atlantic cruise, Tanaka and Niijima resumed their blistering schedule. In Britain Niijima again made arrangements, kept track of receipts, interpreted, wrote official correspondence, made introductions, interviewed educators, and organized and translated the mountain of documents they received daily. He steered interviews with leading educators, asking, "what should be the effect of education on youths, if any institutions of learning simply teach them art, science, language & philosophy and entirely neglect the religious institutions?" He added a request for a "general outline of [the] Christian religion, its necessity, influence & effect."[48] British educators happily complied, and their testimony repeated themes already well-established during the American tour.

Travels on the Continent, however, fueled Niijima's anxieties. "French infidels and German rationalists" rapidly infected the impressionable young men sent abroad for study.[49] "We have now about eighty Japanese students in Berlin," he reported, "but all of them have fallen in the habit of ridiculing Christian people without knowing what Christian truth is." Their European degrees ensured influential government careers, and Niijima feared their secularism would do "great mischief to the country."[50] One student broke from the pack, however, seeking Niijima's guidance, and together they studied the Gospel of John. "I wish you would offer [a] special prayer for that one who has just begun to study with me," he wrote friends, "that the thick unbelieving scales may fall from his eyes and he may see the gentle Saviour standing by him."[51] He also delighted at rumors that under his influence Tanaka had converted. He knew the gossip false, but he thought it planted a seed among students temporarily bedazzled by secularism. He feared, however, that the government's hostility to Christianity would doom these young men to starvation when they inevitably sought spiritual sustenance at home.

More than atheists, Niijima feared Catholics. His Andover Seminary professors passed along their reflexive anti-Catholicism, and several months touring Catholic Europe vindicated his chauvinism. "I can at once," he wrote, "discriminate the Roman Catholic people from the Protestant nations."[52] In Paris the city's opulence dazzled, but Niijima lamented people's taking "so much pain for the outward show and vain glory" while "neglecting the soul's culture." French Sabbaths particularly disturbed him. Not only did he see boys fishing and housewives hanging laundry, he was shocked that "all the drinking saloons are opened as [if] it were some week day."[53] In St. Petersburg Niijima added the Orthodox Church to his list of corrupt faiths. Although he marveled at the sensuous beauty—Raphael's portrait of the holy family arrested him, and St. Isaac's Cathedral left him breathless—he recoiled at the decadence. "I have a great sympathy with those devoted Russians," he mused after visiting a splendid Orthodox church, "for they appear very earnest in their devotion, but am sorry that they are led away by a false method of worship or a false notion of doctrine." He decided the church kept common Russians lazy and ignorant ("I never saw any cabmen reading newspapers"), and he considered it telling that Protestant Germans dominated the city's businesses.[54] His long sojourn outside Protestantism, he reported, left him longing to "breathe once more in the pious atmosphere of New England."[55]

More than simply parroting New England prejudice, Niijima used the Protestant-Catholic split to urge rethinking Japan's ban on missionaries. Catholic sins, he argued, unfairly tarred all Christians. Portuguese Catholics had tainted their early successes by lusting after political power, Niijima argued, and quite rightly the shogun expelled them all in 1614. Now again troublesome Catholics swarmed the newly opened ports, reigniting old animosities and suspicions. Yet "the teaching of God that the Portuguese taught us before is very different from the teaching people follow in Britain, Prussia, and the United States," Niijima pointed out. And, he added, "there is great mistake in the former."[56] Once the government understood that God discriminated between the Catholic and Protestant halves of his communion—and that countries Japan admired most were all Protestant— they could separate the wheat from the chaff. Niijima's anti-Catholicism sounded familiar to his American friends, but he aimed at assuaging Japan's long-held suspicions and assuring Tanaka that Protestant missionaries presented no threat.

European Protestants vindicated Niijima's trust. One Sunday in Mâcon he joined a small Protestant communion, and though he spoke no French and found the parishioners a little scruffy, he admired the pastor's earnestness and thought the congregation "rich in the inward person, though poor in their apparel."[57] In Saxony he delighted at the neat fields and trim homes ("appearing very much like some New England cottages," he could not help adding), and everywhere "men, women, children, even dogs look as if they were engaging to some work."[58] In Holland although he regretted the people were "not so devotedly religious as they used to be in the time of the Republic," he still appreciated the tidy children and their trim little schools.[59] The Scots he admired lavishly, calling them "truly the Bostonians of the British Empire."[60] While New England always remained his gold standard, Europe, too, reaffirmed that Protestant sobriety, thrift, and piety made people good and nations great. He made sure Tanaka took note.

When the embassy headed home, Tanaka invited Niijima to join his new education ministry and privately promised to dare publishing a few Christian books. Returning as Tanaka's friend, confidant, and spiritual mentor certainly seemed "to open a way to the missionaries and shade the national education with the Christian and moral principles."[61] At nearly the same time, newspapers reported Japanese government officials pulling down signboards declaring Christianity illegal. Christ's path seemed open at last. Yet Niijima decided to stay in America and finish his seminary education. He knew not to hurry. God had brought the Iwakura Embassy through modern, Protestant nations, giving all a glimpse of his providence and his instruments. Ever the samurai, Niijima decided he needed only wait until Christ again called him to "give bold and faithful service in his ever-conquering battle-field."[62] The rush of events suggested he should keep himself ever ready.

Back at Andover Niijima began assimilating all he had learned. He had seen every great European capital and visited schools, reformatories, factories, zoos, botanical gardens, universities, churches, orphanages, museums, palaces, and observatories. He understood the Western world better than nearly anyone in Japan. But this knowledge served God rather than his own vanity. In Japan graduates of secular European schools dazzled the unlearned and the untraveled, making it "very necessary for me to keep myself a little ahead of them in modern thoughts, sciences, and language, in order to be a public man religiously."[63] Working with Tanaka convinced him to make the classroom his ministry. Combining Christian devotion and modern knowledge, Niijima could model the inseparable union between faith and national progress. "I want to enlighten Japanese youths by teaching them all the subjects I have studied here, and above all, the teaching of God."[64] Indeed only a few weeks after returning home in 1874, he launched plans for a new school.

The trip also strengthened his claim on his adopted faith. A Japanese convert, he sometimes pondered his own place in the Christian communion. Touring Carlisle Castle, where Queen Elizabeth had stashed Catholic Mary in 1568, and walking the same old Edinburgh streets once trod by Covenanter martyrs, his work for Japan felt connected to a longer Protestant struggle. "I am happy in a meditation on the marvelous growth of Christianity in the world, and believe that if it finds any obstacles it will advance still faster and swifter."[65] He found a voice, too. After returning to America, he was invited to address a congregation about the Japan mission. "But I turned my subject to directly speaking to them," he wrote. Just like any Andover graduate, "I spoke to them about the grace of our Saviour and freeness of his Salvation offered to sinners."[66] And Americans listened. In stretching himself Niijima stretched others. "In him we are brought to see how truly we are one in Christ," an Andover friend marveled, "the whole family of man."[67]

The embassy tour helped Niijima find a trans-Pacific voice that pulled Japan into the broader Christian tradition, part of God's great communion. Christ did not limit his invitation "to any individuals or any nations," Niijima explained. "He offers it to all men and is ready to welcome all."[68] That meant, as he told a Japanese congregation in later years, we "are all sharers in the blessed knowledge."[69]

NOTES

I wish to thank Kojima Yumiko and Ikeuchi Kenji for their invaluable help in translating Niijima's Japanese letters, and the staff at the Doshisha University Archives, especially Fuse Tomoko, for all their assistance. Most of all I owe a lifetime of gratitude for Donald Mathews's intellectual inspiration and friendship.

1. A word about names: During the time period covered in this essay, Niijima's Japanese name was Niijima Shimeta, but in America he used the name Joseph Nee Sima. After returning to Japan in 1875, he changed his name to Niijima Jō and modified his American name to Joseph Hardy Neesima, the two names by which he is best known today. Although he used Shimeta when with other Japanese during the time period covered in this essay, he is so well known by the name Jō that to avoid confusion I use that throughout. Also in the text all Japanese names follow Japanese practice, with the family name first (Niijima) and the given name second (Jō).

Niijima is very well known in Japan, less so in the United States. As a result scholarship in Japanese is rich but sparse in English. The most easily accessible works in English are Arthur Sherburne Hardy, *Life and Letters of Joseph Hardy Neesima* (Boston: Houghton, Mifflin, 1891); Irwin Scheiner, *Christian Converts and Social Protest in Meiji*

Japan (Berkeley: University of California Press, 1970), 127–87; and John E. Van Sant, *Pacific Pioneers: Japanese Journeys to America and Hawaii, 1850–80* (Urbana: University of Illinois Press, 2000), 64–78.

2. Niijima Jō to Susan Hardy, November 7, 1871, *Niijima Jō Zenshū* [hereafter *NJZ*], 10 vols. (Kyoto: Dōhōsha, 1983–96), 6:94.

3. Niijima Jō, "Notes from Professor Park's Class," Item 905, Doshisha University Archives, Doshisha University, Kyoto, Japan.

4. Niijima Jō to Mary E. Hidden, August 21, 1871, *NJZ* 6:91.

5. Quoted in Donald Keene, *Emperor of Japan: Meiji and His World, 1852–1912* (New York: Columbia University Press, 2002), 141. For more on the Iwakura Embassy, see Hirakawa Sukehiro, "Japan's Turn to the West," in *The Cambridge History of Japan*, vol. 5, ed. Marius B. Jansen et al. (Cambridge: Cambridge University Press, 1989), 455–66; Eugene Soviak, "On the Nature of Western Progress: The Journal of the Iwakura Embassy," in *Tradition and Modernization in Japanese Culture*, ed. Donald H. Shively (Princeton, N.J.: Princeton University Press, 1971), 7–34; W. G. Beasley, *Japan Encounters the Barbarian: Japanese Travellers in America and Europe* (New Haven, Conn.: Yale University Press, 1995), 157–77; Ian Nash, ed., *The Iwakura Mission in America and Europe: A New Assessment* (Richmond, Surrey: Japan Library, 1998); Miyanagi Takashi, *Amerika no Iwakura shisetsudan* (Tokyo: Chikuma shobō, 1992).

6. "Confidential Memorandum," January 28, 1870, in U.S. Department of State, *Executive Documents Printed by Order of the House of Representatives, 1870–71* (Washington, D.C.: Government Printing Office, 1871), 474; at "Foreign Relations of the United States," University of Wisconsin Digital Collections, accessed Feburary 6, 2013, http://digital.library.wisc.edu/1711.dl/FRUS.FRUS187071.

7. Niijima Jō to Nikolai Kasatkin, May 24, 1864, *NJZ* 3:16.

8. Niijima Jō to Ephraim Flint, February 16, 1872, *NJZ* 6:95.

9. For examples see Edward E. Andrews, *Native Apostles: Black and Indian Missionaries in the British Atlantic World* (Cambridge, Mass.: Harvard University Press, 2013); Linford D. Fisher, *The Indian Great Awakening: Religion and the Shaping of Native Cultures in Early America* (New York: Oxford University Press, 2012); Tracy Neal Leavelle, *The Catholic Calumet: Colonial Conversions in French and Indian North America* (Philadelphia: University of Pennsylvania Press, 2012); Ryan Dunch, "Beyond Cultural Imperialism: Cultural Theory, Christian Missions, and Global Modernity," *History and Theory* 41 (2002): 301–25; Ryan Dunch, *Fuzhou Protestants and the Making of Modern China, 1857–1927* (New Haven, Conn.: Yale University Press, 2001), esp. 1–47; Daniel H. Bays, *A New History of Christianity in China* (Malden, Mass.: Wiley-Blackwell, 2012), 77–82.

10. Niijima Jō to Iida Itsunosuke, February 25, 1871, *NJZ* 3:88.

11. Niijima Jō to Alpheus Hardy, July 1, 1884, *NJZ* 6:231.

12. Charles Lanman, *The Japanese in America* (New York: University Publishing, 1872), 6–7.

13. Takii Kazuhiro, *The Meiji Constitution: The Japanese Experience of the West and the Shaping of the Modern State*, trans. David Noble (Tokyo: International House of Japan, 2007), 7–11.

174   GAVIN JAMES CAMPBELL

14. Lanman, *Japanese in America*, 11.

15. Kume Kunitake, *The Iwakura Embassy, 1871–1873: A True Account of the Ambassador Extraordinary and Plenipotentiary's Journey of Observation through the United States of America and Europe*, vol. 1, trans. Martin Colcutt (Princeton, N.J.: Princeton University Press, 2002), 266–67.

16. Ibid., 1:292.

17. Kido Takayoshi, *The Diary of Kido Takayoshi*, vol. 2, trans. Sidney DeVere Brown and Akiko Hirota (Tokyo: University of Tokyo Press, 1985), 183.

18. *Cleveland Morning Daily Herald*, May 18, 1872.

19. Kunitake, *Iwakura Embassy*, 1:266.

20. Ibid., 1:278, 350, 349.

21. *Milwaukee Weekly Sentinel*, March 19, 1872. See also *Washington, D.C., Evening Star*, February 29, 1872; Noah Brooks, "Awakened Japan," *Century Magazine*, April 1872, 670.

22. *Chicago Tribune*, February 27, 1872.

23. Kunitake, *Iwakura Embassy*, 1:6.

24. Kido, *Diary of Kido Takayoshi*, 2:149.

25. Ibid.

26. Lanman, *Japanese in America*, 39.

27. Kido, *Diary of Kido Takayoshi*, 2:144–45.

28. Niijima Jō to Ephraim Flint, February 16, 1872, *NJZ* 6:95.

29. Niijima Jō to Alpheus and Susan Hardy, March 8, 1872, *NJZ* 6:98.

30. The student's Japanese name was Kodama Junichiro, and he took the Christian name of John Phillip. For his tour with the embassy, see *Washington, D.C., Evening Star*, March 2, 1872. For news of his baptism, see *Washington, D.C., Daily National Republican*, April 28, 1872.

31. Niijima Jō to Alpheus and Susan Hardy, March 10, 1872, *NJZ* 6:99.

32. Yamazaki Minako, "Iwakura shisetsudan to shūkyō mondai: Amerika shimbun no bunseki wo chūshin ni," in *Meiji ishin to seiyō kokusai shakai* (Tokyo: Yoshikawa kōbunkan, 1999), 179–80.

33. "The Japanese Embassy," *New York Times*, February 20, 1872, 8; "Missionary from Japan," *Baptist Missionary Magazine*, May 1872, 175.

34. *Daily Alta Californian*, January 24, 1872.

35. *Congregationalist*, March 14, 1872, 4.

36. For more on religion and the Iwakura Embassy, see Thomas W. Burkman, "The Urakami Incidents and the Struggle for Religious Toleration in Early Meiji Japan," *Japanese Journal of Religious Studies* 1 (1974): 143–216; Abe Yoshiya, "From Prohibition to Toleration: Japanese Government Views Regarding Christianity, 1854–1873," *Japanese Journal of Religious Studies* 5 (1978): 107–38; John Breen, "Beyond the Prohibition: Christianity in Restoration Japan," in *Japan and Christianity: Impacts and Responses*, ed. John Breen and Mark Williams (New York: St. Martin's, 1996), 75–93; John Breen, "'Earnest Desires': The Iwakura Embassy and Meiji Religious Policy," *Japan Forum* 10 (1998): 151–65; Arjan van der Werf, "Deliberate Non-Communication: The Influence of the Religious Issues on the Diplomatic Talks during the Visit of the Iwakura Embassy to

Belgium," in *Turning Points in Japanese History*, ed. Bert Edström (Richmond, Surrey: Japan Library, 2002), 57–70; Yamaguchi Teruomi, *Meiji kokka to shūkyō* (Tokyo: Tokyo daigaku shuppankai, 1999); Yamazaki Minako, *Iwakura Shisetsudan ni okeru shūkyō mondai* (Kyoto: Shibunkaku Shuppan, 2006).

37. Kunitake, *Iwakura Embassy*, 1:364–67.

38. Kido, *Diary of Kido Takayoshi*, 2:118.

39. Niijima Jō to Alpheus and Susan Hardy, March 19, 1872, *NJZ* 6:103.

40. Niijima Jō to Iida Itsunosuke, February 25, 1871, *NJZ* 3:89.

41. Niijima Jō to Henry Albert Stimson, February 6, 1870, *NJZ* 6:68.

42. Niijima Jō to Alpheus and Susan Hardy, March 19, 1872, *NJZ* 6:103.

43. Ibid.

44. Ibid.

45. Mori Arinori, *Education in Japan: A Series of Letters Addressed by Prominent Americans to Arinori Mori* (New York: Appleton, 1873), 12–13. For more on the confluence of Protestantism and nineteenth-century American education, see David Sehat, *The Myth of American Religious Freedom* (New York: Oxford University Press, 2011), 155–68; R. Laurence Moore, "Bible Reading and Nonsectarian Schooling: The Failure of Religious Instruction in Nineteenth-Century Public Education," *Journal of American History* 86 (2000): 1581–99; Carl F. Kaestle, *Pillars of the Republic: Common Schools and American Society, 1780–1860* (New York: Hill & Wang, 1983), 81–82, 92–99; Robert Michaelsen, *Piety in the Public School: Trends and Issues in the Relationship between Religion and the Public Schools in the United States* (New York: Macmillan, 1970); Timothy L. Smith, "Protestant Schooling and American Nationality, 1800–1850," *Journal of American History* 53 (1967): 679–95. For Tanaka's itinerary and further details of his travels, see N.J., "Travel with Commissioner Tanaka" [diary], *NJZ* 7:49; Karasawa Tomitarō, ed., *Meiji Shoki: Kyōiku kikōsho shūsei* (Tokyo: Yūmatsudō shoten, 1982), vols. 1–2.

46. "The True Ground Work of Education," Julius Hawley Seelye Papers, Amherst College Archives and Special Collections, Amherst College Library; Mori, *Education in Japan*, 70–72.

47. Niijima Jō to Alpheus and Susan Hardy, March 22, 1872, *NJZ* 6:105.

48. Item 1155, Doshisha University Archives, Doshisha University, Kyoto, Japan.

49. Niijima Jō to Alpheus and Susan Hardy, August 10, 1872, *NJZ* 6:118.

50. Niijima Jō to Susan Hardy, October 2, 1872, *NJZ* 6:122.

51. Niijima Jō to Alpheus and Susan Hardy, January 6, 1873, *NJZ* 6:125.

52. Niijima Jō to Alpheus and Susan Hardy, July 21, 1872, *NJZ* 6:117.

53. Ibid., *NJZ* 6:116.

54. Niijima Jō to Alpheus and Susan Hardy, September 3, 1872, *NJZ* 6:118–19. See also Niijima Jō, "Travel with Commissioner Tanaka," *NJZ* 7:80, 81.

55. Niijima Jō to Alpheus and Susan Hardy, December 16, 1872, *NJZ* 6:123.

56. Niijima Jō to Iida Itsunosuke, February 25, 1871, *NJZ* 3:89.

57. Niijima Jō to Alpheus and Susan Hardy, July 21, 1872, *NJZ* 6:116.

58. Niijima Jō, "Travel with Commissioner Tanaka," *NJZ* 7:78.

59. Niijima Jō to Alpheus and Susan Hardy, September 3, 1872, *NJZ* 6:119–20.

60. Niijima Jō to Alpheus Hardy, June 8, 1872, *NJZ* 6:113.

61. Niijima Jō to Susan Hardy, October 2, 1872, *NJZ* 6:122.

62. Niijima Jō to Alpheus Hardy, August 27, 1873, *NJZ* 6:133.

63. Niijima Jō to Susan Hardy, April 6, 1873, *NJZ* 6:128.

64. Niijima Jō to Niijima Tamiharu, April 7, 1872, *NJZ* 3:101.

65. Niijima Jō to Alpheus and Susan Hardy, September 3, 1872, *NJZ* 6:120–21.

66. Niijima Jō to Mary E. Hidden, August 17, 1874, *NJZ* 6:141.

67. Mary Hidden to Susan Hardy, July 11, 1867, in Hardy, *Life and Letters*, 67.

68. Niijima Jō, "God's Love" [1874], *NJZ* 7:124.

69. Qtd. in M. William Steele and Tamiko Ichimata, eds., *Clara's Diary: An American Girl in Meiji Japan* (Tokyo: Kodansha International, 1979), 295.

Mary E. Frederickson

Psychological and Historical Perspectives on the Denial of Death

And should it be my lot to fall in this struggle. . . . I pray God to pardon my many sins, to prepare me for death, and at last to save the poor sinner, of His infinite mercy, through the imputed righteousness of the gracious Savior who died that we might live.

Lt. Charles C. Jones Jr. to Rev. and Mrs. C. C. Jones
Camp Claghorn, Saturday, November 9th, 1861

Three collections of American letters, written over the course of a hundred years by men and women, black and white, old and young, disclose the intimate connections between life, death, violence, and fear evident in the religious and moral struggles that confronted men and women in the American South from the Civil War to the civil rights movement. Seen through the lens of Ernest Becker's work on human nature and religion, the correspondence of the Rev. Dr. Charles Colcock Jones family during the 1850s and 1860s, penned as the conflict between North and South erupted into war, focused on religion and nationalism as sources of strength and permanence in a time of political and personal turmoil. Letters sent to the National Association for the Advancement of Colored People (NAACP) by African Americans in the early twentieth-century South, the virtual if not the actual descendants of the enslaved men, women, and children owned by the Jones family, expose a world of violence and fear that shaped the lives of men and women on both sides of the color line. Letters written to "Dear People at Home in the Safe, Safe North" by civil rights activists participating in the Mississippi Project during Freedom Summer 1964 express the inevitable anxiety that comes from consciously facing one's mortality.[1]

Psychiatrist Ernest Becker in his 1973 Pulitzer Prize–winning book, *The Denial of Death*, argued that individuals have to deny death every single day, even under the most ordinary circumstances, in order to go on living. Becker contends that constant awareness of our mortality, with nothing to suppress the knowledge of our vulnerability, would keep us from functioning. Religion and culture frequently perform this task for us, often by giving us access to what Becker calls an "immortality system" that makes us feel that we are invulnerable. Sacred practices, political affiliations, national allegiance, rituals, and traditions give us access to belief systems that promote as an absolute, inviolable truth, that we are enduring, invincible, and timeless, destined to immortality.[2]

The central tenet of Becker's argument turns on his belief that disastrous consequences often result from individuals and societies taking refuge in an "immortality system" that reinforces feelings of invulnerability and permanence. Ascribing absolute truth to a belief system, Becker argues, "inflates us with a sense of invulnerable righteousness." This, in turn, leads us to insist that "all other absolute truths are false." As a consequence we "attack and degrade—preferably kill—the adherents of different mortality-denying-absolute-truth systems."[3] As Becker protégé Glenn Hughes extrapolates: "Protestants kill the Catholics; the Muslims vilify the Christians and vice versa; upholders of the American way of life denounce Communists; the Communist Khmer Rouge slaughters all the intellectuals in Cambodia; the Spanish Inquisition tortures heretics; and all good students of the Enlightenment demonize religion as the source of all evil." To this seemingly endless list, we could add white enslavement and violation of blacks in the United States and the outbreak of war between the Union and the Confederacy.[4]

Those who penned the letters considered here shared a commitment to a specific cause: Christian evangelicalism, the Confederacy, the NAACP, the civil rights movement. Each group battled an outside force that threatened them with annihilation. Their reactions and language were remarkably similar, but their values were quite different, as were the causes they supported. The enemies these men and women encountered ranged from those who had not been saved as evangelical Christians, to the Union Army, the Ku Klux Klan, and the White Citizen Councils. Rationalizations for action among these correspondents range from a belief in the absolute truth of Christian salvation to a commitment to social justice so deep that it inspired selfless sacrifice.

On the Edge of the Sword

We know a great deal about the life of Rev. Dr. Charles Colcock Jones, a white southern planter, slave owner, and Presbyterian minister trained at Andover and Princeton. From a prominent family in Liberty County, Georgia, Reverend Jones was the grandson of a Revolutionary War hero and the son of a merchant and planter who died before his first birthday. Jones's mother died the year her son turned six. Left an orphan, he was cared for by his uncle Joseph Jones, his father's brother and the family patriarch. Reverend Jones professed his faith as an evangelical Christian at seventeen when a near fatal illness "proved the instrument of his spiritual awakening and he felt the ministry's call." He studied at Phillips Academy, Andover Theological Seminary, and Princeton Theological Seminary.[5]

A follower of Jonathan Edwards, Jones agonized over the morality of owning slaves while he was at Princeton, organized a "Society of Enquiry Concerning Africans," and spoke zealously in favor of Christian missionary work among the slaves of the South. As a theology student at Princeton, Jones adopted the zealous rhetoric of antislavery, writing: "It is high time that our country was taking some measures of some sort, whose ultimate tendency shall be the emancipation of nearly three millions of men, women & children, who are held in the grossest bondage, and with the highest injustice."[6] As Donald Mathews explained, Jones "knew as a young man entering his lifework that he must fight against slavery to destroy it." And then, when the time to act arrived, "he just as clearly decided not to do so." Instead Jones advocated establishing missions for the "poor degraded slaves" throughout the South.[7]

After graduating from Princeton, Jones returned home to Liberty County, Georgia, where he married his first cousin, Mary Jones, and worked to stake out a moral middle ground that combined the theological commitments he made while at Princeton with his heritage as a slave owner. He took on the mantle of southern planter, as his father before him, but he also nurtured the religiosity and spiritual lives of southern slaves, those in his own household and those enslaved by others. Jones forged a Faustian bargain that, on the one hand, provided him (and perhaps his slaves) some personal and intellectual comfort but on the other, embedded him deeply in the system of southern slavery. Jones's compromise, eloquently articulated in *The Religious Instruction of the Negroes in the United States* (1842), committed him and his family to slavery's defense, even as he diligently ministered to those he and his neighbors kept in bondage.[8] Initially Georgia's political elite saw Jones's commitment to providing religious instruction for enslaved men and women as dangerous, largely because it did not preclude teaching slaves to read. But gradually the ground on which Jones stood, both politically and theologically, bolstered the rationale for proslavery paternalism in the 1840s and 1850s. Jones found himself, as Erskine Clarke has argued, "no longer a pioneer in a suspect enterprise but the respected leader of a cause that had been adopted by the South's . . . most influential establishment."[9]

Charles and Mary Jones had conducted their courtship primarily through the mail. Long letters passed in both directions between Liberty County and Princeton as the two sorted out their ideas, beliefs, and deep affection. Once settled in Georgia, they created an unusually close and devoted family constellation with their three children at the center: Charles Colcock Jones Jr., lawyer, historian, and archeologist; Joseph Jones, a physician who settled in Louisiana after the Civil War; and Mary Sharpe Jones Mallard, who moved to Atlanta with her husband during the war and later to New Orleans. Reverend Jones, Mary Jones, and their children remained in close contact through letters that flew back and forth between the three plantations owned by the family in Liberty County and from one relative to the next in Savannah, Columbia, Atlanta, New Orleans, Philadelphia, and Cambridge, Massachusetts.[10]

Wealthy, successful, influential, and prominent, the extended Jones family of Liberty County built their fortune over four generations with the enforced labor, skill, and knowledge of several hundred slaves. Jones family members, and those men, women, and children enslaved by them, lived in a world determined by kinship, shaped by Protestant Christianity, and defined by slavery. Reverend Jones and his family regularly bought and sold slaves, discussing the specifics of these sales, along with those of their livestock and crops, in more than a thousand letters, most of which were carefully preserved by Mary Jones. Reverend Jones ostensibly made an effort not to separate enslaved families and to sell slaves only to people reputed to adhere to the same policy. This commitment did not always hold. Slaves were sometimes sold as punishment for bad behavior, and financial considerations consistently trumped emotional concerns in transactions where human lives and family relationships hung in the balance.[11]

For everyone in the antebellum world of Liberty County, enslaved or free, the fragility of life was a constant. "Disease is ever-present and often frightful, and death is a daily visitor," Myers wrote in the preface to *Children of Pride*. He puzzled over the Jones family's "fascination for lingering illnesses and protracted deathbed scenes," noting this "as excessive, if not bizarre." Bizarre to a late twentieth-century reader, perhaps, but this part of the historical record strikes to the heart of the matter in terms of Becker's analysis in *The Denial of Death*. The effect of so many frequent deaths and near-death experiences bound most in the Jones family to an immortality system that assuaged the effects of the finality of death with promises of ultimate meaning and absolute inviolate truth. One measure of the meaning attached to the importance of Christian evangelicalism as an immortality system can be taken in the time family members devoted to lingering illnesses and deathbed scenes. They lingered, both literally and figuratively, because the moment of passing, for one who had achieved salvation by accepting Jesus Christ as his or her savior, provided affirmation of eternal life. They lingered, too, because of the unbearable pain of mothers dying in childbirth, children succumbing to scarlet fever, typhoid, and measles, and the brutality of fatal accidents that happened with tremendous frequency.[12]

Members of the Jones family knew only too well how quickly the lives of loved ones could come to an end. Six months after the first shots at Fort Sumter, South Carolina, marked the beginning of the Civil War, Charles Colcock Jones's four-year-old daughter, Julia, died of scarlet fever. His wife, Ruth, who had just given birth to a second daughter, died a few days later. Jones sank into a deep depression. Several weeks later, writing to his mother, Mary, who had helped nurse his wife and daughter in their last days, he asked to defer a visit, confiding: "My heart continues very heavy." "Time," he wrote, "heals not at all the deep wounds which sorrow and desolation have made." Anxious and concerned about their son's state of mind in the face of such tragic loss, the Reverend Charles and Mary Jones focused in on their son Charles's perennial refusal to accept Jesus as his personal savior. Reverend Jones used every weapon in his arsenal of Christian faith to persuade his son, now almost thirty years old, to finally give his life to Jesus Christ before it was too late.[13]

Three months after the deaths of his son's wife and daughter, Reverend Jones wrote a harsh letter to Charles reminding him that his beloveds were now covered by the shadows of death, their flesh perishing, their spirits gone to God, their happiness complete because they were with the Lord. Reverend Jones warned his son, "You speak of your hope of reunion with them. . . . but unless you have a real interest in the merits and intercession of the Lord Jesus Christ, such as your dear wife had, you will never meet her in heaven, and your own immortal soul will be eternally lost!" Make use of your deep sorrow, Jones told his son; "nothing short of this can satisfy me." Determined to convince his son to accept Christ as his "only and all-sufficient Redeemer," Jones drove his point home by reconstructing the deathbed scene when Charles's wife, "Dear Ruthie in her dying hours," told her husband "to seek the Lord and seek Him now." She has been gone three months, "lost to your arms in her silent grave," wrote Jones, "and you have not, so far as we know, done it yet!" What would you do, the father continued, if "those tender eyes could once more open upon you, and those dumb lips speak and ask you, '*Why, why* have you not done, my husband, what I begged you to do?' you would be speechless!" In relentless pursuit of his son's soul, Jones persevered: "I cannot but feel that God is dealing very closely with you, my dear son, and am exceedingly anxious that you make your peace with Him, and do it now. Do not postpone so important a matter. He has broken up your precious family by a direct personal affliction; and now your home is to be broken up by a general judgment of a cruel war upon the country. . . . Who knows the issue of war? Do not come out of that home but under the protection and leadership of the Great Captain of our Salvation. And come what will, you will be safe, and saved in Him."[14]

Charles Jr. responded to his father's invective four days later in a letter than reveals the thoughts of a man with nothing left to lose. "I am trying to be a better man," he wrote back. "I would not have you believe that I am trifling with God's dealings with me. . . . I am acting not in my own strength . . . and my daily sins, great and numerous, remind me ever that all human righteousness is but vanity." In repeatedly refusing to take Christ as his savior, Charles had stood up to his father throughout his childhood, adolescence, and young adulthood. A deeply respectful and unusually obedient and affectionate son, he had drawn the boundary between his father and himself at the point of conversion. This line defined his identity in relation to his father, and he would not violate it.[15]

In the depths of his despair and grief, Charles finally addressed his father's relentless order to "seek ye the Lord while he may be found." After the devastating loss of his wife and child, he embraced salvation on his own terms, writing to his father that he knew that hope could only be found "in the free, full, imputed righteousness of the infinitely merciful and all-sufficient Savior, who died to accomplish the salvation of sinners condemned and dying under the law." There will be "no salvation elsewhere," Charles wrote, "nor do I desire that there should be any." He explained that he could only embrace salvation that came "from a sense of sin pardoned and peace made with God." Anything else, he wrote his father, "is valueless." Less than a month after this exchange, Charles declined reelection as mayor of Savannah and also an appointment to the state legislature, in order to serve as senior first lieutenant and chief of the Chatham Artillery. He closed his house in Savannah, emptying the rooms in which he had watched "the triumphant departure of my dearly beloved wife from time into a happy eternity," and left for Camp Claghorn, nine miles from Savannah, on the Isle of Hope.[16]

Wracked with grief and despair, Charles turned from the immortality system that had served his father's needs to one of his own choosing. He fused his need to be sacrificed to the nation's call for service. Seeing himself as "condemned and dying" under the law of God, Charles Colcock Jones Jr. believed that salvation would come only through the "all sufficient Savior," not by joining the church but by actually becoming a heroic Christ figure. Charles planned to put himself on the cross of the Confederacy, to repeat the act of crucifixion. His sacrifice of himself in this way surpassed even his father's expectations. More important he sought forgiveness for the unspoken sins he had committed in not protecting his wife and daughter from God's wrath, a vengeance wrought on him no doubt because of his sinful nature as a man and, perhaps on a more unconscious level, for his transgressions as a slaveholder. "I am of all men most weak," Charles wrote, "My daily sins, great and numerous, remind me ever that all human righteousness is but vanity."[17]

As he left for Hope Island and what he later described as "long and bloody months, fraught with dangers and privations" with the Chatham Artillery, he knew he had a reasonable chance of dying. As Charles became Lt. Colcock Jones Jr., he wrote to his parents: "I will die in the legitimate discharge of the most solemn duty which ever devolves upon a free citizen—the obligation resting upon him to make every sacrifice in support of national honor." He saw himself protecting his homeland from "the infamous pollution of a lawless and inhuman enemy," an enemy that ironically and tragically included those New Englanders his father had once admired, as well as his own classmates at Princeton and Harvard. This was his time on the cross, sacrificing himself so that others might be saved. It was too late to protect and preserve his wife and daughter, but in discharging his legitimate and honorable duty, he thought he could save his nation's honor and in the process redeem his own.[18]

Reverend Jones and his wife, Mary, had long been urging their eldest son to succumb to God, to choose Jesus Christ as his savior, and to join the church. Charles wrote to his father and mother from Camp Claghorn on the night of what would have been his third wedding anniversary: "I pray to God to pardon my many sins, to prepare me for death, and at last to save the poor sinner, of His infinite mercy, through the imputed righteousness of the gracious Savior who died that we might live." While not the conversion they had sought, they accepted their son's heartfelt words, knowing that he had at last seriously considered the possibility of his mortality and made his own peace with God.[19]

Serving in the military, fighting with his beloved Chatham Artillery, Charles did not die a hero's death but expiated his sins enough to live with himself. He married for the second time late in 1863, raised two children, worked in New York City for a decade, and then settled permanently in Augusta, Georgia. Obsessed with death and honor, Charles Colcock Jones Jr., whose father and mother died in 1863 and 1869, spent the rest of his life trying to become a better man. Born again after his time on the cross, he practiced law and pursued a career as a prolific historian, passing judgment on events long past and honoring the lives of the Confederacy's dead heroes. *Honor, good, man,* and *death,* the four words repeated most frequently in his fourteen books and twenty-two articles, became the precepts that bound his life as he watched the world of Liberty County that he had known and loved disintegrate before his eyes.[20]

The Jones family story, as Erskine Clarke has suggested, "is marked by the bitter irony of good intensions gone astray and of benevolent impulses becoming ideological supports for deep oppression."[21] In the last three decades of his life, until his death in 1893, Charles Jones watched with detached passivity as the plantations his family had owned returned to their natural state. Abandoned homes and outbuildings collapsed into ruins. Fields cleared and worked for more than a century by men and women held in chattel slavery rapidly became overgrown with thick forests. As white southerners left the area in the years that followed the Civil War, formerly enslaved men and women continued to work the land, while men like Jones visited their plantations only once or twice a year, had no taste for supervising free labor, and did it poorly. Former slaves who would have become closely supervised sharecroppers in other parts of the South became, in fact, tenant farmers who were eventually given the option to buy acreage of their own. As Peggy Hargis has argued, a complex system of patronage developed as control of the land shifted to the black majority society that remained intact in Liberty County.[22]

When Sherman's cavalry marched through Georgia in December 1864, Brigadier General Kilpatrick established his headquarters at the venerable Midway

Church, where the Jones family had worshipped since the eighteenth century. Union troops foraged in Liberty County for six weeks, stripping the property of whites and blacks alike, during the most extensive raids of the entire campaign. By the time the war ended, most of the white members of the Midway Church attended "daughter-churches" that had been established in the nearby communities of Walthourville, Flemington, Jonesville, and Dorchester. Led by William A. Golding, the son of a slave who had been a local Congregational minister, the freedmen and freedwomen of Liberty County continued to worship at Midway Church, where at Reverend Jones's behest, many had long attended services, sitting in balcony seats designated for slaves. In less than a decade, the African American congregation was estimated at six hundred members. Encouraged by this growth, Golding donated land, called "Golding's Grove," for a new Congregational congregation and contacted the American Missionary Association (AMA) in 1870, asking them to send a teacher into the community. The AMA established the first black school in Liberty County the following year; by 1875, 164 students attended, and more had been turned away. In 1879 a new building and a new name, Dorchester Academy, reflected the institution's growing reputation as a "seat of learning" in coastal Georgia. By 1917 eight buildings, 105 acres, 13 teachers and 500 students, along with the "New" Midway Church, graced "Golding Grove."[23] Out of the travail of slavery had come a New Jerusalem.[24]

Living in This Land of Bigotry

Erskine Clarke's *Dwelling Place*, the epic history of the plantation South set in Liberty County, ends in 1869, "when the entire region appeared strangely and, for the blacks, wonderfully changed." Reconstruction aimed to dismantle the old order, at least theoretically, and change the lives of those who had been enslaved. Black southerners themselves actively claimed freedom, shaped new lives, participated in politics, negotiated wages, established churches, and built schools. Meanwhile white southerners, viewing African American economic and political advancement in light of their own financial ruin, sought to reassert their own dominance in the wake of Reconstruction.[25]

The post–Civil War South, a world of paradox, trepidation, and tremendous hope, was one that Charles Colcock Jones Jr., deeply immersed in studying the past, spent the rest of his life avoiding. He had few benevolent impulses toward the freedmen and freedwomen of the New South; but neither did he resort to violence as a son of the Confederacy who had expected to inherit great wealth.[26] A quiet member of what came to be called the Lost Generation, Jones's retreat to passivity obliquely fostered oppression as many white southerners unleashed their resentment at losing their way of life by turning their rage toward newly freed African American men and women. Reactionary white forces undercut black freedom with the terror of extralegal violence and minimized social and political change by instituting a crop-lien system built on restraining labor, not by bondage, but through indenture and debt.

Ernest Becker's work on the denial of death turns our attention to the anger and aggression that frequently follows an individual's confrontation of his or her own mortality. In the wake of the Civil War and Reconstruction, white southerners who had fought collectively to maintain the Confederacy used aggression as a way to deal with the seeming loss of their own racial superiority and the privileges that emanated from being white. An era of white rage and terror wreaked havoc across the South. Black men and women lost their lives and livelihoods. Lynchings terrorized the free black population. Mobs attacked African American churches, schools, and businesses. The greater black achievement and prosperity, the more virulent the assaults.

The Compromise of 1877 sanctioned the circumvention of the thirteenth, fourteenth, and fifteenth amendments. The White House was delivered to the Republicans in a cynical deal that hinged on returning federal troops to their barracks, removing them as an enforcement factor in the South.[27] The dream of citizenship for all became a nightmare of divided citizenry fragmented by race, ethnicity, and gender. When Reconstruction ended, a wave of newly written laws slowly constricted the lives of African Americans. Restrictions on voting disfranchised blacks; miscegenation laws prohibited racial intermarriage. In 1887 Florida adopted the first "Jim Crow" law applied to railroads. Between 1888 and 1900, ten southern states, including Louisiana, passed similar legislation. One after another newly acquired rights vanished: voting, the right to hold public office, the right of access to public transportation, public schools, and housing. At the same time, a complicated set of legal restrictions and unwritten racial codes developed throughout the South as well as in towns and cities of the Northeast, Midwest, and West. Locally determined, these laws varied from place to place, shifted constantly, and were often improvised and retrofitted in ways that kept black citizens constantly off balance and on edge. Actions acceptable in one location, or at one point in time, could bring serious or even fatal consequences in another place or moment. For example in North Carolina an 1899 statute mandated separate accommodations for white and black passengers on railroads and steamboats but not streetcars. In Alabama blacks and whites could not play pool together; in Georgia blacks and whites could not drink beer or wine in the same room. In Virginia and Tennessee blacks and whites could play pool and drink in shared spaces without breaking the law.[28]

Between 1866 and 1923, thirty major episodes of collective violence occurred across the South, along with an untold number of more isolated incidents. No southern state was spared, as cities from Memphis to New Orleans, from Pulaski, Tennessee, to Yazoo City, Mississippi, and from Wilmington, North Carolina, to Tulsa, Oklahoma, faced terrifying outbreaks of violence against black citizens. The violence unleashed in Atlanta in 1906 foreshadowed the spread of racial bloodshed north beginning in 1908 in Abraham Lincoln's hometown of Springfield and then on to East St. Louis, Illinois. A decade later "a reign of terror" against African Americans racked the nation. Between 1917 and 1923, racial violence raged in Chicago; Omaha, Nebraska; Duluth, Minnesota; and Washington, D.C. Labor strife between white and black workers sparked deadly massacres in Charleston, South Carolina; Longview, Texas; Knoxville, Tennessee; and Elaine, Arkansas.[29]

The Atlanta riot changed W. E. B. Du Bois, then a professor at Atlanta University, in fundamental ways, and a short while later, he left Atlanta and academia. Together with his family, he moved to New York City, where he helped establish the National Association for the Advancement of Colored People (NAACP). Over the years that followed, the NAACP looked South with the goal of securing the rights guaranteed in the Thirteenth, Fourteenth, and Fifteenth Amendments and a commitment to obtaining equal political, social, and economic rights for African Americans. The organization fought racial discrimination and hatred throughout the United States with every weapon they could muster. The NAACP sent field officers to investigate cases throughout the South and founded local chapters across the region, often under the guise of innocuous-sounding organizations such as the "Helping Hand Club." These grassroots groups, often operating undercover and in secrecy and always considered subversive, became the eyes and ears of the national organization. NAACP members throughout the South called for the investigation of hundreds of incidents of racial discrimination, intimidation, and violence reported to the organization in letters written from across the region.[30]

Letters written to the NAACP during these years report threats targeting African Americans, call for investigations, and document lynchings. J. L. Le Flore of Mobile, Alabama, wrote to NAACP headquarters in New York City responding to a request that he help reorganize a NAACP branch in Mobile: "Living in this land of bigotry, where men are judged by the color of their skins and not by merits, where might makes right, where mobocracy dominates and a howling, fiendish mob filled with a lust for human blood may attack any man of color who believes in the equality of all men, I can fully appreciate what the NAACP means to the Negro. And you may rest assured that I shall do my best to see that it becomes active in Mobile, Alabama once again."[31]

One letter reported on a white farmer in Frankfort, Kentucky, who brought an African American boy home and held him in servitude. Another letter came from Durham, North Carolina, where John Flowers had been arrested and shot for not selling sixty-five acres of his land to a white farmer. The Birmingham NAACP chapter reported that "a very fair Negro, as white as any white man so far as color goes, a few days ago was approached by a representative of the K.K.K. who said, 'say fellow you ought to join the Klan.'" The Klansman assured the man that he should not "hesitate to join," because "the first thing we are going to do is . . . get the Capitalist, second, we are going to get the Jew, then third we are going to run every D_____ Nigger in the ocean." NAACP Birmingham chapter president Charles A. McPhillips concluded his letter, "Tension is very high. The police department usually do our lynching for us."[32]

Materials sent to the NAACP national office from Fairfield, Alabama, in 1921 documented that a mob had severely beaten Collins Maddox, an employee of the Tennessee Coal, Iron and Railroad Company. Signed by twenty of "the best citizens among the Negro citizens of Fairfield," Maddox's testimony provided the details of how four men came to his house on the night of April 26: "They forced me to leave home with them and told me that I had to go and sign a peace bond with Mr. Smitherman and take that case out of court. . . . they handcuffed me and drove toward Fairfield for three blocks. Here, they met another big car carrying six other men who wore black covers over their faces. They drove toward the woods and stopped near Oakland cemetery."

At that point, Maddox continues, "they got out of the cars and went to a large tree, placed a rope around my neck." He felt the rope tighten as the men began "to pull my body up from the earth." Then Maddox heard a voice in the crowd beg "that they not lynch me." "Beat hell out of him," the voice insisted. The mob obeyed, tying Maddox to the tree and beating him, as he wrote, "until I was crazy. I was beaten by those men until there was scarcely any feeling left in my body. . . . I was told to remain standing where I was for twenty minutes, that if I moved from there inside of twenty minutes, I would be killed dead in my tracks. . . . After gaining enough strength to leave that place, I wondered about in the woods and darkness until I found my way to the road and finally got back home."

His back raw from the beating, Maddox went into hiding. "I need the protection of good people, who stand for the right," he wrote the NAACP. Maddox concluded his statement: "I have done nothing wrong and feel that somebody needs to help me get the facts before this country." Maddox's testimony, together with statements from "the best citizens among the Negro population of Fairfield," was sent to the NAACP office in New York City. Signed by twenty-two men, the final document read, "We are law abiding and good people out here." The cost of action was high, as reflected in the final line: "Even now we move about this place under threats of death and punishment if we dare to put this matter properly to the public."[33]

Collins Maddox's narrow escape turned on the words "beat hell out of him" spoken by an unknown member of the mob. Most victims waited in vain for that kind of saving grace, as Walter White found when he traveled to Quitman, Georgia, in 1918 to investigate the lynching of six men. As the investigation proceeded, White wrote back to the New York office: "I secured the names of eight who were killed together with the three persons who were found in the river unidentified."

In addition, he continued, "there have been a number of mysterious disappearances which would undoubtedly be classed as lynching." White also obtained the names of two "ringleaders" and fifteen members of "the Mob"—all, he wrote, "prominent Citizens of Quitman."[34]

Spectacles of horror that terrified and mesmerized men and women across the United States in the late nineteenth and early twentieth centuries, lynching incidents embodied the disastrous consequences that Ernest Becker argued often result when individuals and societies ascribe absolute truth to a belief system. The violence and aggression inherent in lynching emanates from the sense of righteousness and invulnerability that fuels the perpetrators' anger and rage, leading them to "attack and degrade—preferably kill" those they see as violating their system of absolute truth.[35] By killing the other, perpetrators can deny their own mortality. In killing a perceived enemy, you get as close to death as possible, without dying yourself. You forestall your own demise.

Many have argued that lynching is a religious ritual that reenacts the crucifixion of Jesus. Countee Cullen published "The Black Christ," an emotionally taut 963-line epic poem, in 1929. Cullen's words of condemnation and shame reverberated from Harlem to the New South capital of Atlanta: "'Lynch him! Lynch him!' O savage cry / Why should you echo, 'Crucify!'" Cullen was not the first to connect lynching to the crucifixion, and he certainly would not be the last. W. E. B. Du Bois had directly related the crucifixion and lynching in "The Prayers of God," published in *Darkwater: Voices from within the Veil* in 1920. Contemporary scholars such as Fitzhugh Brundage, Donald Mathews, Orlando Patterson, and Amy Wood have continued to examine the historical and theological implications of lynching and the analogies between lynching and the crucifixion. In purported reenactments of the crucifixion, members of the lynch mob project their sins onto the victim and then take his (or in rare cases her) life. In the unconscious minds of the perpetrators, the fact that the Christ-figure is black engenders additional fury, anger, and brutal violence. The victim in the lynching spectacle has to sacrifice his life, so that others can remain alive and free. The black other dies, so those perpetrating the lynching can be saved. "This one is dying for me," the thought process goes, "so that I will not die." In this way lynching becomes a ritual act of sacrifice, cleansing, and immortality, an act constructed as an essential requirement, a social imperative. Theologian James Cone has extended this reading, arguing that "the cross and the lynching tree interpret each other. Both were public spectacles, usually reserved for hardened criminals, rebellious slaves, and rebels against the Roman state and falsely accused militant blacks who were often called 'black beasts' and 'monsters in human form' for their audacity to challenge white supremacy in America. Any genuine theology and any genuine preaching must be measured against the test of the scandal of the cross and the lynching tree."[36]

The juxtaposition of Becker's "denial of death" and Cone's "lynching tree" provides historians with a theoretical framework for analyzing the 4,742 lynchings that took place in the sixty-three years between 1882 and 1945. But where does that really leave us? Becker argues that people can avoid the anxiety of facing their own mortality "when they can trustingly live their heroism in some kind of self-transcending drama."[37] He contends that for much of history people sought a "God-ideology that would make sense out of [their] unworthiness and would translate it into heroism." With so many documented lynchings—each one unique; each one the same—we can see how the members of a lynch mob could twist their minds, individually and collectively, to see themselves as heroes in a self-transcending drama. We have also seen how many members of the Jones family used evangelical Christianity to seek forgiveness for their sins and obtain a form of salvation that sustained them as they coped with death "as a daily visitor." As unusually liberal southern Christians, they sought salvation not only for themselves but also for the enslaved men and women who planted their crops and nursed their children. The immortality system that soothed the Joneses' anxiety about death also upheld, reformed, and prolonged the system by which they bought and sold human beings and built a fortune on the backs of men and women they held as property.

Cone argues that "the cross and the lynching tree need each other" because "the lynching tree can liberate the cross from the false pieties of well-meaning Christians"—well-meaning Christians who, like Reverend Jones, used evangelical Christianity as an immortality system that established an inviolate set of beliefs that could not be challenged or used to illuminate the true meaning of the cross in the context of the southern slave system. Becker argues that at some point "psychology has to give way to 'theology'"—meaning that individuals by their very nature seek a worldview that offers the chance of some kind of "heroic apotheosis." Men and women, Becker acknowledges, need to believe in something larger, something that offers a higher level of meaningfulness.[38]

The yielding of Becker, the psychiatrist, to Cone, the theologian, brings us to Cone's interpretation of Reinhold Niebuhr's definition of Christianity as a faith that "takes us through tragedy to beyond tragedy, by way of the cross to victory in the cross." But, asks Cone, "What kind of salvation is that?" He argues that it requires "a powerful religious imagination to see redemption in the cross, to discover life in death and hope in tragedy." A powerful religious imagination, yes, but to find "life in death and hope in tragedy" also necessitates a deep understanding of history. In the United States, to understand the meaning of the cross, Cone contends that "we need to take a good long look at the lynching tree in this nation's history." We have to uncover the meaning of Billie Holiday's "strange fruit" and know the significance of the "blood on the leaves and blood at the root." Cone and Becker would agree that without acknowledging that "the lynched black victim experienced the same fate as the crucified Christ," Christianity will remain a meaningless immortality system that perpetuates a dangerous sense of inviolate righteousness. Psychology, theology, and history converge at the large tree where the mob took Collins Maddox and, in his words, "placed a rope around my neck and was about to pull my body up from the earth."[39]

One year after Maddox wrote his testimony and sent it to the NAACP, a mob of fifty white men lynched African Americans Joe Jordan and James Harvey in Liberty County, Georgia, not far from the Midway Church. There had not been a lynching in coastal Georgia for more than two decades, not since eleven Georgia lynchings in quick succession in 1899 drew national attention and became the focus of Ida Wells-Barnett's *Lynch Law in Georgia: A Six-Weeks' Record in the Center of Southern Civilization.*[40] The men responsible for these murders came from outside the county, and numerous local witnesses, black and white, stepped forward to testify when the Savannah NAACP, with legal help from the Commission on Interracial Cooperation in Atlanta, launched an investigation. The *New York Times* reported that "the people of Liberty County were incensed and at once began making efforts to run down the lynchers." Rev. P. T. Holloway, of the Midway Methodist Church, clearly cognizant of the connection between the cross and the lynching tree, used his Sunday sermon to decry publically the "incompetence and disingenuousness" of the authorities from neighboring Wayne County who were transporting Jordan and Harvey when they were seized by the mob. The quick action of local citizens and the NAACP's investigation, along with Holloway's sermon and his publication of a widely circulated letter denouncing the lynching, resulted in the unprecedented indictment of twenty-two members of the mob and the conviction of four white men on murder charges.[41]

The response of local citizens to the violence of lynching in Liberty County in 1922 came out of a shared history that stretched back to the mid-eighteenth century. A strong sense of identity shaped by longevity and endurance gave blacks and whites in that community the courage to speak their minds collectively. Through slavery, war, and four decades of hard-won freedom, the county's large black population had passed from the days of Reverend Jones's religious instruction meetings for slaves to the American Missionary Association's support of Dorchester Academy in Golding's Grove. Land ownership, literacy rates, school attendance, and church membership across the county surpassed those in other parts of the state.[42] In the 1930s academy alumni put the lessons they had learned about teamwork, cooperation, and community action into practice when they established the Dorchester Cooperative Center. A cooperative store, consumer's cooperative, chicken cooperative, and a producer's cooperative served those who lived in a nine-mile radius of Dorchester Academy. In 1939 the Dorchester Federal Credit Union opened, and in the 1940s, after the first public high school for black children in Liberty County was built, a remodeled boys' dormitory became the Liberty County Hospital Authority for Colored People, a clinic for area residents.[43]

The influence of Liberty County's long emphasis on religion, community, and education continued to spread during the years after World War II when the Dorchester Cooperative Center helped train African American voters and involve local citizens in politics. In 1952 community leaders organized a local branch of the NAACP. In 1961 the Dorchester Cooperative Center began to draw national attention when the Southern Christian Leadership Conference and the American Missionary Association together established leadership training programs and citizenship schools in Dorchester Academy buildings that had opened in 1879. Grassroots leaders from across the South came to Golding's Grove, a stone's throw from the old Midway Church where generations of Jones family members and their slaves had worshipped, to train as organizers for literacy schools and voter registration drives throughout the region. SCLC educational director Dorothy Cotton, teacher training supervisor Septima Clark, and citizenship program administrator Andrew Young set up headquarters in the Dorchester Cooperative Center. In 1962 Martin Luther King, Ralph Abernathy, and Wyatt Walker stayed in the academy's Elizabeth B. Moore Hall while they planned the Birmingham Campaign.[44]

Becker's concept of the denial of death became an important factor for local citizens, grassroots organizers, and regional and national leaders as the civil rights movement gained momentum. The dangerous work of reestablishing the citizenship and voting rights denied black citizens in the segregated South since the end of Reconstruction involved a willingness to put one's life on the line for social justice. As King and his staff filled the classrooms of the old Dorchester Academy in Liberty County, groups of students across the United States began to respond to the movement's call to head south to set up schools and run voter registration campaigns in Mississippi, the most segregated state in the union, during Freedom Summer 1964. The young people who answered this call came face to face with their own mortality in ways that changed their lives, and the lives of those who loved them, forever.[45]

Violence Hangs Overhead like Dead Air

The collection of letters to "Dear People at Home in the Safe, Safe North" were written by civil rights activists who came south to Mississippi during Freedom Summer 1964. This correspondence includes detailed descriptions of freedom schools and voter registration drives, as well as reflections on the courage and dedication of local activists who welcomed students into their homes. These letters also contain tragic stories of violence and sudden death, unexpected and disastrous scenarios that record the experiences of those who came to Oxford, Ohio, for training sessions run by the Congress of Racial Equality (CORE) and the Student Nonviolent Coordinating Committee (SNCC) and then headed to Mississippi in June 1964. References to the denial of death, juxtaposed with comments about everyday life, permeate these personal reports. The mundane became sacred in Mississippi that summer. The ordinary dissipated fear. The everyday became a tangible representation of the continuity of life in the face of death.

The students who headed south in 1964 had come of age in a post-Freudian culture increasingly inclined to acknowledge feelings and fears. Many had been religiously motivated to join the movement, not by belief in an immortality system like the one affirmed by most members of the Jones family, nor by a sense of sacred orthodoxy. Rather the values of these young students, whether overtly religious or intellectually secular, had been shaped by a Judeo-Christian belief system that emphasized social justice and good works; deeds performed, not words spoken. Christian students participating in Freedom Summer, like Casey Cason, active in the YWCA at the University of Texas, and Rick Momeyer of Allegheny College, came from mainstream Protestant denominations—Episcopal, Presbyterian, Methodist, and Lutheran—that had endorsed the Social Gospel, a progressive movement within the churches that worked to establish a Kingdom of God on earth with social justice for all. The Social Gospel movement in the United States, a response to rapid industrialization and urbanization, began in the late nineteenth century and continued throughout the twentieth century. In 1907 Walter Rauschenbusch, an influential Baptist minister in New York City, issued the movement's clarion call when he proclaimed the need for "a democratic cooperative society to be achieved by nonviolent means."[46] The Social Gospel tradition helped shape each of the major twentieth-century initiatives for reform: social welfare, trade unionism, socialism, and civil rights.

Among the many Jewish students who participated in Freedom Summer, most, like young Barney Frank from Harvard and Andy Goodman from Queens College in New York, had been raised by parents who identified culturally as Jewish, not by adhering to a strict religious practice but by retaining a sense of *tikkun olam* that informed their politics. Often translated as "mending the world" and interpreted to mean repairing the shards of a broken world, *tikkun olam* is viewed as a Jewish inheritance, "a mandate to Jews to make the world in which we live a better place." Three ideas converge in the Talmudic and biblical meaning of *tikkun olam:* the first involves the distress of the community and an extrapolation from a particular person being imprisoned to concern about the future of the entire community; the second focuses on the relationship between present and future and an understanding that actions in the present affect the world in the future; the third emphasizes the power of the law to correct systemic injustice.[47]

Regardless of religious identity, the students who signed up to go south in 1964 had all been deeply affected by World War II. Many of the Jewish students had grandparents, aunts, uncles, and cousins who had been victims of the Holocaust. Numbers of these volunteers came from families that had sent fathers, brothers, and sons to fight against Nazi totalitarianism. Some of their relatives had been involved in liberating concentration camps in Germany or Eastern Europe. Every one of these students had grown up in the wake of the atomic explosions at Hiroshima and Nagasaki. They spent their childhood years with the anxiety of nuclear annihilation as the Cold War between the United States and the Soviet Union dominated American politics and culture.[48]

Students from outside the South brought these perspectives with them as they came into the movement. They focused on their own understanding of social justice as they opened their eyes to the suffering of others. The existential gave way to nonviolent action: "I lose patience with people who sit and ponder their belly buttons," wrote one young woman.[49] "It was a time when nobody stopped to wonder, 'What is the meaning of my life?'" wrote another student.[50] Death proved hard to deny even in Oxford, Ohio, after word came that three young men, Michael Schwerner, Andy Goodman, and James Chaney, who had left the training site on the campus of the Western College for Women a few days earlier, had disappeared in Philadelphia, Mississippi. "I felt so bad," wrote one student, I was about ready to forget about going to Mississippi at all. But I still wanted to go; I just didn't feel like giving up my life."[51] Caught in the contradiction between action and the threat of death, students confronted their fears: "June 26 . . . Must write—thoughts are going crazy. Bob Moses just told us now is the time to back out. Should I? I don't know—I am scared shitless. I don't want to go to Mississippi. . . . Tomorrow I am leaving."[52]

Six hundred fifty students attended the training sessions run by SNCC and CORE. More than a thousand volunteers came into Mississippi during the summer of 1964. Students wrote home to explain the training: "A great deal of tension and a great deal of camaraderie here at Oxford." And another student drew the line between North and South this way:

June 17
Dear People at Home in the Safe, Safe North,
Mississippi is going to be hell this summer. Monday, Jim Forman, executive secretary of SNCC, stood up during one of the general sessions and calmly told the staff . . . and the volunteers that they could all be expected to be arrested, jailed, and beaten this summer, and, in many cases, shot at. There is a quiet Negro fellow on the staff who has an ugly scar on his neck and another on his shoulder where he stopped .45 slugs. . . . Another fellow told this morning how his father and later his brother had been shot to death. . . . I'd venture to say that every member of the Mississippi staff has been beaten up at least once and he who has not been shot at is rare. It is impossible for you

to imagine what we are going in to, as it is for me now, but I am beginning to see.[53]

Students who signed on to participate in SNCC's Summer Voting Rights Project in 1964 spent time writing home, describing in detail their experiences for friends and family, for the same reason the family of Reverend Jones in Liberty County communicated so often. Students wanted their parents, friends, and family with them. They wrote to bring them closer. What they chose to write about tells us a lot:

> Dear Mom and Dad,
> A lot of kids are trying to be real casual and cool and funny about everything so they don't worry their folks. This seems silly to me—especially with you—because you're in this with us in the sense that unlike a lot of parents—you realize the significance of this summer as much as I do . . .
> Love, Barbara[54]

They wrote because when terror strikes, we look to our most beloved—parents, spouses, siblings, children—to assuage our anxiety and give us the strength and affirmation we need to go on. An August 24 letter from "Dave" relates to his parents in excruciating detail what happened the Saturday afternoon several young freedom workers went swimming at a farm outside of Laurel, Mississippi. Gathered at the lake's edge, singing and playing guitar, they suddenly saw fifteen white men emerge from the woods. One man approached, kicked the guitar out of Dave's hands, and threw it in the lake. The other men, ranging in age from twenty-two to fifty-five, began beating Dave with a wooden club. As he put it, "so, since I was born for the water, home I went . . . 15–25 feet out, he pulled a pistol from beneath his shirt and began firing . . . . ten or twelve of the other men began shooting with pistols, rifles and shotguns . . . bullets began hitting the water, not five feet from my head . . . thought it was time to make a submarine exit . . . came up 150 feet further out, bullets spattering even beyond me."

Emerging from the water on the other side of the lake, Dave encountered two more men, one swinging a chain at him. As he later wrote his parents, "Deciding it was better to be a live chicken than a dead duck, [I] got the hell out of there." Dodging bullets and barbed wire, he made it back to the farmhouse some five hundred yards away, called the FBI, and reported "that the Civil War was reoccurring and would he please come out—with the rest of the Federal Government." An ambulance finally arrived to take the students to the Jones County Community hospital. "That's all for now," Dave signed off, "take care, don't worry." In those days of few long distance calls, this terrifying experience was over long before Dave's parents received this letter, so skillfully written that even Mom and Dad may have cracked a smile through their tears when they envisioned their son, "born for the water," diving into the lake to escape his tormentors. By the time he wrote of his decision to "be a live chicken, rather than a dead duck," they may have even laughed out loud.[55]

But most accounts of the terrors that were at large in the South in those years (although the extralegal violence was by no means limited to the South) did not have a good ending. The threat of impending violence weighed heavily on the young men and women who wrote these letters:

> June 18th
> Dear family and friends,
> Just the security precautions are scary: beware of cars without tags . . . never go out alone; never go out after dark; never be the last one out of a mass meeting; watch for cops without their badge; listen for an accelerating car outside; if you wake up at night thinking there is danger, wake everybody up.[56]

But waiting for the next strike took the greatest toll:

> Ruleville
> August
> Violence hangs overhead like dead air—it hangs there and maybe it'll fall and maybe it won't. . . . cars have been roaming around; 7 or 8 vigilante trucks with their gun racks and no license plates have been seen meeting at the city dump. What will they do? When? Something is in the air, something is going to happen, somewhere, sometime, to someone.[57]

Fear of death is universal, and when hundreds of student volunteers in Freedom Summer transcended their own culture and looked death in the face, they came head to head with their own mortality. In doing that they made their lives and their work come alive in a particularly compelling way. These letters are suffused with references to the denial of death—the students, SNCC staff members, and those they connected with in Mississippi all worked incredibly hard to hold death, their own and that of those around them, at bay.

As the students trained and prepared themselves to go south, after word came about Chaney, Schwerner, and Goodman's disappearance, one young woman wrote home:

> Dear Mom and Dad,
> I cannot begin to tell you how it feels to be here . . . knowing about them. They were in Oxford only a few days before—they couldn't already be in such danger. But then all of a sudden—the disbelief is countered by a vivid picture of reality—that it could be you. And then there's this weird feeling of guilt because it wasn't you—and here you are on a beautiful campus

trying so hard to understand just what danger is anyway. Everyone suspects the worse . . . but no one says anything. . . . Love, Barbara[58]

Thoughts about death—and life—preoccupied the students of Freedom Summer and all those who participated in the civil rights movement:

Dear Folks,
The past week has been, without doubt, the most amazing of my entire life. Now that I've felt what it is to be involved and committed, it seems hard to believe that I could be content with any other kind of life. I've thought about death a lot and what death means about life, and I know that right now I don't want to live any way but the way I am.[59]

The heart of the matter in these missives home is the connection between death and life—the words contained in them recount the meaning of an authentic life and the significance of living. These young people embraced both the inevitability of death and the potential of life. The students who wrote these letters home looked at the terror going on around them and knew they had to work *consciously* to not be overwhelmed by the possibility of their own death. And in the process they lived authentic lives. Their work was permeated with value and meaning that resonates still. As Becker suggests, we all know we will die, but we go ahead and live, holding death at bay, usually as long as we can, so we can live our dreams, be with those we love, and continue to work for what we believe can be realized now and in the future. Becker asserts that the denial of death, the avoidance of mortality by adherence to an immortality system, is not inevitable. Facing the reality of our own mortality and dealing with the inevitable anxiety that this causes allows us to find something larger than ourselves to which we can devote our attention, not an immortality system that helps us escape by clinging to the unrealistic promise of eternal life but a way of living that brings the self-fulfillment we need to be the heroes of our own lives.[60]

Writing Home

Becker affirms the lives of individuals who, like the students of Freedom Summer, have the strength to break away from cultural networks that keep an awareness of mortality at bay through a series of lies. He argues that those who can face the precariousness of life and the fragility of existence and deal with the inevitable anxiety that follows go through a process of self-realization that requires courage and commitment. Taking a leaf from Martin Luther, Becker asserts: "It is only if you 'taste' death with the lips of your living body that you can know emotionally that you are a creature who will die."[61] Once this has happened—as it did for Charles Colcock Jones Jr. when he watched helplessly as his wife and daughter died; and as it did for Collins Maddox when he felt the lynch rope on his neck; and as it did for

Dave when that guitar flew out of his hands and the shooting began—Becker argues that one can make a choice to avoid "clinging to the supposed absolute truth of an immortality system." Instead, he contends, there is the reality of accepting the unknown and the uncertain knowledge of a transformative faith in life itself.

Jones, steeped in evangelical Christianity since his birth, could not make this happen. Instead he gave himself over to the national furor of war, hoping to die a hero for the Confederate cause. Maddox, unlike those who tried to kill him, sought not an immortality system that promised invulnerability to death but a just legal system that honored and protected the lives of blacks as well as whites. The Freedom Summer volunteers signed on for individual reasons that ranged from the religious to the political, from the exalted to the mundane. Once they arrived in Oxford, Ohio, they realized the gravity of the historical moment of which they were a part and the challenge of the mission that lay ahead of them. That summer these young men and women, together with the SNCC and CORE organizers who recruited and trained them, along with thousands of local activists throughout the South, confronted their own mortality, individually and collectively, and found tremendous meaning in a movement that was changing the country and the world.

Becker draws on Søren Kierkegaard's philosophical tenet that in order to live a meaningful life, one of flexibility and truth, one has to go through the pain, anxiety, and anger of facing the reality of human mortality and come out whole on the other side. Once this process is under way, Becker argues, there is no turning back. It becomes impossible to live another way. "Now that I've felt what it is to be involved and committed, it seems hard to believe that I could be content with any other kind of life," wrote a Freedom Summer student in 1964. "I've thought about death a lot and what death means about life," this volunteer continued, "and I know that right now I don't want to live any way but the way I am." When Maddox made it back home after being beaten and almost lynched by a violent mob in Fairfield, Alabama, in 1921, he contacted the one organization that he believed had the power to transcend what Julian Bond called the "psychological shackles that had kept black southerners in physical and mental peonage." The NAACP responded with a message of *tikkun olam*, that one man imprisoned in a world out of balance in Fairfield, Alabama, endangers the rest of the nation.

Finally, to return to the Jones family in nineteenth-century Liberty County, the decision made by Rev. Charles Colcock Jones Sr. during his time at Princeton had serious ramifications for his family and his community for generations to come. His work to do good went awry. The compromise he articulated in *The Religious Instruction of the Negroes in the United States* perpetuated the slave system he abhorred, even as it perhaps eased the psychological burden of enslavement for those who came to believe in the promise of immortality. The end of slavery's travail was marked by the African American congregation that filled the old Midway

Church after the Civil War and by the construction of the Dorchester Academy nearby. Academy alumni who established the Dorchester Cooperative Center changed the culture in Liberty County for the next generation and prepared the way for the new political order that took more than a century to materialize. The long road to racial justice in Liberty County, Georgia, does confirm, as Becker argues, that there can be salvation on the other side of tragedy: not the type of righteous salvation that Reverend Jones envisioned but rather a slow and painful movement away from a world out of balance toward a new place of fulfillment and realistic hope for the future.

On August 4, 1964, in Meridian, Mississippi, Pete Seeger was giving a concert for Freedom Summer volunteers and local activists when word came that the bodies of the three young men who had left Ohio on June 20 had been found. Just before the final song, Seeger made the announcement. "We must sing 'We Shall Overcome' now," he said quietly. "The three boys would not have wanted us to weep now, but to sing and understand this song." Present when Seeger spoke, one student wrote later, "I had understood death in a new way. Now I realized that Mississippi, in spite of itself, has given real meaning to life. In Mississippi you never ask, 'What is the meaning of life?' or 'Is there any point to it all?' but only that we may have enough life to do all that there is to be done."[62] A narrative of American letters stretching from Liberty County, Georgia, to NAACP branches across the South to Mississippi during Freedom Summer 1964, recounts the profound connection between facing the reality of death and opening oneself to the meaning and sanctity of life.

NOTES

Across place and time, my thanks go out to Donald Mathews, Sarah Knox, Rick Momeyer, and Megan Lloyd Joiner, for introducing me to the diverse historical, psychological, and theological components that came together in this essay. Randall M. Miller generously provided feedback on an earlier draft. Nancy Schick kindly brought her superb research skills to this project. Finally I appreciate Clint Joiner's willingness to join me on a memorable trip to Midway, Georgia, in February 2013.

1. The collections of letters used here include the letters of the Charles Colcock Jones family, published by Robert Manson Myers as *The Children of Pride: A True Story of Georgia and the Civil War* (New Haven, Conn.: Yale University Press, 1972); letters written to the NAACP National Office from the southern NAACP branch offices, 1913–39, National Association for the Advancement of Colored People Collection, Library of Congress; and Elizabeth Sutherland Martínez, ed., *Letters from Mississippi: Personal Reports from Civil Rights Volunteers of the 1964 Freedom Summer* (Brookline, Mass.: Zephyr, 2002).

2. Ernest Becker, *The Denial of Death* (New York: Free Press, 1973), 11–24.

3. Glenn Hughes, "The Denial of Death and the Practice of Dying," lecture, Ernest Becker Foundation, February 4, 1998, http://www.ernestbecker.org/index.php

?option=com_content&view=article&id=215:the-denial-of-death-and-the-practice-of
-dying&catid=19:lecture-texts&Itemid=35.

4. Hughes, "Denial of Death."

5. Myers, *Children of Pride*, 7. For additional biographical information on Jones, see Myers, *Children of Pride*, 1567. As the region's primary proponent of the religious instruction of slaves, Jones has been studied extensively by historians. *Children of Pride* includes more than a thousand letters written by Jones family members and provided the groundwork for a number of remarkable studies of the slaveholding South. Donald Mathews was one of the first scholars to contextualize Jones's work, emphasizing how Jones's devotion to Christian evangelism, combined with his understanding of southern honor, gave him the tools he needed to reform and defend an institution he once abhorred. Erskine Clarke's *Dwelling Place: A Plantation Epic* (New Haven: Yale University Press, 2005) delineates the interwoven lives of black and white men and women in the plantation South. More recently Lacy K. Ford's *Delivery Us from Evil: the Slavery Question in the Old South* (New York: Oxford University Press, 2009) delves deeply into the role religious reform, like that advocated by Reverend Jones, played in the creation of southern paternalism in the decades leading up to the Civil War.

6. Clarke, *Dwelling Place*, 89.

7. Donald G. Mathews, "Charles Colcock Jones and the Southern Evangelical Crusade to Form a Biracial Community," *Journal of Southern History*, 41, no. 3 (1975): 303.

8. Charles Colcock Jones, *The Religious Instruction of the Negroes in the United States* (Savannah: Thomas Purse, 1842).

9. Clarke, *Dwelling Place*, 251. This passage also quoted in Lacy K. Ford, "A Paternalist's Progress: Insurgency, Orthodoxy, and Reversal in the Old South," *Reviews in American History* 35 (2007): 54.

10. Myers includes detailed biographical material on Mary Jones, Charles Colcock Jones Jr., Joseph Jones, and Mary Sharpe Jones Mallard, *Children of Pride*, 1568–76.

11. For discussions of slave sales, see Myers, *Children of Pride*, 183, 240–46, 1008.

12. Myers, *Children of Pride*, preface, 4–5; Becker, *Denial of Death*, 64.

13. Hon. Charles C. Jones Jr. to Mrs. Mary Jones, September 23, 1861, in Myers, *Children of Pride*, 751.

14. Rev. C. C. Jones to Hon. Charles C. Jones Jr., September 27, 1861, in Myers, *Children of Pride*, 755–56.

15. Hon. Charles C. Jones Jr. to Rev. C. C. Jones, October 1, 1861, in Myers, *Children of Pride*, 757.

16. Ibid.

17. Ibid.

18. Lt. Charles C. Jones Jr. to Rev. and Mrs. C. C. Jones, November 9, 1861, in Myers, *Children of Pride*, 792. Drew Gilpin Faust's riveting study of death in the Civil War provides a retrospective look at the intense experiences of death and dying that soldiers on both sides of the conflict endured; Drew Gilpin Faust, *This Republic of Suffering: Death and the American Civil War* (New York: Random House, 2008).

19. Myers, *Children of Pride*, 792.

20. Charles Colcock Jones Jr.'s works include *Historical Sketch of Tomo-chi-chi, mico of the Yamacraws* (Albany, N.Y.: Munsell, 1868); *Dead Towns of Georgia* (Savannah: Morning

News Steam Printing House, 1878); *The History of Georgia*, 2 vols. (Boston: Houghton, Mifflin, 1883); *Gullah Folktales from the Georgia Coast* (Athens: University of Georgia Press, 2000) [orig. Boston: Houghton, Mifflin, 1888]); *Biographical Sketches of the Delegates from Georgia to the Continental Congress* (Boston: Houghton, Mifflin, 1891). For a complete bibliography of his works, see Myers, *Children of Pride*, 1568.

21. Clarke, *Dwelling Place*, 32–34.

22. Peggy G. Hargis, "For the Love of Place: Paternalism and Patronage in the Georgia Lowcountry, 1865–1898," *Journal of Southern History* 70, no. 4 (2004): 825–64.

23. William A. Golding had been a member at Midway Church since birth; his father and grandfather had worshipped there. They all knew the Jones family well. George A. Rogers and R. Frank Saunders, *Swamp Water and Wiregrass: Historical Sketches of Coastal Georgia* (Macon: Mercer University Press, 1984), 111–19; Hargis, "For the Love of Place," 842–45; Historic Marker, 089-26 1983, http://markeroni.com/catalog/display .php?code=GA_GHM_089_026.

24. Noah Andre Trudeau, *Southern Storm: Sherman's March to the Sea* (New York: Harper Collins, 2009), 449–51; Rogers and Saunders, *Swamp Water and Wiregrass*, 112–15, 122; Daniel W. Stowell, *Rebuilding Zion: The Religious Reconstruction of the South, 1863–1877* (New York: Oxford University Press, 1998), 82; "Dorchester Academy Arch, Midway, Georgia," Waymarking.com, accessed May 18, 2014, http://www.waymarking .com/waymarks/WM3DW1_Dorchester_Academy_Arch_Midway_Ga.

25. Clarke, *Dwelling Place*, 10.

26. Charles Colcock Jones Jr.'s grandson, Charles Colcock Jones Carpenter, an Episcopal minister in Birmingham in the 1960s, was born in 1899 and raised in his grandfather's home in Augusta, Georgia. He described Jones as a "bellicose southern patriot" who argued that southern industrialization desecrated "the graves of the Confederate dead" and meant the end of "true civilization in favor of barbarism." Quotations from S. Jonathon Bass, *Blessed Are the Peacemakers: Martin Luther King, Jr., Eight White Religious Leaders, and the "Letter from Birmingham Jail"* (Baton Rouge: Louisiana State University Press, 2002), 31.

27. Eric Foner, *Reconstruction* (New York: Harper & Row, 1988); Paul Alan Cimbala and Randall Martin Miller, eds., *The Freedmen's Bureau and Reconstruction: Reconsiderations* (New York: Fordham University Press, 1999), ix.

28. C. Vann Woodward, "The Case of the Louisiana Traveler," in *Quarrels That Have Shaped the Constitution*, ed. John Garraty (New York: HarperCollins, 1988), 157–74; John Hope Franklin, "History of Racial Segregation in the United States," *Annals of the American Academy of Political and Social Science* 304 (1956): 1–9.

29. Walter C. Rucker and James N. Upton, eds., *Encyclopedia of American Race Riots* (Westport, Conn.: Greenwood, 2007).

30. See Patricia Sullivan, *Lift Every Voice: The NAACP and the Making of the Civil Rights Movement* (New York: New Press, 2009).

31. National Association for the Advancement of Colored People Collection, Library of Congress, Manuscript Division (NAACP Collection), Box 1-G4, Mobile, Alabama.

32. NAACP Collection, Box 1 G75, "Frankfort, KY;" Box 1, G1, Birmingham, Alabama, 1920–26; Box 1, G147, Durham, North Carolina, 1919–26.

33. NAACP Collection, Box 1, G1, Birmingham, Alabama, 1920–26.

34. NAACP Collection, Box 1-G43, Atlanta, 1918.

35. Hughes, "Denial of Death."

36. Countee Cullen, *On These I Stand* (New York: Harper & Row, 1947), 126; W. E. B. Du Bois, *Darkwater: Voices from within the Veil* (New York: Harcourt, Brace & Howe, 1920), 251–52; William Fitzhugh Brundage, *Under Sentence of Death: Lynching in the South* (Chapel Hill: University of North Carolina Press, 1997); Donald G. Mathews, "The Southern Rite of Human Sacrifice: Lynching in the American South," *Journal of Southern Religion* 3 (2000), http://jsr.fsu.edu/mathews.htm; Orlando Patterson, *Rituals of Blood: Consequences of Slavery in Two American Centuries* (New York: Basic Civitas Books, 1999); Amy Louise Wood, *Lynching and Spectacle: Witnessing Racial Violence in America, 1890–1940* (Chapel Hill: University of North Carolina Press, 2009); James Cone, the Charles A. Briggs Distinguished Professor of Systematic Theology, Union Theological Seminary, delivered "Strange Fruit: The Cross and the Lynching Tree," for the 2006 Ingersoll Lecture, at Harvard University on October 19, 2006. The entire text is available on video at: http://www.hds.harvard.edu/multimedia/video/strange-fruit-the-cross-and-the-lynching-tree, accessed 6-10-14. Hereafter cited as Cone lecture.

37. Becker, *Denial of Death*, 198.

38. Cone lecture; Becker, *Denial of Death*, 196.

39. Reinhold Niebuhr, *The Essential Reinhold Niebuhr: Selected Essays and Addresses*, ed. Robert McAfee Brown (New Haven, Conn.: Yale University Press, 1987), 85; Cone lecture.

40. Ida Wells-Barnett, *Lynch Law in Georgia: A Six-Weeks Record in the Center of Southern Civilization* (Chicago: Chicago Colored Citizens, 1899).

41. "White Men Indicted for Lynching Negroes," *New York Times*, September 23, 1922; William Fitzhugh Brundage, *Lynching in the New South: Georgia and Virginia, 1880–1930* (Urbana: University of Illinois Press, 1993), 239; J. William Harris, *Deep Souths: Delta, Piedmont, and Sea Island Society in the Age of Segregation* (Baltimore: Johns Hopkins University Press, 1993), 288. See also Christopher C. Meyers, *The Empire State of the South: Georgia History in Documents and Essays* (Macon: Mercer University Press, 2008), 233–34.

42. Dylan Penningroth, "Slavery, Freedom, and Social Claims to Property among African Americans in Liberty County, Georgia, 1850–1880," *Journal of American History* 84, no. 2 (1997): 405–35; James S. Fisher, "Rural Ownership of Land by Blacks in Georgia: 1920 and 1960," *Review of Black Political Economy* 9, no. 1 (1978): 95–107; William H. Brown, "Financial Support of Secondary Education for Negroes in Georgia," *Journal of Negro Education* 21, no. 4 (1952): 478–83; Stephen G. N. Tuck, *Beyond Atlanta: The Struggle for Racial Equality in Georgia, 1940–1980* (Athens: University of Georgia Press, 2003), 82.

43. "Working Together at the Dorchester Cooperative Center, 1930s–1940s, Dorchester Academy Museum of African American History," Historical Marker Database, http://www.hmdb.org/Marker.asp?Marker=9057, accessed 10 June 2014; National Historic Landmark Nomination, Dorchester Academy Boys' Dormitory, National Register of Historic Places, U.S. Department of the Interior, National Park Service,

February 9, 2006. In 2009 the Dorchester Academy was placed on the National Trust for Historic Preservation's list of the "11 Most Endangered Historic Places in America," http://www.preservationnation.org/travel-and-sites/sites/southern-region/dorchester-academy.html. See also Dawn J. Herd-Clark, "The Role of the American Missionary Association in Liberty County, Georgia, 1867–1950," Ph.D. diss., Florida State University, 1999. On Septima Clark's work at the Dorchester Cooperative Center, see Cynthia Stokes Brown, *Ready from Within: Septima Clark and the Civil Rights Movement* (Trenton, N.J.: Africa World, 1990), 62; and Bettye Collier-Thomas and Vincent P. Franklin, *Sisters in the Struggle: African American Women in the Civil Rights–Black Power Movement* (New York: New York University Press, 2001), 114–15.

44. See "Liberty County Branch NAACP History," https://www.facebook.com/LibertyCountyNAACP, accessed 10 June 2014; Rogers and Saunders, *Swamp Water and Wiregrass*, 120–22. See also "Civil Liberties at Dorchester Cooperative Center, 1940–Present," historical marker, Midway, Georgia, available at Waymarking.com, accessed May 16, 2014, http://www.waymarking.com/waymarks/WM3DV8_Dorchester_Academy_Midway_Ga.

45. On the history of the 1964 Mississippi Summer Project (Freedom Summer 1964), see Doug McAdam, *Freedom Summer* (New York: Oxford University Press, 1990); Sally Belfrage, *Freedom Summer* (Charlottesville: University of Virginia Press, 1990); Herbert Randall and Bobs M. Tusa, *Faces of Freedom* (Tuscaloosa: University of Alabama Press, 2001); and Dick J. Reavis, *If White Kids Die: Memories of a Civil Rights Movement Volunteer* (Denton: University of North Texas Press, 2001).

46. Walter P. Rauschenbusch, *Christianity and the Social Crisis* (New York: Macmillan, 1907).

47. Rabbi Jane Kanarek, "What Does *Tikkun Olam* Actually Mean?" in *Righteous Indignation: A Jewish Call for Justice*, ed. Or Rose, Jo Ellen Green Kaiser, and Margie Klein (Woodstock, Vt.: Jewish Lights, 2008), 15–22; quotation on 15. On Jewish students in Freedom Summer, see Stuart Weisberg, *Barney Frank: The Story of America's Only Left-Handed, Gay, Jewish Congressman* (Amherst: University of Massachusetts Press, 2009), 56–67; and Debra L. Schultz and Blanche Wiesen Cook, *Going South: Jewish Women in the Civil Rights Movement* (New York: New York University Press, 2002), 57–74.

48. On the psychological impact of the nuclear threat and material on the culture of the Cold War in the 1950s and 1960s, see Elaine Tyler May, *Homeward Bound: American Families in the Cold War Era* (New York: Basic Books, 1999), and Allan M. Winkler, *Life under a Cloud: American Anxiety about the Atom* (Urbana: University of Illinois Press, 1999).

49. Martínez, ed., *Letters from Mississippi*, 57.

50. Martínez, *Letters from Mississippi*, ii.

51. Martínez, *Letters from Mississippi*, 12.

52. Martínez, *Letters from Mississippi*, 38.

53. Ibid., 10.

54. Ibid., 31.

55. Ibid., 163–65.

56. Ibid., 15.

57. Ibid., 171.

58. Ibid., 31; on the deaths of Schwerner, Goodman, and Chaney, see Seth Cagin and Philip Dray, *We Are Not Afraid: The Story of Goodman, Schwerner, and Chaney and the Civil Rights Campaign for Mississippi* (New York: Nation Books, 2006), and also the comments of Schwerner's brother Steve Schwerner in Diane Chiddister, "Schwerner Says Questions Remain Unanswered in Slaying of Brother," *Yellow Springs News*, January 13, 2005.

59. Martínez, *Letters from Mississippi*, 28.

60. Becker, *Denial of Death*, 17, 88.

61. Ibid., 88.

62. Martínez, *Letters from Mississippi*, 218–19.

W. Thomas Mainwaring

The Underground Railroad

Deus ex Machina

The Underground Railroad has been doing a booming business in recent years after languishing for a long time. Scores of books ranging from juvenile fiction to scholarly works have appeared over the last twenty years. Harriet Tubman has become a staple of children's fiction, while numerous books have decoded quilts as veiled signposts for the Liberty Line. Another indication of this renewed interest in the Underground Railroad is the recent republication of Wilbur Siebert's pioneering scholarly study, *The Underground Railroad: From Slavery to Freedom*, which first appeared in 1898. Local historical societies during the last two decades have also discovered the Underground Railroad as a way of connecting events in their locality to the national drama of slavery and freedom. The opening in Cincinnati in 2004 of the National Freedom Center, dedicated chiefly to a commemoration of the Underground Railroad, symbolizes the greatly enhanced visibility of the institution in recent years.

Although there are probably many reasons for this resurgence of interest in the Underground Railroad, one stands out: the desire to tell the story of African Americans' participation in securing the freedom of thousands of slaves. As Larry Gara pointed out more than fifty years ago in *The Liberty Line*, the history of the Underground Railroad had largely featured the heroics of white conductors and station masters. The fugitive slaves themselves appeared in this narrative as largely passive passengers who were rescued by stalwart Quakers and other white abolitionists.[1] The television series *Roots* began to challenge this narrative by inspiring African Americans to discover their heritage. Their search led inevitably to a very different picture of the Underground Railroad. More specifically Charles L. Blockson's article in *National Geographic* and two books on the Underground Railroad, one published in 1987 and the other in 1995, provided a new perspective and inspiration for those who saw the true heroes of the institution as the fugitive slaves themselves and the black agents who assisted in their quest for freedom.[2]

This attention to the role that African Americans played in the Underground Railroad has been long overdue. Unfortunately this new narrative that has emerged in the last two decades still suffers from a fatal flaw: the new, biracial

Liberty Line continues to be based more on romanticized legends than on historical evidence. Gara's exposure of Underground Railroad legends has made little impression on more recent portrayals of the institution, particularly in popular culture. Recent works continue to portray the Underground Railroad as an operation that brought vast numbers of slaves to freedom, perhaps hundreds of thousands or even millions. And while they gesture toward the ominous dangers posed by slave catchers and bloodhounds, they ultimately portray travel on the Underground Railroad as very safe by allowing virtually every fugitive to escape. The Underground Railroad thus serves as a deus ex machina—a contrived plot device to "rescue" an impossible situation.

This essay examines three popular works to show how this deus ex machina operates. The first work is Faith Ringgold's children's story *Aunt Harriet's Underground Railroad in the Sky*, published in 1992.[3] Ringgold's book continues to sell well. According to a recent Amazon.com ranking, *Aunt Harriet's Underground Railroad* was the third most popular children's book dealing with slavery. It may well be the first exposure that young students have to the Underground Railroad, just as Parson Weems's story about George Washington and the cherry tree was the first and most memorable tale that generations of young Americans learned about the first president. Ringgold's book may well form a lasting impression in young readers' minds about the nature of the Underground Railroad. Next the essay looks at Jacqueline Tobin's and Raymond G. Dobard's *Hidden in Plain View: The Secret Story of Quilts and the Underground Railroad* (1999). The authors' claim that slave quilts offered hidden messages to slaves contemplating a flight to freedom caused quite a flurry when it was initially published. Although the book has not fared well subsequently with scholars, it remains very influential, particularly in children's literature and popular culture. The very title of Bettye Stroud's book *The Patchwork Path: A Quilt Map to Freedom* (2007) illustrates how the idea of quilts as a secret code for the Underground Railroad has entered the popular culture. Finally the essay examines Edward P. Jones's treatment of the Underground Railroad in his Pulitzer Prize–winning novel, *The Known World* (2003). Set in an imagined county in central Virginia, *The Known World* explores the lives of characters who revolve around Henry Townsend, a former slave who has become the owner of some thirty slaves. Gritty and unsparing in its description of the evils of slavery, especially those connected with a black slave owner, Jones's novel nevertheless relies on stereotypical, sentimental views of the Underground Railroad.[4]

Aunt Harriet's Underground Railroad in the Sky features two young African American children, Cassie and her baby brother, Bebe. Cassie, the heroine of Ringgold's earlier book set in Harlem, *Tar Beach*, has learned how to achieve her dreams by flying and has taught her brother this skill as well. One day Cassie and Bebe are flying high above the earth when they encountered an old passenger train also flying in the sky. This train proves to be Aunt Harriet's Underground

Railroad, which makes its appearance every hundred years, on the anniversary of Harriet Tubman's escape to freedom in 1849. When the train stops, Tubman climbs down from the locomotive to announce that the train is bound for Canada and freedom. Hundreds of footsore slaves board the train, as does Bebe. Cassie warns Bebe to get off the train to avoid trouble, but before he can respond, the train has rapidly pulled away. Soon all that Cassie can see of the train is the blinking message it bears on the last car: "Go free north or die." The voice of Tubman then consoles the weeping Cassie. Tubman explains that during slavery times she led hundreds of passengers to freedom on the Underground Railroad without once ever losing one. Tubman informs Cassie that she must follow the Freedom Train northward to Canada if she ever hopes to see Bebe again. However Cassie must make this journey on the ground and escape from slavery as if it were 1849 again. "Cassie," Tubman explains, "though you can fly, being a slave will suck you to the ground like quicksand." Cassie will have to endure sore feet, hunger pangs, and slave catchers if she is to gain her freedom. Despite these formidable hardships, Tubman reassures the girl that she will be there to guide Cassie every step of the way. In her escape Cassie receives all manner of help. Birds scream to alert her to dangers along the way, kind farmers offer her shelter, and signs such as a star quilt being displayed on a house indicate that it is safe for Cassie to seek shelter there. More than anything else, however, Tubman's voice is a constant presence that directs Cassie to safety. At Tubman's bidding she hides in cemeteries, in secret compartments, and in coffins carried on hearses, eventually making it to Niagara Falls. There the spiritual shackles of slavery fall from her, and Cassie once again can fly across the churning waters to rejoin her brother. In Canada, Cassie and Bebe celebrate the hundredth anniversary of Tubman's own escape from slavery and Tubman's status as "the Moses of her people."

Although Ringgold's story is clearly intended for children, it has a serious historical message and draws explicitly upon the legacy of Harriet Tubman. For this reason her depiction of the Underground Railroad deserves careful attention. *Aunt Harriet's Underground Railroad in the Sky* distorts the historical reality of the Underground Railroad in two fundamental ways. First, Ringgold leaves readers with the impression that vast numbers of slaves were able to find freedom in Canada. Her "freedom train" in the sky is crammed full of passengers. Second, despite warnings to Cassie about the difficulties of escaping from slavery, Ringgold makes the journey to freedom seem relatively easy. Cassie never faces any real danger in her journey northward. Nor do the hundreds of passengers who take the Underground Railroad in the sky.

Accurate estimates of how many African Americans were able to escape from slavery and find freedom north of the Mason-Dixon Line are hard to come by. They have ranged from a low of perhaps 50,000 to more than 150,000 from the inception of the Underground Railroad in the 1780s to the Civil War.[5] But whether one accepts the high or low end of this spectrum, the percentage of slaves who were able to escape was quite low. The census reports from the slave states in 1850 indicated that only 1,011 fugitives had been reported permanently missing by their owners during the previous year. The number reported missing in 1860 fell to 803—out of a slave population of nearly 4 million. Thus in 1860, .02% of the slave population—1 slave out of every 5,000[6]—was reported as having run away permanently. Recent work on the black population of Canada West (modern-day Ontario) also raises questions about how many fugitives were able to find their way north of the border where slave catchers had no authority. Pointing out that previous scholars have erroneously assumed that the vast majority of blacks in Canada West were refugees from American slavery, Michael Wayne has argued that fewer than 5,000 American fugitive slaves ultimately made their home in Canada.[7] *Aunt Harriet's Underground Railroad in the Sky* feeds the popular misconception that vast numbers of fugitive slaves were able to find a safe haven in Canada.

It also fosters the illusion that escaping from slavery was relatively easy. Whereas Cassie has help at every step along the way, most fugitives could not expect to receive any help from sympathetic friends until they reached the free states. The Underground Railroad simply did not exist in most slave states. Some fugitives were even unaware that they could board the Liberty Line in the free states. When Frederick Douglass escaped in 1838, for example, he was unaware of Underground Railroad stations in Wilmington, Delaware, and in Philadelphia. Not until Douglass arrived by train in New York City did he finally seek out help.[8] Tom Stowe, who escaped from Morgantown, Virginia, made it all the way to Franklin, Pennsylvania, a distance of more than 150 miles, before asking for help out of sheer desperation. The biggest part of the journey to freedom was accomplished alone, without any comfort or aid.[9] Ringgold's "Underground Railroad in the Sky" has rendered the real difficulties of escaping from slavery negligible. Her Underground Railroad is truly a deus ex machina that rescues Cassie and hundreds of anonymous slaves from their plight.

Hidden in Plain View was published to considerable fanfare in 1999. The fanfare is understandable, given the claim of the authors, Jacqueline L. Tobin and Raymond G. Dobard, that they had learned how to decode the quilts made by American slaves. They revealed that the quilts offered secret messages for slaves embarking on the Underground Railroad and roadmaps to their ultimate destination. Hung from a window or a fence, these quilts conveyed their hidden messages to slaves even though they were in "plain view." According to Tobin a quilt maker named Ozella McDaniel Williams had confided the secrets of the quilts to her. These secrets had been closely guarded in the oral traditions of African Americans since Emancipation, but Williams, who was then in her seventies, finally opened up to Tobin and urged her emphatically to "write this down."[10] Williams died shortly thereafter. Tobin, a white teacher of writing at a Denver college, subsequently enlisted the help of Dobard, an African American art historian and quilter at Howard University, to coauthor the book. Oprah Winfrey and numerous quilt shop owners subsequently promoted the book and Underground Railroad quilt kits. Educators have also used the premise that quilts offered fugitive slaves secret instructions as part of their lesson plans for teaching black history.[11] Although juvenile works such as Ringgold's book and Deborah Hopkinson's *Sweet Clara and the Freedom Quilt* (1993) had linked quilts and the Underground Railroad previously, *Hidden in Plain View* seemed to establish this connection as a well-documented historical fact.[12]

Historians of quilts and of the Underground Railroad, however, have been increasingly skeptical about the claims made in *Hidden in Plain View*. Quilt historians have noted many problems and contradictions in Tobin's and Dobard's interpretation of the "Underground Railroad code" in slave quilts. The first is that at least fifteen different and mutually exclusive versions of the code have now surfaced in addition to the one that the authors of *Hidden in Plain View* analyzed. Second, some of the quilt patterns that Tobin and Dobard assert were part of the Underground Railroad code did not originate until the 1930s. Equally problematic, these authors assign meanings to African symbols featured in Underground Railroad quilts that directly contradict the meanings of those same symbols in Africa.[13]

Historians of the Underground Railroad have been equally critical of the claims made in *Hidden in Plain View*. Giles R. Wright, director of the Afro-American History Program for the New Jersey Historical Commission, has identified numerous problems with these claims. As he pointed out, the only evidence that Tobin and Dobard cite is the oral testimony Ozella Williams offered before her death. They neglected to consult two obvious sources of oral history regarding quilts and the Underground Railroad—slave narratives and the WPA interviews with former slaves conducted in the 1930s. Tellingly these sources make no mention of quilts as coded messages for the Underground Railroad. Wright also contradicts the impression given in *Hidden in Plain View* that vast numbers of slaves traveled the Underground Railroad to freedom. Noting that most rebels from the plantation remained in the South, he observes the irony that some fugitives actually made Charleston their destination because they could blend into the city's large free black population. Finally he points out that it was far easier for a fugitive who was fleeing Charleston to take a boat for a northern escape rather than the lengthy route through the Appalachians to Cleveland that Tobin and Dobard describe all Charleston fugitives as taking. And as Leigh Fellner points out, it is quite astounding that none of the African Americans who claim the Underground Railroad quilt code as part of their family legacy can identify ancestors who made use of this arcane knowledge to escape from slavery.[14]

Perhaps the most preposterous claims in *Hidden in Plain View*, however, are those that Tobin and Dobard make in regard to the means of escape and route that Charleston slaves followed to freedom. According to the authors, quilts instructed escaping slaves on "how to prepare to escape, what to do on the journey, and where to go." Their interpretation of the monkey wrench quilt pattern at least has a certain plausibility: it signified that it was time to make preparations to escape. (Never mind that the monkey wrench was an American invention dating to about 1850 and was not likely to have made an appearance in plantation blacksmith tool sheds.)[15] But their analysis of the bear's paw quilt pattern stretches credulity: they insist that this quilt was "a visual reference reminding the fugitives to follow the actual trail of a bear's footprints" through the Appalachian Mountains to Cleveland, which Ozella Williams maintained was the ultimate destination of fugitive slaves from Charleston. The authors are adamant that "if the fugitives literally followed the trail of a bear, they would find a route through the mountains." They are silent on how fugitives were to cross the Ohio River. One wonders how many fugitives were able to make their way to Cleveland by following the coded message in the bear's paw pattern.[16]

Tobin and Dobard may have been the dupes of Ozella Williams in more than just this instance. According to Fellner, a fiber artist named Anne Robinson rented a stall in the same tourism market where Williams had sold her quilts until her death in 1998. Robinson began selling *Hidden in Plain View* when the book came out, much to the surprise of her fellow vendors. They were astounded that anyone had believed Williams. "Apparently she was very free with the info that she was telling tales to sell quilts," Robinson related. "According to [the vendors], she used to make up the stories for the tourists and just laugh after they left."[17] It is hard to decide whether the Underground Railroad depicted in *Hidden in Plain View* should be regarded as a deus ex machina or as a magic carpet ride.

Edward P. Jones's depiction of slavery and freedom in his Pulitzer Prize–winning novel *The Known World* is considerably more complicated and sophisticated than that of *Hidden in Plain View*. Whereas Tobin and Dobard assume the existence of a slave community where secret codes can be safely shared, Jones creates a fictional world in antebellum central Virginia where the very idea of community is in doubt. He challenges the reader's expectations by having his central character, a former slave named Henry Townsend whose parents had purchased his freedom, become the eventual owner of thirty-three slaves. A good portion of the novel explains how Henry came to "betray" his people—although Jones makes it abundantly clear that Henry to his dying day considered himself a "good" master. Likewise the small coterie of black families in fictional Manchester County that own slaves perceive nothing wrong with the institution of slavery. As Fern Elston, Henry's teacher, matter-of-factly explained to a Canadian journalist after the Civil

War, "We owned slaves. It was what was done, and so that is what we did." Slavery corrupts virtually everyone in the novel; it knows no racial boundaries.[18]

The Underground Railroad plays a small but significant part in *The Known World*. The first escape in the novel involves Rita, a slave of William Robbins, one of Manchester County's leading planters. Rita becomes Henry's surrogate mother after his parents, Augustus and Maude Townsend, purchase their freedom from Robbins and buy a small piece of property in a distant part of the county. Although Augustus routinely sets aside money from his work as a skilled carpenter to purchase his son's liberty, Robbins's asking price keeps going up, in part because of his greed and in part because of his increasing fondness for the boy. It takes years for Augustus to come up with the money to purchase his son, years during which he and his wife seldom see Henry because of their restricted visiting privileges. When they are finally able to purchase Henry in 1843, Rita cannot bear the thought of parting with him. After watching the Townsends' wagon pull away slowly from Robbins's plantation, she runs after it. She finally catches up to it and begs the Townsends to take her with them. After many tearful entreaties from Rita, Augustus finally relents, even though he knows that one pair of eyes witnessing Rita's climbing aboard his wagon might land him in great difficulties.[19]

Augustus's solution is to send Rita to New York City in a box with a shipment of his elaborately carved walking canes. He has been selling these canes to an Irish merchant in New York for several years. After wrapping the canes in burlap and making provision for food and water, Augustus has the very slight Rita lie in the box with the canes and nails the lid shut. The train to New York takes forty-one hours, but a badly dehydrated and slightly battered Rita emerges at the end of this ordeal and gains her freedom.[20]

Jones must surely have been aware in crafting the story of Rita's escape of Henry "Box" Brown, the slave who mailed himself from Richmond to the Philadelphia Vigilance Committee office in 1849. Brown's escape became one of the most notorious of the era. A widely circulated engraving depicted his resurrection as a free man in Philadelphia. The publicity attending his escape in fact made it very difficult for emulators to follow suit. A subsequent attempt was foiled when suspicious officials pried open the lid of a heavy box bound for Philadelphia and uncovered the would-be fugitive.[21]

Rita's escape is not very plausible historically, even if it is modeled after a real historical incident. According to Jones, Manchester County was located in the middle of Virginia, west of Appomattox, which he specifies was halfway between the fictional county and Richmond. This would place Manchester County in the general vicinity of Roanoke. The difficulty is that his fictional county would lie at least one hundred miles away from Gordonsville, the westernmost railhead in Virginia in the 1840s. Although some of Jones's historical errors (such as having

Millard Fillmore be the president of the United States in 1844) can be dismissed as inconsequential, this one bears some weight. By giving Augustus Townsend access to a railroad freight depot, Jones has made Rita's escape entirely too easy and rendered it suspect. Rita's escape is even more implausible when one considers that it took Henry Brown twenty-seven hours to travel just from Richmond to Philadelphia.[22]

Rita's disappearance has significant consequences for the novel. When she and four other slaves vanish from Manchester County in 1843, William Robbins engineers the incumbent sheriff's ouster, complaining, "Patterson was doing nothing as property just up and walked away." John Skiffington becomes the new sheriff. It is Skiffington who introduces the patrol system in Manchester County to safeguard its bonded property. During his long tenure as sheriff, not a single slave escapes from the county until Townsend's death in 1855.[23]

Jones offers no clear-cut explanations for why the slaves of Manchester County suddenly become less restive. The institution of the patrol system does not suffice for an explanation, as it still exists after Townsend's death, when fugitives begin fleeing the county again. In fact Robbins, not the slave patrol, captures the only slave to run away during the twelve years that Skiffington serves as sheriff while Townsend is alive. One possible interpretation might be that Augustus and Maude Townsend stopped aiding fugitive slaves as long as their son was alive. Jones offers no hint as to whether the Townsends had previously helped runaway slaves or whether shipping Rita to freedom was an isolated act of kindness. However it is striking that no slave escapes from the county between Rita's disappearance and Henry's death. It is also noteworthy that the newly freed Henry had been a witness to his father's preparations for sending Rita to New York. What is certain is that the Townsends could not trust their son. Henry's continued closeness to Robbins and his becoming a slave owner at Robbins's urging may have persuaded his parents that they could not safely aid other potential fugitives. When Henry arrives at their home bearing the news that he is the proud owner of a newly purchased slave, Augustus can only exclaim, "Do you know the wrong of that, Henry?" Henry obviously does not, responding, "I ain't done nothing no white man wouldn't do." The Townsends cannot be sure that Henry would not turn them in if they engineer further escapes, particularly if they involve Henry's or Robbins's slaves.[24]

Henry's early and unexpected death in 1855 leads to the unraveling of the familiar and known world of Manchester County. "Everything was coming apart," Sheriff Skiffington laments soon after Henry's death. Not only do three slaves disappear from Henry's plantation, but so does Augustus Townsend—a kidnapping victim of the county's slave patrollers, who sell him into slavery in the Deep South. The three slaves include Alice, who had seemingly been rendered feebleminded after being kicked in the head by a mule, and Priscilla and Jamie, the wife and son of the hard-driving black overseer, Moses. Moses is complicit in their escape. His long talks about the state of the plantation with Caldonia, Henry's widow, ultimately leads to physical intimacy with Caldonia. Moses has no use for his slave wife and son after he begins to dream that Caldonia will free him and marry him. Careful observation of Alice leads Moses to conclude that her nonsensical answers and constant chanting are part of well-rehearsed act. "Crazy" Alice in fact is quite sane and uses her quirky behavior so that she can wander at night with impunity. Even the slave patrollers get accustomed to encountering the crazy slave muttering to herself on the roads and take no notice of her. Moses urges Alice to take his wife and son to freedom. He lies to them by saying that he will follow later.[25]

Jones offers no explanation of how Alice, Priscilla, and Jamie escaped or of how two other slaves on the Townsend plantation take advantage of the confusion created by their disappearance to steal away. Perhaps we are supposed to construe Alice as a character in the mold of Harriet Tubman. Like Alice, Tubman had been hit in the head at a young age (by a lead weight an overseer aimed at another slave) and was permanently affected by this blow. Tubman suffered from periodic seizures and spells of unconsciousness. But more important, Jones portrays Alice as a woman of steely determination and will. When Moses parts from Phyllis, she breaks down in tears. Alice immediately slaps her: "You just stop all this cryin right now. I won't have it." Alice is also physically tough like Tubman. Jones leaves little doubt that she is perfectly capable of leading two fellow, frightened slaves to freedom. At the end of the novel, Jones reveals that Alice, Priscilla, and Jamie are living in Washington, D.C.[26]

Contrary to his own intentions, Moses ends up trying to follow in Alice's footsteps not long after her escape. Impatient that Caldonia has made no mention of freeing him, Moses one night bluntly asks her after making love when she is going to. Caldonia's reaction immediately makes it clear that she has no intention of doing so. The next time he comes to the house, Caldonia dismisses him with a few curt words. It is then that Moses decides to make his own escape. The next night, he follows a road that he has seen Alice take. But Moses has no sense of direction. "He could have found his way around Caldonia's plantation with no eyes and even no hands to touch familiar trees, but where he was walking now was not that place." In his confusion he goes south, not north. He ends up stumbling onto the farm of Augustus and Mildred Townsend.[27]

Sheriff Skiffington's quest to track down Moses ultimately leads him to this same farm. He has had suspicions about Moses long before he disappears. He does not think that Alice, Priscilla, and her son would have left on their own and quickly infers after a visit that Moses has been sleeping with Caldonia. When his patrollers find no evidence of the escaped slaves, Skiffington speculates that Moses murdered them and buried the bodies. After pondering where Moses might have gone, Skiffington remembers a comment about Moses's being "world-stupid" and guesses that he might have headed south toward the Townsends' home. He sets off with his deputy, Counsel Skiffington, a cousin who has fallen on hard times, to see if Moses has indeed gone in this direction.[28]

The sheriff's quest to find Moses leads to several deaths and the discovery of an Underground Railroad station at the Townsends' house. When Skiffington arrives at the house, he surmises immediately when Mildred comes out of the door with a gun that Moses is hiding in the house. He demands that she "surrender the property." In agony because of a toothache and in no mood to put up with any obstinacy from a free black woman, Skiffington grows impatient when she fails to comply. He attempts to pull his rifle out of its sheath and inadvertently pulls the trigger. The shot hits Mildred in the chest, killing her almost instantly.[29]

Dismayed that he has just killed Mildred, Skiffington delegates his cousin to search the house for Moses. During this search the deputy finds one hundred dollars in gold pieces in a dresser and comes to believe that the Townsend home holds many more riches if he had the proper time to search it. But Counsel Skiffington also knows his cousin as a man of rectitude who will not countenance stealing. So he leaves the house, picks up the blood-stained rifle that Mildred had carried, and shoots the sheriff several times to make sure that he is dead. No one will suspect his story that Mildred and Skiffington killed each other. He threatens Moses, who surrenders after hearing shots, that he will kill him if he ever dares to talk about what he has just seen. Not until several weeks later does Counsel find the opportunity to go back to Mildred's house in search of plunder. Despite repeated searches he does not find any more treasure. He does stumble across "hidden compartments" "designed to hide slaves for the Underground Railroad" but does not recognize these for what they are.[30]

Jones ultimately leaves the operation of the Underground Railroad station at August and Mildred Townsend's house a mystery. Only one sentence in *The Known World* makes reference to it. Although Alice could have led Priscilla and her son to this station, Jones suggests that she made her way north, in the opposite direction. Perhaps the Townsends hid fugitive slaves only from other counties who were fleeing toward freedom. The one thing that is clear is that the station was not used by the slaves of Manchester County from the time of Rita's escape in 1843 until Henry Townsend's death in 1855. Ultimately Jones's mention of an Underground Railroad station serves no useful purpose in the novel.

Jones also resorts to stereotypical views of the Underground Railroad in describing "hidden compartments" at the Townsend house. Although some safe houses probably did have such features, architectural historians have typically found no secret chambers in their investigation of actual stations. Such hidden compartments owe more to melodrama than they do to history. As archaeological student Byron Frueling commented after surveying seventeen Underground Railroad sites in Ohio, "If such constructions existed at all, they must be extremely rare."[31] Locating an Underground Railroad station in central Virginia is equally problematic. Virtually all serious scholars are in agreement that the Underground Railroad began in the free states (or perhaps in the areas contiguous to free states, such as river counties in Kentucky) and did not extend deep into the South. As Fergus Bordewich noted, "But the only place in the inner South where organized underground clearly went on without interruption was the Quaker counties of North Carolina."[32] The romantic image of the Underground Railroad that appears in Jones's novel perpetuates the idea of a large traffic in fugitive slaves.

Edward P. Jones in *The Known World* created a complicated and unconventional portrait of slavery, racial mores, and local habits grounded in gritty realism. Yet Jones's daring and bold examination of the world of slavery in Manchester County unfortunately does not carry over into his treatment of fugitive slaves and the Underground Railroad. He sends Rita on a train ride to New York that could not possibly have taken place. He builds secret chambers for the Underground Railroad in the Townsends' home that are not only highly implausible historically but serve no purpose in the novel. Here the rescue device has turned unwittingly into a trap.

The three popular works considered in this essay all rely on the Underground Railroad as a contrivance to further their narratives. All of them depart considerably from what is known historically about the Underground Railroad in greatly exaggerating the numbers of passengers the Liberty Line carried and in vastly underestimating the difficulties of escape. These works, of course, are not alone in this tendency; they are instead highly representative of much of the literature dealing with the Underground Railroad over the last twenty years. This is unfortunate. The promise of the "new" Underground Railroad was that the real history of African Americans' involvement in the Liberty Line would replace the sentimentalized stories of kindly white conductors "rescuing" fugitives from slavery. But this promise shows few signs of being realized. Even if African Americans are portrayed as being in charge of the Underground Railroad or running away from a black slave owner, such portrayals of the Liberty Line reduce it to little more than a magical device to rescue the plot. It is time to run this particular train back into the roundhouse, where it can be studied as an example of misunderstood and misrepresented history.

NOTES

1. Larry Gara, *The Liberty Line: The Legend of the Underground Railroad* (Lexington: University Press of Kentucky, 1961; repr. 1996), 3–6.

2. Charles L. Blockson, "Escape from Slavery: The Underground Railroad," *National Geographic*, July 1984, 3–39; Charles L. Blockson, *The Underground Railroad: First-Person Narratives of Escapes to Freedom in the North* (Englewood Cliffs, N.J.: Prentice-Hall, 1987); Charles L. Blockson, *Hippocrene Guide to the Underground Railroad* (New York: Hippocrene Books, 1995).

3. Faith Ringgold, *Aunt Harriet's Underground Railroad in the Sky* (New York: Crown, 1992).

4. Edward P. Jones, *The Known World* (New York: Amistad, 2004).

5. Gara, *Liberty Line*, 36–40; Fergus M. Bordewich, *Bound for Canaan: The Underground Railroad and the War for the Soul of America* (New York: Amistad, 2005), 436–37.

6. Wilbur H. Siebert, *The Underground Railroad from Slavery to Freedom* (New York: Russell & Russell, 1898; repr. 1967), 378.

7. Gara, *Liberty Line*, 39; Michael Wayne, "The Black Population of Canada West on the Eve of the American Civil War: A Reassessment Based on the Manuscript Census of 1861," *Histoire Social/ Social History* 28 (1995): 466–70.

8. Gara, *Liberty Line*, 42–58; David W. Blight, ed., *Narrative of the Life of Frederick Douglass, An American Slave*, 2nd ed. (New York: Bedford/St. Martin's, 2003), 111.

9. Eber Pettit, *Sketches in the History of the Underground Railroad* (Fredonia, N.Y.: McKinistry, 1879; repr. Freeport, N.Y.: Books for Libraries Press, 1971), 27–28.

10. Tobin and Dobard, *Hidden in Plain View*, 19–21.

11. Leigh Fellner, "Betsy Ross Redux: The Underground Railroad 'Quilt Code,'" Hart Cottage Quilts, accessed August 20, 2009, http://www.ugrrquilt.hartcottagequilts.com/.

12. Deborah Hopkinson, *Sweet Clara and the Freedom Quilt* (New York: Dragonfly Books, 1993).

13. Fellner, "Betsy Ross Redux," 1.

14. Giles R. Wright, "*Hidden in Plain View: The Secret Story of Quilts and the Underground Railroad*: Critique by Giles R. Wright," accessed August 20, 2009, http://www.antiquequiltdating.com/Hidden_in_Plain_View_-_The_Secret_Story_of_Quilts_and_the_Underground_Railroad.html; Fellner, "Betsy Ross Redux," 1.

15. Wright, "Critique," 3.

16. Wright, *Hidden in Plain View*, 70–92

17. Fellner, "Betsy Ross Redux," 7–8.

18. Jones, *Known World*, 109.

19. Ibid., 45–46.

20. Ibid., 48–51.

21. Bordewich, *Bound for Canaan*, 309–12.

22. Jones, *Known World*, 29, 121, 159; "Gordonsville: Chesapeake & Ohio, Piedmont Subdivision," accessed September 22, 2009, http://piedmontsub.com/Gville.shtml; Bordewich, *Bound for Canaan*, 311.

23. Jones, *Known World*, 3, 39.

24. Ibid., 137–38, 376–77.

25. Ibid., 77, 214–15, 290–98, 337–39.

26. Ibid., 297; on Harriet Tubman's injuries, Bordewich, *Bound for Canaan*, 348–51.

27. Jones, *Known World*, 324–35.

28. Ibid., 322, 359.

29. Ibid., 363–65.

30. Ibid., 369–71, 376–77.

31. Gara, *Liberty Line*, xiv.

32. Bordewich, *Bound for Canaan*, 308.

Emily Bingham

Kentucky in Bloomsbury

*Henrietta Bingham, Black Culture, and the
Southern Gothic in Jazz Age London*

One London night in 1923, Henrietta Bingham carried a southern-style cara-
mel cake to a party at the studio where the artists Duncan Grant and Vanessa
Bell shared space. An artistic cake it was, too, decorated with a fox in a little coat
worrying two ducks. The image was from birthday boy David Garnett's surreal
novella, *Lady into Fox*, then bringing him a burst of literary renown. The assembled artists, intellectuals, and writers were associated with the Bloomsbury Group,
and that evening twenty-two-year-old Kentucky-born Bingham earned her own
succès fou—and an enduring footnote to Bloomsbury history—by seducing two of
Garnett's friends. One, sculptor Stephen Tomlin, would memorialize in bronze
the likes of Virginia Woolf and Lytton Strachey. The other, painter Dora Carrington, became the subject of the 1995 biopic starring Emma Thompson.[1]

Carrington (she hated "Dora") enthusiastically described the scene to her
lover, the writer Gerald Brenan. This letter, from a married woman to a lover
about a lesbian crush—leaving aside Carrington's decades-long attachment to the
homosexual biographer Strachey—suggests what would have scandalized most
Americans about the circle Bingham had stepped into.

> I only know her name is Henrietta. She has the face of a Giotto Madonna.
> She sang exquisite songs with a mandoline [*sic*], Southern State revivalist
> nigger songs. She made such wonderful cocktails that I became completely
> drunk and almost made love to her in public. To my great joy Garnett told
> me the other day she continually asks after me and wants me to go and see
> her. . . . Ralph [Carrington's husband] cut my hair too short last week. When
> it has grown longer and my beauty is restored, I shall visit the lovely Henri-
> etta and revive our drunken passion.[2]

One of Henrietta's songs that night was "Water Boy." Her voice, soft, low,
and "faintly husky," moved over the notes of the chain-gang tune, later recorded
by Paul Robeson and Odetta, exuding extraordinary warmth. So did she.

> There ain't no sweat boy
> That's on a this mountain
> That run like mine boy,
> That run like mine.[3]

So was born Bloomsbury's "Kentucky Princess," who cut a dazzling course through the lives of friends and lovers but whose family legacy was altogether more unsettling. Fittingly for a princess, the story features parties, suitors, and a wedding. As the history of sexuality comes into focus, it is worth glancing back at a lesbian-leaning Henrietta Bingham, standing at a cultural and sexual crossroads, desiring and desirable, performing southernness abroad in the Jazz Age.[4]

Lovable

Henrietta Bingham was my paternal great-aunt. As a child I found her sidesaddles in the attic; as an adolescent I heard she farmed hemp (and maybe marijuana) during World War II; and as a graduate student introduced to women's history, I heard my grandmother diagnose her as, "you know[,] . . . an invert."[5] I had to look that one up, though it was clear enough what she wanted to convey. In early sexologist Havelock Ellis's lexicon, *inversion* describes a psychological abnormality in which a member of one sex behaves, feels, and thinks in ways understood to belong to the opposite sex—in effect reversing gender roles. The slipperiness of this idea, wrapped up as it is with gender conventions as perceived by late nineteenth-century science, is hard to overstate.[6] In any case "Miss Henrietta" of the "violet blue eyes," cropped hair, and long limbs—a "most adorable creature"—was a source of fascination. As one lover recalled, just the memory of her eyes could "turn my bowels to water and send me into orgasms of uncontrollable, delicious weeping."[7] But her insecurities, her unruly sexuality, and, later in life, her addictions produced lingering silences.[8] Born in 1901, she died in 1968. I never knew her, but those who did could not forget her, and the more I heard about her, the less I (a trained historian who knew better than to follow such unprofessional urges) could resist the heat radiating from her memory. Secrecy and sex, love and its limits—all unfurling during a decade of cultural and intellectual ferment—supply the larger storyline. This essay assembles some of what I have learned about her life in the mid-1920s as it intersected with Freudian psychology, with popular ideas about the corrupt but seductive South, and with the rage for African American music.

Had Bingham's path not crossed with the brilliant coterie of Bloomsbury artists and intellectuals (a group that had coalesced before World War I around Virginia Woolf, her sister Vanessa Bell, and their brother's Cambridge friends), it would be difficult to recapture the heady time she had following Garnett's birthday party, for their paintings and sculptures, letters and memoirs document her movements and mark her impact. A Jazz Age "it girl" abroad, she wielded unique allure. Carrington fell under her "magical charm" and shared with her heretofore-unglimpsed "extacy [*sic*]." To Tomlin she was simply "the best companion I have ever had and the most desirable lover."[9] Moving among the broader Bloomsbury circle, the young Kentuckian observed people who, as one scholar has written, consciously rejected "conventions which seemed senseless or irrelevant" while "accepting, without pomposity, the implications of a sharply rational examination of life and art."[10] Sexual norms were set aside, sometimes quietly, sometimes flamboyantly; jealousy was to be avoided and fulfillment celebrated where it was found. The ghastly horrors of World War I had left traditional mores open to their scathing criticism—Henrietta peered over the brink into another world.

Henrietta's sexuality was a subject of personal struggle, family anxiety, and lengthy psychoanalytical treatment. But sex was not the only signifier at work in the making of the "Kentucky Princess." There was also the money. She had one of those American fortunes diminished British heirs regularly set their sights on.[11] It was Jay Gatsby who heard in the voice of the fictional Louisville native Daisy Buchanan the "inexhaustible charm," the perpetual "jingle" of money.[12] Henrietta also possessed a southern legacy that combined gentility with slaveholding, Confederate service, and full-blown General Lee worship—all wrapped up with tragedy, ambition, and neurotic family relationships. Such strands lent her persona a delectable, Poe-like aspect. The cherry on top was the way Bingham channeled (and grooved to) up-to-the-minute African American music and culture. She brought blues and jazz directly into Bloomsbury.

Given that Bingham swam wholeheartedly into the swells of sexual experimentation to a soundtrack a music historian would die for and with enough cash to do as she pleased, it may seem surprising that she spent much of the Roaring Twenties stretched out on an analyst's couch. One reason was the simple one that to live openly as a lesbian (or a gay man) was socially anathema. And yet within certain circles lesbian sex as an expression of bisexuality could excite curiosity and sometimes qualified as radical chic. Henrietta had extended romantic relationships with men who knew of and tolerated her bisexual behavior. And Carrington's lover, Brenan, proffered his rooms in London for her assignations with Henrietta. Lesbian relationships were appearing in plays, novels, and song lyrics. Henrietta could navigate a nascent lesbian and bisexual culture at the theater, where steamy actresses such as Tallulah Bankhead aroused the passions of both sexes; at nightclubs, where blues and jazz divas sang about sex and love both troubled and troubling; and at parties with Woolf and the breakthrough lesbian author Radclyffe Hall. If there was freedom to be had, she would seem the perfect one to seize it.[13]

Historians generally agree that the 1920s were a peak moment of sexual openness followed by backlash and repression in the 1930s. But this was also the decade when Freudian psychology captured the public imagination and psychoanalysis

was established as a profession. Well-off homosexual people gravitated to its prac-
titioners, eager for a place where they could speak about sexual feelings.[14] Henrietta was part of this group, too, seeking greater peace of mind and, following her
analyst's urgings, working to redirect her sexual object choices. Such projects were
not easy nor easily discussed, even in Bloomsbury. No wonder Henrietta's London
persona built on other story lines. There was the juicy gothic literary one. And
there was the spicy Jazz Age one that set her within America's hottest new cultural
creation.

LONDON CALLING

Henrietta spent a prosperous but turbulent childhood in Louisville, Kentucky.
Her father came from a long line of North Carolina schoolmasters, but life as
chief pedagogue at a military boarding school, while respectable, was a narrow
perch for his ambitions. He met Henrietta's mother during her stay at Asheville's
Grove Park Inn a few miles from the Bingham School, where she had come from
Louisville with her ailing father for the mountain air. Besides a warm disposition,
Eleanor Miller brought ballast—her mother's father and brother were prominent
industrialists and breeders of three Kentucky Derby winners. Soon after the couple settled into his mother-in-law's home, Robert Worth Bingham had an L.L.D.
from University of Louisville and helped manage the family's business interests.
He got his feet wet in city politics as county attorney and as mayor after the ouster
of the previous officeholder. As a Progressive, Bingham rankled the established
machine and lost the Democratic nomination for the special election. He and Eleanor had three children, well spaced. Henrietta, who fell between two brothers,
contracted diphtheria as a young child and suffered from an unspecified trauma as
a girl. When she was twelve, her mother died after a collision on the train tracks
(Henrietta was riding in the car). Six years later, in 1918, her father cemented his
political influence with the purchase of two Louisville newspapers.[15]

Smith College brought Henrietta out of the South for the first time. There
she found a confidante in her whip-smart English instructor. Mina Kirstein was a
Smith graduate and first-year professor who later penned several biographies and
translated Proust. Mina's good looks, intellectual prowess, contacts with sometimes flamboyantly Progressive and leftist figures, and department store fortune
(she had been the first girl at Smith to have her own car) made her a notable campus figure. At the same time, she struggled with social anxiety and developed a soft
spot for other outsiders.[16] She recalled Henrietta's behaving "absolutely sure of
herself with a great deal of bravado in her manner." But to this teacher Henrietta
shed her front, revealing a proud, "homesick, frightened" southerner, miserably
out of place in Northampton's "New England atmosphere."[17]

Henrietta's effect on her teacher was such that Mina Kirstein spent much
of the next five years emotionally engaged in her well-being. Her cause was

complicated fairly early on, when, while staying in the Bingham suite at the Wal-
dorf one weekend, she realized that Henrietta had fallen "in love with me and
I with her."[18] Crushes from students were common enough, and indeed David
Garnett teasingly imagined an epitaph for Mina:

> I tried to teach the truth
> To virgins, but forsooth
> All my success in teaching was to see
> My pupils lie with me.

But this crush did not pass and presented not only an emotional entanglement but
also a practical quandary. Mina did not condemn homosexuality but also did not
want to lead the poisoned, secret life that went with it. So she set out to excise the
couple's romantic feelings for one another without compromising the intimacy
they shared.[19]

By second term Henrietta had dropped out of college. A talented writer, she
struggled with her science class, but Mina was sure such challenges could be overcome and remained involved as a tutor.[20] She met the Binghams in England during the summer, and Henrietta returned to Smith in the fall. By spring, however,
the college physician recommended that she drop another course. Her record had
deteriorated in more opaque ways, as well, and the minutes of the Smith administrative board deemed her a "detriment" to the "community." Instead of letting
her problematic pupil slip quietly away, Mina obtained a leave of absence for the
following year to study in Europe and persuaded Henrietta's father that her education should continue abroad.[21]

Henrietta again spent much of the summer in Britain with her family. Her
father took an interest in all things English. He was also a crack shot who loved
grouse hunting and, whenever possible, socializing with members of the landed
gentry. But it was a disastrous holiday for Henrietta, who "could hardly bear to
have him touch her," according to Mina's account, due to "her shame of her homosexuality and her fear of being found out."[22]

Meanwhile Mina was crossing the Atlantic on a luxurious ocean liner. Aboard
was Dr. A. A. Brill, a New York–based physician and psychoanalyst.[23] Mina wanted
treatment for Henrietta in Europe, and Brill supplied an introduction to Ernest
Jones, later Freud's biographer and already a leading psychoanalytical figure in
the English-speaking world.[24] While sojourning at the luxurious Hotel Meurice
in Paris with Henrietta, Mina laid out in an eight-page letter to Jones the case of
the young woman she considered her "charge." This letter remains in the archives
of the British Psychoanalytical Society.[25]

The extensive correspondence between Henrietta and Mina themselves has
not, however, survived. This should not surprise us, as "prudence dictated that
[homosexual people] remain unobtrusive and leave behind as little incriminating

evidence as possible." In fact Mina acted purposefully with respect to her papers and destroyed those she did not donate to well-known repositories. Among the latter were communications from Henrietta Bingham.[26] On Henrietta's side little correspondence had been found until I opened a forgotten trunk in the garret of her father's house. Carefully tied up at the bottom were almost two hundred love letters from Tomlin and another lover from the 1920s, John Houseman. But her many relationships with women are represented almost exclusively in photographs she kept.[27] Discovering the Tomlin and Houseman letters only underscored for me the complexities of Mina and Henrietta's bond, and why they preferred that others not see them spilled on paper.

Mina's plea from Paris reached Jones, whose practice in 1922 was scarcely overbooked. The general population rejected psychoanalysis as lewd, and the BBC listed him among figures "dangerous to the public morality." Writing to Freud, he described his new case, "an actively homosexual girl" seeking treatment "both for her inversion and for neurotic symptoms." The young woman had soon been joined by "her feminine partner," and both were "well educated and highly intelligent." Such subjects were "specially interesting."[28] Yet another stroke of luck came his way when Eleanor Chilton (a recent Smith graduate from West Virginia then living in London and romantically entangled with Henrietta *and* Mina) sought his help for sexual and other neuroses.[29] The early days of psychoanalysis were not known for establishing clear professional boundaries around relationships with patients. One letter from Jones to Mina assured her of his strong attraction to each of the trio: "Your allotment of my feelings for the three of you contrasts with Eleanor's dictum that I 'liked' her, 'loved' you, and 'adored' Henrietta. . . . I really love you all in different ways. Of course, H has an enormously strong and deep femininity—that's the trouble. It doesn't show very easily but some day when I've finished some lucky man will get the benefit of it. And you needn't tell me how sweet and lovable she can be." Henrietta enjoyed such warm regard, and Mina considered Jones "my father, my father confessor, my guardian angel and my lover," under whose sure hand she aimed to psychological resolution.[30]

Jones produced a paper, "The Early Development of Female Sexuality" (1927), based on "five cases of manifest homosexuality in women," in hopes of shedding light on what "differentiates the development of homosexual from that of heterosexual women." In all instances he observed an unusually strong infantile fixation in regard to the mother succeeded by a strong father fixation. He found that adult heterosexual women dreaded the mother, whereas lesbians focused their fear of punishment on the father and/or the removal of his love. In effect women whose sexuality was inverted resolved the Oedipus complex by sacrificing their own sex rather than sacrificing their father as their love object. The published paper does not report the outcome of the analyses in the cases in question, but unlike Freud, who cautioned that converting a fully developed homosexual person to heterosexuality was as likely as converting a practicing heterosexual to homosexuality, Jones at least in the clinical setting took on the task of reversing inversion. These Americans, two of whom hailed from southern states, were the clay he tried to reshape.[31]

While Jones had no problem taking on such "interesting" patients, most participants in the Bloomsbury circle strenuously avoided Americans. When Mina met Virginia Woolf's brother, Adrian Stephen, he addressed her in loud, slow tones, as if she spoke a foreign language.[32] And when Lytton Strachey—the transformative biographer, author of *Eminent Victorians* (1918)—wanted to lease his house in the country, Garnett sent Mina and Henrietta to look it over. Carrington, who shared the house, trailed along behind these "two exquisite American girls." But after they sped away in a "blue motor car," Strachey declared he "couldn't bear to have them," and Carrington acceded to the dictum.[33] To be American by definition risked vulgarity. Respectful treatment in Bloomsbury (Woolf counted abolitionists among her ancestors) was less likely still for someone from the South, a land notorious for anemic culture and racial brutality.[34]

Meantime Confederate talismans were arriving by post. That spring Henrietta received a cross and anchor inlaid with shells, items her North Carolina grandfather, Col. Robert Bingham, carved while a prisoner of war on Johnson's Island. An accompanying letter described wartime heroics and claimed that most of his men "could knock a squirrel out of the highest tree in the woods." Outnumbered thirteen to one, his company fought off the enemy for hours before surrendering. Released in a prisoner exchange, her grandfather returned to the front in time to fight again and witness the surrender at Appomattox. Each week Henrietta devotedly sent the Confederate schoolmaster cut flowers; he, in turn, wanted her to have these "symbols" of her legacy.[35]

She grew up on Reconstruction stories, too. Her father claimed that his "earliest memory was of clutching my mother's skirts in terror at a hooded apparition, and having my father raise his mask to relieve me." As the elder Bingham grew up in the 1870s, Robert E. Lee commanded such awe for him that he once felt honor bound to alert a rival boy who had "whipped" him in a fight that he was taking boxing lessons with the express intention of dispatching him next time. Such southern shadows might fascinate or repulse her English acquaintances, and it is difficult to ascertain exactly how Henrietta herself felt about them. Whatever the case, people were reminded of her roots every time she spoke.[36]

"Anything Is Nice if It Comes from Dixieland"

Henrietta sounded southern, but in Bloomsbury it helped that the sounds she made were sometimes coded "black."[37] As a high school senior, she charged a saxophone—hardly considered a suitable instrument for "young ladies"—to her father's account at Louisville's Krausgill Piano Company. Possibly she dreamed of playing in an all-female combo like the ones that began appearing in the late 1920s.[38] But the anomaly in 1923 of a southern belle in London (two years before Josephine Baker swept away Paris) singing and playing what were considered "negro" songs in "negro" styles translated into instant cachet.

Henrietta's love affair with the world of African American music and theater is traceable over the late 1910s and early 1920s. At home in Louisville, she engaged local jug bands and "combos," sometimes from as far as New Orleans, to play at parties.[39] On trips to New York she attended the theater and collected sheet music of Ziegfeld Follies numbers, Sophie Tucker and Al Jolson hits, and "Darktown Strutters' Ball," considered the first jazz record.[40] She would have witnessed Broadway's historic step circa 1921, when full-blown musical theater productions began to feature African American casts instead of whites in blackface. Though the roles often replayed minstrel show stereotypes, a new generation of black performing artists was thriving in America.[41] Some would soon be the toast of London, where Henrietta ushered them directly into her social circle.

With these musicians as her unlikely regional brethren, Henrietta coordinated a degree of racial mingling that would have been scandalous in Louisville and highly irregular even in New York. On an early summer night in 1923, she and Mina threw a party at Grove House, their "pretty regency villa."[42] Perhaps the most remarkable guests were the principal stars of the controversial, just-opened stage sensation *From Dover Street to Dixie*. The "Dixie" portion was lifted from Lew Leslie's 1922 New York success *Plantation Revue*, backed by a superior black jazz orchestra—among the first to be heard in England.[43] There is no record of what Henrietta wore to the show's gala opening, but the petite, birdlike headliner, Florence Mills, dressed in a plantation boy's hobo costume, mesmerized the audience, as would Edith Wilson, a recorded blues vocalist also known for her "hot" (as in sexy) jazz numbers.[44] Henrietta's cross-racial social life was edgy, even for London, where in the later 1920s society hostesses objected to a party with a "negro band." The young ladies might, after all, talk to the musicians. Nearly forty years afterward, Garnett got a thrill from the memory of Henrietta's introducing "Miss Wilson" to him. He had been talking to Henrietta's father, then visiting London. The elder Bingham knew of Wilson, having treated his younger son to the New York version of the show. At the party the trio remained "for some time" conversing across the color line.[45] Having grown up in segregated Louisville, Edith Wilson knew about Bingham, too. Her mother worked as a cook and laundress for white families; her father was descended from famed Kentucky politician, U.S. vice president, and Confederate general John C. Breckinridge. "It was an education for me to listen to their conversation," wrote Garnett, impressed by the "exquisite," "slow ease, the perfect courtesy," between two people separated by a racial gulf.[46]

Even as London set the stage for greater freedom and appreciation for Henrietta's charms, success there established Mills and Wilson as more than just "brilliant entertainers," a position black Americans were by then permitted in the United States. They were granted "the status and respect of the high arts." Londoners embraced these performers in part due to the popular interest in primitivism, a concept shaped by racially muddled art criticism and psychology to which Bloomsbury members contributed. The music, singing, and dancing of the American entertainers appealed to audiences as delightfully exotic yet also profound.[47] James and Alix Strachey (James was Lytton Strachey's brother, and Alix, James's wife, was a confidante of Carrington's who later engaged in a flirtation with Henrietta) were psychoanalysts and Freud's English translators. They collected African artwork because they thought it offered "a more direct expression of the Freudian unconscious." A white southerner who keenly followed, supported, and herself interpreted African American music, Henrietta Bingham had hitched her wagon to a cultural meteor shower.[48]

That late spring evening the party lasted into the wee hours. Henrietta, dressed in lavender, perched on the piano and played her saxophone. The French windows were thrown open, and the revelers turned the lights toward the flower-filled garden. Mina's younger brothers, then visiting from Boston, were rousted from their beds, hustled into "the girls'" pajamas, and led in a dance with Russian ballerina Lydia Lopokova, who arrived from her appearance at Covent Garden.[49] Lytton Strachey—apparently not above accepting American hospitality—served drinks to Mina's brothers, and painter Duncan Grant called the gathering "absolutely perfect . . . beautiful to look at and delicious to taste."[50]

DANGER AND DECADENCE: A SOUTHERN DEBUTANTE IN DISTRESS

Now to the gothic—the taboo, the looming hysteria surrounding Henrietta's 1920s profile. Everyone around Henrietta in those months would have been familiar with Edgar Allan Poe's grotesque antebellum tales of decadence and irrationality and with Harriet Beecher Stowe's 1856 "counter-pastoral," *Uncle Tom's Cabin.* Garnett's memoir with its appreciative rendering of Henrietta's father mingling graciously with his slightly darker countrywoman clashes with other images of the "Judge"—so called after serving briefly on Jefferson County's circuit court—as a manipulative man, a "sinister" force in his daughter's complicated emotional life.[51]

Mina was chief among those who took this dark view. It had not started that way. Bingham's letters to Henrietta at Smith were regularly signed "Love to Mina & best love to you."[52] The young professor had "a bully time" with the Kentucky family in London in 1921, attending the theater and ballet, shopping at Selfridge's department store, and taking jaunts to Sussex. Mina's ostensible hosts that trip were Frida and Harold Laski, friends from her postgraduate studies at Harvard, now attached to the London School of Economics. Frida, a Fabian socialist and birth control reformer, vainly wished Mina would give up the "Southern crowd."[53]

Notable for his high regard for Jews, Robert Worth Bingham appreciated Mina as an intellectual guide to his daughter. He made regular deposits into Henrietta's account at the Guaranty Trust, thereby supporting their life in London. In return Henrietta posted commentaries on British politics. He was certain she would "make a real writer." Indeed he viewed all her activities as preparing her to share and eventually to inherit his roles as newspaper publisher and Democratic Party power broker. His involvement in the state- and national-level cooperative agricultural movement—an outgrowth of his progressivism—had made him "the most popular, and possibly the most powerful, figure in the Commonwealth of Kentucky." One package from home contained Walter Lippmann's *Public Opinion* (1922) because it was important for "us newspaper owners." When she got back the two of them "should read the news daily and then consider apt subjects for editorials."[54] Such seemingly feminist convictions from a southern patriarch, even of the New South variety, are astonishing. For years Henrietta had yearned for, and generally secured, his approval. She also harbored or at least absorbed her father's enormous ambition. The newspapers supplied an ample field on which they could play—together.

But in 1922, just as the young women were settling into their service flat around the corner from the Ritz, Judge Bingham had called Henrietta home. Her elder brother's alcoholic benders were too much; in Asheville her grandfather's health was suffering; he needed her, Henrietta, to "save something from the wreck."[55]

Henrietta wavered. She had "saved" him before and suffered the psychic consequences still—consequences she was trying to unravel in sessions with Jones. The story went that after her mother's death, father and daughter locked together for consolation and companionship in ways that were for her both enormously empowering and confusing. Well before she entered high school, Henrietta was house manager and hostess. Two and a half years later, her father married Mary Lily Kenan Flagler, Standard Oil magnate Henry Flagler's widow, then considered America's wealthiest woman. She and Bingham had met during his college days but renewed their acquaintance in Asheville, where she and her family were staying at the new Grove Park Inn. Off to boarding school went Henrietta. Eight months into the marriage, Mary Lily Bingham, aged fifty, was dead, having signed a codicil to her will that left Bingham five of her many millions. Vicious rumors swirled. Years later President Franklin Roosevelt called Bingham, a hefty political supporter, his favorite murderer.[56]

In the scandal's wake, Henrietta returned to Louisville—to her reign at home and to the security of being the most important woman in her father's life. During the same time, she began to date, but sexual attractions to girls and at least one relationship with an adult woman followed. I was told of a debut party around the time of World War I at which a flower of Louisville society came running from the ladies' room and shouted over the grand staircase, "Henrietta Bingham just kissed me on the lips!"[57]

It seemed clear that a father-daughter complex lay at the root of her troubles, indeed had crippled her for years. Mina watched Henrietta panic when her father bade her return. She became distraught, pinioned by conflicting emotions. Ernest Jones vowed that Henrietta would one day understand "how insecure are incest and homosexuality to build [a life] on."[58]

A play Henrietta wrote with her younger brother dramatized the forces at the center of her relationship with her father and suggests the level of her anger, bounded as it was by pity. In "Shadows," the widowed father, a well-to-do "Southern gentleman," "had an ideal of a woman so independent mentally that she could do whatever she chose with her life." He had raised his daughter "as a new sort of creature." And so she is. His "experiment" is a success, for Gordon, as she is called, has more ambition and independence of mind than any other woman around. But a family friend questions whether the father was capable of facing his daughter's "independence if it means she will leave [him]." He cannot say. The "prospect of loneliness overwhelms me," he replies. He dreads her working, or, worse, marrying. For then they would "never be as close together again."[59]

But in the fall of 1922, Henrietta stood her ground against her father and remained in London to complete what the family referred to as "courses in psychology." The Judge accused her of neglecting her duty to him, then tried to apologize for hurting her.[60] After a full year in England, Henrietta returned to Kentucky and opened a bookstore in Louisville. Mina was teaching again in Northampton, but her sense of responsibility for and even ownership of her friend's well-being was reaching a peak. One winter evening, after a visit from Henrietta, Mina picked up an old journal and wrote of how "under my care she has changed from a frightened, rebellious child to an independent, reliable girl. Her judgment is unsurpassed. The keenness and directness of her mind carve out infallible opinions. By her alone, could any of my decisions be influenced."[61]

Predictably Mina and Bingham came to loggerheads. So long as she and the Judge wanted the same thing for Henrietta, all was "bully"; but they planned to spend the summer together in England, and Mina was pressing Henrietta to complete her analysis and break from her father's grip. Soon there was a full-blown feud.

Varying accounts of the rift survive. In one the jealous, vengeful, window-peeping, alcoholic brother witnessed an act of lesbian "perversion" and informed the outraged father. In another the bisexual bluestocking (Mina), being already in love with Henrietta, seduced her father and angled to marry the older man as a way to have them both. And in yet another the father approached Mina with a proposal and was rebuffed. Mina was in any case "banned from the family circle."[62] No wonder Grant, the thirty-nine-year-old veteran of countless affairs and personal dramas, enjoyed Mina's visits that summer of 1924 to his studio, where she was sitting for her portrait. He eagerly anticipated the next installment in Henrietta's "hair-raising" "history."[63] It was as good as "The Fall of the House of Usher."

Meanwhile Dora Carrington and Lytton Strachey had a new house, and Carrington organized weekend parties where friends painted the walls, breaking for rides and walks evening games, and drinks. As a laborer Henrietta almost won Strachey over. "I liked her more than before," he wrote to Garnett. "She whitewashed unceasingly and never said a word."[64] The affair with Carrington had been bumpy, and Carrington hungered for time alone with her. One afternoon they slipped off after tea and walked far across plowed fields, "through little conifer plantations until we came onto "Sheepless Down," and saw faraway in the distance the downs of Tidworth and Salisbury. She won me by being completely captivated by my down. . . . She dresses badly, talks American, and has a hundred faults but somehow they don't matter, she is so beautiful, and so charmingly sensitive."[65]

Also present for many of the painting parties was Stephen Tomlin. He had weathered Henrietta's return to Kentucky over the previous winter, but cables and Christmas "pekon nuts" did not make up for the lack of long letters. Surely she was "the triumphant success you always are everywhere" and had been "surrounded by adorers of every sex." Tomlin realized Henrietta had gotten him "to my knees at the start and I suppose that is where I shall remain." The person who first brought Henrietta to the painting parties may have been Stephen Tomlin, He had fallen for Henrietta in early 1923 and produced an impressive bronze head of his lover that year. Her return to Kentucky in the fall of 1923 had spawned a flood of heartsick letters from the young sculptor. He was not jealous, per se, indeed he assumed that at home she was "surrounded by adorers of every sex" and "the triumphant success you always are everywhere." She sent him a great box of bourbon and "pekon nuts" at Christmas, but this did not make up for her failures as a correspondent. Tomlin tried to forget her, but couldn't. She had gotten him "to my knees at the start and I suppose that is where I shall remain." Tommy, as he was called, was tolerant of Henrietta's lesbian adventures (he engaged in homosexual flirtations of his own) and by the time she came back to England in June of 1924 the couple was talking about marriage. She left both Tomlin and Carrington miserable when Henrietta's "dreadful father and brothers" took her off to a Scottish castle for grouse season.[66]

Casualties littered the battlefield. Mina retired, crushed by her treatment at the hands of the Judge. Henrietta was caught between. Then the gothic spectacle reached its climax with an unexpected announcement. Ernest Jones informed his wife that "Judge Bingham is here and is suddenly to marry on Wednesday.

Henrietta vomited for 5 hours at the news. General frightful crises with Bing-hamesque scenes." The word around Bloomsbury was that the father had mar-ried to spite Henrietta "for her coldness toward him," for not remaining at his side in Kentucky. [67] But the marriage hardly eased their entanglement. Emotions were running high when the Judge demanded an interview with Jones. It was "dramatic," but Jones believed that both parties left his office "equally relieved" by the understanding the doctor had been able to broker.[68] In the wake of this confrontation, a friend noted that Henrietta took care to wear skirts in public. But the calm was fragile if not fictive, and as Christmas approached Judge Bingham again insisted that she return home. Jones alerted Mina that Henrietta "dreads he might think she is still h - l [homosexual] if she doesn't come. A mass of guilt, poor child."[69] Henrietta remained in Europe.

Granting that living openly as a lesbian in 1924 was (in her sister-in-law's words) "beyond the pale," Henrietta might have steered a safer course: there could easily have been another wedding that year. She could have married Tomlin. He was well-born, well-educated, delightfully conversational, artistically talented, and sexually tolerant (albeit emotionally unstable). He wished they had tied the knot the day after they met at Garnett's *Lady into Fox* party. For more than a year, he had begged for her hand while expressing his horror of any kind of "posses-sion" that might cause her to "lose your own identity."[70] Indeed she proved almost as elusive a love as the vixen in the story, remaining the "Kentucky princess," at-tracting admirers, performing southernness, and finding pleasure and meaning at cultural and racial intersections. Lovable and beloved, Henrietta was perfection—when she was with her lovers. She "lacked no quality." But she seemed always to be leaving and would send only "corseted little lines" in too-infrequent letters.[71] At some point these were discarded. The desires, drama, and distress trace the line Henrietta Bingham walked between freedom and fear. It was a tightrope.

NOTES

1. *Carrington*, written and directed by Christopher Hampton, was based on Michael Holroyd's biography *Lytton Strachey* (New York: Holt, 1980). Hampton expressed regret at not including Bingham in the story despite her pivotal role in Carrington's "polymor-phous period"; see Malcolm Lawrence, "Interview with Christopher Hampton," *Cin-ema Stardust*, November 1995, http://towerofbabel.com/sections/film/cinemastardust/hampton.htm. In *Lady into Fox* (London: Chatto & Windus, 1922), a young English wife presents her husband with a dilemma when she transforms into a vixen. Garnett used the parable-like tale to address the problem of fidelity and love's changeability. It was dedi-cated to his one-time lover Duncan Grant. This essay is part of a larger project focusing on the life of Henrietta Bingham.

2. Dora Carrington to Gerald Brenan, May 31, 1923, Gerald Brenan Collection, Harry Ransom Humanities Research Center, University of Texas at Austin [GBC-HRC].

3. David Garnett to Mina Kirstein Curtiss, March 9, 1962, Berg Collection, New York Public Library, New York [Berg, NYPL]; John Houseman, interview with Susan E. Tifft and Alex S. Jones, in possession of the author; David Garnett, *The Familiar Faces: Being Volume Three of the Golden Echo* (London: Chatto & Windus, 1962), 9, 11.

4. During the 1920s lesbian, bisexual, and gay culture and community, much less "identity," were not widely conceptualized or developed, and Henrietta Bingham's evolving self-understanding is impossible to ascertain, though there are indicators. For examples of scholarship around these concepts, see for instance the "failed lesbian" narrative attached to writer Vernon Lee, as explored in Sally Newman, "The Archival Traces of Desire: Vernon Lee's Failed Sexuality and the Interpretation of Letters in Lesbian History," *Journal of the History of Sexuality* 14 (2005): 51–77, and Anna Clark's "Twilight Moments," *Journal of the History of Sexuality* 14 (2005): 139–60. The work of uncovering the lives of southern lesbians has begun. See Pippa Holloway, "Searching for Southern Lesbian History," in *Women of the American South: A Multicultural Reader*, ed. Christie Anne Farnham (New York: New York University Press, 1997), 258–72. In the same year, John Howard, ed., *Carryin' On in the Gay and Lesbian South* (New York: New York University Press, 1997), was published. The cardinal points of gay history have been framed as identity, community, politics, and desire. This project highlights that final aspect of homosexual life.

5. Henrietta Worth Bingham [HWB] to Barry Bingham, January 22, 1943, Mary Caperton Bingham Papers, Filson Historical Society, Louisville, Kentucky; Mary Caperton Bingham, interview with the author, 1994.

6. Havelock Ellis (1859–1939) published his study *Sexual Inversion* in 1897 and continued to write on the subject in his last decade. George Chauncey Jr. parses the evolution of medico-scientific terminology in "From Sexual Inversion to Homosexuality: Medicine and the Changing Conceptualization of Female Deviance," *Salmagundi* 58–59 (1983): 114–46.

7. John Houseman, *Front and Center* (New York: Simon & Schuster, 1979), 109; Dr. Hugh Young to Robert Worth Bingham [RWB], Robert Worth Bingham Papers, Library of Congress, Washington, D.C. [RWB-LOC].

8. Joan Schenkar places Bingham among the women whose lives went awry in the shadow of their family members' wealth and/or fame; Schenkar, *Truly Wilde: The Unsettling Story of Dolly Wilde, Oscar's Unusual Niece* (New York: Basic Books, 2000), 406–11. As Schenkar has noted, many "dissolved their disappointments in acid baths of chemicals and liquids" (410).

9. Tomlin to HWB, August 27, 1923, in possession of author; Dora Carrington to Gerald Brenan, August 6, 1924, in *Carrington: Letters and Extracts from Her Diaries*, ed. David Garnett (New York: Holt, Rinehart & Winston, 1970), 299, 403.

10. David Gadd, *The Loving Friends: A Portrait of Bloomsbury* (London: Hogarth, 1974), xiii. The literature about the members of this loose-knit group is immense. For other helpful looks at the group and their approach to living, see Janet Malcolm, "A House of One's Own," *New Yorker*, June 5, 1995, 58–79, and Frances Partridge, *Love in Bloomsbury: Memories* (Boston: Little, Brown, 1981).

11. Even before the devastation of World War I, "many a duke looked around for ways and means to supplement his income. One of these was the American wife." Susanne Everett, *London: The Glamour Years: 1919–1939* (New York: Gallery Books, 1985).

12. F. Scott Fitzgerald, *The Great Gatsby* (New York: Scribner, 1925), 120.

13. Lesbian sex as chic, see Lillian Faderman, *Odd Girls and Twilight Lovers: A History of Lesbian Life in Twentieth-Century America* (New York: Columbia University Press, 1991), 85–88, Houseman, Tifft, and Jones, 14, and Stephen Tomlin to HWB, July 11, 1924, in author's possession. The nascent lesbian and bisexual culture, see Faderman, *Odd Girls*, 66, 69–77, 91), and, somewhat later, Robert A Schanke, *"That Furious Lesbian": The Story of Mercedes de Acosta* (Carbondale: Southern Illinois University Press, 2003). Among the Bloomsbury Group, male homosexuality was more prevalent and more accepted than lesbianism.

For theatrical intersections with lesbianism, see also Robert A. Schanke, *"That Furious Lesbian": The Story of Mercedes de Acosta* (Carbondale: Southern Illinois University Press, 2003). The overweighting of literary representations in cultural history is apparent in our greater familiarity with novels such as Woolf's androgynous fable *Orlando* (1928) and Hall's defiant *The Well of Loneliness* (1928). Hazel V. Carby, who has focused on black women writers of the Harlem Renaissance, addressed this shortcoming in her essay on women's blues music of the 1920s, "'It Jus Be's Dat Way Sometime': The Sexual Politics of Women's Blues," in *Unequal Sisters: A Multicultural Reader in U.S. Women's History*, ed. Vicki L. Ruiz and Ellen Carroll Dubois, 2nd ed. (New York: Routledge, 1994), 330–41.

14. On the 1920s see Faderman, *Odd Girls*; Florence Tamagne, *A History of Homosexuality in Europe: Berlin, London, Paris, 1919–1939* (New York: Algora, 2004); and Carroll Smith-Rosenberg, "The New Woman as Androgyne," in her *Disorderly Conduct: Visions of Gender in Victorian America* (New York: Oxford University Press, 1985), 245–96. On psychoanalysis see Tamagne, *History of Homosexuality in Europe*, 225–26; Henry L. Minton, *Departing from Deviance: A History of Homosexual Rights and Emancipatory Science in America* (Chicago: University of Chicago Press, 2002); Peter Gay, *Freud: A Life for Our Time* (New York: Norton, 1998); and Brenda Maddox, *Freud's Wizard: Ernest Jones and the Transformation of Psychoanalysis* (Cambridge, Mass.: Da Capo, 2007).

15. Bingham (1871–1937) was born in Alamance County, North Carolina. The family school moved to Asheville in 1891. William E. Ellis, *Robert Worth Bingham and the Southern Mystique: From the Old South to the New South and Beyond* (Kent, Ohio: Kent State University Press, 1997), 1–2, 9, 14–16, 52–53, 63.

16. Mina Stein Kirstein (1896–1985) spent most of her childhood in Rochester, New York, and moved to Boston when her father assumed a partnership role in Filene's department store. She taught at Smith from 1922 until 1934 and again in 1940–42. In 1926 she married Henry Tomlinson Curtiss. For her Smith days, see her essay on the challenges of intellectual life at college, "One of the Little Foxes," *Seven Arts Chronicle* 1 (1916): 667–68; Mina Kirstein Curtiss [MKC], "The Past and I," 125–28, unpublished memoir, Papers of Mina Kirstein Curtiss, Sophia Smith Collection, Smith College, Northampton, Mass. [MKC-SSC]. Her friends included journalist Franklin P. Adams, publisher Benjamin Heubsch, and Walter and Faye Lippmann (see Frida Laski to MKC, December

19, 1921, MKC-SSC). On her experience as a Jew, see MKC, "Chosen," *Massachusetts Review* 24, no. 2 (1983): 425–32. In 1949 she published the first English translation of *The Letters of Marcel Proust* (New York: Random House). Biographies followed: *Bizet and His World* (New York: Knopf, 1958) and *A Forgotten Empress: Anna Ivanovich and Her Era, 1730–1740* (New York: Ungar, 1974). Her *Other People's Letters: A Memoir* (Boston: Houghton Mifflin, 1978) was reissued in paperback by Helen Marx Books in 2005.

17. MKC to Ernest Jones [EJ], September 23, 1922, Ernest Jones Papers, Archives of the British Psychoanalytical Society, London [EJP-APBS].

18. MKC to EJ, September 23, 1922, EJP-ABPS; John Houseman, draft manuscript of his memoir *Run-Through*, John Houseman Papers, University of California at Los Angeles Library, box 51, folder 7. The women's sexual and emotional attachment was a closely guarded aspect of Curtiss's life; many years later she named Henrietta as the first of her three great loves (the others were her husband and the poet and French Nobel laureate Saint-John Perse). Stephen Pascal, ed., *The Grand Surprise: The Journals of Leo Lerman* (New York: Knopf, 2007), 408, 408n2.

19. David Garnett to MKC, August 18, 1924, Berg, NYPL; MKC to EJ, September 23, 1921, EJP-ABPS. A contemporary who knew Henrietta well in Louisville, London, and, later, New York reported that Mina, unlike Henrietta, seemed to be heterosexual. See Susan Tifft and Alex Jones, interview with Sophie Preston Albert and Jacques Albert, Louisville, Kentucky, February 27, 1987, 24, in author's possession. Mina's discomfort with homosexual relationships was apparent in her letters to Jones and others about her brother, Lincoln Kirstein. For a full treatment of his life, see Martin Duberman, *The Worlds of Lincoln Kirstein* (New York: Knopf, 2007).

20. Academic difficulties were par for the course for southern women at elite northern institutions such as Smith. See Joan Marie Johnson, *Southern Women at the Seven Sister Colleges: Feminist Values and Social Activism, 1875–1915* (Athens: University of Georgia Press, 2008), 42–52.

21. Henrietta entered Smith in the fall of 1920. She dropped out after Christmas but returned as a freshman for the 1921–22 academic year. See Catalogue of Smith College, 1920–21 and 1921–22, MKC-SSC. The records of dropped classes and the "detriment" statement come from Administrative Board minutes, 1920–22, Dean's Office, Smith College.

22. MKC to EJ, September 23, 1922, EJP-ABPS.

23. Abraham Arden Brill (1874–1948) pioneered American psychoanalysis, translated Freud's works, treated many Greenwich Village bohemians, and in 1921 published *Fundamental Conceptions of Psychoanalysis* (New York: Harcourt Brace). He was likely on his way to attend the International Congress of Psychoanalysis, held in September in Berlin.

24. Alfred Ernest Jones (1879–1958) was born in Wales and studied medicine in London. On his influence see Maddox, *Freud's Wizard*, 1. Vincent Brome critiqued his views on homosexuality in *Ernest Jones: Freud's Alter Ego* (New York: Norton, 1983).

25. MKC to EJ, September 23, 1922, EJP-ABPS.

26. John D'Emilio, *Sexual Politics, Sexual Communities: The Making of a Homosexual Minority in the United States, 1940–1970* (Chicago: University of Chicago Press, 1983),

20. The bulk of Curtiss's papers went to the Sophia Smith Collection. She also donated Bloomsbury-related correspondence to the New York Public Library, including several letters from David Garnett to Henrietta. She placed letters from Jones with the Freud Archive at the Library of Congress and her own literary correspondence at Yale. She burned a great deal, too. "These past two evenings she has been tearing and burning letters from [Antoine de Saint Exupéry translator] Lewis Galantiere and others," her friend Leo Lerman wrote. "Some feel of social history, but she doesn't want anyone to read them. How very odd for a biographer to do this—and how selfish"; journal entry, September 5, 1965, in Pascal, *Grand Surprise*, 278.

27. A handful of Henrietta's letters to family members survive, along with a set of mysterious transcriptions of her father's letters to her in college and abroad. Perhaps Henrietta kept the records of her relationships with men as reminders of the choices she had. Female partners included Smith graduate Jeanette Young of Chicago, English actress Beatrix Lehmann, American tennis player Helen Hull Jacobs, stage actress Hope Williams, and, later in life, Dorothie Holland, who had been on stage in the 1920s.

28. "Ernest Jones," Wikipedia, April 29, 2009, http://en.wikipedia.org/wiki/Ernest_Jones; EJ to Sigmund Freud, February 15, 1923, in The Complete Correspondence of Sigmund Freud and Ernest Jones, 1908–1939 ed. R. Andrew Paskauskas (Cambridge, Mass.: Belknap Press of Harvard University Press, 1993), 510.

29. Eleanor Carroll Chilton (later Agar), Smith College, 1922 (1900–1948). An anonymous handwritten volume of her poetry is in the MKC-SSC. The same poems may be found (along with others) in the Eleanor Chilton Agar Collection, Smith College Archives, and include writings about Mina and Henrietta. The volume is inscribed to "M.S.K." and opens with a dedication: "Dearest, remind me: it is true/That you have given me all but love;/And that I've love enough for two;/And love is all I have for you." MKC, "Slices of Life," unpublished memoir, and different version, "The Past and I," MKC-SSC, 9–10.

30. EJ to MKC, April 7, 1925, and MKC to Jones, December 27, 1924, EJP-APBS.

31. Jones described three of the patients as being in their early twenties, corresponding with Kirstein, Bingham, and Chilton. He noted that "only two" of the five "had an entirely negative attitude toward men," implying a better chance of success in reversing their homosexual behavior. Ernest Jones, "The Early Development of Female Sexuality," read at the Tenth International Congress of Psycho-Analysis, Innsbruck, September 18, 1927, *International Journal of Psycho-Analysis* 8 (1927): 459, 460. Freud's skepticism about "converting" sexuality is laid out in "The Psychogenesis of a Case of Homosexuality in a Woman" (1920), in *The Standard Edition of the Complete Psychological Works of Sigmund Freud*, vol. 18 (1920–22), trans. James Strachey et al. (London: Hogarth, 1955), 151.

32. MKC, "Past and I," 9–10.

33. Carrington to Brenan, March 1, 1923, GBC-HRC.

34. Quentin Bell, *Virginia Woolf: A Biography* (London: Hogarth, 1973), 4.

35. Robert Bingham (1838–1927) to HWB, March 14, 1923, Southern Historical Collection, Wilson Library, University of North Carolina at Chapel Hill.

36. RWB to Margaret Mitchell, February 16, 1937, RWB-LOC.

37. "Anything Is Nice if It Comes from Dixieland," by Grant Clark, George W. Meyer, and Milton Ager, New York: Leo Feist, 1919. Sheet music, HBR collection, in author's possession.

38. March 1, 1920, 309 West Walnut Street, Receipted Bills G-P, Robert Worth Bingham Papers, addition, Filson Historical Society, Louisville, Kentucky. For resistance to female saxophonists, see the *New York Times* obituary for Peggy Gilbert (1905–2007), Sunday, February 25, 2007. For Henrietta's sax playing in London, see, for instance, Garnett, *Familiar Faces*, 10.

39. RWB to HWB, February 24, 1923, Pineland, Georgia, to London; Tifft and Jones, Albert interview, 11. For more on jug band music, which originated and flourished in post–World War I Louisville, see "Jug Bands," in *The Encyclopedia of Louisville*, ed. John E. Kleber (Lexington: University of Kentucky Press, 2001), 454.

40. Tifft and Jones, Albert interview, 11. The all-white Original Dixieland Jazz Band recorded "Darktown Strutters' Ball" in 1917 and took New York by storm. Betty Nygaard King, "Darktown Strutters' Ball," *Encyclopedia of Music in Canada*, May 8, 2009, http://www.thecanadianencyclopedia.ca/en/article/darktown-strutters-ball-emc (accessed June 20, 2014). HWB's copy of the sheet music in author's possession.

41. Allen Woll, *Black Musical Theatre: From Coontown to Dreamgirls* (1989; New York: Da Capo, 1991), 81–82; Bill Egan, *Florence Mills: Harlem Jazz Queen* (Lanham, Md.: Scarecrow, 2004), 66–73; Steve Tracy, "Stafford and Wilson: Trailblazers in a Brave New World," liner notes to *"Ain't Gonna Settle Down": The Pioneering Blues of Mary Stafford and Edith Wilson*, Archeophone Records, 2008.

42. It is a well-documented gathering, appearing in the writings of David Garnett, Duncan Grant, John Houseman, and Lincoln Kirstein (Mina's brother). Lincoln Kirstein, "Villa," in *Mosaic: Memoirs* (New York: Farrar, Straus & Giroux, 1994), 59.

43. For the influence on jazz in England of the Plantation Orchestra and an overlapping production called *Plantation Days*, with musicians led by James P. Johnson (whom Houseman noted Henrietta knew, as well), see Howard Rye and Jeffrey Green, "Black Musical Internationalism in England," *Black Music Research Journal* 15 (1995): 101–5. For a description of the show, see Egan, *Florence Mills*, 86–88; for its impact on music in England, see Egan, *Florence Mills*, 91.

44. Mills opened with "Down among the Sleepy Hills of Ten-Ten-Tennessee," and Wilson sang "Yankee Doodle Blues." On the production see Egan, *Florence Mills*, 77–98.

45. D. J. Taylor, *Bright Young People: The Lost Generation of London's Jazz Age* (New York: Farrar, Straus & Giroux, 2007), 6, 130–31; RWB to HWB, November 22, 1922, New York [Waldorf-Astoria] to London, transcribed letters bulk 1921–23, from Sam Thomas, in author's possession. Garnett refers to "Miss Wilson" in his *Familiar Faces*, 14.

46. Wilson, finding herself with a novelist, might have talked that night about her grandmother, a slave who ran away from Breckinridge and whom she said inspired the character of Eliza in Harriet Beecher Stowe's *Uncle Tom's Cabin*. See Tracy, "Stafford and Wilson," 10; Garnett, *Familiar Faces*, 14–15.

47. Wilson, Mills, and the musicians of the Dixie part of *Dover Street to Dixie* were in demand at London parties all that summer—another was thrown by poet and shipping

heiress Nancy Cunard, whose relationship with a black jazz pianist and writer became a scandal later in the decade. Egan, *Florence Mills*, 92–93. For more on the high art critical argument, see Gretchen Gerzina, "Bushmen and Blackface: Bloomsbury and 'Race,'" *South Carolina Review* 38 (2006): 46–64, 279. Virginia Woolf portrayed Jazz Age dance and music as destabilizing; for many it promised an authenticity shell-shocked Europeans craved after the Great War. A close reading of the place of dance in Woolf's writings appears in Rishona Zimring, "'The Dangerous Art Where One Slip Means Death': Dance and Literary Imagination in Interwar Britain," *Modernism/Modernity* 14 (2007): 707–27.

48. Perry Meisel and Walter Kendrick, eds., Bloomsbury/Freud: The Letters of James and Alix Strachey, 1924–1925 (New York: Basic Books, 1985), 47. Houseman noted that her close relationships with black performers continued during her residence in New York in 1925–26. Tifft and Jones, Houseman interview, 8, 5, 28.

49. Garnett, *Familiar Faces*, 14; John Houseman, *Run-Through: A Memoir* (New York: Curtis Books, 1972), 46; David Garnett to Constance Garnett, July 1, 1923, David Garnett Collection, HRC; Lincoln Kirstein, *Thirty Years: The New York City Ballet* (New York: Knopf, 1978), 6–7. Mina's brother, Lincoln, went on to found the New York City Ballet with George Balanchine, though he erred in dating this memory from 1922; it was 1923.

50. Duncan Grant to MKC, August 12, 1923, Berg, NYPL.

51. "Gothicism," in *The Companion to Southern Literature: Themes, Genres, Places, People, Movements, and Motifs*, ed. Todd W. Taylor, Joseph M. Flora, and Lucinda Hardwick MacKethan (Baton Rouge: Louisiana State University Press), 311–16; Lucinda Mac-Kethan, "Genres of Southern Literature," *Southern Spaces*, February 16, 2004, http://www.southernspaces.org/contents/2004/mackethan/5a.v2.html; Susan E. Tifft and Alex S. Jones, *The Patriarch: The Rise and Fall of the Bingham Dynasty* (New York: Summit Books, 1991), 43; MKC to EJ, September 23, 1922, EJP-ABPS; Tifft and Jones, House-man interview. Garnett, conscious of tension between father and daughter, avoided Bingham, without, however, threatening the checks he received for contributions to the *Courier-Journal* book page. Samples of his submissions are found scattered in the Sunday editions, 1924–26. Garnett remained on friendly terms with Bingham despite his concerns about Henrietta, inscribing John Evelyn's *Memoires for My Grand-Son*, transcribed by Geoffrey Keynes (Oxford: Nonesuch, 1926) to Bingham (in author's possession). David Garnett to MKC, August 10, 1923, Berg, NYPL.

52. RWB to HWB, October 5, 1921, and March 4, 1922.

53. Louis E. Kirstein [LEK] to MKC (in London), July 26, 1921, Louis E. Kirstein Papers, Baker Library, Harvard University School of Business, Cambridge, Mass.; MKC to LEK, July 5, 1921, MKC-SSC; Frida Laski to MKC, March 16, 1922, MKC-SSC.

54. Philo-Semitism, RWB to HWB, March 4, 1922 and undated "Expression of Esteem on behalf of American citizens of Jewish faith in Louisville," in Mary Caperton Bingham Papers, courtesy Eleanor Bingham Miller. Financial indulgence and expectations of Henrietta's political and publishing future, Sophie and Jacques Albert, Tifft and Jones, 8, 11, 28, interview with Mary Caperton Bingham, 1994, by author, and Houseman, Tifft and Jones, 4, 6, 9, 11. "Popular," Ellis, Robert Worth Bingham and

the Southern Mystique, 81. "Writer," RWB to HWB, November 29, 1922, in author's possession. On her future in Kentucky, see RWB to HWB, March 4, 1922, February 25, 1923, and March 9, 1923 (which came with Lippmann).

55. RWB to HWB, October 30, 1922, in author's possession.

56. MKC to EJ, September 22, 1922, EJP-ABPS. The story is repeated in the Tifft and Jones interview with Houseman, and the problematic father-daughter relationship became a source of tension when Henrietta and Houseman were together in 1925–27. On Mary Lily Kenan Flagler Bingham, see Tifft and Jones, *Patriarch*, 56–71, which argues that she died from complications of syphilis, while Robert Worth Bingham's biographer suggests (more convincingly) that alcoholism caused her death. Ellis, *Robert Worth Bingham*, 59–61, 214–15 n. 25, 214. Travis J. Tysinger, headmaster of Stuart Hall, confirmed in a February 26, 1987, letter to Tifft Henrietta's attendance from September 1916 until December 1917, when she left midyear (copy in possession of author); Stuart Hall's yearbook, *Inlook*, detailed her participation in tennis, basketball, volleyball, and the missionary society. She passed her courses and earned honors in English and German.

57. Sarah McNeal Few to author, ca. 2004.

58. EJ to MKC, January 27, 1925, Ernest Jones Papers, Sigmund Freud Archives, Library of Congress, Washington, D.C. [FA-LOC].

59. "Shadows," by H.W.B and G.B.B., n.d. [1926?], in possession of Eleanor Bingham Miller.

60. RWB to HWB, October 30, 1922, and November 22, 1922, in author's possession.

61. Diary entry, January 6, 1924, MKC Diary 1918–19, MKC-SSC.

62. Tifft and Jones, Houseman interview, 26; Frida Laski to Benjamin Huebsch, February 24, 1933, Benjamin Huebsch Papers, Library of Congress; Mary Caperton Bingham interview. David Garnett ran interference between Mina and the elder Bingham; HWB to Garnett, June 10, 1924, Garnett Family Papers, Charles Deering McCormick Library of Special Collections, Northwestern University, Evanston, Ill.

63. Duncan Grant to MKC, August 31 and September 16, 1924, Berg, NYPL.

64. Frances Partridge, *Memories* (London: Clark, 1982), 98–99; Lytton Strachey to David Garnett, June 23, 1924, Robert Taylor Collection, Series 3, Modern Manuscript Collection, Box 18, Manuscripts Division of the Rare Books and Special Collections Department of the Princeton University Library, Princeton, N.J.

65. Carrington to Brenan, June 23, 1924, GBC-HRC. For a description of life at Ham Spray, Ham Spray was the home, beginning in 1924, of Lytton Strachey, Dora Carrington, and Ralph Partridge. see David Garnett, *Great Friends: Portraits of Seventeen Writers* (New York: Atheneum, 1980), 157.

66. "Pekon," and "triumph," Tomlin to HWB, September 15, 1923, author's possession; "surrounded," Tomlin to HWB January 1, 1924, author's possession. "Dreadful," Dora Carrington to Gerald Brenan, August 6, 1924, Carrington: Letters and Extracts from Her Diaries, 369. Miserable, Carrington to Brenan, August 24, 1924, GBC-HRC.

67. Bingham married Aleen Muldoon Hilliard (1877–1953) at St. Margaret Church, Westminster, in London; EJ to Mrs. Ernest [Katherine] Jones, August 7, 1924, EJP-ABPS;

September 27, 1924, James Strachey to Alix Strachey, Strachey Papers, British Library, London.

68. EJ to MKC, October 21, 1924, Jones Papers, FA-LOC.

69. EJ to MKC, November 12, 1924, Jones Papers, FA-LOC; Tifft and Jones, Albert interview, 25. Laura Doan, in *Fashioning Sapphism: The Origins of a Modern English Lesbian Culture* (New York: Columbia University Press, 2001), 97, cautions against ahistorical assumptions that women's masculine clothing signified sexual identity.

70. Mary Caperton Bingham, interview with the author, 1994; Tomlin to HWB, January 1, 1924, and November 25, 1923.

71. Carrington to Brenan, July 8, 1924, GBC-HRC; MKC to EJ, December 27, 1924, EJP-ABPS.

Daniel R. Miller

Nationalism, Marxism, and the Christian Reformed Church in Cuba

Nationalism has been a key determinant of the Cuban Revolution. Fidel Castro famously complained that even to toast the nation's independence with a Cuba Libre, one had to imbibe a soft drink imported from the United States. More broadly and seriously, the Fidelista revolution has as one of its principal aims to promote a more authentically Cuban society by weaning the Cuban people away from dependence on the economy and the culture of North America. Another key element of the revolution, Marxist Leninism, is expressed not only in political and economic structures, but also in the materialist and antireligious tenor of public discourse. Both aspects of the Cuban Revolution have posed serious challenges for Cuba's Protestant and Catholic churches. They have felt various types of pressure to cut financial and institutional ties with North America in order to become more "Cuban" and to adjust their beliefs and practices to conform more closely to the ideals and expectations of the revolution. The experience of the Cuban Christian Reformed Church illustrates how state influence in the life of Cuba's religious community has waxed and waned since the start of the revolution. It also reveals how one small denomination has attempted to balance these competing influences.

Prior to the revolution, Cuba's Christian churches were characterized by a degree of pluralism unusual in Latin America at that time. They were also highly dependent on foreign resources and ideas. The Catholic Church was an imposing institution, but its roots were shallow. High rates of nominal affiliation could not obscure the fact only a minority of Cubans had meaningful contact with the church. Much of the clergy was foreign born and unfamiliar with life as it was experienced by the poor majority of Cubans. The hierarchy, anxious to preserve the institutional privileges of the church, expressed only tepid concern about issues of poverty and injustice prior to 1959. Lay activism generally took forms that appealed to the sensibilities of upper- and middle-class Cubans. Among the poorer classes and in the rural areas, religious identity was only weakly tied to the Catholic Church.[1] The weakness of the Catholic Church in Cuba along with the island's proximity to the United States made it an attractive mission field to

North American Protestants in the early twentieth century. Although Protestants did preach a message of personal uplift through education and righteous living, the theology they brought, like the theology of the Catholic Church, largely ignored issues of social justice. And like the Catholic Church, Protestants focused their attention on middle-class Cubans, some of whom had already broken away from Catholicism. By the middle of the twentieth century, most of Cuba's Protestant churches were highly dependent on North America for resources and theological ideas.[2]

While a number of individual Christians were prominent in the struggle against the military regime of Fulgencio Batista, most churches of whatever stripe avoided taking an official position on the legitimacy of Batista's government or the insurrection that was attempting to overthrow it. Many church leaders expressed relief at Batista's overthrow, but their enthusiasm for Castro's government faded quickly as state and churches clashed on a broad range of issues. By the mid-1960s Cuban church members found themselves under great pressure to identify themselves either as Christians or as supporters of the revolution. The immense popularity of Castro and the revolutionary movement he led, coupled with the narrowness of the churches' prerevolutionary social base, guaranteed that by almost any measure the churches would end up the losers in this clash of loyalties. Cubans who continued to identify themselves as Christians by such public acts as attending worship services endured marginalization in many spheres of life, and some suffered overt forms of discrimination. The churches lost conservative clerical and lay members to exile and progressive members to the Communist Party. A few denominations went out of existence entirely; most retreated into survival mode, hoping to ride out the storm.[3]

Far from fading away, however, the revolutionary government institutionalized its relations with the churches in the Constitution of 1976. The document explicitly guaranteed freedom of conscience in matters of religion.[4] However it undermined this right in other sections, such as Article 39, paragraph 1 ("The education of children and young people in the spirit of communism is the duty of all society"), and Article 54, paragraph 3 ("It is illegal and punishable by law to use religious faith or belief to oppose the Revolution or education, or to oppose compliance with the duty to work, to defend the homeland with arms, to revere its symbols, or any other duties established by the Constitution").[5] Civil and criminal codes elaborated on these limitations, prohibiting teachers from engaging in religious activities, excluding religious believers from a variety of employments, and criminalizing expressions of pacifism or attendance at unregistered associations such as house churches.[6]

Once it became clear that the revolution was not going to be a brief historical aberration but an ongoing reality, the Cuban clergy began expressing a more conciliatory attitude toward the government. At the end of the 1960s, the Catholic hierarchy, which had kept its peace in the wake of the Bay of Pigs debacle, issued a pair of pastoral letters condemning the U.S. embargo and calling upon lay Catholics to take an active role in the Cuban government's efforts to improve the material lot of the people.[7] In a similar fashion the Cuban Council of Evangelical Churches (Concilio Cubano de Iglesias Evangélicas) met in September 1972 to reflect on "the dual responsibility of Cuban Christians to their churches and to society."[8] In both Catholic and Protestant congregations, lay members were less enthusiastic about these olive branches than were their leaders. Catholic laity accused their bishops of selling out to Castro; conservative Protestants elected less conciliatory officials to the next meeting of the CCIE and, when progressives recaptured the organization, many conservatives withdrew from it.[9] Still it was becoming clear to all but the most intransigent anticommunists that the Fidelista revolution was here to stay and that a modus vivendi with it would have to be reached if the churches were to continue to play a significant role in Cuban society.

On the side of the government, a similar process of rapprochement was visible. In 1972 Castro addressed a meeting of Christians for Socialism in Chile, saying, "Where do the contradictions between Christian teachings and socialist teachings lie? Where? We both wish to struggle on behalf of man, for the welfare of man, for the happiness of man."[10] Seven years later the vocal support given to the Sandinistas by a "popular" faction of the Nicaraguan Catholic Church was acknowledged by Fidel and the official Cuban press as a sign that a certain kind of religion could be useful to the revolution.[11] Then in 1984 Rev. Jesse Jackson went to Cuba to seek the release of some prisoners of conscience. During the visit he invited Castro to accompany him to a Methodist church in Havana, an act that undermined the widespread perception that communists must avoid contact with religion.[12] In the following year, Castro granted an extensive series of interviews to Frei Betto, a Brazilian bishop who was eager to find common ground between Cuba's revolution and the Catholic Church. A transcript of their talks was published in Cuba under the title *Fidel y la religión*, further eroding the antireligious stance of the Cuban government.[13]

The collapse of the Soviet bloc and the onset of the "special period in time of peace" resulted in a significant shift in the balance of power between the government and the churches. With greatly reduced economic resources, the Cuban government found itself dependent on the churches to augment public social programs using relief supplies, which the churches were receiving from abroad.[14] At the same time, many churches were gaining members as Cubans who were disenchanted with the revolution began to seek meaning and comfort in religious observance. Not coincidentally, perhaps, the Cuban Communist Party dropped the word *atheist* from the list of requirements for membership. One result of this relaxation was that by 1998 four Protestant ministers had been elected to the national assembly.[15] The visit of Pope John Paul II to Cuba in 1998 was another milestone in the government's acknowledgment of religion's importance, as was an ecumenical council of Protestant churches that met in 1999. Both produced expressions of religiously based protest against the excesses of the government, indicating that Catholic and Protestant leaders were beginning to find their voices after a generation of embarrassed and intimidated silence.[16]

THE CASE OF THE CHRISTIAN REFORMED CHURCH IN CUBA

The Cuban Christian Reformed Church was a very young denomination at the time of the Fidelista revolution. Its first church building was not even a decade old, and its denominational character had just been finalized. It owed its origins quite literally to a marriage of Cuban and North American religious influences. The North American contribution to the Cuban CRC began with a determined young woman named Bessie Vander Valk. In 1940 Vander Valk was just twenty years old, unmarried, and a member of Bethel Christian Reformed Church in Paterson, New Jersey. Despite the fact that she did not speak Spanish, she became convinced that God wanted her to go to Cuba to spread the gospel. Her family and her home congregation were dubious about the wisdom of Vander Valk's calling, but she went anyway, arriving in the province of Matanzas, east of Havana, in the fall of 1940.[17]

Vander Valk was not the first Protestant missionary to come to this part of Cuba; Quakers had been active in Matanzas since the turn of the century and had established a number of educational and philanthropic enterprises there. Vander Valk began her missionary endeavors by serving in an orphanage founded by the Quakers in the western part of the province. As her competence in Spanish improved, she began working as an aide in the hospital at Matanzas, the provincial capital.[18] An irrepressible evangelist, she witnessed to the patients she encountered there. One of her first converts was Virginia Gómez, a woman from Jagüey Grande, a town in the southern zone of Matanzas Province. Gómez urged Vander Valk to begin evangelistic work there and offered her free lodging. Vander Valk accepted the offer and began teaching English classes and conducting Sunday school in Jagüey Grande in 1943.[19]

About a year and a half after Vander Valk's arrival in Jagüey Grande, a charismatic young Cuban came to establish a church there. The newcomer, Angel Vicente Izquierdo Alonso, was a student at Los Pinos Nuevos Evangelical Seminary, which was a joint enterprise of the Baptist and Presbyterian denominations.[20] Just as they had with Vander Valk, the Quakers of Matanzas played an important role in helping Izquierdo get established in Christian ministry. In his case their support consisted of financial aid during his seminary studies. The two young evangelists began to collaborate, with Vander Valk's teaching children and women and Izquierdo's teaching men. Within five months they were married, a development that proved crucial to the formation of the Christian Reformed denomination in

Cuba some years later. Appropriately enough a Quaker officiated at the wedding ceremony.[21]

Their burgeoning ministry had no formal affiliation with any of the other Protestant denominations on the island, but Izquierdo called it "La Misión Evangélica al Interior."[22] A milestone was reached on December 8, 1951, when a church building was inaugurated in Jagüey Grande.[23] During the next few years, Izquierdo recruited six evangelistic workers to extend the mission to new places. At the end of 1958, there were twelve formally organized congregations.[24] By that time the Jagüey Grande church was also supporting a day school with seventy-five students and two teachers. The Ebenezer School offered free instruction through sixth grade with additional courses for adults in English and business.[25] Barely a decade after its inauguration, the mission had become what could only be described as an independent Cuban denomination.

Independence had its price, however, one that became more burdensome as the work expanded. The Misión Evangelica al Interior was registered in the province of Matanzas, but it had no official standing with the national government. This circumstance made it difficult to begin work in the neighboring province of la Habana, something that Izquierdo was eager to do. He concluded that affiliation with a North American denomination would make it easier to obtain the needed government recognition. Another concern was the low level of education, theological and otherwise, possessed by the mission's evangelists. Izquierdo did not feel himself adequately prepared to provide what they lacked, but he hoped that an established denomination would be able to offer the needed theological training. Most pressing of all was the need for money. Izquierdo and Vander Valk received irregular contributions from Bethel CRC and from the Baptist Tabernacle in Paterson, but the mission's six full-time evangelists had almost no support as most of the mission's converts were people of limited means. Once again the solution seemed to lie in the mission's attachment to a larger, better-financed denomination.[26]

Izquierdo first approached the Southern Baptists. They were willing to provide him with a regular salary but would not take responsibility for the six evangelists he had recruited. At that point Vander Valk intervened. She remarked that there was a "very rich" Christian Reformed Church in Grand Rapids, Michigan— La Grave CRC—and she encouraged her husband to write to them to see whether they might be willing to take on the financial burden of supporting the seven pastors of the young Cuban denomination.[27] The North American congregation took an immediate interest in Izquierdo's request and commissioned four members to investigate the Cuban mission to see whether it merited their support.[28] After a three-week visit to the island, the delegation recommended to the La Grave congregation that it sponsor the mission, at least until the Cubans' needs could be presented to the Synod of the Christian Reformed Church in North America.[29]

For the Cubans the willingness of La Grave CRC to sponsor their seven pastors was decisive: they agreed to identify themselves as "Christian Reformed" and to seek financial support and theological instruction from the North American denomination. Their decision reflected more than just immediate financial need, and it portended more than a mere name change. Izquierdo had already encountered Reformed ideas at Los Pinos Nuevos Seminary because one of the teachers there was a Presbyterian. Vander Valk's influence was probably even more crucial. Her spiritual formation had been in the Christian Reformed Church, and her approach to evangelism and discipleship involved heavy doses of the Heidelberg Catechism, a mainstay of the Christian Reformed Church. Hence the basic ideas of Reformed Christianity were already familiar to some of the older members of the denomination whom Vander Valk had had a hand in converting and catechizing.[30] Moreover the support that she and her husband had received over the years from her home church had also helped to familiarize him with the CRC, and, of course, it was her suggestion to write La Grave CRC.[31] These influences made the Cuban mission more receptive to Reformed theology than it might otherwise have been.[32]

For its part the Christian Reformed Church in North America also took the budding relationship with the Cuban mission seriously. At its annual synod in the summer of 1958, the denomination put off formal adoption of the Cuban mission, opting instead to commission Rev. Clarence Nyenhuis, a recent graduate of the denomination's seminary, to go to Cuba to offer theological instruction to both pastors and laypeople, whom they viewed as excessively "fundamentalistic."[33] The 1958 synod also commissioned a missionary with prior experience in Latin America, J. Jerry Pott, to visit the Cuban churches and bring a report to the next synod about their suitability for adoption by the North American denomination. Pott spent nine weeks on the island at the close of 1958, and the report he filed on his return to the United States strongly recommended adoption of the Cuban churches as a mission of the CRC in North America. The synod agreed in the summer of 1959, and so the Misión Evangelica al Interior became the Interior Gospel Mission of the Christian Reformed Church.[34]

We can only speculate about what this new relationship might have meant for the Cuban church had it continued uninterrupted for many years, but it seems likely that it might have become quite dependent on the North Americans. The Synod of the Christian Reformed Church in North American assumed responsibility for three-quarters of the annual budget of the new "Gospel Mission," including salaries and rental housing for the evangelists with most of the money to come from La Grave CRC.[35] It approved a continuation of the catechetical work being done by Nyenhuis. And it voted to send a teacher trainer to the Ebenezer School in order to align it more closely with the North American denomination's conception of what a Christian school should be like.[36] Whatever this ecclesiastical collaboration might have produced, it was cut short by the Cuban Revolution, which triumphed just as the new partnership was being launched.

The members of the newly denominated Christian Reformed Church of Cuba were not all of one mind about Castro and his revolutionary movement. Bessie Vander Valk began describing Cuba's new government as "communistic" and warning about its aims almost from the start. Rev. Ramón Borrego remembers thinking that the men who showed up to take charge of the municipal government in Alacranes on January 1, 1959, were led by a very unsavory character. He and Izquierdo had come from families that owned small farms, and so it is not too surprising that both were highly critical of the new government's collectivist ideals. On the other hand, Rev. Domingo Romero was urged by a parishioner to join Ché Guevara's forces as a chaplain, an opportunity Romero tactfully declined.[37] Several pastors and many lay members in the denomination believed that the revolution represented a change for the better, not only for the nation but for the churches as well.[38] Nyenhuis was undoubtedly reflecting their views when he wrote to his supporters in the United States at the beginning of 1959: "It's the year of the bearded rebel soldier coming to national power, the year of Cuban national peace with the promise of economic prosperity. It's a year in which evangelical churches are receiving official recognition and favors from the revolutionary government."[39] As it turned out, the revolution presented the Cuban Christian Reformed Church with the challenge of a drastically narrowed space for religious activities and expressions of belief.

The first decade of the revolutionary period was probably the most stressful for the Cuban CRC. The deterioration in relations between the governments of the United States and Cuba made life increasingly awkward for North Americans living in Cuba. Clarence and Arlene Nyenhuis remained in the country through 1959, but the approaching birth of their third child in the summer of 1960 prompted them to leave for Miami, and, with the concurrence of the North American Mission Board, they decided not to return.[40] Izquierdo left the country in 1961 and was prevented from returning by the Cuban government. His North American wife, Bessie, remained in Cuba for another year, but she found herself having to cope with material privations and constant surveillance by members of the local Committee for the Defense of the Revolution. After months of appeals for permission to emigrate, she was allowed to leave for Miami with her children in the fall of 1962.[41]

The strained relations between the United States and Cuba also made it increasingly difficult for the Christian Reformed Churches in Cuba and North America to remain in contact with each other. In December 1960 the CRC in North America sent Nyenhuis back to Jagüey Grande to sign papers granting full autonomy to the Cuban CRC and giving it legal title to all of the denomination's assets so that they could not be confiscated as foreign-owned property.[42]

Meanwhile problems with mail delivery and wire transfers made it difficult for the Christian Reformed World Missions Board to provide pastors in Cuba with the funds they had promised. A temporary solution was found in the large number of Cubans who wanted to leave the island and who needed plane tickets. Christian Reformed pastors let such people know that, in exchange for pesos paid to the Cuban pastors, their partners in North America would obtain plane tickets for them. In this roundabout way, Cuban pastors received their support. However as the number of Cubans departing by air dwindled in the mid-1960s, so too did this avenue for paying their salaries.[43]

Relations between the churches and the Cuban government took a decisive turn for the worse in the spring of 1961. Jagüey Grande is only fifteen miles from the Bay of Pigs and, when the exile forces came ashore on April 16, members of the Christian Reformed churches found themselves in the front lines of the battle between communism and counterrevolution. The Cuban government pressed many members of the Cuban CRC into service to provide first aid and emergency transportation for wounded soldiers while the Ebenezer School became a field hospital.[44] Immediately following his victory over the invaders, Castro declared that the Cuban Revolution was and always would be Marxist Leninist. Because the counterrevolutionaries had justified their opposition to Castro on religious grounds, the churches now fell under suspicion. Restrictions were placed on all kinds of religious activities. The importation of Bibles was prohibited.[45] Religious events had to occur in legally registered church buildings, and the events had to be announced to local authorities in advance, sometimes by as much as a year. Any violation of the rules, such as hosting a Bible study in a private home, could lead to draconian penalties including loss of the home.[46] In May the government ordered the closing of all three hundred Christian schools on the island, Protestant as well as Catholic, often accompanied by the confiscation of their facilities.[47] While the Cuban Christian Reformed Church was spared the loss of its property because the building doubled as a sanctuary, the closing of the Ebenezer School meant a loss of employment for the wives of several pastors.[48] Their dismissal, coupled with the loss of financial support from North America, made the economic situation of the Cuban pastors nearly impossible since their congregations were in no position to support them financially. Izquierdo applied to the CRC Missions Board for an assignment in Mexico. Four other pastors immigrated to the United States during the ensuing decade, in part because of the practical difficulty of doing pastoral work under the new circumstances. Fifteen years after the triumph of the revolution, only three Christian Reformed pastors remained in Cuba.[49]

Even after the Bay of Pigs fiasco, anti-Castro guerrillas remained active in the nearby Escambray Mountains for several years. Naturally this made the Cuban government nervous, and it kept the entire area under very tight security. On one occasion more than six hundred residents of the area were rounded up on suspicion of supplying the rebels with provisions. Pastors were regarded with especial suspicion because of their presumed counterrevolutionary inclinations and their influence with parishioners. Religious meetings were confined to official church buildings, and evangelistic trips into the countryside were forbidden. Both Ramón Borrego and Domingo Romero were called to party headquarters and questioned closely for hours about what they were preaching. Under the circumstances otherwise small matters could assume a very sinister guise. Borrego remembers hitchhiking home from a farm where he had bought bananas to supplement his family's legal food ration. He was picked up by a car full of local communist party officials. The officials said nothing about the bananas, which had obviously been obtained in violation of the government's prohibition of private food sales, but Borrego was so shaken by the experience that when he got home he told his wife, Norma, that they should begin making arrangements to emigrate as soon as possible.[50]

Given the fact that Cuba was a nation under siege during this time, it may be that the government's restrictions on the work of the pastors had as much to do with perceived threats to its security as to ideology; however it is also true that pastors were often characterized as "worms" and "parasites."[51] Young men who applied to go to seminary were told that they must first do three years of military service.[52] One Christian Reformed pastor, Rev. Pedro Suárez, was drafted into the Unidades Militares en Apoyo de Producción (UMAP), an agricultural brigade supposedly reserved for social deviants. He acquitted himself well under the circumstances and was released after less than a year when the Cuban government closed the program in response to complaints of abuse, but the experience cast a pall on his reputation because of the supposedly unsavory nature of the people who were drafted into the brigade. A later president of the Cuban Christian Reformed Church, Rev. David Lee Chang, was called to the UMAP office on several occasions, though he was never actually inducted. Cuban CRC historian Eduardo Pedraza speculates that such actions may have constituted a sort of psychological warfare directed against religious leaders by overzealous local officials.[53]

Even after the threat of counterrevolution had faded, church members faced close scrutiny from revolutionary officials. Jobs involving a degree of responsibility, such as school teacher or sugar refinery manager, required membership in the Communist Party, which at that time meant that one had to be an atheist.[54] Church members were faced with difficult choices about what to say and whether to go to church. Jorge Fontrodona was fired from his job at a radio station when he acknowledged that he was a Christian. His employers told him they would prefer "someone who was not very smart, but was not a Christian, [while] you would rather remain a Christian than have a good job." Later, while filling out an application for a teacher training program, he confronted a question that asked him whether he attended church. He answered yes and was the only young person from his school to be rejected by the program.[55] Ramón and Norma Borrego recall that during the 1960s the Christian Reformed churches lost many members who feared that continued attendance at church might jeopardize their employment. At one point the main congregation at Jagüey Grande counted only four official members.[56] Some congregations became almost entirely defunct. In a couple of cases, church buildings escaped confiscation as abandoned properties only because two or three faithful women gathered in them each Sunday to pray.[57]

Cuba's new public education system created one of the most agonizing issues that Reformed Christians had to confront. While the instruction was technically excellent, it was also secular and at times even antireligious. Vander Valk recalled that her daughter was singled out unfavorably by a teacher for admitting that she believed the Bible.[58] Students attended schools in their neighborhoods through the eighth grade, but after that they were assigned to boarding schools in the countryside where they spent half the day in study and half in agricultural work. This situation created a terrible dilemma for Reformed parents. Without a secondary education, their children would be seriously handicapped as adults. However they worried that, once removed from the home, their children would be more vulnerable to indoctrination, and they had heard rumors that the barracks in which the students lived were places of great moral laxity. Moreover in high school there was much more pressure on students to join the Communist youth organization but, like the Communist Party, it required members to forswear belief in God. A great many families and young people left the church over this issue.[59] Some abandoned the church and accommodated themselves to the new order of things while others immigrated to the United States, including Ramón Borrego, who had led the denomination for five years after the departure of Vicente Izquierdo. Borrego's replacement as head of the Cuban Christian Reformed Church was Rev. Erelio Martínez.[60] It would be his task to find a way to combine loyalty to Christ with loyalty to the revolution.

Martínez represented a new generation of leadership in the Cuban CRC. He was a teenager at the time of the revolution, finished seminary training in the early 1960s, was ordained in 1963, and became head of the denomination when Borrego left Cuba in 1967.[61] Martínez combined a fervent evangelical spirit with sympathy for the goals of the revolution. Norma Borrego recalls Martínez as a nonconfrontational person who grew up with the revolution and was determined to remain in Cuba. In support of that opinion, her husband, Ramón, describes a particularly difficult official at the local Committee for the Defense of the Revolution with whom Borrego had frequent run-ins. Years later when Borrego returned from the United States to preach at the Jagüey Grande church, that official was in attendance having been befriended and converted in the meanwhile by Martínez.[62]

Under the leadership of Martínez and two other young pastors, Rev. David Lee Chang and Rev. Pedro Suárez, the Cuban CRC developed a progressive theological emphasis that was more attuned to the contemporary Cuban situation. For example they dedicated the year 1979 to the study of the Old Testament prophets for the light their writings shed on issues of justice and concern for the material needs of the poor.[63] They also sought theological instruction from the Presbyterian Seminary of Matanzas, which was considerably more open to the insights of Liberation Theology than was the Evangelical Seminary of Los Pinos Nuevos. According to Martínez some of the more "fundamentalist" members of the Cuban CRC objected to being taught by "communists," but the CRC pastors were unfazed by the criticism, and the church continued to pursue a progressive theological orientation.[64]

In fact the Cuban CRC sought to make a name for itself as a church whose social vision was compatible with the new society that the revolutionary government was seeking to build. With the aid of foreign donors in the United States, Canada, and Europe, the denomination developed an ambitious array of social programs that provided services and benefits such as interest-free loans to enable home owners to improve their properties, free meals delivered to seniors in their homes, rides for people with medical appointments in distant cities, and distribution of relief supplies for victims of tornadoes and hurricanes.[65] Often these services were provided in collaboration with the Cuban government. For example the seniors who received free meals were selected by a committee comprising church members, city council members, and representatives of the Ministry of Public Health.[66] Summarizing his denomination's approach to matters of social concern at the first annual workshop, "The Social Responsibility of the Christian," in 1998, Martínez stated:

> We know how to do evangelism without having to say to anybody: "Here is a plate of food for you if you come to our worship service tonight." We believe that this [approach] is immoral and not worthy of a Christian, but we know that many people are going to ask themselves about the faith . . . they are going to wonder in their mind what the connection is between the Christian faith and what we are doing. Many have asked: Why are you so crazy and foolish? . . . A communist said to me: "Why, after you have been discriminated against, are you doing these things?" Well, they don't understand our philosophy of forgiveness and love and that is what we are going to keep practicing.[67]

The Cuban CRC also supported causes that expressed solidarity with other socialist countries, such as contributing money to a nationwide collection for the reconstruction of Vietnam in the mid-1970s and collecting toys for children in Nicaragua during the 1980s.[68] In 1998 the synod of the Cuban CRC expressed its opposition to the U.S. embargo against Cuba and called on its sister churches in North America to do what they could as citizens to have the policy changed.[69]

While cooperative in its approach to the Cuban government, the Cuban CRC also defended its religious identity. Martínez refused to participate in a public ceremony with a local official who had been depicting him as a "parasite" until the official agreed to respect Martínez's pastoral ministry as a legal and honorable profession. He and other leaders in the denomination protested strongly when members of their denomination were prevented from enrolling in the University of Havana because of their religious affiliation.[70] They based their appeals on the letter of Cuban law, which guaranteed freedom of conscience. In the 1990s, as material privations worsened and popular support for the government waned, the church's protests became more pointed. At a meeting with Castro in 1990, the Cuban Ecumenical Council, of which the Cuban CRC was a member, informed the president that while conditions were improving, "as Christians we still do not have access to radio, television, and press. Education and job opportunities for many of our youth are limited, even though we contribute to the health of our nation."[71] These complaints brought a measure of relief. Castro himself admitted that Christians had suffered from discrimination, and he promised to defend their right to worship.[72] By the early years of the twenty-first century, the government had dropped most restrictions on religious meetings and was even providing support for the construction of new church buildings, although, in a manner similar to its dealings with the private economic sector, the government was prone to retract such privileges without notice or explanation.[73]

Like most other churches on the island, the Cuban CRC has experienced considerable numerical growth during the last two decades. Formal membership increased from six hundred to more than one thousand, and the number of fully organized congregations grew from twelve to twenty between 1980 and 2000. In addition, after the government dropped its ban on house churches and prayer cells, that number exploded to more than one hundred. The proliferation of these informal, geographically dispersed gathering places has permitted a large increase in participation by nonmembers so that the actual number of individuals connected in some way to the denomination is now around five thousand.[74] Erelio Martínez died in 2005, but the church continues to grow under the leadership of President David Lee Chang and fifteen other full-time pastors, aided by many laymen and -women who have shown remarkable stamina in doing the work of the church under difficult circumstances over many years.[75]

This period of growth has coincided with and been aided by the restoration of close ties with the Christian Reformed Church in North America. Telephone contact was restored between the two denominations in 1974, and members of the CRC in North America began visiting the island in the 1980s to offer Bible training and bring needed resources. La Grave CRC has provided substantial funds for the repair of old buildings and the construction of new ones.[76] Finally in 2001 ties between the Cuban CRC and the CRC in North America were formally reestablished.[77] Ironically the biggest impediment to the restoration of the Cuban CRC's dependent relationship on the CRC in North America is the United States–imposed embargo with its restrictions on travel and the transfer of funds to the island.

The influence of Cuban nationalism and Marxist atheism on one side and their own religious identity and attachment to North American resources and ideas on the other are the competing factors that have determined the shape of the Christian Reformed Church in Cuba. Early on, the Fidelista revolution drastically curtailed the denomination's external dependence and over time it also prompted a significant revision of the church's beliefs and practices. Since the onset of the "special period in time of peace," the balance of forces has shifted considerably. The church has become a stronger competitor with the state for the loyalty of the Cuban people, and it has also become an alternative source of material resources due to its access to foreign donors. The first developments suggest the remarkable resiliency of religious identity—a humbling lesson for Marxist revolutionaries. The second suggests the remarkable resiliency of North American influence, an even more humbling lesson for Cuban nationalists. Yet there has been adjustment as well as resistance on the part of the denomination. Church leaders have embraced progressive theological ideas disseminated by the Presbyterian Seminary in Matanzas as part of a general rethinking made urgent by the challenge of Cuba's revolutionary ideology. The ambitious social endeavors of the church also reflect the influence of the Cuban government's relentless focus on bettering the material conditions of poor Cubans. In sum, while it has shown remarkable staying power, the Cuban Christian Reformed Church also appears to have learned a few things from the revolution.

NOTES

1. Margaret E. Crahan, "Cuba: Religion and Revolutionary Institutionalization," *Journal of Latin American Studies* 17, no. 2 (1985): 319–40, esp. 319–21; Margaret E. Crahan, "Salvation through Christ or Marx: Religion in Revolutionary Cuba," *Journal of Interamerican Studies and World Affairs* 21, no. 1 (1979): 156–84.

2. Theo Tschuy, "Protestantism in Cuba, 1868–1968," in *Christianity in the Caribbean: Essays on Church History,* ed. Armando Lampe (Barbados: University of the West Indies Press, 2001), 229–68, esp. 259–60.

3. Theron Corse, *Protestants, Revolution, and the Cuba-U.S. Bond* (Gainesville: University Press of Florida, 2007), esp. chap. 5; Marcos A. Ramos, *Protestantism and Revolution in Cuba* (Coral Gables, Fla.: University of Miami, 1989), 68–73; Tschuy, "Protestantism in Cuba," 260–64.

4. Cuban Constitution of 1976, Article 54, accessed August 26, 2005, http://www .georgetown.edu/pdba/Constitutions/Cuba/cuba1976.html: (1) El Estado socialista, que basa su actividad y educa al pueblo en la concepción científica materialista del universo, reconoce y garantiza la libertad de conciencia, el derecho de cada uno a profesar cualquier

creencia religiosa y a practicar, dentro del respeto a la ley, el culto de su preferencia ((1) The socialist state, which bases its activities and educates the people in the scientific materialist conception of the universe, recognizes and guarantees liberty of conscience, the right of everyone to profess any religious belief whatsoever and to practice, within the limits of the law, the religion of their choice).

5. From the Cuban Constitution of 1976, Article 39, accessed August 26, 2005, http://pdba.georgetown.edu/Constitutions/Cuba/cuba1976.html (accessed June 23, 2014): "(1) La educación de la niñez y la juventud en el espíritu comunista es deber de toda la sociedad"; Article 54: "(3) Es ilegal y punible oponer la fe o la creencia religiosa a la Revolución, a la educación o al cumplimiento de los deberes de trabajar, defender la patria con las armas, reverenciar sus símbolos y los demás deberes es tablecidos por la Constitución."

6. Hiram Abi Cobas, "*Annex XXIV: Legal Coercion and Religious Freedom in Cuba,*" in United Nations, Commission on Human Rights, E/CN.4/1989/46, February 26, 1989, reproduced in "Documents, Religious Freedom in Cuba," *Religion in Communist Lands* 18, no. 1 (1990): 64–72, esp. 69–71.

7. John M. Kirk, *Between God and the Party: Religion and Politics in Revolutionary Cuba* (Tampa: University of South Florida Press, 1989), 127–31; Crahan, "Salvation through Christ or Marx," 175–76.

8. Margaret E. Crahan, "Cuba," in *Religious Freedom and Evangelization in Latin America: The Challenge of Religious Pluralism*, ed. Paul E. Sigmund (Maryknoll, N.Y.: Orbis, 1999), 87–112, esp. 101.

9. Crahan, "Religion and Revolutionary Institutionalization," 330–32; Corse, *Protestants, Revolution,* 125–26.

10. Crahan, "Cuba," 104.

11. Milay Gálvez, "Church and State in Cuba Today," lecture given at Calvin College, Grand Rapids, Mich., February 11, 2004.

12. Tim DeVries, "The Mighty Work of God in Cuba: Interview with Obed Martínez," unpublished typescript, World Bible League, September 1992; Corse, *Protestants, Revolution,* 136; Kirk, *Between God and the Party,* 150.

13. Corse, *Protestants, Revolution,* 137. The English version of their conversations is *Fidel and Religion: Castro Talks on Revolution and Religion with Frei Betto* (New York: Simon & Schuster, 1987).

14. Crahan, "Cuba," 111; Tim DeVries, personal interview with the author, Grand Rapids, Mich., July 25, 2003; Gálvez, "Church and State"; Geraldine Lievesley, *The Cuban Revolution: Past, Present and Future Perspectives* (New York: Palgrave Macmillan, 2004), 148.

15. Lievesley, *Cuban Revolution,* 137; Crahan, "Cuba," 107.

16. James C. Dekker, "Thanks, Christians in Cuba," *Banner,* August 21, 1991, 6–7; James C. Dekker, "Cuba's CRC Nurtures Harvest in Rocky Soil," *Banner,* May 25, 1998, 24–26.

17. Eduardo B. Pedraza, *Con las espaldas llenas de ardor* (Jagüey Grande, Cuba: Iglesia Cristiana Reformada, 2002), 3; Rev. Ramón Borrego and Norma Borrego, personal interview with the author, Miami, May 28, 2005; Rev. Jake Eppinga, personal interview with the author, Grand Rapids, Mich., July 26, 2005.

18. Eppinga interview.

19. Pedraza, *Con las espaldas llenas de ardor*, 9, 14; Eppinga interview.

20. Borregos interview.

21. Pedraza, *Con las espaldas llenas de ardor*, 16–17.

22. Ibid., 109.

23. Ibid., 20.

24. Rev. W. Thomas De Vries, "Some Information Regarding the Christian Reformed Church in Cuba," typescript, Christian Reformed Church in North America, Interchurch Relations Committee, September 2000; Rev. Vicente Izquierdo, personal interview with the author, Miami, May 29, 2005.

25. Pedraza, *Con las espaldas llenas de ardor*, 24.

26. Christian Reformed Church in North America, Agenda, 1958, 90–91; J. Jerry Pott, Report on Assignment to Cuba, Christian Reformed Church in North America, Acts of Synod, 1959, 346–53.

27. Izquierdo interview.

28. Eppinga interview.

29. Izquierdo interview.

30. Eppinga interview.

31. Borregos interview.

32. Eppinga interview.

33. The Christian Reformed Church in North America originated in the middle of the nineteenth century as a denomination overwhelmingly comprising Dutch immigrants. Its Calvinist theology and worship practices drew on European traditions rather than the evangelical and revivalistic forms of Protestantism that were flourishing around them. The denomination's leaders criticized fundamentalism for its Arminianism and anti-intellectualism. See James D. Bratt, *Dutch Calvinism in Modern America: A History of a Conservative Subculture* (Grand Rapids, Mich.: Eerdmans, 1984), 131–34.

34. Christian Reformed Church in North America, Acts of Synod, 1959, 17.

35. Ibid., 348.

36. Ibid., 17.

37. Rev. Domingo Romero, personal interview with the author, Grand Rapids, Mich., July 27, 2005.

38. Ramón Borrego mentioned Rev. Felix Reynoso as one pastor who was hopeful about the new government, and his wife, Norma, mentioned that many church members were supportive of Castro's government; Borrego interview.

39. Clarence J. Nyenhuis, "Cuba," pamphlet (n.p.: Women's Missionary Union of Grand Rapids Christian Reformed Church, [1959]).

40. Arlene Nyenhuis, personal interview with the author, Grand Rapids, Mich., October 8, 2005.

41. Bessie Vander Valk-Izquierdo, "Out of Cuba," audiotape of talk given at the [Baptist] Tabernacle in Paterson, New Jersey, November 27, 1962; Pedraza, *Con las espaldas llenas de ardor*, 102.

42. Clarence J. Nyenhuis, "Cuba," in *Lengthened Cords: A Book about World Missions in Honor of Henry J. Evenhouse*, ed. Roger S. Greenway (Grand Rapids, Mich.: Baker Book House, 1975), 145.

43. Borregos interview.

44. Pedraza, *Con las espaldas llenas de ardor,* 39.

45. Ramos, *Protestantism and Revolution,* 73–74.

46. Romero interview.

47. Crahan, "Cuba," 95; Gálvez, "Church and State"; Ramos, *Protestantism and Revolution,* 70–74.

48. Borregos interview.

49. Romero interview.

50. Borregos interview.

51. Romero interview; Borregos interview. See also the account Eduardo Pedraza gives of his own interrogation by local police in 1964. He and a friend had just come from a worship service. They were wearing suits and carrying tracts while riding on a bus. A policeman took them to the station where they were interrogated for several hours and told that their literature was "trash." Pedraza comments that the experience was the result of overzealous local officials who misconstrued the revolution's attitude toward religion. Pedraza, *Con las espaldas llenas de ardor,* 138–39.

52. Romero interview.

53. Romero interview; Pedraza, *Con las espaldas llenas de ardor,* 139–40.

54. Borregos interview.

55. Jorge Fontrodona, personal interview with the author, Miami, May 27, 2005.

56. Tim DeVries and Kathy DeVries, personal interview with the author, Benton Harbor, Mich., August 4, 2003.

57. James C. Dekker, "Cuba's CRC Nurtures Harvest," 24.

58. Vander Valk/Izquierdo, "Out of Cuba."

59. Borregos interview; Romero interview; Fontrodona interview.

60. Nyenhuis, "Cuba," 145–46.

61. Eppinga interview; Pedraza, *Con las espaldas llenas de ardor,* 98; Nyenhuis, "Cuba," 146.

62. Borregos interview.

63. Pedraza, *Con las espaldas llenas de ardor,* 48.

64. Ibid., 165–66.

65. Ibid., 58–61.

66. Ibid., 64.

67. Ibid., 57.

68. Ibid., 50, 78.

69. Ibid., 149.

70. James C. Dekker, "How Can There Be Christian Reformed Churches in Cuba?" *Banner,* January 27, 1986, 1, 6–8, 7–8.

71. Qtd., in English, in Dekker, "Thanks, Christians," 7.

72. Rafael Cepeda, Elizabeth Carrillo, Rhode González, and Carlos E. Ham, "Changing Protestantism in a Changing Cuba," in *In the Power of the Spirit: The Pentecostal Challenge to Historic Churches in Latin America*, ed. Benjamin F. Gutiérrez and Dennis A. Smith (Guatemala City: Centro Evangélico Latinoamericano de Estudios Pastorales, 1996), 99.

73. "Fidel Castro Offers Support to Build Evangelical Churches," *Christian Courier*, September 12, 2005, 24; Michelle A. Vu, "Cuba House Churches Face New Restrictions," *Christian Post*, September 20, 2005, http://www.christianpost.com/news/cuba-house -churches-face-new-restrictions-15872/.

74. James C. Dekker, "Thanks, Christians." "Some Information Regarding the Christian Reformed Church in Cuba," typescript of a report presented to the Interchurch Relations Committee of the Christian Reformed Church in North America, September 2000.

75. Luis Pellecer, "Cuban CRC Leader Dies," *Banner*, October 2005, 17; DeVries interview.

76. Pedraza, *Con las espaldas llenas de ardor*, 166–67.

77. "Synod Establishes Ties with Cuban CRC," *Banner*, July 9, 2001, 17.

Gerald Lee Wilson

Preachers and Politics

The Religious Issue in the North Carolina Presidential Campaign of 1960 — A Footnote on Al Smith

Twice in the twentieth century the Democratic Party has nominated a member of the Roman Catholic Church for the presidency of the United States. In 1928 the party chose as its standard-bearer Gov. Alfred E. Smith of New York, who joined the ranks of the also-rans. In 1960 the party nominated Sen. John F. Kennedy of Massachusetts, who became the thirty-fifth president of the United States.

Much has been written about how and to what extent the Roman Catholic faith affected the presidential campaign and election of 1928. Relatively little has been written specifically addressing how the same issue affected the presidential campaign and election of 1960. Nor is it difficult to reason why: Smith lost, and became to many something of a martyr; Kennedy won and became an almost mythic figure. The purpose of this study is to assess the role of religion and religious prejudice in the campaign of 1960 in one southern state, North Carolina. Will Herberg, in a footnote, makes an observation about North Carolina that renders the state as an especially fertile field for this study: "Thus in North Carolina there are said to be fewer Catholics proportionately than anywhere else in the world, including Africa and the Far East."[1]

The "religious issue" as it refers to the presidential campaign of 1960 in North Carolina is, for the most part, a euphemism for prejudice. The word *prejudice* itself needs defining. For purposes of this study, a definition offered by Gordon W. Allport in his classic work, *The Nature of Prejudice*, will serve more than adequately. Allport takes as his starting point *The New English Dictionary*'s definition of prejudice: "A feeling, favorable or unfavorable, toward a person or things, prior to, or not based on, actual experience."[2] "Ordinarily," Allport continues, "prejudice manifests itself in dealing with individual members of rejected groups." Therefore we might define prejudice as "an avertive or hostile attitude toward a person who belongs to a group, simply because he belongs to that group, and is therefore presumed to have the objectionable qualities ascribed to the group."[3]

In assessing the role of religious prejudice in the 1960 presidential campaign in North Carolina, special attention will be given to the official journals of the two largest Protestant denominations in the state, the Southern Baptist *Biblical Recorder* and Methodist *North Carolina Christian Advocate*, because these journals represented so large a part of the religious population of the state.[4] Also cited, for obvious reasons, is the *North Carolina Catholic*, which effectively responded to many of the questions and issues raised in the campaign.

In 1928, faced with opposition from both religious and political leaders in North Carolina and elsewhere in the South, Al Smith lost both North Carolina and his bid for the presidency. In this campaign both the *North Carolina Christian Advocate* and the *Biblical Recorder* took strong, often vehement, stands against Smith. Thirty-two years passed before the Democratic Party again nominated a member of the Roman Catholic Church for the presidency of the United States. During that time national Prohibition was repealed, and what C. Vann Woodward called the "Bulldozer Revolution" came to North Carolina.[5]

Early in the election year 1960, as Senator Kennedy began to round up delegates for the Democratic nomination for president, it became apparent that religion once again would be an issue in the campaign. On January 23, 1960, the *Biblical Recorder*, in an editorial titled "The Presidential Ambitions of Senator John Kennedy," stated its position: "We predict that in the end Democrats will turn to Adlai Stevenson or Senator Lyndon Johnson to oppose Richard Nixon in the Presidential election. If he chooses, Kennedy may be the vice-presidential candidate, and that will be too close to the Presidency to suit many Americans."[6] The *North Carolina Christian Advocate*, on the other hand, was making no mention of Kennedy but publishing articles "friendly" to the Catholic Church. On January 14, in the article "A Catholic View of Tithing," the Methodist editor said, "Too often we look down our noses at our Catholic friends. . . . They have much to teach us as we have much to teach them."[7] A subsequent article in the same newspaper stated that anyone who read the Catholic magazines would find a "new emphasis" in the Catholic Church and would realize that they can no longer rely on their old prejudices concerning Catholicism.[8]

It soon became evident that the *North Carolina Christian Advocate* in 1960 simply did not choose to comment on the campaign other than in general terms of voting "responsibly" and "without prejudice."[9] Other than two letters to the editor that spoke of "bondage to Rome" should Kennedy be elected, there was no negative mention of Catholicism or Kennedy.[10] One minor incident that occurred within the pages of the *Christian Advocate* evidently caused the editor great concern and illustrated just how far he would go to keep from saying anything that even hinted of anti-Catholicism. In the August 11, 1960, issue, a small advertisement appeared that asked, "Should a Catholic be President?" In order to help readers answer the question, the Biblical Publishing Corporation of Detroit was offering a new book titled *A Foreign Monarchy in America*.[11] Evidently the editor of the *Advocate* received some adverse comment on this advertisement, for in an issue of the magazine published a few weeks later, he apologized for it and proclaimed his neutrality in all things except morals. He felt that both sides of all questions should be heard.[12]

In the last issue of the *Advocate* published before the election the editor again asserted his neutrality, stated his reasons for it, and took occasion to frown on those religious publications that did get involved in the campaign:

> Some church papers have taken sides and as a result stirred up quite a furor among their people. . . .
>
> It has been our policy to stay clear of all political commitments. We regard the *Advocate* as a religious periodical devoted to the work of the church.[13]

Little time had passed in the presidential year before it became evident that an incident that had occurred some twelve years previously would feature prominently in the campaign. In 1948 Kennedy, then a congressman, had accepted an invitation to attend the consecration of the Chapel of the Four Chaplains in Philadelphia. Kennedy, acting on the advice of Cardinal Dougherty of Philadelphia, then canceled his acceptance of this invitation. Kennedy stated that he had canceled because he had been invited as a representative of the Catholic faith. If he had been invited merely as a public official or private citizen, he could have accepted the invitation.[14] Dr. Daniel Poling, the noted Baptist minister in charge of the consecration of the chapel, maintained that Kennedy had been invited as a public official and not as a spokesman for the Catholic faith.[15]

The first mention of this incident in the North Carolina religious press came as early as January 30, 1960. The *Biblical Recorder* in an article dealing with Kennedy's refusal to speak at an interfatith meeting in Philadelphia, asked "Whether his Roman Catholic faith would restrict his appearances at non-Catholic events if he were elected President."[16]

In February the president of the Southern Baptist Convention, Dr. Ramsey Pollard of Knoxville, Tennessee, announced his opposition to Kennedy. Pollard said that he could not "stand by and keep my mouth closed when a man under control of the Roman Catholic Church runs for the Presidency of the United States."[17] In its March 5, 1960, issue, the *Biblical Recorder* printed "An Anonymous Letter: A Catholic in the White House." The editor of this journal said that it was not his policy to print anonymous letters but that the special nature of this letter urged him to publish it. The letter discussed Roman Catholic persecutions in Spain and expressed concern about the Roman Catholic hierarchy's direction of Kennedy's religious life. The editor of the *Biblical Recorder* stated that he would "have more to say" about Kennedy's religion in subsequent issues of the paper.[18]

Meanwhile a national magazine was conducting a nationwide survey, which revealed that southerners were not the only ones concerned with a president's faith. *Newsweek* for March 14, 1960, ran the results of a poll in its "Listening Post" section titled "Protestants and a President's Faith." In summary, the poll found that clergymen throughout the nation had "strong reservations" about electing a Catholic to the presidency; politicians were badly split about the practicality of nominating a Catholic; and laymen seemed very "receptive to the idea." Most clergymen conceded that any citizen ought to have the right to seek the highest office in the land, "but once this point was conceded many Protestant churchmen proceeded to voice in no uncertain terms their worries over the constitutional separation of Church and State."[19]

On the other hand, there was a highly vocal minority of Protestant ministers who saw no threat in a Catholic president. These ministers urged that people look at the man himself and not his Catholic religion. For example in Raleigh, North Carolina, the Reverend W. W. Finlator, liberal pastor of a Baptist church, said, "It's unrealistic to think there won't someday be a Catholic President. How can 40 million people never be allowed the honor of seeing one of their number President?"[20]

The *Newsweek* survey found that "Protestants of the Bible Belt South—and notably the Baptists—are perhaps the strongest of all in their opposition to a Catholic President." As a result, "Protestant Democratic leaders in the South who normally can count on a Democratic vote are inclined to worry. In states like Alabama, North Carolina, Kentucky, and Arkansas, the politicos feel his religion will definitely be a factor against Kennedy." In its summary of the South, *Newsweek* found that clergymen were strongly against and laymen mostly against a Catholic president, and that politicians thought Catholicism might hurt.[21] This was a major concern in a double sense: some Southern clergy worried that a Roman Catholic might not carry traditional Democratic states in the South, and at the same time, for many, it reflected their anxiety over the constitutional issue of separation of church and state.

In March the first of many verbal exchanges between the editor of the *North Carolina Catholic* and the editor of the *Biblical Recorder* began. In an editorial titled "Killing Straw Men," the editor of the *North Carolina Catholic* wrote:

> In preceding likely changes of policy in the *Biblical Recorder* last fall we lay no claim to clairvoyance. We regretted the choice of Mr. J. Marse Grant as the new editor because of his record with *Charity and Children*, a Baptist publication from Thomasville. In the past we took occasion two or three times to point up the unfactual and biased editorial policy of (in all unlikely spots) *Charity and Children*.
>
> In ten weeks now as the editor of the *Biblical Recorder*, Mr. Grant has brightened the format, enlarged the type, and undertaken to whoop up circulation with fervid anti-Catholicism.

Bigotry is far more subtle when broadcast under the guise of a profound political problem. The present political campaign, with Kennedy running loud and strong, offers a ready springboard to rehash and rewarm the old pottage of religious prejudice.

For the sheer sake of repetition we say again that the Catholics of the United States regret many things done in the name of religion in countries like Spain or Russia. We believe that the record speaks clear and loud for the United States citizens who are Catholics. Let Mr. Grant point out where any of the scores of Catholic Supreme Court Justices, Senators, Cabinet members, federal and state judges, generals and admirals . . . have failed the country because of their Catholicism. Or let Mr. Grant point to Ireland as a typical Catholic country with a Protestant president. We Catholics of the United States are Americans, not Spaniards or Swedes.[22]

The *Biblical Recorder* on April 9, 1960, reprinted this *Catholic* article in full and accompanied it with an editorial of its own. This editorial defense ended with two questions: What about the persecutions of Protestants in Spain? And what about House Majority Leader John McCormack's steering of thirty thousand dollars' worth of aid to the Catholics?[23]

On May 14, 1960, the *Biblical Recorder*'s editorial page asked the question "Does the Roman Catholic Church participate in politics?" The answer: "It is the right and the duty of the Church to guide Catholics in political activities. Catholics must unite their strength toward a common aim, and the Catholic hierarchy has the right and the duty of guiding them."[24] This "answer" was attributed to Pope John XXIII, and the source from which this information came was the *Capital Baptist*.[25] The *North Carolina Catholic* lost no time in replying to this article, and May 29 commented: "Latest, and typical, piece of malarky appears in the May 14 issue of the *Biblical Recorder* as an insert from some source called 'Capital Baptist.'" The editor added, "This is a straight forgery and obviously libelous." He concluded: "To cite obscure sources (Capital Baptist), and omit date and source of the alleged papal statement on such a serious issue is dishonest journalism to say the kindest thing possible. We repeat our deep regret over the bigotry mongering role recently assumed by the *Biblical Recorder*."[26]

On May 16–19 the Southern Baptists held their convention in Miami Beach, Florida. The Reverend G. Wendell Davis of Charlotte presented to the convention the resolution of the Christian Citizenship Committee.[27] Section 1 of the resolution reaffirmed the historic Baptist stand on church and state separation. Section 2 of the resolution read:

We reaffirm our conviction that a man must be free to choose his own church and that his personal religious faith shall not be a test of his qualification for public office. Yet, the fact remains that when and if a public official is inescapably-bound by the dogma and demands of his church, he cannot consistently separate himself from these. This is especially true when that church maintains a position in open conflict with our established and constituted American pattern of life as specifically related to religious liberty, separation of church and state, the freedom of conscience in matters related to marriage and the family, the perpetuation of free public schools and the prohibition against the use of public monies for sectarian purposes.

Section 3 of the resolution got to the crux of the matter: "Therefore, the implications of a candidate's affiliations, including his church, are of concern to voters in every election. In all cases a public official should be free from sectarian pressures that he may make individual decisions with the rights and privileges of all citizens." The resolution was adopted by the convention. In the presidential address to the convention, Pollard reaffirmed his earlier statements about the Catholic Church: "I want to tell you Roman Catholicism must repent of its sins and must come with clean hands and confession and admitting its own sin in the field of religious persecution and bigotry before it can dare raise its finger at us who claim that religious freedom is not only for Baptists, and Protestants, but religious freedom is for all men. I am a bit tired of hearing certain groups in this country fold their hands and piously cry out against bigotry and persecution in America."[28] Thus the largest single Protestant denomination in the nation, and the strongest in the South, had, in effect, put itself on record as opposing the nomination of a Roman Catholic for the highest office in the land.

While the Baptists were making it clear that they would follow the same path they had followed in 1928, the Methodists in North Carolina were voicing quite a different attitude. The *Christian Advocate* in an editorial titled "Religion and Politics," published in the June 16, 1960, issue, stated, "our only advice to Methodists is to vote according to their best knowledge and conscience when the election comes next November. . . . Prejudice, either religious or sectional, should not determine the way we cast our ballots."[29] In the next few weeks, both the Western North Carolina Conference and the North Carolina Conference of the Methodist Church met and made no official mention of the presidential campaign.[30]

By midsummer 1960 another element had entered the campaign: the use of "converted" Catholic priests and ex-nuns by groups who were strongly opposed to the election of a Roman Catholic to the presidency. At the Buncombe County Baptist Pastors' Conference on June 13, a Rev. Walter Zvoda, a converted Catholic priest, spoke on the four ways Catholicism endangered western North Carolina. According to this ex-priest, Catholics were dangerous in four areas of concern: in education they were trying to take over school boards; in economics Catholics were being sent from the North to take over business in the South; in politics the Vatican was trying to get a Catholic in the White House; and in religion the church wanted to gain religious domination in America. The editor of the *Biblical Recorder* expressed the hope that this message would be spread throughout the state.[31]

July 1960 was convention month for the Democrats. It was generally assumed that the North Carolina delegation to the national convention would follow many of the other southern states in supporting Lyndon B. Johnson. Early in July the Democratic nominee for governor, Terry Sanford, indicated that he might not support Johnson. Sanford said that whatever he did would be for the best interests of the state.[32] On July 6 it was announced that Sanford would support *either* Johnson or Kennedy.[33] Meanwhile Governor Hodges reaffirmed his support of Johnson. Four days later Sanford announced that he would support Kennedy, and he predicted that Kennedy would get one-third of the state's thirty-seven votes at the convention.[34] Sanford immediately received criticism from various religious groups in the state, including a telegram from the four-thousand-member convention of the Church of God, then meeting in Charlotte, which stated the church's unyielding opposition to the nomination of a Roman Catholic.[35] On July 14 Sanford made one of the seconding speeches for Kennedy's nomination, referring to Kennedy as another Franklin D. Roosevelt.[36]

Kennedy received the presidential nomination on the first ballot, but his vote in the North Carolina delegation did not quite reach the one-third Sanford had estimated. The Tar Heel State voted 27.5 votes for Johnson, 6.5 for Kennedy, 3.5 for Stevenson, and 0.5 for Sen. George Smathers of Florida.[37] At the same time, Sanford had to fight a rearguard action at home. Drew Pearson reported that Sanford had met with Robert Kennedy in a Raleigh motel sometime before the runoff North Carolina gubernatorial primary on June 25 and had promised to support Senator Kennedy for a quid pro quo agreement that the Kennedys would give him financial aid in his campaign against I. Beverly Lake. Though he admitted that he had met with Robert Kennedy, Sanford denied that any deals were made.[38]

On July 7, 1960, the *Biblical Recorder* published an editorial called "A Revealing Survey," which charged that most of the leaders of the Democratic Convention were Catholics. This editorial observed that every Democratic national chairman since 1928 had been a Roman Catholic and that among the present leaders of the party, Mayor Richard Daley of Chicago, Gov. Edmund (Pat) Brown of California, Gov. Michael DiSalle of Ohio, Mayor Robert Wagner of New York, Gov. David Lawrence of Pennsylvania, Tammany Hall leader Carmine DeSapio of New York, and House Majority Leader John McCormack were all members of the Catholic faith.[39]

The *North Carolina Catholic* on August 14, 1960, answered this *Biblical Recorder* editorial with an editorial of its own, "The Catholic Plot," which challenged the intent of the *Biblical Recorder* article. The editor mentioned some of the non-Catholic supporters of Kennedy at the convention: governor nominee Sanford,

Gov. Herschel C. Loveless of Iowa, W. Averill Harriman, and Congresswoman Edith Green of Oregon. "It would seem rather obvious from the names listed, and their nominee choices, that Catholics did not gang up to put in their candidate . . . as implied in the *Biblical Recorder*."[40]

Shortly after the nomination of Kennedy, the "bogus" Knights of Columbus oath, which appeared during the 1928 campaign, reappeared in North Carolina.[41] A Baptist pastor in Stanley, North Carolina, the Reverend James C. Honeycutt Jr., reprinted this "oath" in his Sunday Church bulletin.[42] Honeycutt later apologized for this, saying that since the oath had appeared in the *Congressional Record*, he had assumed it to be authentic.[43] In September two Baptist churches in Waynesville circulated copies of the so-called oath throughout the western part of North Carolina.[44] On August 6, 1960, the *Biblical Recorder* continued its anti-Catholic attack in an article titled "Not Afraid of the Man, but the System. . . ," which admitted that the average Catholic layman was a good neighbor, a good friend, and a good citizen but that the Roman Catholic hierarchy was quite another matter.[45]

At the same time, forty Baptist ministers in Gaston County were organizing an "Informational Center on Catholicism," which promised to mail out literature and to broadcast "information about the Roman Catholic Church."[46] This group was led by Dr. Ward Barr, minister of the First Baptist Church of Gastonia, who stated, "I fear Catholicism more than I do communism."[47] This group was to come under heavy fire even from some ministers of the Baptist denomination. Dr. Claude Broach, minister of St. John's Baptist Church of Charlotte, declared that the Catholic Church was not the candidate but rather Kennedy. Broach criticized the Informational Center and declared, "Many Roman Catholics have served and do now serve the public good in high offices of trust, and there is no reason to assume Senator Kennedy is unworthy merely because of his religion."[48]

The August 20, 1960, issue of the *Biblical Recorder* carried an advertisement for a tract called "Baptists, Roman Catholics, and Religious Freedom," which could be obtained from the Baptist Sunday School Board free of charge, in quantities, for distribution in churches. This tract, according to the advertisement, "effectively describes how the principle of separation of Church and State is being threatened by the Roman Catholic Church in this Country."[49] Throughout the late summer and early fall, local Baptist associations were meeting and declaring their opposition to Kennedy because of his Catholic faith. One of these, the Carolina Association, rapped the "foreign ties" of Kennedy and declared that if a Catholic were elected president there would be no public school system within twenty years.[50]

Democratic leaders in the state, much as they had in 1928, were beginning to take to the stump in an effort to combat the rising tide of opposition to Kennedy on religious grounds. One of the most effective defenders of Kennedy's faith was a prominent Charlotte woman long active in political affairs, Mrs. Charles W.

Tillett. Typical of her approach to the question was the speech she delivered in Huntersville, North Carolina, on September 6, 1960. Tillett told the Democratic Woman's Club of that town that "a recent poll, as reported in the press, gave the religious issue the number one spot for the campaign in the South." She continued: "God forbid that we say to the Gold Star Mother—(Mrs. Rose Kennedy) your son can die for his country, but your son cannot be President unless he belongs to the right denomination."[51]

Theodore H. White reported that throughout the August session of the U.S. Senate in 1960, Kennedy was "restless" and anxious to get out on the campaign trail as reports drifted up from the South that Baptist ministers "had begun to preach against the Church of Rome and its candidate."[52] White said that early in the campaign Kennedy decided to meet the religious issue head on: "There was, as the Kennedys had learned in West Virginia, only one way to separate the bigots from the honestly fearful: that was to face the issue of religion frankly and in the open, stripping it of the darkness, incense and strange rituals that so many Protestants feared."[53] The only question that remained was the tactical one: when and where. Kennedy's original strategy was to wait until late in October, close to the election, when the question could most effectively be dealt with. But the rising tide of anti-Catholic sentiment and the opposition of prominent Protestant leaders such as Dr. Norman Vincent Peale persuaded Kennedy that the issue should be dealt with at once. He decided to accept the invitation of the Greater Houston Ministerial Association to discuss his religion on September 12, 1960. At this meeting he would make a statement and then open the floor for any and all questions. His aide Ted Sorenson commented to a friend, "We can win or lose the election right there in Houston on Monday night."[54]

White's version of the decision to bring the religious issue out in the open early in the campaign has persisted as the more or less standard interpretation. However in January 1961 Thomas B. Morgan, writing in *Harper's Magazine*, suggested a different version of the process by which this decision was made. According to Morgan's version, early in the 1960 campaign the Kennedy forces obtained use of an IBM 704, a "people machine" that, when fed the proper information, "described a simulation of future human behavior in terms of voters' reaction to the religious issue." The "people machine" was asked "What would happen on election day if the issue of anti-Catholicism became 'much more salient' in the voters' minds?"[55] The machine's answer would direct the Kennedy camp's thinking on how to deal with the issue. On the basis of this machine's projections, Robert F. Kennedy was given this report on August 25, 1960:

> Kennedy today has lost the bulk of the votes he would lose if the election campaign were to be embittered by the issue of anti-Catholicism. The net worst has been done. If the campaign becomes embittered he will lose a

few more reluctant Protestant votes to Nixon, but he will gain Catholic and minority group votes. Bitter anti-Catholicism in the campaign would bring about a reaction against prejudice and for Kennedy from Catholics and others who would resent overt prejudice. It is in Kennedy's hands to handle the religious issue during the campaign in a way that maximizes Kennedy votes based on resentment against religious prejudice and minimizes further defections.[56]

This report went on to suggest that since Kennedy had already lost most of the votes he would lose because of the religious issue, the best course of action would be to use the issue to his advantage: "On balance, he would not lose further from forthright and persistent attention to the religious issue, and could gain. The simulation shows that there has already been a serious defection from Kennedy by Protestant voters. Under these circumstances, it makes no sense to brush the religious issue under the rug. Kennedy has already suffered the disadvantages of the issue even though it is not embittered now and without receiving compensating advantages inherent in it."[57] The Kennedy forces now had an informational basis for "a clear-cut tactical decision." They could either follow Al Smith's policy of trying to avoid the issue, or Kennedy could pay "forthright and persistent attention" to it. Morgan concluded by saying that he did not know what role this report had in the thinking of the Kennedy strategists, but their subsequent handling of the issue was parallel to the suggestions of the report of the "people machine."[58]

Of course either interpretation of why and to what extent Kennedy chose to deal with the religious issue early in the campaign is open to question. It is quite possible that both interpretations are correct. That is, because of increasing attacks by Protestant groups on Kennedy's religion *and* in view of the findings of the survey, Kennedy decided not "to sweep the issue under the rug" but to feature it prominently. If this is the case, then there is some reason to believe that these increasing attacks by religious groups and by such publications as the *Biblical Recorder* may actually have *helped* the Kennedy cause.

In any case Kennedy met with the Greater Houston Ministerial Association on the evening of September 12. At that meeting he stated his credo in much the same way Smith had in the *Atlantic Monthly* in 1928:

> I believe in an America where the separation of Church and State is
> absolute—where no Catholic prelate would tell the President (should he
> be a Catholic) how to act, and no Protestant minister would tell his parish-
> ioners for whom to vote—where no church or church school is granted any
> public funds or political preference—where no man is denied public office
> merely because his religion differs from the President who might appoint
> him or the people who might elect him. . . .

That is the kind of America in which I believe. And it represents the kind of Presidency in which I believe—a great office that must be neither humbled by making it the instrument of any religious group, nor tarnished by arbitrarily withholding its occupancy from the members of any religious group. I believe in a President whose views on religion are his own private affairs, neither imposed upon him by the nation or imposed upon him as a condition to holding that office.[59]

Though this statement may have silenced some of the critics of Kennedy's religious faith, it gave added strength to others. By September 24, 1960, things had evidently reached such a point that the North Carolina State Baptist Convention's Committee on Public Affairs through its chairman, W. W. Finlator, felt compelled to release a statement that expressed regret over the circulation of "slanderous, scurrilous and defamatory statements which are circulated to incite the basal emotions of hostility and to appeal to the uninformed prejudices of many of our citizens." The report continued: "Though this is being engaged upon by many persons, some of whom are Baptists, the committee regards this spirit as being contrary to the genius of our Baptist practice and faith."[60]

The same issue of the *Biblical Recorder* also contained an editorial titled "Where's All the Flood of 'Hate Literature'?," that was obviously aimed at the committee and that made it clear that it did not speak for all Baptists. The editor commented, "If this loose talk about hate literature is designed to curb free and open discussion of the issue, this objective should be made clear too."[61]

This air of righteous indignation on the part of the editor of the *Biblical Recorder* continued when, in the same issue, he criticized statements that had been made by Dr. John Bennett of the Union Theological Seminary in New York in the Catholic publication *America:* "Dr. Bennett said that religious opposition to Senator Kennedy came from a 'kind of religious underworld.' *America* said that Dr. Norman Vincent Peale and Dr. Daniel A. Poling had been 'maneuvered into a position where they could be used as a respectable front for the theologically bankrupt Protestant underworld of bigotry.' That's pretty strong language from those who preach tolerance so loudly."[62] While the editor of the *Biblical Recorder* continued to pursue his attack on Kennedy's religion, other North Carolina Baptists were taking quite a different stance. Early in October a statement heralded as a "Declaration of Conscience" was released by twenty-eight leading Baptist professional people in North Carolina, including Hubert Olive, Henry Belk, Irving E. Carlyle, L. P. McLendon Sr., and John R. Jordan. This statement declared their belief that Kennedy would honor his statements on church and state if elected and warned of the dangers of a denomination allying itself with one political party: "If any organization, including any church, works to defeat the candidate of one political party it thereby inevitably and automatically makes itself to some extent the ally or agent of the other political party—with all the dangers to its spiritual unity, its prestige, progress and growth which such a definite political alliance could bring for a full generation to come."[63]

In the final month of the campaign, activity by anti-Catholic religious groups and leaders increased. On October 5, 1960, the Reverend H. Gordon Weekley, minister of Providence Baptist Church of Charlotte, mailed out four hundred anti-Kennedy letters.[64] On October 10 the South Fork Baptist Association meeting in Maiden was told by the Reverend Kermit Caldwell that "we must face the threat of a Catholic hierarchy with its expressed dogmas."[65] The Hickory Grove Baptist Association meeting in Cherryville was told by the Reverend Waldo Mullen of the Second Baptist Church in that city that Baptists were engaged in a great struggle "against communism and Catholicism." Mr. Mullen also pointed out to the five hundred delegates at this meeting that 68 percent of higher federal employees are Roman Catholics. He warned them that if the Catholic Church gained control, there would no longer be any religious freedom or public education.[66]

On October 27, 1960, shortly before Reformation Day, Bishop Nolan Harmon of the Methodist Church spoke from his Charlotte office urging all Methodist ministers not to let the religious issue of the campaign be a subject of their sermons for Reformation Day. The Bishop said that the Methodists must not do what others accuse Catholics of doing—interfering with politics.[67]

The *Charlotte Observer* for October 27 reported that the Justice Department was investigating anti-Catholic literature in North Carolina. Close attention was being given to the bogus Knights of Columbus oath and a pamphlet then being circulated called "The Reasons Why," which listed ten reasons why a person should not vote for a Roman Catholic.[68] On October 31 Dr. Casper C. Warren of Charlotte, former president of the Southern Baptist Convention, claimed that the election of Kennedy would be "nothing short of a great tragedy." He added, "And I have no doubt whatever that a Catholic President would be under the constant influence if not the actual control of the Roman Catholic Church." The election of Kennedy, he said, was part of a "well-organized, long-planned, well-financed Catholic plot to gain control in America and there's no doubt about it."[69]

Shortly before election day, an incident happened that seriously threatened Kennedy's campaign. Two bishops of Puerto Rico denounced reform-minded Gov. Luis Marins in a pastoral letter and told the Catholics of Puerto Rico: "It is our obligation to prohibit Catholics from giving their vote to a party that accepts as its own the morality of a 'regime of license' denying Christian morality."[70] Kennedy immediately issued a statement saying that he considered it "wholly improper and alien to our Democracy for Churchmen of any faith to tell the members of their Church for whom to vote or for whom not to vote."[71]

This situation was not lost on the editor of the *Biblical Recorder.* The issue of November 5 carried six articles on the Puerto Rico incident and said that "American citizens, faced with a crucial election in their own nation, will observe developments closely in Puerto Rico."[72] The *North Carolina Catholic* observed that the bishops' letter was most "impolitic." The editor wrote, "Catholics in the United States, aware of civic responsibility, and thankful for the democratic privilege and function of a two-party system, have prevented the dangerous necessity of forcing their bishops to interpose their religious authority into the highly emotional and controversial sphere of practical politics."[73]

The editor of the *North Carolina Catholic* called his readers' attention to an advertisement that appeared in Raleigh newspapers during the closing weeks of the campaign that sounded a little like a Protestant version of the Puerto Rico incident. This advertisement urged voters, "whether Protestant or Catholic," to "consult your pastor . . . if you are undecided how to vote on November 8." The *North Carolina Catholic* objected vigorously to this suggestion. If the undecided voter goes to his pastor, the editor countered, "odds are 13-to-one" that the minister "will groan in spirit and come up with the anti-Catholic fixation-revelation that the Pope will rule America with racks and iron virgins in the F. B. I. basement—if a Catholic got the White House pass key." The editor continued, "The Catholic Church does not want Catholic priests telling people how to vote, whether from the pulpit, from the pastor's study, and most certainly not from the confessional. . . . Catholics want no union of Church and State, notwithstanding the obvious fact that some near-hysterical lunatic fringe anti-Catholics do!"[74]

In the last issue before the election, the editor of the *Biblical Recorder* wound up his efforts in an editorial titled "And Finally Brethren." It read:

> Regardless of which Party wins the election on November 8, the winner and the loser already seem to be evident.
>
> If the Democratic candidate wins, the Roman Catholic hierarchy will have the first member of its faith in the White House.
>
> If the Republican Party wins, the Roman Catholic hierarchy already has commitments from both the Presidential and Vice-Presidential candidates that they will support Federal aid to parochial schools, on the elementary level as well as in college.
>
> One of the losers of the election, regardless of who wins, will be America's 62,534,502 Protestants who have been the object of a campaign that has sought to picture them as narrow, bigoted, selfish and intolerant. Through skillful manipulation of public opinion, Roman Catholicism has been pictured as tolerant, broad-minded and understanding.[75]

On November 8, 1960, 68,832,818 Americans voted. In one of the closest presidential elections in history, Kennedy defeated Nixon by a vote of 34,221,463 to

34,108,582. The electoral vote was 303 to 219. North Carolina gave Kennedy 52.1 percent of its votes. Kennedy received 713,318 votes in North Carolina, and Nixon 655,648.[76]

On November 26 the Baptists of North Carolina, meeting in convention in Asheville, sent a message to the President-elect assuring him of their "full cooperation in his effort to keep our government true to its historical principles of complete religious liberty and separation of Church and State." The Baptists promised Kennedy their "sincere remembrance in prayer as we together seek to make our Country an instrument for the promotion of peace and complete religious liberty among the nations of the earth."[77]

The *North Carolina Catholic* had the last word on this resolution:

Tar Heel Don Quixote
Possibly Mr. John Kennedy was vaguely relieved to hear that the Asheville Baptist Convention had the savoir-faire to water-down the sour-grapes resolution of J. Marse Grant. Had the *Biblical Recorder* editor had his way, the Baptist Convention would have gone on record as promising qualified cooperation and prayers for the President-elect . . . if he lived up to his campaign promises to maintain separation of Church and State, a la Grant, and restricted any attempts of the Roman hierarchy to influence his decisions. It was simply another of those "Will you stop beating your wife?" mousetraps that set so easily for the Baptist editor.

Happily the Convention turned down Mr. Grant's effort to posture as the great crusader for religious freedom, and substituted a less bristling, if not mild, resolution to cooperate and to pray for the president-elect, "We had hoped that the election returns would have convinced Mr. Grant that his virulent Anti-Catholicism in the *Biblical Recorder* was roundly ineffective in stirring up religious intolerance in North Carolina. Obviously and sadly Mr. Grant is hard to convince that the effort to create a religious test act for the Presidency directly contradicts the United States Constitution."[78]

The final question is, of course, what was the significance of the religious issue in the 1960 presidential campaign in North Carolina, and as a footnote, why did the religious issue fail to make the impact on the voters that it did in 1928? It is somewhat easier to determine that significance in terms of the 1960 campaign than it has been for the 1928 campaign for the obvious reason that the issue of Prohibition was absent from the campaign. It can be concluded that organized religious groups were not as effective against Kennedy as they had been in 1928 against Smith. Four tentative reasons for this ineffectiveness can be offered.

First, as already mentioned, the anti-Catholic forces in the state lacked an emotionally charged supporting issue such as Prohibition by which they could raise vigorous support among the people. Second, the anti-Kennedy forces in the state failed to solidify their efforts and enlist the aid of strong religious leaders. An integral part of this failure was the fact that many of the religious leaders in the state, with the exception of Baptist leaders, were either publicly neutral or acted as Bishop Harmon did in urging others not to make religion an issue in the campaign.

Again the anti-Catholic forces were without political backing from either party and had no defectors from the regular Democratic organization to aid them as Senator Simmons had done in 1928. What few defectors there were came largely from the conservative group in the state identified with unsuccessful gubernatorial candidate I. Beverly Lake, and their break with the Democratic Party was primarily over the race issue and not the religious issue.

The third reason is stated here. A combination of the "image" of the Democratic Catholic candidate and the increase of mass communications helped to defeat the anti-Catholic efforts. With television the voters, some of whom might possibly never have seen a Catholic in their whole lives, could have the Catholic candidate in their living room. Kennedy himself did much to quell fears of Catholicism in that he had none of the traditional characteristics and mannerisms about him that would suggest the image of a Catholic to those who were prejudiced against them. Kennedy did not look "foreign." Indeed he looked like an "all-American boy." For these reasons religion as an issue did not gain enough support to deny Kennedy the state's electoral votes.

The role of religion in the 1928 campaign has been far more difficult to assess. The Prohibition issue clouds any really accurate analysis. Anti-Smith "dry" Democrats at the time maintained that Smith was defeated because of his liquor stand. Regular Democrats claimed that he was defeated because he was a Catholic. Shortly after the election, an editorial in the *Charlotte Observer* stated that religion was the chief cause of Smith's defeat: "The Democratic schism was the only reason for Hoover's success in North Carolina. And the Democratic split developed mainly because of Smith's Catholicism."[79]

Time and the perspective of history have not settled the argument. Reinhold Niebuhr stated some years ago that he "believed the real issues in the campaign were hid under the decent veil of loyalty to a moral ideal—prohibition."[80] Robert Moats Miller, who examined the question extensively, reached the opposite conclusion: "Prohibition was not a straw man; it was the factor that more than any other determined the votes of many Americans in the election of 1928."[81]

However a strong case can be made for the fact that religion was the chief factor in Smith's defeat in North Carolina. First, if Prohibition was the real issue, then why did the state vote for the "wet" Cox in 1920, the "wet" Davis in 1924, and the "wet" Roosevelt in 1932? Second, with so much anti-Catholic prejudice evident in 1960, is it not likely that thirty-two years earlier a less well-informed people were more apt to carry anti-Catholic sentiments in their hearts and into the voting booth? Finally, Smith himself "talked" like a Catholic: that is, his voice fitted the preconception that many people had of Catholics in general. With so few Catholics in the state in 1928 (fewer than seven thousand), it is possible that many people had never seen an actual Catholic and were accordingly fearful of the unknown. Without television all these people had to judge Smith by was his East Side of New York, "Fulton Fish Market" accent, which grated on the ears of southern voters. Smith's voice seemed to give concrete substance to their macabre images. In view of all of this, there is some justification for saying that anti-Catholic sentiment was indeed the major factor in Smith's 1928 defeat in North Carolina.

The second question that should be considered is that of the degree of influence that anti-Catholic preachers and publications exerted in these two campaigns. Did they actually influence people, or were they merely reflecting what the people already felt? Miller again offers an interesting viewpoint: "[Powerful clergymen] did not coerce, dupe, or otherwise force their congregations to assume unwittingly an anti-Smith position. Such a position was already held, and in a very real sense clergymen simply shared the attitudes (or prejudices, if you will) of their people." Protestants listened to their pastors' warnings against Smith and nodded their heads in approval. They did so not because they were cowed by their clergymen but because what they heard agreed with convictions they long held.[82]

Miller's assumptions about the role of the clergy does not adequately recognize the fact that southern clergymen in the 1920s, and to some extent even today, exercise a great deal of influence over their flocks and are quite capable of persuading them with respect to political issues. Of course the truth of the matter is that this was probably a two-way street. Undoubtedly many clergy were simply reflecting the views of their congregations, but there is much that supports the argument that many of the clergy led members of their congregation into the anti-Smith camp.

Finally, two observations need to be made in order to place the issue in its proper perspective. First, in the matter of motives of the individual voter in the 1928 election, it is important to note that undoubtedly many people who opposed Smith on religious grounds did use Prohibition as an effective cover for their religious prejudices. It is just as likely that many "wets" turned to the religious issue and voted for Smith in the name of tolerance. It is impossible for one person to be sure of another person's motives, and indeed a person often cannot even be sure of his or her own motives.

Second, though this study has been directed toward religious prejudice, it should be remembered that not all of the questioning of the Catholic candidates in both elections was on the level of bigotry. The history and thought of the Catholic Church did give rise in the minds of many to some honest questions about civil and religious authority, and many who asked these questions asked them quite sincerely and awaited the answers with open minds. Perhaps this study should end where it began, with Gordon Allport's simple definition of prejudice: "A feeling, favorable or unfavorable, toward a person or things, prior to, or not based on, actual experience." And that has been the focus of this study.

The final word on the election of 1960 was best expressed by White, who wrote: "No American prejudice faded, I think, more quickly than the religious prejudice that vexed and underlay the election of 1960. It began to fade within weeks after Kennedy's election, even before his inauguration as it became clear that what he wanted to do with power was connected to neither Papal nor to Protestant purpose. . . . That old issue religion, which had cost so many thousands of lives in the history of the Anglo-American tradition, vanished in the light."[83]

Stability and Change in 1960

Shortly after the 1960 election, a team of political scientists at the University of Michigan examined in depth the effect of the religious issue on the election. The results of their study suggest that in general "Catholicism gave a very slight net advantage to Kennedy outside the South" and "penalized him heavily within the South."[84]

More specifically this study found that the defection rate of those who traditionally voted Democratic to Nixon was strongly correlated with regular attendance at a Protestant church.[85] This was especially significant for the South in that the region as a whole was 95 percent Protestant and southerners were more faithful churchgoers than northerners. More than 50 percent of the total vote in the South was cast by Protestants who went to church "regularly," whereas less than 20 percent fell in the same category in other regions outside the South. Narrowing this down a bit more, the study revealed that outside the South, regular churchgoing Protestant Democrats cast about 5 percent of the total vote. In the South, however, regular churchgoing Protestant Democrats accounted for 35 percent of the total vote. It was this fact that accounts for the large anti-Catholic vote in the South in 1960. The table reproduced below reveals that approximately 40 percent of the regular Protestant Democratic churchgoers defected to Nixon. The general average of defectors in this category for any election is about 6 percent. While the 40 percent figure is comparable to the 38 percent of regular Protestant Democratic churchgoers outside the South who defected, in the South, again, that category comprises a greater proportion of the total vote. Note especially that in the table under "South-never," there are no figures. This is explained by the authors in an interesting footnote: "The number of Protestant Democrats who 'never' attend church in the South is too small for inclusion."[86]

The authors of the study concluded with the observation that they felt the importance of religion in the 1960 campaign had been underestimated.[87] If it is assumed that the above findings are reasonably accurate, then it is evident that Kennedy's Catholicism cost him quite heavily in North Carolina even though it did not cause him to lose the state.

Defections to Nixon among Protestant Democrats as a Function of
 Church Attendance

Church attendance	Regular	Often	Seldom	Never
North	38%	27%	12%	6%
South	40%	37%	19%	??

SOURCE: The table given here is not an exact reproduction of the original but rather a simplified version containing the information essential for this study.

NOTES

1. Will Herberg, *Protestant-Catholic-Jew* (Garden City, N.Y.: Doubleday, 1960), 24.

2. Gordon W. Allport, *The Nature of Prejudice* (Garden City, N.Y.: Doubleday, 1958), 7.

3. Ibid., 8.

4. A National Council of Churches survey released in 1957 listed a total statewide church membership in North Carolina of 1,620,339 (out of a total general population of 4,061,929). Of these church members, 781,037, or 49.2 percent, were Baptists; 339,069, or 21.4 percent, were Methodists; and 29,565, or 1.68 percent, were Catholics. Overall North Carolina in 1957 was 97.9 percent Protestant and 1.8 percent Catholic. Furthermore in twenty-one of the state's one hundred counties, there were no Catholics. In twenty-two other counties, there were less than fifty. In only one county in the state did Catholics exceed 7.4 percent of the church population. In coastal Onslow County, Catholics accounted for 46.3 percent of the church population, with 6,000 communicants. See *Churches and Church Membership in the United States: An Enumeration and Analysis by Counties, States, and Regions* (New York: National Council of Churches, 1957), series C, no. 34.

5. C. Vann Woodward, *The Burden of Southern History* (New York: Vintage Books, 1961), 6. Woodward uses the phrase "Bulldozer Revolution" to describe the spread of cities into suburban areas. "It [the bulldozer] encroaches upon rural life to expand urban life. It demolishes the old to make way for the new."

6. "The Presidential Ambitions of Senator John Kennedy," *Biblical Recorder,* January 23, 1960, 3.

7. "A Catholic View of Tithing," *North Carolina Christian Advocate,* January 14, 1960, 4.

8. "Roman Catholicism: A New Emphasis," *North Carolina Christian Advocate,* May 19, 1960, 4.

9. "Facing our Responsibilities as Citizens," "Christian Responsibility in 1960 Elections," *North Carolina Christian Advocate,* July 14, 1960, 4; August 4, 1960, 3; August 18, 1960, 15.

10. *North Carolina Christian Advocate,* September 1, 1960, 13; September 22, 1960.

11. "Should a Catholic Be President?" (advertisement), *North Carolina Christian Advocate*, August 11, 1960, 16.

12. "The Editor's Position," *Carolina Christian Advocate*, September 15, 1960, 3.

13. "November 8 Can be a Day of Destiny," *North Carolina Christian Advocate*, November 3, 1960, 3.

14. Theodore H. White, *The Making of the President, 1960* (New York: Pocket Books, 1962), 312.

15. "On Chapel of Four Chaplains Incident . . . Statements by Dr. Poling, Senator Kennedy Differ," *Biblical Recorder*, October 1, 1960, 14, Quoting from the *Atlanta Constitution*, September 13, 1960.

16. "On Bishop's Order-Kennedy Confirms Poling's Report Note:" *Biblical Recorder*, January 30, 1960, 11.

17. "Pollard Opposition to Kennedy Voiced," *Biblical Recorder*, February 27, 1960, 6.

18. "An Anonymous Letter: A Catholic in the White House," *Biblical Recorder*, March 5, 1960, 3.

19. "Protestants and a President's Faith," *Newsweek*, March 14, 1960, 33, 36, 38, 40.

20. Ibid., 36.

21. Ibid., 38.

22. "Killing Straw Men," *North Carolina Catholic; Edition of Our Sunday Visitor*, March 20, 1960. Hereafter cited as *North Carolina Catholic*.

23. "Editorially-This Isn't 'Flapdoodle'" *Biblical Recorder*, April 9, 1960, 4–5. Not signed, but in space reserved for editorials.

24. "Simple Question-Straight Answer" *Biblical Recorder*, May 14, 1960, 3.

25. Ibid.

26. Editorials: "Even After West Virginia," *North Carolina Catholic*, May 29, 1960, 4.

27. "Charlotte Pastor Did Good Job Framing Resolution," *Biblical Recorder*, May 28, 1960, 7.

28. "Religious Freedom Is for All Men . . . Catholicism Must Repent of Sins, Pollard Declares," ibid., 24.

29. "Religion and Politics," *North Carolina Christian Advocate*, June 16, 1960, 13.

30. *Minutes of the Western North Carolina Annual Conference of the Methodist Church, 1960*, and *Journal of the North Carolina Annual Conference of the Methodist Church, 1960*.

31. "Buncombe Pastors Hear Converted Catholic Cite Fourfold Dangers," *Biblical Recorder*, July 2, 1960, 10.

32. "Sanford Decision Delayed-He'll Pick Johnson or Kennedy in LA," *Charlotte Observer*, July 6, 1960, 1–24.

33. Ibid. It is worth noting at this point that at the 1956 Democratic Convention, Kennedy had been something of a favorite with the southerners. When Kefauver was nominated for the vice-presidency on the second ballot, he received little southern support. The entire delegations of Arkansas, Georgia, Kentucky, Louisiana, Mississippi, South Carolina, Tennessee, Texas, and Virginia cast their votes for Kennedy. North Carolina voted 7.5 for Gore of Tennessee, 9.5 for Kefauver, and 17.5 for Kennedy. See *Official Report of the Proceedings of the Democratic National Convention, 1956* (Chicago: Democratic National Committee, 1956), 480–81.

34. "Sanford Move Gives Kennedy Big Break-Johnson's 'Solid' Dixie Cracks," *Charlotte Observer*, July 10, 1960, 1

35. "Churchmen Tell Sanford Not to Back Kennedy," *Charlotte Observer*, July 11, 1960, 1B.

36. "Kennedy is Nominated in First Ballot Sweep-Convention Goes Wild," *Charlotte Observer*, July 14, 1960, 1.

37. "This is How the Vote Went," Ibid, 6A.

38. "Hits Pearson Charge-Terry Says No Deal Made. He Denies Money Given by Kennedy," ibid., 4A.

39. "A Revealing Survey," *Biblical Recorder*, July 23, 1960, 3.

40. "Editorials-The Catholic Plot," *North Carolina Catholic*, August 14, 1960, 4A.

41. This bogus "oath," which had appeared in a congressional campaign early in the century, read, in part, "I now in the presence of Almighty God . . . declare and swear that His Holiness, the Pope is Christ's vice regent and is the true and only head of the Catholic or Universal Church throughout the earth. . . . I do now denounce and disown any allegiance as due to any heretical king, prince, or state, named Protestant or Liberals, or obedience to any of their laws, magistrates, or officers. . . . I do further promise and declare that I will, when opportunity presents, make and wage relentless war, by secret and openly, against heretics, Protestants and Masons, as I am directed to do, to extirpate them from the face of the whole earth; and that I will spare neither age, sex, or condition, and that I will hang, burn, waste, boil, flay, strangle, and bury alive these infamous heretics; rip up the stomachs and wombs of their women, and crush their infants' heads against the walls in order to annihilate their execrable race." See 62 Cong. Rec., 3rd Sess. (1913), 3216.

42. "One Pastor Already Embarrassed . . . So Called 'Oath' of Columbus is Not Authentic," *Biblical Recorder*, August 6, 1960, 15.

43. Ibid.

44. "Editorials-Church Authority," *North Carolina Catholic*, September 11, 1960, 4A. The use of the bogus oath seems to have been quite wide spread in the state in 1960. As early as 1959, a Winston-Salem Bible college published and distributed the oath. The editor of the *North Carolina Catholic, 4A* suggested that some criminal libel action should have been taken then. See "Editorials-Truth Serum By Court Order," *North Carolina Catholic*, August 28, 1960, 4A.

45. "Not Afraid of the Man, But the System. . . , Average Catholic Laymen Good Neighbor, Friend, Citizen; Hierarchy Another Matter," *Biblical Recorder*, August 6, 1960, 16.

46. "Ward Barr Takes Lead . . . Information Center on Catholicism Being Opened in Gastonia," *Biblical Recorder*, August 13, 1960, 2.

47. "Editorials-American Protestant Assn.-1844–1960," *North Carolina Catholic*, August 14, 1960, 4A.

48. "Dr. Claude Broach . . . Church Not Candidates, Charlotte Pastor Says," *Biblical Recorder*, September 3, 1960, 5.

49. "Baptists, Roman Catholics, and Religious Freedom" (advertisement), *Biblical Recorder*, September 20, 1960, 14.

50. "Carolina Association Raps 'Foreign Ties' of Presidential Nominee," *Biblical Recorder*, August 27, 1960, 21. See also issues for October 15, 1960, 22, "Our Readers Write-From Rocky Mount" and "Our Readers Write-From Central Association," November 5, 1960, 21.

51. Mrs. Charles W. Tillett, *Religious Freedom and the Ballot Box* (n.p., n.d.), North Carolina Collection, Wilson Library, University of North Carolina at Chapel Hill.

52. White, *Making of the President*, 301.

53. Ibid., 311.

54. Ibid.

55. Thomas B. Morgan, "The People Machine," *Harper's Magazine*, January 1961, 53.

56. Ibid., 54.

57. Ibid.

58. Ibid.

59. White, *Making of the President*, 312.

60. "Convention's Committee on Public Affairs Releases Statement Deploring Hate Material," *Biblical Recorder*, September 24, 19601, 8.

61. "Where's All the Flood of 'Hate Literature'?" *Biblical Recorder*, September 24, 1960, 3. The editor, Marse Grant, and W. W. Finlator have long been at odds over many issues since each represents an opposite end of the scale, Finlator, of course, being quite liberal." On several occasions in 1960, Finlator spoke out on the religious issue. In an address titled "Conscience in the South," he said, "I believe that opposition to, or support of, a candidate for civil office on account of his religion constitutes, in itself, a violation of the principle of Church-State separation. . . . It also does violence to the civil nature of the Presidency." "Editorial-Orchids To:," *North Carolina Catholic*, October 16, 1960, 4A. Italics added by the editor.

62. "Editor's Notebook-Those Prominent TV Signs; Term 'Protestant Underworld' is Bad;" *Biblical Recorder September 24*, 1960, 2

63. "A Declaration of Conscience for Baptists to Consider" *Biblical Recorder*, October 8, 1960, 6–7.

64. "Nixon Impresses Baptist Ministers," *Charlotte Observer*, October 5, 1960, 6A

65. "Baptists told of 'Dangers' to Freedom," *Charlotte Observer*, October 7, 1960, 12A.

66. "Preacher Calls on America to End Spiritual, Moral Fall," *Charlotte Observer*, October 19, 1960, 11B.

67. "Keep Politics Aside-Reformation Day Stressed," *Charlotte Observer*, October 27, 1960, 4A.

68. Ibid.

69. "Great Tragedy-Warren Speaks out Against Kennedy," *Charlotte Observer*, October 31, 1960, 14B.

70. "Fuss in Puerto Rico," *Time*, October 31, 1960, 11.

71. Ibid, 12.

72. Under the Heading "The Puerto Rican Story," "Separation of Church and State is Fundemental," "Methodist Bishop, Criticizes Pastoral," "Glenn Archer Denounces Clerical Interference in Puerto Rico," "Perfectly within Their Rights . . . Vatican Upheld Bishops in Puerto Rico," "Washington Post Takes Issue with Puerto Rico Bishop," "Asks

Their Transfer . . . San Juan Paper Blasts Letter from Bishops," *Biblical Recorder,* November 5, 1960, 18–19.

73. "Editorials 'Puerto Rican Affair,'" *North Carolina Catholic,* November 6, 1960, 4A.

74. "Editorials-Vote Without Your Pastor," *North Carolina Catholic,* October 30, 1960, 4A.

75. "Editorially-And Finally Brethren," *Biblical Recorder,* November 5, 1960, 3.

76. White, *Making of the President,* 461.

77. "Editorially-Asheville Adjectives: Courageous, Harmonious," Resolution to New President was Positive, Constructive," *Biblical Recorder,* November 26, 1960, 3.

78. *North Carolina Catholic,* November 27, 1960, 4A.

Appendix A

Dissertations Directed by Donald G. Mathews

Gerald Lee Wilson, "Nathaniel Beverley Tucker, Aristocratic Paternalist: The Search for Order and Stability in the Antebellum South." 1973.

Larry Edward Tise, "Proslavery Ideology: A Social and Intellectual History of the Defense of Slavery in America, 1790–1840." 1974.

Robert Francis Martin, "The Early Days of American Pentecostalism, 1900–1940: Survey of a Social Movement." 1975.

Roberta Gail O'Brien, "War and Social Change: An Analysis of Community Power Structure, Guilford County, North Carolina, 1848–1882." 1975.

Kathryn A. Pippin, "The Common School Movement in the South, 1840–1860." 1977.

Keith Robert Burich, "The Catholic Church and Intellectuals: From Cooper to Santayana." 1979.

James M. Becker, "Was Randolph-Macon Different? Revivalism, Sectionalism, and the Academic Tradition: The Methodist Mission in Higher Education, 1830–1880." 1980.

Mary Evans Frederickson, "A Place to Speak Our Minds: The Southern School for Women Workers." 1981.

Dennis Lee Frobish, "The Family and Ideology: Cultural Constraints on Women, 1940–1960." 1983.

Ruth Alden Doan, "The Miller Heresy: Millennialism and American Culture." 1984.

John Scott Strickland, "Across Space and Time: Conversion, Community and Cultural Change among South Carolina Slaves." 1985.

Daniel R. Miller, "A History of the Cedral Mine under United States Ownership, 1870–1930." 1987.

Wayne K. Durrill, "Uncivil War: Washington County, North Carolina in the Great Rebellion." 1987.

W. Thomas Mainwaring, "Community in Danville, Virginia, 1880–1963." 1988.

Richard Eugene Rankin Jr., "Evangelical Awakening and Episcopal Revival: Cultural Change and the Development of Genteel Piety among North Carolina Episcopalians, 1800–1860." 1989.

Philip N. Mulder, "Choosing God's People: Religious Identity in the Era of Awakenings." 1995.

Emily Simms Bingham, "Mordecai: Three Generations of a Southern Jewish Family, 1780–1865." 1998.

Gavin James Campbell, "Music and the Making of a Jim Crow Culture, 1900–1925." 1999.

Regina Diane Sullivan, "Woman with a Mission: Remembering Lotte Moon and the Woman's Missionary Union." 2002.

David Joseph Voelker, "Orestes Brownson and the Search for Authority in Democratic America." 2003.

Monte Harrell Hampton, "'Handmaid or Assailant': Debating Science and Scripture in the Culture of the Lost Cause." 2004.

Cheryl Fradette Junk, "'Ladies, Arise: The World Has Need of You': Frances Bumpass, Religion and the Power of the Press, 1851–1860." 2005.

Kenneth Joel Zogry, "The House Dr. Pope Built: Race, Politics, Memory, and the Early Struggle for Civil Rights in North Carolina." 2008. [James Leloudis, codirector]

Nancy Gray Schoonmaker, "Mystery and Possibility: Spiritualists in the Nineteenth-Century South." 2010.

Appendix B

Select Bibliography of Donald G. Mathews's Writings, 1965–2015

BOOKS

Lynching Religion: Evangelical Protestantism in the New South and the Lynching of Sam Hose. [forthcoming]

With Jane Sherron De Hart. *Sex, Gender, and the Politics of ERA: A State and the Nation.* New York: Oxford University Press, 1990.

Religion in the Old South. Chicago: University of Chicago Press, 1977.

Slavery and Methodism: A Chapter in American Morality, 1780–1845. Princeton, N.J.: Princeton University Press, 1965.

EDITED BOOKS

Religion in the American South: Protestants and Others in History and Culture. Edited by Beth Barton Schweiger and Donald G. Mathews. Introduction by Donald G. Mathews. Chapel Hill: University of North Carolina Press, 2004.

Agitation for Freedom: The Abolitionists. Edited and introduction by Donald G. Mathews. New York: Wiley, 1971.

ARTICLES

"The Southern Rite of Human Sacrifice: Lynching in the American South." *Mississippi Quarterly* 61 (2008): 27–70.

"The Southern Rite of Human Sacrifice: Lynching in the American South." *Journal of Southern Religion* 3 (2000). http://jsr.fsu.edu/mathews.htm.

With Samuel S. Hill, Beth Barton Schweiger, and John S. Boles. "Forum: Southern Religion." *Religion and American Culture* 8 (1998): 147–77.

"'We Have Left Undone Those Things Which We Ought to Have Done': Southern Religious History in Retrospect and Prospect." *Church History* 67 (1998): 1–21.

"'Spiritual Warfare': Cultural Fundamentalism and the Equal Rights Amendment." *Religion and American Culture* 3 (1993): 129–54.

With Jane De Hart-Mathews. "The Cultural Politics of ERA's Defeat." *Organization of American Historians Newsletter,* November 1982, 13–15. Rpt. in *Rights of Passage: The Past and Future of the ERA,* edited by Joan Hoff. Bloomington: Indiana University Press, 1986.

"Women's History/Everyone's History." In *Women in New Worlds: Perspectives on the Wesleyan Tradition*, edited by Rosemary Skinner Keller and Hilah Thomas, 29–47. Nashville: Abingdon, 1981.

[Coauthor] "Women and Politics in the Contemporary South: The ERA in North Carolina." *Furman Studies*, December 1980, 15–17.

"Charles Colcock Jones and the Southern Evangelical Crusade to Form a Biracial Community." *Journal of Southern History* 40 (1975): 299–320. Rpt. in *Articles on American Slavery*, vol. 16, *Religion and Slavery*, edited by Paul Finkelman, 489–510. New York: Garland, 1989.

"Religion in the Old South: Speculation on Methodology." *South Atlantic Quarterly* 73 (1974): 34–52.

"The Second Great Awakening as an Organizing Process: An Hypothesis." *American Quarterly* 20 (1969): 23–43. Rpt. in *Religion in American History: Interpretative Essays*, edited by John F. Wilson, 199–217. Englewood Cliffs, N.J.: Prentice-Hall, 1977.

"The Methodist Schism of 1844 and the Popularization of Antislavery Sentiment." *Mid-America* 51 (1969): 3–23.

"The Abolitionists on Slavery: The Critique behind the Social Movement," *Journal of Southern History* 33 (1967): 163–82. Rpt. in *Articles on American Slavery*, vol. 14, *Antislavery*, edited by Paul Finkelman, 335–55. New York: Garland, 1989.

"The Methodist Mission to the Slaves, 1829–1844" *Journal of American History* 51 (1965): 615–31. Rpt. in *Articles on American Slavery*, vol. 16, *Religion and Slavery*, edited by Paul Finkelman, 511–28. New York: Garland, 1989.

CHAPTERS IN BOOKS

"The 'Translation' of Lundy Harris: Interpreting Death out of the Confusion of Sexuality, Violence and Religion in the New South." In *Death in the American South*, edited by Craig Thompson Friend and Lorrie Glover. New York: Cambridge University Press, 2015.

"Corra Harris: The Story Teller as Folk Preacher." In *Georgia Women: Their Lives and Times*, vol. 1, edited by Ann Short Chirhart and Betty Wood, 341–69. Athens: University of Georgia Press, 2009.

"Lynching Religion: Why the Old Man Shouted 'Glory!'" In *Southern Crossroads: Perspectives on Religion and Culture*, edited by Walter H. Conser and Rodger M. Payne, 318–53. Lexington: University Press of Kentucky, 2008.

"Lynching '. . . is Part of the Religion of Our People': Faith in the Christian South." In *Religion in the American South: Protestants and Others in History and Culture*, edited by Beth Barton Schweiger and Donald G. Mathews, 153–94. Chapel Hill: University of North Carolina Press, 2004.

"Crucifixion—Faith in the Christian South." In *Autobiographical Reflections on Southern Religious History*, edited by John Boles, 17–38. Athens: University of Georgia Press, 2000.

"United Methodism and American Culture: Testimony, Voice, and the Public Sphere." In *The People(s) Called Methodist: Forms and Reforms of Their Life*, edited by Dennis Campbell and Russell Richey, 279–304, 336–39. Nashville: Abingdon, 1998.

"Religion and the South: Authenticity and Purity—Pulling Us Together, Tearing Us Apart." In *Religious Diversity and American Religious History*, edited by Walter H. Conser Jr. and Sumner B. Twiss, 72–101. Athens: University of Georgia Press, 1997.

"'Christianizing' the South—Sketching a Synthesis." In *New Perspectives in American Religious History*, edited by Harry S. Stout and Daryl G. Hart, 84–115. New York: Oxford University Press, 1997.

"Evangelical America—The Methodist Ideology." In *Perspectives on American Methodism*, edited by Russell E. Richey, Kenneth E. Rowe, and Jean Miller Schmidt, 17–30. Nashville: Kingswood Books, 1993.

"Women and Evangelicalism in the Early Nineteenth-Century United States." In *The Languages of Revolution*, edited by Loretta Valtz Mannucci, 65–82. Milan: Instituto di Studi Storici, Universita degli Studi di Milano, 1990.

"Religion and Slavery—The Case of the American South." In *Anti-Slavery, Religion, and Reform: Essays in Memory of Roger Anstey*, edited by Christine Bolt and Seymour Drescher, 207–33. London: Dawson, 1980.

"North Carolina Methodists in the Nineteenth Century: Church and Society." In *Methodism Alive in North Carolina*, edited by O. Kelly Ingram, 59–74. Durham, N.C.: Duke Divinity School, 1976.

"'I Will Be Heard': The Abolition Campaign." In *The American Destiny*, vol. 6, edited by Henry Steele Commager and Maldwyn Jones, 60–83. London: Danbury, 1976.

"Orange Scott: The Methodist Evangelist as Revolutionary." In *The Antislavery Vanguard: New Essays on the Abolitionists*, edited by Martin B. Duberman, 71–101. Princeton, N.J.: Princeton University Press, 1965.

REVIEW ARTICLE

"American Millennium: A Review Essay." *Religious Studies Review* 5 (1979): 15–21.

Contributors

EMILY BINGHAM is an independent historian in Louisville, Kentucky. She holds a B.A. in history from Harvard and an M.A. and Ph.D. in history from University of North Carolina at Chapel Hill and has taught most recently as a visiting professor at Centre College. She is the author of *Mordecai: An Early American Family* (2003) and *The Southern Agrarians and the New Deal: Essays after "I'll Take My Stand,"* edited with Thomas Underwood (2001). Her essays have appeared in the edited volumes *Neither Lady nor Slave: Working Women in the Old South* (2002), *Rethinking Religion in the American South* (2004), and *Jewish Roots in Southern Soil: A New History* (2006). Her essay in this volume is from her current project on the life of Henrietta Bingham.

GAVIN JAMES CAMPBELL is professor of American studies at Doshisha University in Kyoto, Japan. He has written widely on the subject of southern music, including *Music and the Making of a New South* (2004). More recently he has published on Americans in Japan, and he is currently completing a book on the trans-Pacific life of Niijima Jō (1843–90), a samurai, educator, and Japan's first ordained Protestant minister.

RUTH ALDEN DOAN is professor emerita and the former Batten Professor for the History of Women and Leadership at Hollins University. Her publications include "Worship, Experience, and the Creation of Methodist Place," in *By the Vision of Another World: Worship in American History,* ed. James D. Bratt (2012); "John Wesley Young: Identity and Community Among the People Called Methodist," in *The Human Tradition in Antebellum America,* ed. Michael A. Morrison (2000); *The Miller Heresy, Millennialism, and American Culture* (1987); and "Millerism and Evangelical Culture," in *The Disappointed: Millerism and Millenarianism in the Nineteenth Century,* ed. Ronald L. Numbers and Jonathan Butler (1987).

WAYNE K. DURRILL is professor of history at the University of Cincinnati. His publications include *War of Another Kind: A Southern Community in the Great Rebellion* (1990; paperback, 1994), plus a number of articles on the American South and Africa. He is currently finishing a book tentatively titled "Nat Turner and the Great Slave Revolt of 1831."

MARY E. FREDERICKSON is professor of history at Miami University, Oxford, Ohio, and a visiting professor in the Graduate Institute of Liberal Arts at Emory University. She is the author of *Looking South: Race, Gender, and the Transformation of Labor* (2011) and coeditor of *Gendered Resistance: Women, Slavery and the Legacy of Margaret*

Garner (2013). During 2012–13 Professor Frederickson was a Mellon fellow at the James Weldon Johnson Institute at Emory University, where the essay in this volume was completed.

MONTE HARRELL HAMPTON is adjunct assistant professor of history at North Carolina State University. His publications include *Storm of Words: Science, Religion, and Evolution in the Civil War Era* (2014), "Navigating Modernity: The Bible, the New South and Robert Lewis Dabney," in *Virginia's Civil War*, ed. Peter Wallenstein and Bertram Wyatt-Brown (2005).

CHERYL F. JUNK is an assistant dean for academic advising at the University of North Carolina at Chapel Hill. Her publications include "To Become a Power in the Land: The Burwell School and Women's Education in Antebellum North Carolina, 1837–1857" (1999) and "Good Soldiers of Christ: North Carolina Quaker Resistance to the Civil War" (1993).

W. THOMAS MAINWARING is chair and professor of history at Washington & Jefferson College, where he has taught since 1989. He is the abridging editor of *Making America: A History of the United States*, first and second brief editions. He has lectured and written about a variety of local history topics in western Pennsylvania, including the Whiskey Rebellion and the Underground Railroad. He is at work on a book about the Underground Railroad.

ROBERT F. MARTIN is professor of history and head of the department at the University of Northern Iowa. His publications include the foreword to *The Sawdust Trail: Billy Sunday in His Own Words* (2005); *Hero of the Heartland: Billy Sunday and the Transformation of American Society, 1862–1935* (2002); and *Howard Kester and the Struggle for Social Justice in the South, 1904–77* (1991).

DANIEL R. MILLER received a Ph.D. from the University of North Carolina at Chapel Hill (1987) and is currently professor of Latin American history at Calvin College in Grand Rapids, Michigan. He writes on the subject of Protestantism in Latin America and is translator of *Like Leaven in the Dough: Protestant Social Thought in Latin America, 1920 to 1950*, by Carlos Mondragon (2010).

PHILIP N. MULDER is professor of history at High Point University. His publications include *A Controversial Spirit: Evangelical Awakenings in the South* (2002). He is currently tracking the early nineteenth-century ministers and congregants who dreamed of making the Ohio River Valley an ecumenical paradise but who ended up just building more churches and denominations.

NANCY GRAY SCHOONMAKER holds a Ph.D. from the University of North Carolina at Chapel Hill (2010), where she was Donald G. Mathews's final student. She is working on a book, "Mystery and Possibility: Christians and Spiritualism in the Nineteenth-Century South," based on her dissertation.

REGINA D. SULLIVAN is dean of Global Education at Carson-Newman University. She holds an M.A.R. from Yale Divinity School and an M.A. and a Ph.D. from the University of North Carolina at Chapel Hill. She is the author of *Lottie Moon: A*

Southern Baptist Missionary to China in History and Legend (2011). Her essays have appeared in the journal *Historically Speaking* (2012) and the collections *Entering the Fray: Gender, Politics, and Culture in the New South*, ed. Jonathan Daniel Wells and Sheila R. Phipps (2010), and *Women in the American Civil War: An Encyclopedia*, ed. Lisa Tendrich Frank (2007).

LARRY E. TISE is the Wilbur & Orville Wright Distinguished Professor of History at East Carolina University. He has previously served as the executive director of the North Carolina Division of Archives and History, the Pennsylvania Historical and Museum Commission, the American Association for State and Local History, and the Benjamin Franklin National Memorial. He is the author of more than fifty articles and books on many facets of history and historical work, including *Proslavery: A History of the Defense of Slavery, 1700–1840* (1987), *The American Counterrevolution: A Retreat from Liberty, 1783–1800* (1999), *Benjamin Franklin and Women* (2000), *Conquering the Sky: The Secret Flights of the Wright Brothers at Kitty Hawk* (2009), and *Neyuheruke 300* (2013).

DAVID J. VOELKER is an associate professor of humanistic studies and history at the University of Wisconsin-Green Bay. His publications on the early national period include "Church Building and Social Class on the Urban Frontier: The Refinement of Lexington, 1784–1830" (2008); "Thomas Paine's Civil Religion of Reason" (2009); and "Cincinnati's Infernal Regions Exhibit and the Waning of Calvinist Authority" (2008). He has also authored and coauthored numerous articles on teaching and learning history, including "The End of the History Survey Course: The Rise and Fall of the Coverage Model" (2011), which was winner of the 2012 Maryellen Weimer Scholarly Work on Teaching and Learning Award.

GERALD LEE WILSON is the senior associate dean of Trinity College of Arts and Sciences at Duke University, prelaw adviser, and adjunct professor of history. He is coeditor of *Teaching Social Studies: Handbook of Trends, Issues, and Implications for the Future,* (1993) and coeditor of an annual publication, *The Book of Lists*, which collects data on law school programs. Additional articles have appeared in religious, historical, and prelaw publications. At Duke he has been honored with two of the university's highest awards, the Presidential Award (2010) and the University Medal (2013). He received his A.B. degree from Davidson College, B.D. from Duke Divinity School, M.A. in religion from Duke University, and, of course, Ph.D. from the University of North Carolina at Chapel Hill. An ordained minister in the Presbyterian Church (USA), he was Donald Mathews's first Ph.D. student at Chapel Hill.

CPSIA information can be obtained at www.ICGtesting.com
Printed in the USA
LVOW11*0334270815

451676LV00005B/7/P